Technoliteracy, Discourse and Social Practice:
Frameworks and Applications in the Digital Age

Darren Lee Pullen
University of Tasmania, Australia

Christina Gitsaki
University of Queensland, Australia

Margaret Baguley
University of Southern Queensland, Australia

INFORMATION SCIENCE REFERENCE

Hershey · New York

Director of Editorial Content: Kristin Klinger
Senior Managing Editor: Jamie Snavely
Assistant Managing Editor: Michael Brehm
Publishing Assistant: Sean Woznicki
Typesetter: Sean Woznicki
Cover Design: Lisa Tosheff
Printed at: Yurchak Printing Inc.

Published in the United States of America by
    Information Science Reference (an imprint of IGI Global)
    701 E. Chocolate Avenue
    Hershey PA 17033
    Tel: 717-533-8845
    Fax: 717-533-8661
    E-mail: cust@igi-global.com
    Web site: http://www.igi-global.com/reference

Library of Congress Cataloging-in-Publication Data

Technoliteracy, discourse and social practice : frameworks and applications in the digital age / Darren Lee Pullen, Christina Gitsaki and Margaret Baguley, editors.
    p. cm.
  Includes bibliographical references and index.
  Summary: "This book provides a unique and important insight into the diverse approaches to, and implementation of, technoliteracy in different contexts, presenting the significance and value of preparing students, educators and those responsible for information technology to use IT effectively and ethically to enhance learning"--Provided by publisher.

  ISBN 978-1-60566-842-0 -- ISBN 978-1-60566-843-7 (ebook) 1. Technological
literacy. 2. Computers and literacy. 3. Educational technology. I. Pullen,
Darren L. II. Gitsaki, Christina. III. Baguley, Margaret, 1966-
  T65.3.T44 2009
  303.48'34--dc22
                    2009017413

British Cataloguing in Publication Data
A Cataloguing in Publication record for this book is available from the British Library.

Table of Contents

Section 1
Leadership

Chapter 1

Amanda Walker, Tasmanian Department of Education, Australia
Bridgette Huddlestone, Tasmanian Department of Education, Australia
Darren L. Pullen, University of Tasmania, Australia

Chapter 2

Donna Mahar, State University of New York, USA

Chapter 3

Candance Doerr-Stevens, University of Minnesota, USA

Chapter 4

Laurie A. Henry, University of Kentucky, USA

Chapter 5

Thao Lê, University of Tasmania, Australia
Quynh Lê, University of Tasmania, Australia

Section 2
Technoliteracy in Practice

Section 3
The Literacy of Gaming

Detailed Table of Contents

Section 1
Leadership

Chapter 1

Amanda Walker, Tasmanian Department of Education, Australia
Bridgette Huddlestone, Tasmanian Department of Education, Australia
Darren L. Pullen, University of Tasmania, Australia

This chapter examines how being literate is vital for learning and working, with a focus on the digital age. The reliance on technology however has created problems and opportunities particularly in regards to who has access to technology and how it is used. The authors propose that the interconnectedness of digital technologies ultimately transforms how and when we communicate resulting in another form of literacy known as technoliteracy. This chapter provides a brief overview of technoliteracy in addition to its more theoretical and practical applications.

Chapter 2

Donna Mahar, State University of New York, USA

This chapter focuses on Colleen, who took part in a two year qualitative study designed to explore young adolescents' use of information communication technology and popular media texts to make sense of themselves and their world. Through a framework based on the concept of multiliteracies and activity theory, the study looks at the overlaps and schisms between adolescents' use of ICT and popular media texts in their everyday lives (home, community, peer group) and how adolescents' engagement with ICT and popular media texts affects established social institutions, while at the same time it illustrates the non-linear, non-hierarchical complexity of the pedagogy of multiliteracies.

Chapter 3

Candance Doerr-Stevens, University of Minnesota, USA

This chapter explores the hybrid identity design online, i.e. how native English speakers intermix local and global resources in strategic ways in a process the author has termed *glocal appropriation*. The chapter presents a case study of one native English speaker's use of local and global resources to design an online identity and how through this hybrid identity practice of glocal appropriation, he is able to design new imaginaries of self, which promotes continued participation and, in turn, allows for literacy learning and spaces of civic pluralism.

Chapter 4

Laurie A. Henry, University of Kentucky, USA

This chapter presents a comparative, qualitative study that explored social equity issues related to technology integration among middle schools located in the United States of America in order to determine if inequalities related to technology integration generally, and the development of multiliteracies specifically, exist. The author identifies several contextual factors that may impede the development of the new literacies including the use of the Internet as an information resource.

Chapter 5

Thao Lê, University of Tasmania, Australia
Quynh Lê, University of Tasmania, Australia

This chapter explores, using a Critical Discourse Analysis (CDA) perspective, how Information Technology (IT) has permeated many fields and aspects of modern society particularly through the use of the Internet. The introduction of the Internet has brought in a range of new areas such as e-commerce, e-health and e-learning. The authors argue IT is socially situated and its role and impacts cannot be divorced from its socio-cultural context as evidenced when using a CDA approach. The authors challenge experts in IT, educators and users to consider the instrumental power of IT and how to use it responsibly to enhance humanity.

Section 2
Technoliteracy in Practice

Chapter 6

Abbad Alabbad, The University of Queensland, Australia
Christina Gitsaki, The University of Queensland, Australia
Peter White, The University of Queensland, Australia

This chapter investigates the impact of computers and the Internet on both the achievement of learners of English as a foreign language (EFL) and their attitudes toward learning EFL. The findings of the study indicate a strong positive shift in the subjects' attitude and motivation toward learning EFL after using the new technology-based approach. These findings provide strong support for the effectiveness of a technology-enhanced learning environment for second language teaching and learning.

Chapter 7

With digital communications and technological media becoming an integral part of the new professional workplace and everyday lives of the younger generation (especially in post-industrial societies), comes the clarion call for educators to develop a more complex understanding of language and literacy and how to go about designing pedagogies that equip students with 21st Century skills. This chapter presents two case studies that examine the complex interaction of teachers, students, writing pedagogies, language curriculum and Information and Communication Technologies (ICT). The study explored students' experiences of using ICT in second language writing and the impact of ICT on writing pedagogy and the curriculum, producing in-depth descriptions and interpretations to answer a set of focused research questions.

Chapter 8

This chapter explores how senior visual arts students engage with and utilise technology in the creation of art works during their program of study. Interpreted through a social constructivist perspective, the findings revealed that the senior visual arts students regularly used technology as part of their process, but often reverted to using traditional media with some technological aspects in the creation of their final work.

Chapter 9

This chapter describes a research project, which explores the challenges and concerns preservice teachers face when teaching complex literature such as Shakespeare. The main question this chapter attempts to answer is: is there room for technology in the study of the bard? Through a repertoire of literacy practices and interactions with a set of digital vodcasts featuring an 'expert teacher' teaching Shakespeare's

Hamlet, the preservice teachers in this study effectively engaged in a 'cognitive apprenticeship' on their way to becoming reflective practitioners.

Chapter 10

This chapter describes a study that took place at a Catholic PreK-8 school/parish where pre-service teachers worked with elementary students to create a range of multi-media projects. These projects showcased the oral histories of the people, places, and events of the school and church community and allowed the pre-service teachers to integrate technology into their teaching. The pre-service teachers' attempts at learning through and teaching with technology, revealed a multiplicity of enactments of fast literacies and reflected the notion of the "intersection" between school, community, and technology.

Chapter 11

This chapter describes a study that took place at a Catholic PreK-8 school/parish where pre-service teachers worked with elementary students to create a range of multi-media projects. These projects showcased the oral histories of the people, places, and events of the school and church community and allowed the pre-service teachers to integrate technology into their teaching. The pre-service teachers' attempts at learning through and teaching with technology, revealed a multiplicity of enactments of fast literacies and reflected the notion of the "intersection" between school, community, and technology.

Section 3
The Literacy of Gaming

Chapter 12

This chapter examines the multiliteracies associated with Massively Multiplayer Online Games (MMOGs). Specifically, it desrcibes the nature and affordances of the associated technologies as they pertain to the multiliteracies of consumption and production in an effort to provide an understanding of the nature of skills necessary to function in a multiliterate and multimodal world.

This chapter explores the way in which educators in a multi-literate society must find opportunities for students to interact and interpret the multitude of new literacies. This chapter discusses how multi-literacies are bound up in computer games and how educators can employ these games through play, study and creation to shift students from consumers to creators of interactive narratives. The chapter also raises questions about computer game use in the primary classroom, and calls for an integrated approach to teacher and trainee teacher professional development in the area of computer gaming.

This chapter explores the author's journey of literacy learning from a player's perspective. The author created an avatar and joined the online community of the Massively Multiplayer Online Game, the *World of Warcraft™* produced by Blizzard Entertainment®. An autoethnographic approach was undertaken to explore the game's linguistic, visual, audio, spatial and gestural elements of design to provide an insider's perspective of the meaning-making resources that were on offer. The chapter concludes with a tentative consideration of how understandings about the literacies used within a virtual world might inform the learning of literacies in schools and other educational institutions.

Foreword

Technoliteracy, Discourse and Social Practice: Frameworks and Applications in the Digital Age by Pullen, Baguley and Gitsaki is about future citizenship and the need to embrace a diversified range of literacies to interact, communicate, learn and survive in the 21st century. To be productive in a modern world it is necessary to prepare multi-literate students by providing educational experiences that embrace linguistic, visual, auditory, gestural and spatial modes of communication.

Previous traditional connotations of literacy focused on text-based reading and the ability of the reader to comprehend, interpret and evaluate the text for understanding and communication. With the advent of more complex media through the internet, three-dimensional environments, mobile technology and the need to socially connect across national borders, literacy in the 21st Century needs to be re-conceptualized. Literacy in the digital age has now become multi-faceted, and its diversified nature means that global citizens require a range of skills to effectively communicate and interact in the modern world. Ubiquitous technology and unprecedented levels of access by privileged users mean that technology is fundamentally reshaping how people interact in the world. There has also been a blurring of our personal and professional lives as we have become network connected 24/7 both wirelessly and socially through our mobile devices as well as being geographically located through our GPS enabled accessories. To be functional and literate in the digital age requires a change in mindset from all community members as there is a widespread need to embrace multi-literacy. This involves embracing a new language that is intertwined with the internet, new media and new thought processes. We all need to become proficient in the new literacies; all levels of education will need to be cognisant of this shift in learning and teaching where students become designers and creators not consumers.

Technology is a fundamental component of new literacies, offering networking, access, rich media and immersive engagement in three dimensional network games that embrace millions of users across the globe. Technology has changed the way we interact, communicate, network and the language that we use. However the way we approach technology is essential for acquiring literacy. Technology skills are insufficient to assist this process and it is no longer relevant to perceive technology as a skill. Our mindset needs to recognize technology as a tool that is shaped and molded to suit the situation. This change in perception needs to occur at both the educator and student levels as teachers need to change their perceptions of technology, develop expertise and technology confidence in order to educate the next generation of student designers. What it means to be educated is fundamentally changing and it is essential that society does not create a wider digital divide between the multi-literate and the mono-literate. Access and equity is still a key concept in relation to internet technologies and there is still inequity of access due to socio-economic status and the infrastructure available within a country.

Chapters in the book cover a diverse range of topics related to technology, literacy, techno-literacy and multi-literacy which is a key concept throughout the book. Social inequality in relation to access to technology and access to innovative education create a digital divide which is eloquently examined within the book. Users are generating new meaning through their use of new media as the affordances allow new ways of thinking and new ways of expressing ideas and thoughts across the global network of professional and social networks. This book is an essential tool for engaging with the key areas of multi-literacy and the digital age and will provoke wide discussion on communicating as a global citizen in a modern world.

Professor Mike Keppell
Professor of Higher Education
Director, The Flexible Learning Institute
Charles Sturt University

Mike Keppell *is Professor of Higher Education and Director, The Flexible Learning Institute, Charles Sturt University, mkeppell@csu.edu.au BHMS (Ed)(Qld); B.Ed (PG) (Qld); M.Ed (Calgary); Ph.D (Calgary). Professor Keppell is currently working in the roles of Director, The Flexible Learning Institute and Professor of Higher Education at Charles Sturt University. The Flexible Learning Institute, newly established within Charles Sturt University, has as its aim to promote and foster excellence in flexible learning and teaching, through pedagogical scholarship, promotion of exemplary practice and policy advice. Prior to this, he worked at the Hong Kong Institute of Education as Associate Professor and Head of the Centre for Learning, Teaching and Technology (LTTC) from 2003 – 2007. Before joining the Institute of Education, he was Head of the Biomedical Multimedia Unit, Faculty of Medicine, Dentistry and Health Science, The University of Melbourne from 1998 – 2002 and Head of the Interactive Multimedia Unit, Division of Distance and Continuing Education, Central Queensland University from 1994 –1998. He has a background in teaching and learning, curriculum, evaluation and more specifically instructional design. His expertise lies in his ability to combine the operational and development tasks of educational technology with the academic study of curriculum, instructional design and evaluation. He has worked as an instructional designer on hundreds of technology-enhanced initiatives in areas as diverse as coal-mining, medicine, science, nursing, dentistry, physiotherapy, psychology, multimedia, human movement studies and education. His research focuses on blended learning, learning oriented assessment, authentic learning and transformative learning using design based research.*

Preface

The nature of the education system is becoming increasingly more complex and more globally focused. Today, most effective teaching would incorporate a variety of different media types, or combinations of, as result of this interconnection of media learning and teaching has become much a more complex set of events (CISCO, 2008).

Given the changes that are occurring as a result of globalisation and the proliferation of digital technologies the nature of what is considered 'core' educational skills is also evolving. For instance, the nature of literacy has evolved from being able to 'simply' decode written information through to acquiring the basic knowledge and skills in reading and writing (Baker & Street, 1994). However the advent of the Internet and increasing access to information and communication technology (ICT), specifically computers, in the late 1990's has necessitated a broadening of the concept and notion of what is literacy and what it means to be literate in the 21st Century (Lonsdale & Curry, 2004). In recognition, or perhaps as a result of the increasing globalisation and increasing use and reliance on technology, the United Nations (UN) proposed a need to redefine the term 'literacy' to acknowledge that the uses of literacy is rapidly being altered in the face of a new economy - the knowledge economy - which is seeing individuals from different social and cultural groups interacting via the use of technology (Lonsdale & Curry, 2004). With this increase use of technology-based communication societies and individuals are bringing into the conversation their own cultural processes, personal circumstances and literacy demands.

These communicative changes led a group of literacy academics in 1996 to coin the term *Multiliteracies*. Brought together in New Hampshire, New London the proponents of multiliteracies considered the future of literacy teaching and made predictions on how and what should be taught in a rapidly changing world. The New London Group, as they were to be called, believed that multiliteracies best described the emerging, cultural and institutional order of the day. They believed the term encapsulated the 'multiplicity of communication … and media' available to learners, whilst also recognising the increasing cultural and linguistic diversity between and amongst learners (Cope & Kalantzis, 2000). However, the New London Group could not have foretold the rapid advances of technology and new communication mediums that have developed in the proceeding years. Accordingly the notion of multiliteracies has evolved.

Reasons for the evolution of multiliteracies, and hence literacy, include the developments of technology, globalisation of national economies, the proliferation of information, lifelong educational experiences, the diversity of cultural perspectives, new teaching and learning practices, a move to make learning possible anywhere and anytime, flexible modes of delivery and the critical dimension of questioning traditional practices. This broadening of traditional notions of literacy led Lonsdale and McCurry (2004) to believe that literacy "is multiple with multiple purposes" (p. 10), meaning that to be literate in a digital world learners need to be able to use a variety of literacy sources, or modes, such as print, visual, auditory, kinaesthetic or any combination thereof. The Internet is a good example of a text which is multimodal as it not only supports print, it also supports sound and pictures - and often with interconnections (hyperlinks) between several different literacy sources at once. As such, learners are presented with a range of ways to make meaning of their world and given the interactivity of the technology to also be able to contribute to the world at a personal and global level. For instance, wikis (i.e. Wikipedia) and social networking sites (i.e. FaceBook) allow individuals to communicate to their friends whilst also giving them the opportunity and some might say power, to 'talk' to anyone who visits their site.

Chapters of the Text "Technoliteracy, Discourse and Social Practice: Frameworks and Applications in the Digital Age"

This text commences with an introductory overview in **Chapter One** of how society has become increasingly reliant on technology titled *An Overview of Technology in Society: An Introduction to Technoliteracy*. Amanda Walker, Bridgette Huddleston and Darren L. Pullen highlight how a range of digital technologies are interconnected resulting in another form of literacy known as 'technoliteracy'. This brief overview of technoliteracy is supported by an investigation of both its theoretical and practical applications.

Chapter Two is *Designs of Meaning: Redesigning Perceptions of School and Self Using Tactics of Resistance*. In this chapter Donna Mahar has conducted a two year investigation into young adolescents' use of information communication technology and popular media texts to make sense of themselves and their world. The subject of her study 'Colleen' utilises a range of technologies and multiliteracies to challenge social conventions and expectations of behaviour. During this journey Colleen eloquently explains her choices and rationalises her interactions. Her expertise in utilising multiliteracies is an important factor in her ability to defend and support peers who do have the capacity to do so.

Chapter Three is named *Hybrid Identity Design Online: Glocal Appropriation as Multiliterate Practice for Civic Pluralism*. Candace Doerr-Stevens investigates the concept of *glocal appropriation*. This is explained as the process native English speakers use to combine local and global resources in strategic ways. This phenomenon is investigated through the case study of one native English speaker and how he has designed new images of self which enables him to participate in and find a space in which to engage in literacy learning in addition to exploring and participating in civic pluralism.

Chapter Four is titled *Unpacking Social Inequalities: How a Lack of Technology Integration may Impede the Development of Multiliteracies among Middle School Students in the United States*. Laurie A. Henry examines how limited or no access to technology may result in inequalities for students. The ramifications of this situation, particularly in terms of how it can affect the future of young people is examined along with a range of contextual factors.

Chapter Five by Thao Lê and Quynh Lê titled *Information Technology: A Critical Discourse Analysis Perspective* examines the field of Information Technology through a Critical Discourse Analysis (CDA) perspective. In addition to describing a range of new areas which information technology has developed such as e-commerce, e-health and e-learning the authors argue that IT is socially constructed and therefore cannot be divorced from this context. Therefore IT experts, educators and those who utilise IT in instrumental ways are challenged to consider the responsibility they have.

The second section of the text focuses on the practice of technoliteracy. **Chapter Six** by Abbad Albbad, Christina Gitsaki and Peter White titled *CALL Course Design for Second Language Learning: A Case Study of Arab EFL Learners* investigates the impact of computers and the Internet on how English Foreign Language (EFL) students learn and how they feel about learning English as a foreign language. The study found that the participants motivation increased substantially when they were able to use a technology based approach when learning a foreign language. The authors therefore propose that a technology-enhanced environment is an important requirement when teaching a foreign language.

Chapter Seven titled *ICT in Malay Language Learning: Lessons Learned from Two Case Studies* written by Abduyah Yaakub, Christina Gitsaki and Eileen Honan also investigates the complexities involved in learning another language. The authors argue that educators are required to develop a more complex understanding of language and literacy in order to design pedagogies that equip students with 21st century skills. This study is presented via two case studies which examine the complex interaction of teachers, students, writing pedagogies, language curriculum and Information and Communication Technologies (ICT). This chapter builds on the previous one by exploring how students' experience using ICT to assist them in their writing in a foreign language and also how ICT impacts on writing pedagogy and the curriculum.

Chapter Eight written by Martin Kerby and Margaret Baguley is titled *A Snapshot View of how Senior Visual Arts Students Encounter and Engage with Technology in Their Arts Practice*. This study investigated three senior art students from two different schools in order to compare and contrast the findings. Although technology is firmly embedded in the daily lives of these students the findings revealed that even though the schools were well resourced, the students often reverted to using traditional media with some technological aspects in the creation of their final work. Interviews were conducted at the beginning, middle and end of the year to provide a snapshot view at these critical stages of how the students work was developing in this critical year of their visual arts studies.

Chapter Nine titled *The Bard and the Web: Using Vodcasting to Enhance Teaching of Shakespeare to Pre-Service English Teachers* written by Anita Jetnikoff explores the challenges and concerns teachers face when teaching literature considered to be more complex for students such as Shakespeare. The author ponders whether technology can be effectively utilised to engage students in the study of Shakespeare. A series of digital vodcasts utilised by an expert teacher with pre-service English teachers are examined to consider whether using technology participants are familiar with will provide a greater connection with, and insight into, learning about Shakespeare. The 'cognitive apprenticeship' model adopted in this study is also examined in its potential to enhance the reflective aspect of professional identity.

Chapter Ten titled *Developing Literate Practices in Design and Technology Education* by Mike Brown examines how literate practices are demonstrated in the field of Design and Technology. The context of this study is Victorian Year 12 Design and Technology students. This study reveals that there is an increasing demand for literacy skills and expertise from both students and teachers in this area. To support this finding the author has analysed the curriculum and pedagogical practices associated with the mandated Year 12 Design and Technology program in Victoria and has illustrated how multimodal texts in particular are being utilised as an important aspect in this area.

Chapter Eleven concludes this section and is titled *Multimedia, Oral History, and Teacher Education: From Community Space to Cyberspace*. Jenifer Schneider, James R. King, Deborah Kozdras, James Welsh, and Vanessa Minick have conducted a study at a Catholic PreK-8 school/parish community where pre-service teachers have worked with elementary students to create a range of multi-media projects. These projects, in addition to showcasing the oral histories of the participants, places and events of the school and church community, have allowed the pre-service teachers to integrate technology into their teaching. The study revealed that the pre-service teachers utilised 'fast' literacies when learning to incorporate technology into their teaching. In addition it became evident that there was an intersection evident through the use of technoliteracies between the school and the community.

Section Three of the text investigates the literacy of gaming. **Chapter Twelve** titled *The Hidden Literacies of Massively Multiplayer Online Games* written by P.G. Schrader and K.A Lawless, examines the multiliteracies associated with Massively Multiplayer Online Games also known as MMOGs. This chapter describes the nature of and examines the type of technologies used in these types of games. The games are based on the idea of supply and demand and therefore the study investigates the multiliteracies of consumption and production in an effort to provide an understanding of the nature of skills necessary to function in a multiliterate and multimodal world.

Chapter Thirteen written by Pam Wright and David Skidmore is titled *Multiliteracies and Games: Do Cybergamers Dream of Pedagogic Sheep?* In this chapter the authors examine the way in which educators in a multi-literate society are expected to engage students to interact and interpret a multitude of new literacies. The authors explore how multiliteracies are bound up in computer games and consider how educators can employ these games through play, study and creation to shift students from consumers to creators of interactive narratives. This chapter also considers how computer games can be used in the primary classroom and in this process argues for an integrated approach to teacher and pre-service teacher professional development in the area of computer gaming.

Chapter Fourteen, the final chapter in this text, is written by Robyn Henderson and is titled *Learning from Computer Games: Literacy Learning in a Virtual World.* Through an autoethnographic approach the author investigates the Massively Multiplayer Online Game the *World of Warcraft* ™ produced by Blizzard Entertainment®. During this process the author created an avatar and joined the online community of the *World of Warcraft*™. The chapter explores the strategies the author used to access and navigate this MMOG with particular attention given to the game's linguistic, visual, audio, spatial and gestural elements of design to provide an insider's perspective of the meaning-making resources that were offered. The chapter concludes with some considerations given as to how a virtual world might inform the learning of literacies in schools and other institutions.

CONCLUSION

Each of the chapters in *Technoliteracy, Discourse and Social Practice: Frameworks and Applications in the Digital Age* provides a unique and important insight into the diverse approaches to and implementation of technoliteracy in different contexts. It is evident that the authors comprehend the significance and value of preparing students, educators and those responsible for Information Technology to use effectively and ethically to enhance learning. These dimensions are particularly evident in the first section of the book. An examination of the practical applications of ICT is of interest to practitioners and others interested in this area. How ICT is utilised in the classroom to enhance the way students learn and to utilise a form of communication many of them are comfortable with provides important information for educators. The building upon of research in this way results in a richer and more comprehensive understanding of how this important field is being utilised in education. The final section provides an important examination of how gaming combines a range of literacies and in the process develops quite sophisticated skills in its players. The ability to navigate complex levels of multimedia text and interactive elements requires advanced skills in multiliteracies. These skills are imperative to function in an increasingly visual world which relies on tacit understandings of a number of conventions to function effectively. The multilteracies approach advocated by The New London Group has been transformed into a technoliteracies approach which complements their concern that young people need to be prepared so that they can operate in a world in which their quality of life is enhanced by whatever means they use to communicate.

REFERENCES

Baker, D. & Street, B. (1994). Literacy and numeracy: Concepts and definitions. In T Husén, & T Postlethwaite, *The international encyclopedia of education* (vol.6, pp. 3453–3459). London: Pergamon.

CISCO, (2008). *Multimodal learning through the media: What research says.* Paper commissioned by CISCO (pp. 1-24). Retrieved February 2, 2009 from http://www.cisco.com/web/strategy/docs/education/Multimodal-Learning-Through-Media.pdf.

Lonsdale, M. & McCurry, D. (2004). Literacy in the new millennium. Report prepared for National Centre for Vocational Education Research (NCVER). *Australian Council for Educational Research* (pp. 1-50). Adelaide: Department of Education, Science and Training.

Cope, B. & Kalantzis, M. (Eds.). (2000). *Multiliteracies: Learning and the design of social futures.* London: Routledge.

Acknowledgment

Deep gratitude goes to the contributing authors who generously shared their work in this handbook. Their response to our call for chapters demonstrates the willingness of educators to share and 'tell their stories'.

We are grateful to the many peer reviewers, whose careful reading and constructive comments enabled the authors to improve and develop their chapters. Nonetheless, the co-editors take full responsibility for any errors, omissions, or weaknesses in this work.

We also acknowledge that without the continual support of IGI Global, the *Handbook of Technoliteracy, Discourse and Social Practice: Frameworks and Applications in the Digital Age* would not have been possible. In particular we would like to acknowledge the important contributions given to us by the IGI editorial team. To Tyler Heath, Heather Probst and Kristin Roth we thank you for your continued support and encouragement.

Finally, we thank you, the reader, for giving this book your attention. We hope that after reading this handbook you will be motivated and inspired to use digital technologies in your own teaching. We hope that when a future call for chapters goes out, you will be ready to share your discoveries by contributing a chapter.

Sincerely,

Darren Lee Pullen, Christina Gitsaki & Margaret Baguley

Co-editors

Section 1
Leadership

Chapter 1
An Overview of Technology in Society:
An Introduction to Technoliteracy

Amanda Walker
Tasmanian Department of Education, Australia

Bridgette Huddlestone
Tasmanian Department of Education, Australia

Darren L. Pullen
University of Tasmania, Australia

ABSTRACT

Being literate is vital for learning and working, possibly more so in the digital age than in the industrial age, given society's reliance on digital technologies. Individual and societal reliance on technology has in turn created problems and opportunities. The associated problems concern who has access to what forms of technology and when and how it is used. The opportunities centre on the interconnectedness of digital technologies, which ultimately transform how and when we communicate. When technology and communication are joined together they form another literacy commonly referred to as technoliteracy. This chapter will provide a brief overview of some of the ways in which literacy and technology interconnect and will provide the reader with sufficient understanding of the field to enable them to grasp some of the more theoretical and practical applications of technoliteracy discussed in the following chapters.

INTRODUCTION

We live in times of rapid technological change. New forms of technology--such as the Internet, personal digital assistants and mobile phones, to name but a few--require further understandings and capabilities to comprehend and conform to new ways of doing things. New technology has the capacity to shape and reform societal norms, often dictating how things are done. It can also be said that the reverse is often true, in that society shapes and forms new technologies (Pullen, 2008). In this information rich society information and communication technologies (ICT) are at the heart of human life and social developments. People have always worked together and communicated via speech, writing and the printed word (Scouter,

DOI: 10.4018/978-1-60566-842-0.ch001

2003). The rapid advancement of computers and communication technologies has reached a point where technology is omnipresent in almost every facet of our lives. This has enabled individuals and society to become interconnected in ways that were previously unimaginable, making access to information easier and transforming how we communicate (Finger, Russell, Jamieson-Proctor & Russell, 2007).

The advancement of the Internet in the early 1990s, resulted in the concept of the global village and subsequently new ways of teaching and learning involving hypertext, multimodality and virtual classrooms. This rapid rise in fast, mass communication has reached the point that in order to live, learn and work successfully we must learn to use technology efficiently and effectively. This has lead to a new term called *technoliteracy* which in effect refers to how literate one is with technology and how they use the technology to communicate.

Strongly associated with the rise of digital technologies, specifically computers, which are becoming more affordable and available, society has had to change to keep pace with technological developments. This upsurge of technologies can be attributed to how society has changed from an 'industrial-based' economy, referred to as the *industrial age*, to a 'knowledge-based' economy, known as the *information age* (Cepeda, 2006; Davenport & Prusak, 2000). As a result of these technologically driven changes, labour markets are changing from an industrial base to a knowledge production process, where work practices are being transformed. This context demands a more specialised, highly educated, flexible and technologically savvy workforce (Meredyth, Russell, Blackwood, Thomas & Wise, 1999). Corresponding with the transformation from an industrial age to an information age, society in general has also had to adapt to technological advancements, just as labour markets have and are continuing to do. The implications and global scale of this change have significant global, regional,

local and individual repercussions. To varying degrees, all individuals, organisations and societies are affected by this change and "only those who realign their practices most effectively to the information age ... will reap ... benefits. Those who do not will be ... diminished by ... competitors" (Dolence & Norris, 1995, p. 2).

Parallel to the increase in technology in our workplaces and homes is the presence of technology in schools. Technologies such as computers and the Internet are increasingly being made available to teachers and schools, to the point that their presence in schools would be considered to be normal and their absence would be a rarity. Indeed many governments around the world have made the public provision of technology, specifically computers, fundamental education policy. For instance, in the United States, the No Child Left Behind Act of 2001 has the goal of maximising technology's contributions to improving education (US DoE, 2009), whilst in Australia the focus is on a one-to-one student to computer ratio for every student from grade nine onwards (Australian Labor Party, 2007). Whilst both policies have their merits and faults each has a common fundamental belief that technology access and skill development is an essential requirement for a well-rounded education and the subsequent advancement of a country's economic prosperity.

Within an educational environment the classroom is no longer a room within a school that is isolated from other classrooms or indeed from its local context or global society. Indeed it could be argued that the classrooms of today are global. That is to say that the classrooms of today are places where the educational uses of technology are coming together in terms of development and application and new ways of teaching and learning are becoming apparent. At the cutting edge of this change is the relationship between human users of technology and the technology itself. This relationship between humans and technology, or machines, is termed *humachine*. For example, recent technological innovations have increased the speed and *reach* of communicative endeavours. For instance, newer digital technologies do not operate in isolation from each other. An example of this convergence is the use of the Internet for local and international phone calls by using local area phone lines connected to the Internet's network of networks. Besides the convergence of networks the phone example also indicates how technologies are becoming increasingly interconnected and interrelated. In this example a phone call can be made using a standard landline which uses the service provider's physical landlines and then peripheral line or satellite transmission. Furthermore, a caller could alternatively use their computer (or normal phone) and their Internet connection (via a modem) to make a call over the Internet. This is called voice over internet protocol (VOIP) and offers users the advantage of cheap phone calls locally and internationally.

Technically the phone example illustrates convergence at a binary digital form in which data is transmitted from point A to point B but it also illustrates how communication has become global. Communication of data in a binary form allows for the transmission of data or information in any format, whether that is sound, images, text or any multimedia combination. Therefore communication is no longer confined to any one media format allowing a user to communicate with one or many individuals in a variety of media formats simultaneously. This mass communication using multimedia allows individuals to not only get their messages across in different literacy modes it also gives the receivers an opportunity to manipulate the data into a format that is suited to their learning or work needs. The users' ability to send, receive and reformulate digital data into different literacy modes is the essence of being technoliterate.

An example of the evolving nature of technology convergence, and the interconnected nature of technology to the human users, is that of learning communities that one finds online or in social networking programmes, such as SIMS, Facebook or World of War Craft, which are both a part of the complex identity units and distribution facilities for ideas about current culture. Teachers in these situations need to be aware of how new forms of language, values, group dynamics and shifts in behaviour will change the learning requirements of their students. This does not mean that teachers should become immediately conversant in SMS (short message service) messaging to teach - but that understanding about how cultural homogeny mediated through technology determines the ways in which students may take a stance or hold attitudes that have previously been part of face-to-face performances (Pullen, Baguley & Marsden, 2009).

Accordingly it is important that the education sector not only respond to these labour market changes, but redefine the education landscape - from one of merely educating students to one of instigating and sustaining a passion for life-long learning. With ICT attributed as being the catalyst for current education reform (Australian Council of Deans of Education, 2001; Meredyth et al. 1999; Office of Educational Research and Improvement, 1998), the Australian Council of Deans of Education (2001) describes this as '*new learning for new time*'. It is quite feasible that the career paths for today's students do not even exist in current labour markets (Papert, 1998). The education sector has to accommodate for this and critically look at the way students are being prepared and trained for life in today's world, as well as their futures (Twigg & Oblinger, 1996).

These teaching, learning and job changes have occurred within a very short period of time (Taylor, 1998). The rapid advancement and innovation of technology places an expectation, at least according to Mumford (1979), that humans "should and would adapt to the demands of the technology" (p. 2). However this can only occur effectively when technology is made to suit the requirements of the users as well. A recent example of this is the mobile phone that was primarily a tool for verbal communication; however the change from analogue to digital transmission allowed users to quickly take advantage of the alpha-numeric nature of data to create SMS or text messaging. Telecommunication companies and manufacturers responded in turn by adding additional phone features such as cameras, Internet connectivity and more recently options to pay for goods and services. As a result of these technological advancements users in turn are finding new and novel ways to utilise the technology for personal and social communication.

BACKGROUND

The modern world is one of constant change that is currently undergoing a shift from the industrial age to that of a new technological or information age. This shift has far reaching implications for all areas of our society, including that of education. As the world progresses into this technology rich environment, our ways of living, communicating and educating are also transforming. Traditional means of teaching and understanding literacy is shifting from traditional forms of printed and visual text, mainly in the forms of reading and writing, to the more technologically advanced ways of the world. According to Lankshear, Snyder & Green (2000) these technologies are becoming fundamental to our modern society and the shift towards the technological age is becoming more apparent in all areas of society, including the education sector. Children born into this technological age are exposed to a diverse range of technologies from birth and quickly become literate in new techniques, strategies and processes. Prensky (2001) labelled today's students as 'digital natives' referring to the way in which they are using ICT in their everyday lives and how their attitude towards ICT and technology differs from those who were born before this digital age. Prensky (2001) also described people not born during the digital age as 'digital immigrants', indicating that they are not native

to the culture, but have adopted the practices at a later stage and certainly are not as comfortable with the technology as the 'natives'.

To define technology as one single element is difficult. Many have defined technology as the devices and processes used to assist with communication (Moursund, 2005; Tinio, 2007; UNESCO, 2003). Defining literacy is also challenging, but is usually described as the ability to communicate with others through, speaking, listening, reading and writing (Hill & Mulhearn, 2007). The common factor in these two definitions is that of communication. It is this common factor linking both technology and literacy together that creates the notion of technoliteracy. Technoliteracy can be described as the use and understanding of technological devices, such as home and mobile telephones, personal computers, personal digital assistants (PDAs), the Internet and World Wide Web, faxes, scanners, digital still and video cameras and multimedia programmes (Moursund, 2005).

The majority of students in western schools today have access to these types of equipment and in many cases, are more familiar with the technology than their teachers. Peck, Cuban and Kirkpatrick's (2002) study of teachers use and understanding of ICT and recent investigations by Huddlestone (2008) and Walker (2008) revealed that teachers were not as comfortable or as confident in using ICT as their students. Furthermore the aforementioned studies were in accordance with Lankshear, Snyder & Green's (2000) study that found students often taught their teachers how to use newer technologies. These findings relate directly to the notion of technoliteracy, where students of today are becoming increasingly technologically savvy and use ICT in their everyday lives with ease.

The development and widespread use of technologies, along with the greater understanding of their importance as a communication tool has occurred across all sectors including the education sector. This has resulted in a growing need amongst organisations to adopt practices that promote the use of technologies in order for individuals and organisations to achieve their individual and corporate strategies more efficiently and effectively (Lin & Pervan, 2003; Peppard & Ward, 2004). The current trend and future focus, particularly in western societies is for increased efficiencies in the workplace, which is contributing to the further deployment of digital technologies in schools (Finger et al., 2007).

As a consequence of this increase and integration of the use of technology in society, the education sector has had to re-evaluate its role in preparing students for their future lives, necessitating reconstruction of teacher-student relationships and changes in the culture of the classroom learning environment (Meredyth et al., 1999). This requires teachers to participate in continuous professional development and training to assist their understanding of new technologies and how they can be used to introduce, support and extend traditional and current content and context in the classroom. In Australia these changes have been implemented in all states and territories making the use of technology in schools a high priority and part of school policy. Over the past decade, and more recently, the education sector has made considerable investments in technology and ICT infrastructure and training a priority. For example, the recent Australian federal government's *Education Revolution* (2008) is funding schools for the provision of digital technologies, typically computers, and associated infrastructure and training. This investment of time and resources demands a huge financial commitment that the school as an organisation needs to recognise and manage in order to justify and prioritise its ICT investment (Kumar, 2002; Milis & Mercken, 2004).

One of the cornerstones of the Australian government's *Education Revolution* is the need for literacy in its various guises to assume an increased prominence, an aspect that has been supported in the mainstream literacy sector (Davis, 2008; Lankshear & Knobel, 2003). Over time various

forms or models of literacy and literate practices have been advocated. For example, during the 1980s theorists such as Hirsch (1987) proposed cultural literacy, and more recently the concept of critical literacy (Freebody & Luke, 1990) have been advocated and supported. However, advances in technology, specifically multimedia capable computers and the World Wide Web, together with workplace and educational reforms have meant a reconceptualising of what literacy is and what literate skills are required for the twenty-first century. Given the aforementioned changes a group of literacy academics proposed the concept of "multiliteracies" in 1996 (New London Group, 1996). Since the characterisation of multiliteracies much has changed in the field of literacy education. The fundamental aspect of multiliteracies was to make a connection between the multiplicity of literacies that are present in learning contexts, and the wider plane of social change, so that teachers may make sense of this multiplicity of literacies and utilise it in the form of new pedagogies that correspond to diverse learning options with special reference to evolving technological applications. In addressing these evolving domains the proponents of multiliteracies suggested that literacy educators need to re-orient their pedagogical practices in fundamental ways. These were explained as the processes of meaning-making as design, which were translated into a pragmatic pedagogy of situated practice, overt instruction; critical framing and transformed practice (see Pullen & Cole, forthcoming for a more detailed description and analysis of multiliteracies in theory and practice).

Following on from multiliteracies Lankshear, Snyder and Green (2000) proposed the concept of technoliteracy in order to address how newer technologies are shaping literacy practices, such as SMS and icon driven mobile phone messaging. However, regardless of the terminology - multiliteracies or technoliteracy - the advent of technology, in particular personal computers, mobile phones and the internet, has enabled communication to spread rapidly from the local to the international context. This rapid and global proliferation of technologies and communication mediums has not only increased the multiplicity of communication channels but has led to an increasing awareness of, and exposure to, cultural and linguistic diversity. The proliferation of technology and communication has in turn moved the notion of literacy and what it means to be literate from being a singular concept which has historically centred on written and oral language through to the notion of literacy practices which encapsulates a broader notion of literacy inherently related to specific socio-cultural contexts. In effect, to be literate in a technologically rich global society requires literacy practices to extend beyond formal school learning to be inclusive and supportive of productive participation in wider social and community contexts which are inherently technologically orientated and enhanced.

Defining Technoliteracy in the Digital Age

The shift from the industrial to the digital age has great significance, particularly in the education sector. According to Zammit and Downes (2002) students of this era need more than just being able to read and write - their world is full of technological change, which in turn demands them to be multiliterate or technoliterate. This natural interest in and exposure to technology has immeasurable social and economic benefits within the school environment. Recently the Australian education sector, like other western countries, has adopted the widespread introduction of digital technologies in the education sector which address these economic, social and educational reform agendas to move from the industrial age into the knowledge economy. The education sector has recognised the importance of technology use and with funding is implementing policy within schools to establish life-long learning with technology to achieve desired education outcomes.

The implementation of these policies is in line with the interests of today's students who have a natural affinity for technology and see it as an absolute facet of their lives. The ease in which students use technology in their personal lives should be embraced and extended in schools to complement classroom content and curriculum. Today's students are connected with their technologies in ways that may not have been imagined a few years ago, or indeed when the technology they are using was devised. When students use technology to communicate they enter into an informational relationship with their machines in terms of locating materials and performing the logical sequential steps to enable them to make choices (Cole & Moyle, 2009). The use of these mental strategies and interest in technology could be harnessed in schools to the educational practitioners' advantage. Students' natural interest in the use of the technology and ICT has the potential to increase student engagement, shifting the focus from one of traditional teacher-centred, lecture-based instruction, to one where student learning is supported by inquiry and exploration, scaffolded and supported by the teacher; and one where students are given more responsibility for their own learning (Saville, 2009).

Long acknowledged as an essential skill, being multiliterate is necessary for modern day personal life and employment, as well as being a key element for successful global citizenship (Cope & Kalantzis, 2000). Supporting this notion, Hill and Mulhearn (2007) insist that having multiliterate skills, or rather technoliteracy skills reflecting the technological and digital nature of modern day literacies, are crucial for effective communication and work practices in this era.

The identification of multiliteracies with the use of educational technology has perhaps been its most abiding relationship in practice. In the United Kingdom, the term technological literacy is more readily employed to explain this situation. In the United States digital literacies are more frequently referred to; however in Australia multiliteracies has been the prevailing term. In the field of educational research and practice there has been a blossoming of new literacies which sit somewhere between multiliteracies and actual technological applications as a type of map that shows how the field of ICT innovation and knowledge formation are creating new ways to enable and enhance communication and relationship building. The questions about how technology changes and potentially enhances education and where literacy fits into this process are therefore complex and never ending.

IDENTIFYING KEY AREAS AND ISSUES ASSOCIATED WITH TECHNOLOGY AND LITERACY IN THE DIGITAL AGE

Some might argue that the introduction of ICT into the curriculum heralds a new dawn of educational practice or the advent of an educational revolution in that any knowledge field can be uploaded and transmitted instantaneously to anyone anywhere. Indeed educational technologists or zealots might advocate personal computers for every student, enabling students to access their files, work though the curriculum in an electronic form, and make their designs, calculations and explanations given available knowledge on the subject focus and any corresponding syllabus outcomes. However technology antagonists or luddites might throw up their arms at this suggestion and point to the lack of social and communal contact that this situation would encourage, together with the lack of teacher control on student learning. It could also be argued that the wide-scale introduction of this kind of individualised computer technology might also be a ploy on the part of computer and software manufacturers to sell and supply products. However, the truth of the matter lies somewhere in between these two scenarios. Education has been enhanced and is still being enhanced through new developments in ICT. At the same time users of

that technology are finding new and unimagined ways to utilise the available technologies for personal, work and educational pursuits.

As a consequence of newer technologies and innovative ways of communicating with that technology the notion of what is considered to be a *text* has evolved. Ask a layperson to describe a text and they will probably respond that a text is anything that can be written using the symbols of their language. For instance, a book, newspaper and magazine are possible examples offered by the layperson as examples of texts (Kress, 2003). However, ask the same person to describe the internet and they would probably describe an environment that is comprised of the written word (text) but also incorporates sound, still and moving images all of which is interconnected and allows for user interactivity via hyperlinks. In effect they have described a multimodal text (Anstey & Bull, 2004; Kress & Van Leeuwen, 2001) which they may have daily exposure to via the Internet and interactive TV (e.g. TiVo). All of these advances in technology have in turn challenged the very nature of what literacy is and what it means to be literate in the digital age (Davis, 2008; Goldman, 2004; New London Group, 1996).

The emergence of new forms of literacy has led to new ways of communicating, making meaning, being understood and expressing one's self to others on an intimate and global level. All of this has been made possible by the convergence of digital technologies with the human desire to communicate. As a consequence of the technology-human relationship (humachine) new digital literacy skills are required in order for users to negotiate an increasingly multi-modal communicative environment. However the need for users to be able to decode alphabetic print, know how to make and construct meaningful written and visual texts for particular audiences and generally have access to a range of linguistic resources has not changed from the pre-digital age (Kress, 2003; Larson & Marsh, 2005; Unsworth, 2001). What have changed are the social conditions and expectations for becoming literate and the reliance on technology to achieve a literate status in society.

The broadening of the concept of literacy in the digital age has required educators to re-encapsulate their understanding of "what is literacy" and what technoliteracy skills students will require to operate efficiently and effectively in the new global economy - often referred to as the "knowledge" economy or "information age". Associated with this redefinition of the term literacy is the notion that literacy, or more precisely communication has changed. Given the ease at which technology enables or facilitates communication, it no longer is constrained to an activity which is confined to a local context. Instead, digital technologies enable individuals from all 'walks of life' to communicate on a mass global scale. As such users of global technologies need to be aware of their own and others social and cultural values and beliefs. Which at least according to Gee (1994) requires a "change of identity" (pp.168-169), which given the multimodal nature of digital technologies often necessitates the user to take on a "new identity" (Gee, 2003, p. 51).

The multimodal nature of digital technologies readily allows for the technology to cross-cultural and social divides, as communication is no longer restricted to the dominate language of the country nor is communication restricted to alphabetic scripts (Cope & Kalantzis, 1997; New London Group, 1996, 2000). This cross-cultural aspect in turn causes an ongoing change and reconstruction of meaning being offered by this form of communication. This continual process of transformation brings with it uncertainty and a major cultural shift that is contributing to changing identities and a change in literary practices from print to visual (Green & Bigum, 1993) to multimodal (Kalantzis, Cope & Harvey, 2003; New London Group, 1996; 2000). These changes in turn are further influenced by the speed of technological development and proliferation into our homes and lives. All of which means that as the technology

develops users will find traditional and more unexplored uses for the available technology. For example, mobile phones whilst conceived to enable mobile voice communication have quickly evolved to the point where television news stations encourage viewers to use their phone's camera and video capabilities to record news worthy events. In effect the audience has become the reporter, film and production crew making the old adage of technology supporting learning anywhere at anytime to become reporting anywhere at anytime by anyone.

In a practical sense to prepare students for this new technology savvy and information hungry world they should have access and training in the most relevant and useful ICT applications, as the contemporary workplace increasingly requires such entry skills. However, schools and educators need be wary of the tendency to overload the curriculum with computer mediated activities that might take away from the students' abilities in physical forms of learning and performance. Educational enhancement could therefore be sketched out as a balance between digital mediation and the physical embodiment of ideas (Cole & Throssell, 2008). Furthermore, educators need to move beyond the adoption and adaptation of the technical and move into the sociocultural aspects of the technology. By this we mean that the educational use of the technology needs to meet the socio-cultural aspects and needs of the users. Lankshear, Snyder and Green (2000) consider this understanding the technology (medium), the message and the impact on sociocultural relationships. An understanding of the human-technology relationship (or humachine) is necessary if the education sectors, and others, are to efficiently utilize the available technology, modify content and delivery to meet the challenges of providing life-long education to students in the digital age (Cope & Kalantzis, 2000; Dolence & Norris, 1995; Ehrmann, 1995).

Emerging Trends

As the world is changing so too is the field of education, producing a continuously changing literacy which further evolves with the introduction of new multimedia devices, designed to assist society in global communication. Traditional compulsory education and post-compulsory education are in the process of providing quality education for a rapidly diversifying student cohort (Middlehurst, 2003). While traditionalists worry that *'sms'* or text messaging is having a damaging effect on the English language skills of the younger generation, Snowden (2006) argues that this is not necessarily the case. The ways in which students are connecting with the language means that it is the role of the teacher that requires change from the traditional *'sage on the stage'* to that of a *'guide on the side'*, reflecting the need to become a more flexible provider of education with new delivery methods, new contacts between schools and other partners, and the globalisation of education (Dyril & Kinnaman, 1994; Guri-Rosenblit, 1998; Perkins, 1991; See, 1994). In order for the teachers to facilitate this change they must be supported in an organization that is also willing to change and embrace innovation (Hall & Hord, 1984).

Widely promoted within the education sector since the early 1980's, technology is recognised as a valuable tool to transmit curriculum content through a variety of formats to improve access to and increase knowledge, as well as being a medium to improve collaboration and interactions between teachers, their colleagues and students (Jenkins, 1999). At the forefront of the educational technology revolution is the belief that teaching with ICT is "an important catalyst and tool for introducing educational reforms that change ...students into productive knowledge workers" (Pelgrum, 2001, p. 163). This kind of revolutionary change indicates, for many, that the introduction of ICT will transform teaching and learning (Dawes, 2001; Massy & Zemsky, 1995). This anticipation may in part explain why, many individuals, such as

politicians, educational policy makers, as well as parents, employers and the general public give great credit to the transformative capacity of technology.

Supporting the assertion that the education sector is coming under increasing market pressures almost all member countries of the Organisation for Economic Co-operation and Development (OECD) have experienced an increased exposure to market forces. These changes are multifaceted and include catering for a more transient population, a population that is becoming increasingly technologically capable and a population that has increasingly more leisure time and disposable income. What this means is that in a global economy all economies are interconnected. This interconnectedness is evident today with the global down turn of financial markets and numerous countries entering into recession. Within the education sector globalisation and technolisation has meant that schools and teachers have to deal with the fact that the characteristics of their students are changing. More and more students, particularly in the secondary level are requesting changes to the curriculum to accommodate their broader social and career prospects, such as matriculation and vocational education and training. Primary aged students are coming to the classroom with a broader understanding of the world around them and their particular place within the world, which has mainly come about by the increase use of technology and mass communication such as television and the Internet. This in turn means that students are coming to school with a broader understanding of how to use technology. This immediately implies that these learners need a higher level of flexibility of time, space, content, types of study materials and assignments so that schooling reflects the students' learning and use of technology outside of school.

Associated with the increasing use of and reliance on technologies at school commercial interest has been generated in the technological literacy area. This is no more evident than in the creation of numerous game-based programs, such as World of War Craft (see section three of this book). Education providers seeking to remain current with, and provide the most effective and innovative teaching and learning environments in turn try to assimilate these games into their curriculums. These game-based programs ostensibly seek to attract the technologically literate skills of 'digital natives' yet also are cleverly marketed to appeal to a perceived need in the educational context. Lankshear, Snyder and Green (2000, p. 132) note that this trend is especially apparent in education "where commercial developers, freelancers and university 'researcher-consultants' fight it out for the chance to 'deliver' off-the-shelf, packaged approaches to literacy, remedial intervention programs, diagnostic kits, together with training in their use". Further aspects of the commercial interests and perceived educational benefits of gaming in the curriculum are established and expanded on in section three of this title (see also Freebody, 2007).

As a cautionary note a students ability to navigate around Internet sites such as Facebook or Google or in downloading music and video files form the Internet does not attest to their ability to ethically use the available technology. Nor does their downloading imply that they have mastered the technology. Their use merely depicts an affinity to utilise those aspects of the technology which appeal to them. Indeed, Scanlon (2009) warns that from his experience the ability of 'digital natives' to navigate around youth orientated websites does not necessarily mean that they are technoliterate. This 'narrow' understanding and use of technology by 'digital natives' is supported by Solvie (2008) who found that whilst pre-service teachers in his course had access to course specific wikis, many students chose not to use them. In this respect educators need to ensure that they work with students to examine the wider personal and social roles that technology can play in their lives, and why you would utilise one form of technology over another. This necessary encompasses technoethics

and understanding the role and function of various forms of technology and how they can be used. In essence this becomes technolitearcy.

Despite findings of mixed results with technology (see Russell, 1999) and 'digital natives' not being as competent or as fluid with the technology (Scanlon, 2009; Solvie, 2008) as it was believed governments and schools are still pouring money into providing more and more technology to schools. For example, in our home country, Australia, the Prime Minister Kevin Rudd has introduced a one billion dollar "education revolution", which is currently in the process of being instituted. The aim of the Australian education revolution is to make a computer available to every student from grade 9 to 12 (Archer, 2007; Australian Labor Party, 2007; Coorey, 2007). The federal government's *digital revolution* is the Australian government's attempt to improve economic and perhaps social prosperity by linking technology firmly to the education of its younger citizens. This linking is in part due to the belief that "there is now incontrovertible evidence that education should be understood as an economic investment" (Coorey, 2007). As such the Australian *"education revolution"* appears to be in part supporting a 'push' for a broader increase and perhaps foundation in the technoliteracy skills of its populace, in the hope that it will eventually lead to a strengthening of the economy. The notion of economic prosperity ridding on the back of a technoliterate society is not a new concept, nor will it be the last.

New Ways of Learning and Interpreting the World

The axiom that technology will change the way we teach and learn has been widely accepted for many decades. Indeed in the 1920's Thomas Edison predicted that the motion picture would transform the education system and that within a few short years it will "supplant largely, if not entirely, the use of textbooks" (Oppenheimer,

1997, p. 45). Motion picture like radio, television, computers and now internet and multimedia capable computers have all been seen as a panacea for improving teaching and learning. However the rhetoric of technology transforming the education sector has not been realized (Cuban, 2001). Despite this, technology provides a tool for lifelong learning which the United Kingdom's ICT advisory agency (BECTA- British Educational Communications and Technology Agency) believes can be fostered though linking school use of technology with outside school use. In this regard technology is seen to provide opportunities for not only strengthening home-school links ICT is also seen as a "rapprochement between formal education and the learning that takes place outside the school" (BECTA, 2001, p. 101), in effect facilitating lifelong learning.

The need for individuals, especially teachers and students to utilise and work with digital media has been emphasised since the early 1990's. For example, the International Society for Technology in Education (ISTE) established standards for technological literacy for teachers (ISTE, 2008) which recommended that teachers should be confident to:

- Facilitate and Inspire Student Learning and Creativity
- Design and Develop Digital-Age Learning Experiences and Assessment
- Model Digital-Age Work and Learning
- Promote and Model Digital Citizenship and Responsibility
- Engage in Professional Growth and Leadership

Indeed the current CEO of ISTE has said that "teachers must become comfortable as co-learners with their students and with colleagues around the world. Today it is less about *staying ahead* and more about *moving ahead* as members of dynamic learning communities. The digital-age teaching professional must demonstrate a vision

of technology infusion and develop the technology skills of others. These are the hallmarks of the new education leader" (Knezek, 2008). Furthermore teachers themselves are demanding that technology be brought into the classroom so that school use of technology better matches student access and usage of technology at home (Stokes, 2001). This trend is being hastened by younger teachers wanting to use technologies which they themselves are more familiar with (Stokes, 2001).

Change as a result of technology, in particular computers and the Internet have been recognized as providing opportunities for lifelong learning and improving social and economic productivity. This is dependent on the education sector appropriately preparing students to take advantage of the diverse range of technologies available. For schools to prepare students for the information age they must move away from their relatively insular state and embrace the outside world. In order to achieve this many government education departments have shifted from a centralized management approach of schools to a more decentralized approach. In the decentralized model the school principal has a greater say and level of daily responsibility for the decisions made in managing the school, including staffing and technology (Williams, Harold, Robertson & Southwood, 1997). In relation to principals making technology based decisions it is suggested that they are now faced with making "complex decisions" (Schiller, 1997, p. 136) in an area in which they have little expertise or knowledge (Schiller, 1997; Sharpe, 1996).

However, the changes in education as a result of digital technologies are an adjunct to change not the *raison d'etre*. This point is particularly pertinent given Moore's Law (Hutcheson, 2005) which implies that technology will continue to increase in capacity whilst decreasing in costs. This in turn makes the technology more accessible but it also means that users must be constantly learning how to use and adapt to the new technology.

Given the proliferation of digital technologies many schools are now equipped with computers, Internet connections, networked applications and continuing professional development programs to upskill teachers in the use of learning technologies for teaching and administrative purposes. As a result schools and education authorities are continuing to develop policies that support teaching and learning. With the digitalization of learning or e-learning there is the belief that the technology will revolutionise the way teaching and learning occurs (Clarke, 2003). Clarke maintains that a great deal of progress has been made but he also believes that much more needs to occur.

In a report to the President and the Congress of the United States of America Kerrey and Iskason (2000) mentioned that the power of the Internet for learning is that learning can be more student-centered, with a focus on the needs of the individual learners. These ideas relate to lifelong learning which Guri-Rosenblit (1998) believes is made more accessible by making use of new technology. The technology in turn can be used to promote a move from individualized learning to collaborative learning (Reil, 2000) though to autonomous or self-directed learning (Forsyth, 1996). Within the compulsory educator sector studies have shown that students are able to mediate their own learning away from the school (BECTA, 2001; Robertson & Williams, 2004). Given the changes to teaching and learning made possible by digital technologies it is inevitable that the teacher must change their role and how they teach (Wheeler, 2000) with the technology.

The main catalytic drivers for this change are the technocentric beliefs that ICT is essential for producing a technically capable workforce to underpin economic growth; the premise that technology has the potential to improve the quality of education; and its ability to address and improve social inequalities (Aviram, 2001; Cuban, 2001; Dede, 1997; Katz, Rice & Aspden, 2001). As Dolence and Norris (1995, p. 2) note *"All people, organizations, societies and nations are affected, although not at the same pace or to the same degree. Those who realign their practices most effectively to the Information Age... will reap substantial benefits. Those who do not will be replaced."*

In response to the social and economic benefits being purported by technology use Australia, like other western countries, has adopted the widespread introduction of digital technologies in the education sector as a means of addressing economic, social and educational reform agendas to move from the industrial age into the knowledge economy. To achieve this transition governments and schools have adopted technology policies and allocated technology specific funds to achieve their desired outcomes. To date several ways have been used to report on this technology transition. Firstly there is the resource or mechanistic approach which measures success in terms of measuring the physical deployment of technologies (Cuban, 2001). This measure is often reported in terms of student/computer ratio and the number of peripheral devices such as data projectors and interactive white boards (IWBs) that the school has (Newhouse, Trinidad, & Clarkson, 2002). The resulting measurements are then used by some (i.e. governments and schools) to indicate technological progress (Bligh, 2002).

For instance a decade ago a United Kingdom report to the Houses of Parliament recommended that all schools have access to internet connected computers and that by the year 2004 all school students should have their own laptops (Dearing, 1997). To date this objective has not been met with the most recent UK reports indicating that on average there was one computer for every 7.5 primary students and one for every 4.9 secondary students in 2004. However the report did indicate that all schools had access to the Internet (DCSF, 2004). Within the Australian context Federal Government reports mirror the same aspirations (DETYA, 2000); however like the UK sector the one computer per student ratio has yet to be realized.

To overcome the dichotomy between technology as a skill to be learnt versus technology as a tool to facilitate teaching and learning a change in mindset is required by those who use and make decisions to incorporate technology into the school. This may be the elephant in the room, or the elephant in the education sector, because to a large extent the education sector has been myopically teaching "people how to use…technology [rather than] how to solve educational problems [with] technology [as appropriate]" (Kearsley, 1998, p. 50). Kearsley lamented that the technology being used has become a distraction to effective learning and teaching which gave rise to him labeling technology as the "great siren song of education" (p. 47).

Many researchers indicate that the learning process has been significantly changed by the introduction of technology (BECTA, 2001; Bonk & King, 1998; Marina, 2001; Shelly, Cashman, Gunter, & Gunter, 1999; Smith, 2002). Technology advocates believe that learning with, and through, technology will better equip students for life and work in the Information Age (Butzin, 2000; Marina, 2001). Associated with the rapid spread of technology in schools is the proliferation of digital technologies in the home. For schools to maximize the educational benefits offered by technology they need to capitalize on the school-home technology link. This has been termed formal learning and informal learning. In a recent study in the UK it was found that ICT has an impact on "home-school relations" as well home use of technology improves "motivation" and "school effectiveness" (BECTA, 2001, p. 32).

Home technology opens the door for new and innovative ways for learners to learn. Indeed home learning also creates educational opportunities for students who may not have had ready access to education before (Bates, 1997). Ultimately school based learning, home based learning or a blend of the two can enhance the curriculum and subsequently student learning but this is dependent on the effective use of digital technology resources as tools to support teaching and learning. In this regard student technology use, skills, confidence and level of involvement in decision-making is as relevant as it is for teachers. Similarly access to technology, specifically a computer and the Internet at home is becoming essential for student success in a technology rich culture. Moreover home access to technology is quickly dividing the world into those who "have" access and those who "have-not" (Aviram, 2000).

CONCLUSION

Given the impetus from governments, the business sector, and social commentators for digital technologies, it has become ubiquitous in modern society and therefore its absence in schools and workplaces in developed countries would be a rare exception. The pervasiveness of technology represents both a major challenge and an exciting opportunity for the education system, particularly as digital technologies are shaping and being shaped by global communications.

This chapter has provided an overview of literacy and the general changes that have occurred as the concept of literacy has converged with technology to form technoliteracy. The history of literacy is complex and has been affected by human development and a range of innovations such as developments in communication technology. The incorporation of digital technologies in the workplace and home environment, resulting in rapid social change, has necessarily affected the education sector. Therefore it is evident that the traditional approach to literacy, based solely on reading and writing, is not appropriate for effective engagement in the digital economy. Additionally, the emergence of the digital native and the digital immigrant is changing the traditional positioning of the teacher as the sole source of information to one where the students are becoming the teachers.

In response to these global and school-based changes educators have to be willing to learn about and engage with new technologies so that, as with any discipline area, they are aware of new developments and how these developments can be incorporated into their teaching repertoire and curriculum areas. The complex role of the educator has been made more difficult by pressures which can occur both within and outside of the classroom. This can result from externally imposed expectations on teaching and learning, for example through the benchmarking of results; issues of equity and access in relation to funding between schools; commercial gain related to technological innovations and the pressure to use particular programs; and the disparity between students of particular competencies related to their learning. There is also the extreme case when personal use of technology in class disrupts the learning environment of others, such as the recent case of a 14-year old Wisconsin girl who was arrested by police after refusing requests by her teacher to stop texting during her maths lesson (Cellular-news, 2009). In this example school policy, social etiquette and 'common sense' should have prevailed. As such technology brings with it new and rebadged issues which schools, teachers and students need to work through in order to maximise the educational benefits offered by technology. In the mobile phone example, as with all uses of technology, users need to be educated in technoethics (see Pullen, 2009) which concerns the ethics associated with using technology.

Unless schools tackle the issues associated with technoethics (see Luppicini & Adell, 2009) strategies such as providing computers to every student are only beneficial if supported by the whole school, adopted into policy and practice with significant professional development given where it is needed. Educators also need to acknowledge that some students are a vital resource in terms of technological literacy and may be able to provide mentoring within the school, both for their peers and teachers. Once these aspects are

discussed, polices and practices associated with using technology for literacy endeavours can be tackled.

REFERENCES

Anstey, M., & Bull, G. (2004). *The literacy labyrinth* (2nd Ed.). Sydney: Pearson Education Australia.

Archer, L. (2007). Kevin Rudd promises computers for every student. *news.com.au*. Retrieved January 20, 2009, from www.news.com.au/story/0,23599,22754187-2,00.html?from=public_rss

Australian Council of Deans of Education. (2001). *New learning: A charter for Australian education*. Canberra, Australia: Australian Council of Deans of Education.

Australian Labor Party. (2007). *The Australian economy needs an education revolution* (Policy paper). Retrieved January 20, 2009, from www.alp.org.au/download/now/education-revolution.pdf

Aviram, A. (2001). The integration of ICT and education: From computers in the classroom, to mindful radical adaptation of educational systems to the emerging cyber culture. *Journal of Educational Change*, *1*, 331–352. doi:10.1023/A:1010082722912

Bates, J. M. (1997). Measuring predetermined socioeconomic 'inputs' when assessing the efficiency of educational outputs. *Applied Economics*, *29*, 85–93. doi:10.1080/000368497327434

BECTA. (2001). *Primary Schools of the Future– Achieving Today*. London: British Educational Communications and Technology Agency.

Bligh, A. (2002). *Qld State schools to share in more than $18 million to boost ICTs*. Retrieved September 20, 2008, from http://www.education.qld.gov.au/itt/learning/docs/ictl-grant-1instal.doc

Bonk, C. J., & King, K. S. (Eds.). (1998). *Electronic Collaborators: Learner-Centered Technologies for Literacy, Apprenticeship, and Discourse.* Mahwah, NJ: Lawrence Erlbaum Associates.

Butzin, S. M. (2000). Project CHILD: A decade of success for young children. *Technology Horizons in Education Journal, 27*(11). Available online http://www.thejournal.com/magazine/vault/A2882B.cfm

Cellular-News. (2009). *Student Arrested for Refusing to Stop Texting in Class.* Retrieved February 22, 2009, from http://www.cellular-news.com/story/36173.php

Clarke, C. (2003). *Towards a unified e-learning strategy.* Consultation Document, Department for education and skills. UK: UK Department of Education and Skills.

Cole, D., & Moyle, V. (In press). Cam-capture literacy and its incorporation into multiliteracies. In D. Pullen, & D. Cole (Eds.), *Multiliteracies and Technology enhanced Education: Social Practice and the Global Classroom.* Hershey, PA: IGI Global.

Cole, D. R., & Throssell, P. (2008). Epiphanies in action: Teaching and learning in synchronous harmony. *The International Journal of Learning, 15*(7), 175–184.

Coorey, P. (2007). Rudd vows education revolution. *The Sydney Morning Herald*, Jan 23, 2007. Retrieved January 20, 2009, from www.smh.com.au/news/national/rudd-vows-education-revolution/2007/01/22/1169330827940.html?page=fullpag

Cope, B., & Kalantzis, M. (1997). *Productive diversity: A new Australian model for work and management.* Annandale, Australia: Pluto Press.

Cope, B., & Kalantzis, M. (Eds.). (2000). *Multiliteracies: literacy learning and the design of social futures.* London: Routledge

Cuban, L. (2001). *Oversold and underused: Computers in the classroom.* Cambridge, MA: Harvard University Press.

Davis, D. (2008). *First we see: The national review of visual education.* Canberra, Australia: Australian Government.

Dawes, L. (2001). What stops teachers using new technology? In M. Leask (Ed.), *Issues in teaching using ICT* (pp. 61-79). Florence, KY: Routledge.

DCSF. (2004). Department for Children, Schools and Families (UK). *ICT in schools survey 2004.* Retrieved January 10, 2009, from http://publications.teachernet.gov.uk/default.aspx?PageFunction=productdetails&PageMode=publications&ProductId=DFES-1122-2004& Dearing, R. (1997). *Higher education in the learning society. London, United Kingdom: National Committee of Inquiry into Higher Education.* Retrieved July 26, 2007, from http://www.leeds.ac.uk/educol/ncihe/

Dede, C. (1997). Rethinking how to invest in technology. *Educational Leadership*, (November): 12–16.

DETYA. (2000). *Learning for the knowledge society: An education and training action plan for the information economy.* Canberra, Austrailia: Department of Education, Training and Youth Affairs. Retrieved November 4, 2007 from http://www.dest.gov.au/sectors/school_education/publications_resources/summaries_brochures/learning_for_the_knowledge_society.htm

Dolence, M. G., & Norris, D. M. (1995). *Transforming Higher Education: A Vision for Learning in the 21st Century.* Ann Arbor, MI: Society for College and University Planning.

Dyril, O. E., & Kinnaman, D. E. (1994). Integrating technology into our classroom curriculum. *Technology & Learning, 14*(5), 38–42.

Ehrmann, S. (1995). New technology, old trap. *Educational Review*, *30*(5), 41–43.

Finger, G., Russell, G., Jamieson-Proctor, R., & Russell, N. (2007). *Transforming learning with ICT: Making IT Happen!* Sydney: Pearson.

Forsyth, I. (1996). *Teaching and learning materials and the Internet*. London: Kogan Page.

Freebody, P. (2007). Building literacy education: pasts, futures, and "the sum of effort". In A. Simpson (Ed.). *Future Directions in Literacy: International Conversations conference 2007*, (pp. 96 – 114). Sydney: Sydney University Press.

Freebody, P., & Luke, A. (1990). Literacies programs: Debates and demands in cultural context. *Prospect: Australian Journal of TESOL*, *5*(3), 7–16.

Gee, J. (1994). Orality and literacy: from the savage mind to ways with words. In J. Maybin & J. Clevedon (Eds), *Language and literacy in social practice*. Multilingual Matters Ltd & The Open University.

Gee, J. (2003). *What video games have to teach us about learning and literacy*. New York: Palgrave Macmillan.

Goldman, S. R. (2004). Cognitive aspects of constructing meaning through and across multiple texts. In N. Shuart-Ferris & D. M. Bloome (Eds.), *Uses of intertextuality in classroom and educational research* (pp. 313-347). Greenwich, CT: Information Age Publishing.

Green, B., & Bigum, C. (1993). Aliens in the classroom. *Australian Journal of Education*, *37*(2), 119–141.

Guri-Rosenblit, S. (1998). Future agendas of distance-teaching and mass-orientated universities. Universities in a digital age: Transformation, innovation, and tradition. *Proceedings of the seventh EDEN (European Distance Education Network) Annual Conference* (June 1998). Budapest: European distance education network.

Hall, G. E., & Hord, S. M. (1984). *Change in schools: Facilitating the process*. New York: State University of New York Press.

Hill, S., & Mulhearn, G. (2007). Children of the new millennium: Research and Hirsch, E. D. (1987). *Cultural literacy: What every American needs to know*. Boston: Houghton Mifflin.

Huddlestone, B. (2008). *Teachers' attitudes and beliefs: a case study of ICT use in a catholic classroom*. Unpublished honours thesis. University of Tasmania, Locked Bag, Australia.

Hutcheson, G. D. (2005). Moore's Law: the history and economics of an observation that changed the world. *Electrochemical Society Interface*, *14*(1), 17–21.

Jenkins, J. (1999, March). Teaching tomorrow: The changing role of teachers in the connected classroom. Paper presented at the *EDEN 1999 Open Classroom Conference*, Balatonfured, Hungary. Retrieved June 28, 2007 from http://www.eden-online.org/papers/jenkins.pdf#search=%22%22EDEN%201999%20Open%20Classroom%20Conference%22%22

Kalantzis, M., Cope, B., & Harvey, A. (2003). Assessing multiliteracies and the new basics. *Assessment in Education: Principles . Policy & Practice*, *10*(1), 15–26.

Katz, J., Rice, R., & Aspden, P. (2001). The Internet 1995-2000: Access, civic involvement and social interaction. *The American Behavioral Scientist*, *45*(3), 405–419.

Kearsley, G. (1998). *A guide to on-line education*. Retrieved November 28, 2007, from http:www.gwis.circ.gwu.edu/~etl/online.html

Kerrey, B., & Iskason, J. (2000). *The power of the internet for learning. Final report of the web-based education commission*. Retrieved November 5, 2007, from http://www.ed.gov/offices/AC/WBEC/FinalReport/index.html

Knezek, D. (2008). *NETS statement. ISTE*. Retrieved January 28, 2009, from http://www.iste.org/AM/Template.cfm?Section=NETS

Kress, G. (2003). *Literacy in the New Media Age*. London: Routledge.

Kress, G., & van Leeuwen, T. (2001). *Multimodal discourse: The modes and media of contemporary communication*. London: Arnold.

Kumar, R. (2002). Managing risks in IT projects: An options perspective. *Information & Management, 40*(1), 63–74. doi:10.1016/S0378-7206(01)00133-1

Lankshear, C., & Knobel, M. (2003). *New literacies: Changing knowledge and classroom learning*. Philadelphia: Open University Press.

Lankshear, C., Snyder, I., & Green, B. (2000). *Teachers and Technoliteracy: Managing literacy, technology and learning in schools*. St. Leonards, Australia: Allen & Unwin.

Larson, J., & Marsh, J. (2005). *Making Literacy Real: Theories and Practices for Learning and Teaching*. London: Sage Publications.

Lin, C., & Pervan, G. (2003). The Practice of IT Benefits Management in Large Australian Organizations. *Information & Management, 41*(1), 13–24. doi:10.1016/S0378-7206(03)00002-8

Luppicini, R., & Adell, R. (Eds.). (2009). *Handbook of Research on Technoethics*. Hershey, PA: IGI Global.

Marina, S. (2001). Facing the challenges, getting the right way with distance learning. *At a Distance, 15*(30), 1-8.

Massy, W., & Zemsky, R. 1995. Using Information Technology to Enhance Academic Productivity. Paper presented at *Wingspread Conference*, June. EDUCOM.

Meredyth, D., Russell, N., Blackwood, L., Thomas, J., & Wise, P. (1999). *Real time: Computers, change and schooling*. Canberra, Australia: Australian Key Centre for Cultural and Media Policy & Macmillan printing group.

Middlehurst, R. (2003). Competition, collaboration and ICT: Challenges and choices for higher education institutions. In M. Van der Wende & M. va der Ven (Eds.). *The use of ICT in Higher Education: A mirror of Europe* (pp. 253-276). Utrecht: Lemma Publishers.

Milis, K., & Mercken, R. (2004). The use of the balance scorecard for the evaluation of information and communication technology projects. *International Journal of Project Management, 22*, 87–97. doi:10.1016/S0263-7863(03)00060-7

Moursund, D. G. (2005). *Introduction to Information and Communication Technology in Education*. Retrieved January 20, 2009, from http://uoregon.edu/~moursund/Books/ICT/ICTBook.html

Mumford, E. (1979). *Systems design and human needs. In Bjorn-Anderson et al. The impact of systems change in organizations*. Netherlands: Sijhoff & Noordhoff International Publishers.

New London Group. (1996). A pedagogy of multiliteracies: Designing social futures. *Harvard Educational Review, 66*(1), 60–92.

New London Group. (2000). A pedagogy of multiliteracies: Designing social futures. In B. Cope & M. Kalantzis (Eds), *Multiliteracies: Literacy learning and the design of social futures* (pp. 9-38). South Yarra, Australia: Macmillan.

Newhouse, P., Trinidad, S. & Clarkson, B. (20002). *Quality pedagogy and effective learning with information and communications technology (ICT).* Western Australian Department of Education.

Oppenheimer, T. (1997). The computer delusion. *Atlantic Monthly, 280*(1), 45–62.

Papert, S. (1998). *Child power: Keys to the new learning of the digital century.* Talk given at the Imperial College London. Retrieved from http://www.ConnectedFamily.com/frame4/cf0413seymour/recent_essay/cf0413_cherry_2.html

Peck, C., Cuban, L., & Kirkpatrick, H. (2002). Techno-promoter dreams, student realities. *Phi Delta Kappan*, (February): 472–480.

Pelgrum, W. (2001). Obstacles to the integration of ICT in education: Results from a worldwide educational assessment. *Computers & Education, 37*(2), 163–178. doi:10.1016/S0360-1315(01)00045-8

Peppard, J., & Ward, J. (•••). (n.d.). Beyond Strategic Information Systems: Towards and IS Capability. *The Journal of Strategic Information Systems, 13*(2), 167–194. doi:10.1016/j.jsis.2004.02.002

Perkins, D. (1991). Technology meets constructivism: Do they make a marriage? *Educational Technology, 31*(5), 18–23.

Prensky, M. (2001). Digital Natives, Digital Immigrants. *On the Horizon, 9*(5), October 2001. Retrieved January 20, 2009, from http://www.marcprensky.com/writing/Prensky%20-%20Digital%20Natives,%20Digital%20Immigrants%20-%20Part1.pdf professional learning into practice [Electronic Version]. Australian Research

Pullen, D. (2008) Technoethics in Schools. In R. Luppicini & R. Adell (Eds.), *Handbook of Research on Technoethics* (pp. 680-698). Hershey, PA: IGI Global.

Pullen, D., Baguley, M., & Marsden, A. (2009). Back to Basics: Electronic Collaboration in the Education Sector. In J. Salmons & L. Wilson (Eds.), *Handbook of Research on Electronic Collaboration and Organizational Synergy* (pp. 205-222). Hershey, PA: IGI Global.

Pullen, D., & Cole, D. (Eds.). (Forthcoming). *Multiliteracies and Technology enhanced Education: Social Practice and the Global Classroom.* Hershey, PA: IGI Global.

Reil, M. (2000). The future of technology and education: Where are we heading? In D. Watson & T. Downes (Eds.). *Communication and networking in Education* (pp.9-24). Boston: Kluwer Academic Press.

Robertson, M., & Williams, M. (2004). *Young People, Leisure and Place: Cross Cultural Prespectives.* New York: Nova Science Publishers.

Russell, T. (1999). *The no significant difference phenomenon.* Chapel Hill, NC: Office of instructional telecommiunications.

Saville, M. (forthcoming). Robotics as a vehicle for multiliteracies. In D. Pullen, & D. Cole (Eds.). (Forthcoming). *Multiliteracies and Technology enhanced Education: Social Practice and the Global Classroom.* Hershey, PA: IGI Global.

Scanlon, C. (2009). The natives aren't quite so restless. *The Australian*, 33.

Schiller, J. (1997). What do principals do when implementing computer education? *The Practicing Administrator, 14*(4), 36–39.

Scouter, C. (2003). Foreword. In C. Nicol (Ed.), *ICT Policy: A beginner's handbook.* Paris: Association for Progressive Communications.

See, J. (1994). Technology and outcome-based education: Connection in concept and practice. *The Computing Teacher, 17*(3), 30–31.

Sharpe, F. (1996). Towards a research paradigm on devolution. *Journal of Educational Administration, 34*(1), 4–12. doi:10.1108/09578239610107138

Shelly, G. B., Cashman, T. J., Gunter, R. E., & Gunter, G. A. (2006). *Teachers Discovering Computers: Integrating technology and digital media in the classroom* (4th Edition). Boston: Course Technology, Thomson Learning.

Smith, R. *(2002)*. Successfully incorporating Internet content and advanced presentation technology into collegiate courses: Lessons, Methodology, and Demonstration. *Massachusetts.*

Snowden, C. (2006). *'Casting a Powerful Spell: The Evolution of SMS', The Cell Phone Reader - Essays in Social Transformation.* New York: Peter Lang Publishers Inc.

Solvie, P. (2008). Use of the Wiki: Encouraging Preservice Teachers' Construction of Knowledge in Reading Methods Courses. *The Journal of Literacy and Technology, 9*(2), 58–87.

Stokes, S. (2001). Visual literacy in teaching and learning: A literature perspective. *Electronic Journal for Integration of Technology in Education, 1*(1). Retrieved January 21, 2009, from http://ejite.isu.edu/Volume1No1/Stokes.html

Taylor, P. (1998). Institutional change in uncertain time: Lone ranging is not enough. *Studies in Higher Education, 234*, 269–279. doi:10.1080/03075079812331380246

The International Society for Technology in Education (ISTE). (2008). *National Educational technology Standards (NETS) for teachers.* Retrieved January 21, 2009, from http://www.iste.org/AM/Template.cfm?Section=NETS

Tinio, V. (2007). *ICT in education.* Retrieved June 27, 2008 from http://www.apdip.net/publications/iespprimers/ICTinEducation.pdf

Twigg, C., & Oblinger, D. (1996). *The virtual university.* Retrieved January 8, 2009, from http://www.educom.edu/nlii/VU.html

UNESCO. (2003). *Developing and using indicators of ICT use in education.* Retrieved December 22, 2008 from www.unsecobkk.org/ips/ebooks/documents/ICTindicators.pdf

United States of America Department of Education. (2009). *No child left behind act of 2001.* Retrieved January 15, 2009, from http://www.ed.gov/nclb/landing.jhtml

Unsworth, L. (2001). *Teaching multiliteracies across the curriculum: Changing contexts of text and image in classroom practice.* Buckingham, UK: Open University Press.

Walker, A. (2008). *Early childhood education (ECE) supporting it with ICT.* Unpublished honours thesis, University of Tasmania, Locked Bag, Australia.

Wheeler, S. (2000). *The role of the teacher in the use of ICT.* Bohemia, Czech Republic: University of Western Bohemia.

Williams, R., Harold, B., Robertson, J., & Southwood, G. (1997). Sweeping decentralization of education decision-making authority: Lessons from England and New Zealand. *Phi Delta Kappan, 78*(8), 626–631.

Zammit, K., & Downes, T. (2002). New learning environments and the multiliterate individual: A framework for educators. *The Australian Journal of Langauge and Literacy, 25*, 24–36.

Chapter 2
Designs of Meaning:
Redesigning Perceptions of School and Self Using Tactics of Resistance

Donna Mahar
State University of New York, USA

ABSTRACT

This chapter focuses on Colleen, one of 22 youths who took part in a two year qualitative study designed to explore young adolescents' use of information communication technology (ICT) and popular media texts to make sense of themselves and their world. The rationale for the study stemmed from limited research concerning the overlaps and schisms between adolescents' use of ICT and popular media texts in their everyday lives (home, community, peer group) and how adolescents' engagement with ICT and popular media texts affects established social institutions. The New London Group's (1996) conception of multiliteracies (Cope & Kalantzis, 2000) and an activity theory-influenced framework (Beach, 2000; Cole, 1996; Engestrom & Miettinen, 1999) were used to guide the study. Colleen's use of ICT and popular media texts, both in and outside of school, illustrates the non-linear, non-hierarchical complexity of the pedagogy of multiliteracies (Cope & Kalantzis, 2000).

INTRODUCTION

Subj: **Something That Might Interest You**

Date: 6/10/2003 10:17:20 PM Eastern Daylight Time

From: kittie48@xxx.com

DOI: 10.4018/978-1-60566-842-0.ch002

To: Author

My god! It's almost the end of the year! my last day of class is tomorrow and then i just have to finish finals. Blah. Well, I'll get to the point. Lately, I've been watching this really great cult 60's show called The Prisoner starring Patrick McGoohan. the plot goes something like this: a man resigns his position from a top-secret British intelligence agency and is immediately kidnapped and taken away to a strange "village" which is totally isolated from the rest of the world. the people here are taken to either protect or to extract the information in their heads. They have no names-just a number. The man I speak of is number six. in this place, cameras are everywhere-nothing goes unnoticed and no one has yet escaped. Conformity is the key in this community-but the prisoner doesn't want to crack or conform- he just wants to escape. so in every episode, a new tactic is used to try and break number six's will-and fails. The perimeter is guarded by this killer weather balloon thing called "rover" It's job is to knock out and retrieve or kill the escapees-but since number six is so valuable to the people of the village, his encounters with the rove are merely a "nasty experience", as they are called there. i though you might be interested because the principles of the village reminded me of life in middle school-keep the students happy, but don't give them any real freedom. Squash out their individuality like a bug and if they try and be different or stand up- god forbid! So-in sort of a conclusion, i give you number six's statement to number two in the arrival episode:

"I will not be pushed, filed, stamped, indexed, briefed, debriefed or numbered! My life is my own!"

sigh

(I'm hopelessly addicted to that show now:)

"I AM NOT A NUMBER-I'M A FREE MAN!"

Colleen dePointe du Lac, the Anti-Britney, aka rocket queen

high priestess of ozz, disposable teen, Taltos, sister of Ashlar, mistress of axl rose & professional builder of mechanical animals hail to the almighty ozz god! (They call me Mr. Tinkertrain, so come along and play my game, you will never be the same!) "you know where you are? you're

in the jungle baby! you're gonna die....

From September 2001 to June of 2003, 22 suburban adolescents ranging in age from 12 to 15 shared with me how they interpreted aspects of their world, as well as how they worked to resist and change aspects of established social systems they encountered. Due to their age and the various positions they held within these social systems, many of the changes and challenges they initiated were of a covert nature. The preceding email was composed by Colleen. This chapter highlights Colleen's use of information communication technology and popular media texts to define herself and her place in the world.

For Colleen and her peers, interpreting the multiplicity of messages surrounding them resulted in what at times appeared to be disorganized rips in an existing social order. These adolescents are different than the youths of the 1960's and 1970's who directly confronted political and social hierarchies with the intent to change them. This early 21st century cohort of suburban teens caused disruptions in social systems by the very nature of who they are and the world they live in. Rather than being intent on "raging against the machine," Colleen and her peers were willing to work within existing social systems in order to achieve their personal goals. "Disorganized rips" refers to the individual challenges and changes that occurred within existing social systems as these adolescents designed ways of reading both their world, as well as establishing their role within it. These rips became identity markers noting changes in how these adolescents interpreted their world as well as the often-unintended changes they brought to the world they lived in and the texts that supported it.

Although Colleen and the other students in this study would fit into the definition of "middle class" it is important to note the wide socioeconomic range this term covers. Colleen's parents were successful professionals who prioritized their daughter's education above all else. Several students came from families who "just" qualified as middle class, or rather, "just" missed out on being able to participate in the federally funded free lunch program. Economics and social status apparently have a significant influence on the choices these students made. However, it is fair to say that all 22 participants had knowledge of what Delpit (1995) refers to as "the culture of power" (p. 24). "Issues of power are enacted in classrooms; there are codes or rules for participating in power; that is there is a culture of power" (Delpit, 1995, p. 24). Colleen's parents have a strong awareness and engagement with issues of social justice which they have shared with their daughter. Colleen is therefore explicitly aware of how power can be misused thereby creating imbalances in society. Although her peers in the study could not articulate this concept, they were clearly aware of who was privileged and who was disadvantaged within their school system.

The rips and identity markers left by these students became a palimpsest for individuals, groups, and cultural trends within their suburban school. Frequent use of the Internet, along with daily access to popular culture through television, advertisements, malls, music, and movies, allowed groups, or communities, to form around interests that were not indigenous to their suburban milieu. The ready access to a wide variety of information, consumer goods, and cultural icons via the Internet also allowed Colleen to explore an array of cultural groups and communities that at times were complementary and overlapping and at other times appeared to be in dissonance with each other. Just as Number 6, referred to in the opening e-mail, resists the efforts by those in charge to make him crack or conform, Colleen also devised ways to resist those she perceived as being in power, while at the same time using the texts and tools of hegemonic institutions to her advantage.

BACKGROUND

The expanded conception of literacy beyond traditional alphabetic text (Lapp & Flood, 1995) offers a multiplicity of terms to capture the spatial, audio, visual, gestural, semiotic, and multimodal aspects (New London Group, 1996) involved in constructing meaning of both the world and the self. The following definitions represent the lenses I used to experience Colleen's wide array of cultural codes and interactions. By defining key terminology at the onset of this chapter, I hope to provide the topography of my two-year journey through the "geographies of youth culture" (Skelton & Valentine, 1998).

Disorganized Rips and Identity Markers

As reading and writing rapidly move beyond the traditional linear concept of alphabetic text on a printed page (Alvermann, 2002; New London Group, 1996), the concept of reading moves beyond print to include gestures, actions, signs, symbols, and emotions. This multiplicity of interactive communication and interpretive tools has expanded the variety of ways individuals read both the word and the world (Freire & Macedo, 1987). Technology allows for active, and at times immediate, interaction and interpretation of cultural surroundings that can lead to "rips" in conventional literacy practices. Websites, chat rooms, blogs, and fan sites devoted to cultural icons have not only introduced new ways of reading and composing both the word and world, they have also provided a new way to create virtual identities. These online identities allow a degree of creative freedom and personal expression that is not possible in the concrete world of real-time interactions. Colleen was able to embody her online explorations of fan sites and music blogs by reading them as literacy events (Barton & Hamilton, 2000) which she then performed by employing multimodalities.

Within the context of this chapter, literacy is seen as engagement with both the word and the world. "Reading the world always precedes reading the word, and reading the word implies continually reading the world" (Freire & Macedo, 1987, p. 35). Reading the world that Colleen engaged with constitutes more than reading traditional print-based alphabetic texts. Performative, visual, aural, and semiotic understandings all become tools to read the world (Alvermann, 2002). At the same time they compose an autobiography that reflects individual choices and cultural values. Although an autobiography changes as an individual "reads" more of the world and makes subsequent choices, markers are left that note a particular juncture in that individual's life. Looked at in retrospect, these markers signify cultural changes that are often too subtle to be noted as they occur.

This ongoing exploration and interpretation of self and environment is critical in the fast-paced world of production and consumption that Colleen and her peers populate:

In defining their own identities in a media culture, adolescents often perceive their everyday local experience and identities in terms of links to larger global media. Given the globalization of youth market consumer goods, adolescents throughout the world mark their identity as consumers through purchase of brand-name items or participation in homogenized global media. At the same time, they may also hold allegiances to the unique culture of their own local community, creating a tension between participation in global and local cultures. (Beach, 2000, p. 11)

The allegiances that Colleen and her peers hold toward their local community, peer group, and, perhaps most importantly, interest groups are what result in the disorganized rips in the larger global culture. These rips result in identity markers that subsequently can affect the composite of the global community. An example of this is Colleen's patronage of a mall-based store called Hot Topic

designed to appeal to a gothic, or alternative, adolescent style. Adolescent rips and identity markers can be found on the Hot Topic website, where adolescents are asked to send in their current interests as well as local trends in alternative style. As with most cultural issues, this can be looked at from two perspectives: adolescents having significant impact on corporate culture, or adolescents being co-opted and commodified for corporate gain.

ICT: INFORMATION AND COMMUNICATION TECHNOLOGIES

This chapter refers to the media and cultural texts used by Colleen and her cohorts as popular media texts. The operational tools that these young adolescents use to locate, read, manipulate, and redesign both traditional print texts and popular media texts will be referred to as information and communication technologies (ICT). ICT will encompass basic computer operational skills as well as Internet use and the use of other technologies related to text creation and manipulation (Holloway & Valentine, 2001; Valentine, Holloway & Bingham, 2002). ICT practices allowed Colleen and her peers to manipulate, transform, and create texts as well as alter existing cultural text forms.

In the context of this chapter, the term multiliteracies will refer to the framework proposed by the New London Group (New London Group 1996; Cope & Kalantzis, 2000) that attends to "the increasing salience of cultural and linguistic diversity" as well as the "multiplicity of text forms" (Cope & Kalantzis, 2000, p. 5) that these adolescents use to interpret their world. Multiliteracies encompass how Colleen and her peers use popular media texts and ICT to make sense of the world around them as well as to create spaces in that world for their own interests that at times are marginalized or unsanctioned by established social systems. Colleen's opening e-mail offers a snippet of this. Her engagement with the 1960's television show *The Prisoner* led to her creating drawings of the characters accompanied by her annotated comments. Her analogy between the subject of the show and her middle school experience alludes to interpretations of the original text in ways most likely not envisioned by the show's creators. Her use of the Internet to share her interpretations of the show suggests a multiplicity of text forms and demonstrates her linguistic diversity in conveying her interpretations.

Communities of Practice and Activity Theory

In exploring how these young adolescents used both the traditional and popular media texts, it became apparent that they were adept at creating locations where they could explore acts of pleasure, resistance, and manipulation. This can be seen in their creation of websites, collaborative online stories based on popular media icons, online and real-time groups formed to pursue popular video games, and styles of dress that set them apart from other adolescents of their age in their suburban middle school. Rather than being constrained by configurations of space, especially during the school day, these adolescents "approached the relations of context as much more fluid - not to think of school over here and homes over there, but to follow how literacy practices themselves bound and unbound contexts" (Leander, 2003, p. 4).

The term communities of practice refers to a social theory of learning that integrates four components seen to characterize "social participation as a process of learning and knowing: meaning, practice, community, identity" (Wenger, 1998, pp. 4-5). By interacting with Colleen and her peers for over two years I found that their communities of practice were dynamic, changing, and overlapping. "Through their participation in an activity, participants transform the nature of the activity, and in the process, are transformed by their participation" (Beach, 2000, p.5). Consumption and

production of popular media texts as well as the use of ICT within various and overlapping communities of practice defined Colleen as a certain "type" in the eyes of school personnel, peers, and corporate consumer cultures. At the same time, how Colleen used both popular media texts and ICT within communities of practice allowed her to redesign adult domains to incorporate her interests and priorities. Membership in various and overlapping communities of practice allowed Colleen to create space for her interests in previously forbidden territories.

Activity theory offers a set of terms to discuss how adolescents utilize ICT and popular media texts to construct a sense of self and meaning in their world. Some activity theorists, especially those concerned with literacy and communication (Beach, 2000; Russell, 1997) use the following components in their analysis: object/purpose for participation in the system; genres, sometimes seen as types of tools on which the community members draw; identities that participants define and construct through participation; codes/conventions, or social scripts within the system; and division of labor amongst participants to achieve the desired objective as well as ensure the viability of the community (Beach, 2000; Cole, 1996; Lave & Wenger, 1991; Wenger, 1998; Wertsch, 1998). Shared perspectives on joint activity as the unit of analysis and the importance of tools to mediate that activity are fundamental tenets of activity systems.

Activity theory allows ICT and popular media texts to be tools for creating meanings that are open to being defined within the various systems by the various participants. By seeing these tools as open to new ways of being used and defined, the tools become one of many symbolic resources that mediate what Wertsch (1991) termed "higher mental functioning" (p. 21). This higher mental functioning allows the tools themselves to be subject to redesign and new interpretations as the other components of the activity system interact. "Having a tool to perform an activity changes the nature of the activity" (Wenger, 1998, p. 59) and participating in a changed activity will change the members of the community in terms of how they see themselves and their world.

Colleen and her cohorts have learned how to use their ability to create, alter, and interpret popular media texts and ICT to their advantage, also known as tactics of resistance. Since both the school texts and corporately produced popular media texts adolescents engage with are manufactured by dominant power systems, Colleen and her peers became adept at creating ways to resist, as well as employ, traditional texts and tools to design new texts and spaces that hold personal meaning. Michel de Certeau (1984) uses the term *tactics* to describe such action contrasting the strategies used by those in power to the tactics used by those without power. The idea of tactics is especially relevant to young adolescents who are often seen as lacking knowledge of, or access to, corporate codes of power and dominance (Delpit, 1995).

COLLEEN: PERSONA AS IDENTITY MARKER

Colleen's e-mail about *The Prisoner* provides a glimpse into how Colleen defined herself and her world. Her online signature:

Colleen dePointe du Lac, the Anti-Britney, aka rocket queen high priestess of ozz, disposable teen, Taltos, sister of Ashlar mistress of axel rose & professional builder of mechanical animals hail to the almighty ozz god! (They call me Mr. Tinkertrain, so come along and play my game, you will never be the same!)

"you know where you are? You're in the jungle baby! you're gonna die…!

This online autobiographical snippet is in stark contrast to the picture that would emerge if you were to read Colleen's school records without

meeting her. To read a profile of Colleen without an accompanying physical description or Web signature would paint a picture of a traditional all-American youth as depicted by mainstream media culture: a straight-A student, first chair in the prestigious school marching and jazz bands, regular attendee at her church and confirmation classes, participant in a community soccer club, summer counselor at a church-related camp, and devoted daughter who spends weekends with her parents and twin sister. She also is an avid reader and writer; at least one evening a week she goes to her community library to order books via inter-library loan as well as to research topics of personal interest.

The advantages that Colleen had from being part of an upper-middle class family were mediated by certain restrictions her parents placed on ICT within the home. In a home without cable TV or broadband Internet access, Colleen's trips to the library allowed her to visit her favorite on-line fandom sites. Her conversations with the local librarian, who was less than enthusiastic about some of Colleen's online reading, provided her with practice negotiating with adults in order to support her media choices. This real-time negotiation proved to be advantageous when she negotiated space for her media and multimodal textual preferences. Colleen's literacy enactment included negotiation, multimodal texts, and integration of print sources with ICT, items noted by Jenkins, Clinton, Purushotma, Robinson and Weigel (2006) as critical components of twenty-first century literacy. "First, textual literacy remains a central skill in the twenty-first century … Youth must expand their required competencies, not push aside old skills to make room for the new. Second, new media literacies should be considered a social skill" (Jenkins et al., 2006, p. 19). Colleen's interactions at the local library, selecting her favorite Ann Rice books, researching nineteenth-century philosophers, and engaging in conversations on fan sites that give her a voice in a larger social network, allow her to negotiate social skills across media, genre, age, and gender. The skills she garnered with her weekly banter with the librarian served her well beyond gaining access to print and electronic texts.

Colleen's use of de Certeau's tactics or what constitutes her "guileful ruse" (de Certeau, 1984, p. 37) is the initial profile provided in the opening paragraph as well as how she constructs her public persona. She is white, with a pale, Northern European complexion; her use of dark, pronounced eyeliner, black lipstick, and thick, chalky foundation at times is similar to the aesthetic of actors in Kabuki theater. This serves as an interesting analogy since this popular form of Japanese theater is traditionally acted by males, unintentionally supporting Colleen's desire to at times appear androgynous. Her makeup also made her a high-profile anomaly in the school hallways, primarily populated by students wearing jeans, khakis, and shirts with logos from popular mall retailers.

Although Colleen occasionally would wear long, flowing black skirts accompanied by black ruffled tops with corsets over them, completing the outfit with chunky lace-up military boots, a reoccurring theme in many interviews was her desire to be androgynous. Her usual daily garb consisted of the chunky boots, often laced over jeans with rips through which could be seen assorted fishnets, band T-shirts with logos promoting heavy-metal bands such as Ozzy Osbourne or Marilyn Manson, and spiked necklaces and bracelets along with dangling crystals and pendants. Her nails were often painted black or dark red, and her shoulder-length hair was usually highlighted a dark, unnatural henna. The contrast between Colleen's public persona, autobiographical signature, and all-American guidance folder dossier presented her as an adolescent anomaly when considered from a media perspective. Did she belong in *Twilight, The Osbournes,* or *The Wizards of Waverly Place?* Colleen's ability to "expand her required literacy competencies, by redesigning old literacy skills to incorporate new ICT in social

contexts (Jenkins et al., 2006) illustrates how the recursive elements of the multiliteracies pedagogy (New London Group, 1996) problematize the flat characterization of contemporary adolescents in mainstream media texts.

Multiliteracies

Colleen's use of popular media texts and ICT can be analyzed by using the multiliteracies framework. Colleen created meaning within the various communities of practice she engaged in, as well as creating a sense of her identity and agency within these various communities or systems. Colleen's design/redesign process focused on her physical appearance as the text involving "re-presentation and recontextualisation" (Cope & Kalantzis, 2000, p. 22). By upholding all the traditional expectations attributed to a stellar student, while at the same time creating a physical presentation of self that was counter-intuitive to these expectations, Colleen was not just transforming how she defined herself. Colleen was challenging how those she came in contact with made sense of their relations with her and previously held notions of what constitutes a "good student".

Colleen incorporates gestural design to create and display her identity markers and the subsequent rips they make in existing groups and systems. Elements that constitute gestural design include: "behavior, bodily physicality, gesture, sensuality, feelings and affect, kinesics, and proxemics" (Cope & Kalantzis, 2000, p. 26). Colleen used her favorite pop-culture texts to create a bodily physicality, gestures, and affect that directly challenged traditional views of how a "good student" should look in school. In regard to the pedagogy of multiliteracies - situated practice, overt instruction, critical framing, and transformed practice - Colleen's interaction with texts illustrates the recursive, non-linear, non-hierarchal constructs of the pedagogy.

Colleen appeared able to intuit the "six major areas in which functional grammars, the metalanguages that describe and explain patterns of meaning with multiliteracies - linguistic design, visual design, audio design, gestural design, spatial design, and multimodal design" (Cope & Kalantzis, 2000, p. 25) allowed her to expand her personal definition of literacy beyond reading and writing. Colleen's design became her online and real time physical personas, which reflect aspects of all six design areas that contribute to her making meaning of her world and the place she holds in it. Colleen's design process, particularly the aspect of the Redesigned, had significant ramifications on both student and adult communities of practice within the school.

Colleen's status as a high honor-roll student, athlete, and band member allowed her to question certain practices that more mainstream student groups, such as the student council and character education group, espoused. In September of 2001, these two groups, in conjunction with the vice principal, coordinated a fashion show that would be put on during the lunch periods. The purpose of this show was to illustrate appropriate school clothes. Colleen voiced concern about this. She had several previous conversations with the vice principal regarding her choice of dress. The vice principal asked Colleen not to wear her spiked necklace and bracelet to school anymore as they, "looked to be a sign of ownership and degraded women" (Field notes, September 17, 2001).

Colleen's choice to use her physical presentation as a type of textual identity marker put her at odds with the codes and conventions sanctioned by the majority of school personnel and students. In trying to create a community of practice within the space and locations of school where her personal pursuits would be valued, Colleen was willing to challenge the dominant structure using its own tools, codes and conventions as her tactics of resistance. Colleen responded to the vice principal's comment as follows:

Dress codes allow girls to wear tight tops, to show their navels, to wear short shorts. But they don't allow me to wear my spiked necklace or bracelet because the vice principal feels that these "are degrading to women." Well, I am the one who puts those on myself. The girls in the revealing clothes wear them because that is what the generic girl does. It is kind of an odd way of seeing what is feminine. (Interview, May 30, 2002)

Colleen wrote the vice principal a letter in September asking to be part of the fashion show. In the letter she cited passages from the student handbook and dress code that supported her clothing selections as appropriate. When discussing this choice to be in the fashion show prior to the actual event, Colleen recognized that she would face derision and ridicule from her peers. When asked why she would put herself through that, she replied, "Otherwise by not doing something to show what I feel is appropriate, I am then agreeing that their way is not only the best, but really the only way to dress. I want to show that there are many ways you can be; I want to do this for the people who are picked on who can't do this for themselves" (Field notes, September 19, 2001).

Colleen's involvement in the fashion show can be interpreted as an attempt to gain validation for a marginalized community of practice within the school, those referred to by others as "losers." Using her physical presentation as a way to validate some of the codes and conventions of appearance often associated with this marginalized group, Colleen was also challenging the physical identity of a "good student" as well as introducing an unexpected ideological tension within the intended fashion show discourse.

In the context of the fashion show, Colleen's object/purpose, conventions/codes, identity, and challenge to the intended discourse can be analyzed from the lens of the multiliteracies pedagogy. Colleen's participation in the fashion show was a form of overt instruction, where she was attempting in a "systematic, analytic, and conscious" way to explain to the larger school community her personal choices in terms of presentation, performance, and identification. She employed critical framing both before and after the fashion show. She "stood back" from the generally negative responses to "view them critically in their context." "I knew that the kids in the cafeteria would laugh. My point was that a school event needs to be inclusive. We have all these signs on the walls [throughout the school] about respect and responsibility, and then there is this [the fashion show]. To me that is more about conformity than inclusion" (Field notes, September 24, 2001).

The multiliteracies pedagogy affords an interesting interpretation of the fashion show in terms of the duality that transformed practice had on Colleen and her peers. Colleen's insistence on being a part of the fashion show brought a marginalized group to the forefront. Rather than continuing this event as an annual fall and spring tradition as the administration had planned, complaints from the more mainstream students and parents regarding Colleen's inclusion led to its dissolution. The irony is that Colleen followed the dress code as it was explicitly written, where many of the more privileged outfits showed bare midriffs, tight shirts, and short shorts that actually challenged the code more than Colleen's baggy black pants, black T-shirt, lace gloves, and black work boots did.

Colleen's participation as an eighth-grade student in the fashion show also made her a type of cult figure to seventh- and especially sixth-grade students in the school. Informal conversations with these students revealed that for one reason or another they felt on the margins of in- and out-of-school communities. By January, a community of "Colleen wannabes" had formed, imitating her dress. Much like *Xerox*, *Jello*, and *Kleenex*, Colleen's last name became a common noun for what these students saw as a counterculture commodity. When asked to describe how they presented themselves, they did not use the term, "goth" or refer to Hot Topic, the popular mall store where most of their clothes and accessories were

purchased. Rather they referred to Colleen and her twin sister as a collective of their last name: "We're like the Bridgers."

This group of marginalized younger students did not share Colleen's affiliations with the school band or soccer team, nor did they share her academic success or personal reading, research, and political interests. In looking at the socio-economic backgrounds of Colleen's followers, a power differential became apparent. Colleen was comfortable and adept challenging school policies because of the situated practice, overt instruction, and critical framing (New London Group, 1996) she had received through interacting with her parents and the local librarian. Her followers were students from lower income housing, foster homes, and a local group home for transient youth. Lacking the practice with both traditional academic discourses, negotiating with adults through conversations, and ICT resources, these students looked to Colleen as their voice. When I spoke to Colleen about these followers (I hesitate to use the term mentee as that suggests a mutually agreed upon relationship where growth is the outcome) in terms of the components of an activity system: object/purpose, tools/genres, identities, conventions/codes, and discourses, rather than speak disparagingly about her young followers, Colleen looked at the components as they applied to her.

My purpose for wearing the logos I do is that they represent the music I like. Music is something that is important to me; that's why I'm in marching band and jazz band. The logos and clothes are all tools or symbols of what I believe. I don't wear Marilyn Manson stuff because I want to be different, I wear it because the person behind the Marilyn Manson stage name, Brian Warner, sticks up for people like the kids who are dressing like me. That's why I have this quote by him on my notebook, "There is no one marching in front of the Democratic Convention saying, 'What about the outcast pimply faced white teenager who gets beatup in school every day?' That's who I was. There was no one to stick-up for me." Those kids are not my friends, or as you say, communities, but I am glad they saw me as sticking up for them. That is part of who I want to be *(Field notes, February 13, 2002).*

Colleen's outfits became an identity marker for her, as well as for younger students who only knew her through what evolved as her mythic icon status. However, Colleen was clear in both defining the personal choices her physical presentation represented, as well as stating that the personal meaning that her clothing choices held did not transfer to the younger Colleen wannabes. *"People might copy my jewelry, but my Kitty necklace is more to me than a necklace. Kitty was the first female rock band that I started to listen to in sixth grade. They had a lot to do with how see I what it means to be feminine"* (field notes, February 13, 2002). Photo albums Colleen's mother shared with me on home visits showed a very different Colleen prior to sixth grade. In elementary school Colleen and her twin sister dressed in the preppy style that predominated their school community. Colleen was also a bit chunky and lacked the direct, almost defiant look that more recent photos depicted.

When discussing these changes with both Colleen and her mother, they noted that Colleen's summer between fifth and sixth grade proved to be a pivotal one in her development. *"This was the summer I spent as an exchange student in England. I also decided to stop eating butter; I was tired of being fat"* (Field notes, July 2001). England was where Colleen became acquainted with *Kitty's* music and upon returning to the United States she shared the music with her parents for their approval.

Colleen's change in how she perceived and presented herself after spending the summer in England signified to her peers that she had acquired cultural knowledge not readily available to most of her suburban peers. Colleen's budding feminist interest in *Kitty* was at this point a disorganized rip in her prior identity. She did not attribute her eschewing of butter to be for health reasons, but rather for "being sick of being fat," and as she elaborated, being identified as such. When looking at her weight loss from an eighth-grade perspective, Colleen stated that, *"being thin helps me to achieve a more androgynous look"* (Field notes, June 12, 2002).

Colleen's wish to be perceived as androgynous was something that would ebb and flow during the two years I spent with her. It appeared that Colleen was at times more concerned with disrupting established social patterns than with consistently presenting a uniform version of who she was to the world. Like a chameleon, she would change her presentation when it best suited her needs. Wearing the mandatory band and soccer uniforms allowed her to participate in activities that held personal interest. Her choices of how she presented herself to the world were much like her choices of other texts: conscious, deliberate, and part of a larger design.

SUMMARY

The multiliteracies framework provided a lens from which to view Colleen's design and redesign of her physical appearance as more than adherence to the latest fashion trends. Colleen's gestural design was grounded in her philosophical interests and beliefs. Marilyn Manson, Ozzy Osbourne, and Kitty were more than just music icons for Colleen. Colleen was willing to look behind the music to see how these individuals fashioned their public presentations. Rather than replicate what had been done by these media mentors, Colleen drew from the available designs they offered to produce for herself, and subsequently her followers, "new constructions and representations of reality" (Cope & Kalantzis, 2000, p. 22).

Colleen's conscious selection of clothes that challenged the accepted notion of what a "good" student looked like challenged the school community to reevaluate what was privileged both in terms of apparel and the more subtle interpretations that were made based on appearance. Colleen's direct confrontation of the social messages embedded in the school fashion show provided a type of critical framing for the students and staff who planned this event. Colleen's challenge redesigned the show. In so doing, she provided an opportunity for everyone involved to "interpret the social and cultural context of this particular design of meaning…by standing back from the original intent and viewing it critically in relation to its context (Cope & Kalantzis, 2000, p. 35).

Activity theory also provided a lens through which to analyze how Colleen chose to interact with her surroundings and the subsequent interpretations she made. Colleen's object/purpose in selecting how she presented herself was based on challenging not just the accepted practices of the greater school community; she also challenged members of her own communities of practice. Her fluency with the discourses of academics, band, church, and accepted middle-class culture allowed her to challenge these communities while at the same time being successful within them. Colleen's tools/genres were grounded in her fashion choices and popular media texts. However, she was not willing to lose acceptance in established communities, such as the school marching band, that were important to her. She was insightful enough to know the codes and conventions of established communities, as well as the parameters within which her redesigns would be accepted.

FUTURE TRENDS

Colleen was able to recognize the value of established literacy practices and cultural norms that provided her with useful services and pleasure. At the same time she was willing to challenge and redesign aspects of conventional wisdom, and conventional schooling that struck her as

being counterproductive. Moje (2008) cautions against, "the trend toward romanticizing youth literacy practices in a way that overlooks the social, political, and economic importance - indeed necessity - of developing strong academic literacy skills and practices, particularly those focused on print" (p. 207). Colleen's knowledge and mastery of academic codes and conventions allowed her to negotiate a space for her out of school interests within the school day. Lacking this knowledge and proficiency would have negated her ability to redesign established aspects of the school culture to allow space for her texts of choice.

Much has been written by researchers concerning the creation of "third spaces," areas where ICT and popular texts intersect with academic literacies, ideally to benefit the goals of both students and teachers (Gutierrez, Baquedano-Lopez, Alverez, &Chiu, 1999; Kirkland, 2008; Moje, 2008; Moje, Ciechanowski, Kramer, Ellis, Carrillo, & Collazo, 2004). Moje (2008) questions whether these third spaces are always "valuable and desirable" (p. 216); however, for Colleen this intersection was both. Having the opportunity to reflect on her thoughts regarding the fashion show and music assignment with her peers both online and in the research focus groups, as well as formulating her thoughts through the metacognitive reflection our interviews allowed, provided Colleen with a scaffold for her design/redesign process.

There are limited opportunities during the school day to discuss the intersections and overlaps of in-school and out-of-school literacy practices. Although many universal and local factors influence the allocation of time, the current standards movement in the United States that focuses on bringing adolescents who struggle with literacy to the norm via print measures (Moje, 2008) takes time away from all students to focus on the critical thinking and design/redesign abilities necessary in a global market place. When viewed from a multiliteracies perspective, the critical framing component of the New London Group's Pedagogy of Multiliteracies is lost. Since critical framing allows for "interpreting the social and cultural context of particular Designs of meaning" which "involves the students' standing back from what they are studying and viewing it critically in relation to the context" (Cope & Kalantzis, 2000, p. 35) adolescents' involvement with ICT and popular media design is relegated to a "messing around" status. Likewise, merely having ICT tools in the school is not enough to ensure that they are being used to help scaffold adolescents for the unique demands of 21st century literacy (Dressman, O'Brien, Rogers, Ivey, Wilder, & Alvermann, 2006).

When considering future trends for the global classroom, scaffolding by a more capable other (Vygotsky, 1978) must be available for critical reflection and non-print literacies. Doing so will require schools to reconceptualize their definitions of literacy, as well as what is necessary to be literate and employable in a global marketplace. In addition to participating in a longitudinal research study, Colleen was privileged in another way. Coming from a home where both parents were professionals who promoted reading over television, Colleen had a rich background in print literacy and Standard English that was not dependent on school acquisition. If all adolescents are to participate and compete in the global economy, schools need to provide critical scaffolding in ICT and popular media texts, as well as a strong foundation in the print language that continues to control social, economic, and educational advancement.

Students with out-of-school ICT access and mentorship such as Colleen are not dependent on the school system to support or sustain this aspect of their personal pursuits. For interested, motivated, and creative designers who may lack out-of-school ICT tools, as well as support necessary for both overt instruction and sustained practice, school becomes a critical space. In a global economy that is more and more dependent on ICT practices to conduct even basic activities

of daily living, schools can no longer view ICT proficiency as an enrichment experience. Although not a measurable part of the standards movement that has been embraced by United States education policies in the first decade of the twenty-first century, being literate in ICT is crucial to being a functional and productive citizen.

Todd Oppenheimer (2003), a San Francisco-based journalist reporting on the allocation of money to technology within the United States public school system noted that it was the underlying school culture, not the amount of technology tools available, that established how and for what purpose these tools were utilized. This echoes Carmen Luke's (1997) statement "that if schooling refuses to deal with the texts of everyday life, which include media and school texts, then educators will indeed widen, not bridge, the experiential knowledge gap between both teacher and student" (p. 47). It is not enough for schools to have ICT tools; teachers, administrators, and community members would be well served to look at how these tools are allocated and used within the school community.

By observing how successful student-centered communities of practice formulate and sustain themselves, educators can glean insight into how classroom practice can utilize student-centered, as well as student-generated tools and conventions to address aspects of literacy that are outside the realm of linear, alphabetic, printed texts. This invites new genres into the classroom (Labbo, 2004) that position students in the role of an ICT expert, whilst also strengthening the role of the teacher as a critical framer to the often subliminal messages found in popular cultural texts. By acknowledging that there can be new ways to use existing tools and texts, teachers can open their classrooms to the design/redesign process rather than replicate existing designs in a rote fashion. Research that focuses on how ICT and popular media texts are incorporated into classroom curricular goals, research on "what constitutes literacy?" could explore how the current national standards movement is addressing the global literacy demands that often necessitate both ICT and popular media proficiency. Studies on ICT and popular media have often been located in the areas of media studies, communication, and cultural studies (Hagood, 2003). The effects of hypertext, online genres (Chandler-Olcott & Mahar, 2003), nonlinear text links, semiotic sign systems, and online composition offer researcher possibilities in the areas of reading, composition, and linguistics. Moving beyond the socio-cultural and socio-historical (Alvermann, 2002) perspectives that reading research has focused on in regard to ICT and popular media texts would afford researchers the opportunity to consider how these tools and genres influence emergent and developmental reading both on the independent and instructional levels.

Finally, research that looks at how the effects of adolescents' design and redesign of ICT practices and use of popular media texts reaches beyond the adolescents' personal and local nexus could provide research-driven data to an area that has previously been dominated by journalistic observations (Katz, 2000; Lewis, 2002; Nussbaum, 2004; Singer, 2004). Michele Knobel and Colin Lankshear (Knobel & Lankshear, 2002; Lankshear & Knobel, 2002) have acknowledged how ICT practices, with their ability to quickly garner both attention and feedback, are changing not only how adolescents choose and change ICT practices, but how these practices have the ability to shape larger social, political, and economic issues.

CONCLUSION

Just as the original Luddites of the early nineteenth century feared that the Industrial Revolution would displace artisans, neo-Luddites of the present fear that technology will come to dominate and control the systems that employ it. Colleen and her peers were able to illustrate how ICT and popular media

texts are tools and genres they utilize in a complex and recursive design process. This design process values individual human input and mentorship, resulting in communities of practice that in turn support the individual designers in creating a sense of meaning regarding their world and the place they hold in it.

It appears disingenuous to approach evolving ways of reading both the world and the self from the structural, linear, assembly-like communication lenses that drove academic curricula through the last century. As comfortable as this academic model may be to the boomers who see education as a commodity to be obtained, rather than a system to be negotiated, maintaining this antiquated model does a huge disservice to young people facing an ever changing global market place.

Adolescents who, like Colleen, are fortunate enough to have adult mentors who can model the literacy skills needed for negotiating power differentials both online and in real time have the opportunity to develop social skills that will serve them in the global arena. These mentors are not necessarily determined by socioeconomic status. It was Colleen's parents' resistance to cable television and broadband Internet access that led her to the local library. However, it was also her parents' knowledge of the social infrastructure of school and the importance that outside enrichment holds that allowed Colleen the luxury of being a successful student, band member, athlete, and advocate for social justice.

Attending to the ICT and popular media practices of adolescents offers a venue from which to study evolving ways of being and understanding the world. Attending to ICT and popular media practices, as well as how these practices design and reconceptualize traditional notions of what it means to be literate, is of critical importance if we are to avoid reinforcing a class system where power and privilege are rapidly becoming options only to those who can obtain tools and mentorship in ICT practices beyond what the majority of public schools can offer.

Courtney Cazden (2000) addresses the need for adults to reconceptualize what it means to be literate in the twenty-first century by citing Basil Bernstein's advice that, "If the culture of the teacher is to become part of the consciousness of the child, then the culture of the child must first be in the consciousness of the teacher" (p. 323). Rather than shy away from adolescents' ICT and popular media practices in favor of less controversial, standards-based curricula, educators need to facilitate dialogues where the impact that certain ICT and popular media texts have on individuals, local communities, and global concerns can be explored by all stakeholders in the debate on what constitutes literacy in the twenty-first century.

Harkening back to Colleen's opening e-mail about *The Prisoner*, adults who fail to recognize the effects that adolescents' design and redesign of ICT and popular media texts has on public, private, global, and online spaces may find themselves in the position of Number 6, inhabitants in a strange village that is totally isolated from the rest of the world. Unlike Number 6, who rails against conformity, the neo-Luddites of today may find that their inability to move beyond linear thoughts and expression forms a self-imposed prison where they are isolated from new trends, news, and economic opportunities. To inhabit spaces walled off from media texts, information communication technologies, and cultural practices of youth is akin to creating a cultural and linguistic ghetto. By continuing to privilege twentieth century literacy practices, especially in high- stakes assessments, public schools are in danger of creating a work force that is illiterate in regard to ICT unless mentorship is available outside of the school setting.

At one end of the social divide, aging baby boomers may have the financial means to reside in ICT isolation, or arrested technological development, where they can hire mentors to service their ICT needs. At the other end of the social spectrum, the tools needed for ICT proficiency may be luxuries well beyond the means of our ever-increasing ranks of working poor. When food, shelter, and health care are daily concerns, there is little time, space, money, or energy left to engage in ICT design processes. Whether it is for a lack of interest, or a lack of tools, it is questionable whether the generation currently writing and enforcing educational policies has the authority to relegate younger generations to a communication ghetto, especially when the solvency of established communities depends on the creativity, innovation, and genius of youth.

Although they may be skilled in ICT and popular media texts, Colleen and her peers were often naïve in the ways of corporate manipulation and appropriation. They can benefit from mentors who help them to read both the word and the world, even if these mentors lack ICT proficiency. It will take a partnership involving the best practices of twentieth century literacy initiatives, and the creative genius of new design possibilities, to ensure that all individuals avoid the fate of Number 6, prisoners in a village of conformity, "totally isolated from the rest of the world" (Colleen, e-mail, June 10, 2003).

REFERENCES

Alvermann, D. E. (2002). *Adolescents and literacies in a digital world*. New York: Peter Lang.

Barton, D., & Hamilton, M. (2000). Literacy practices. In D. Barton, M. Hamilton, & R. Ivonic (Eds.), *Situated literacies: Reading and writing in context (pp. 7-15)*. New York: Routledge.

Beach, R. (2000). Using media ethnographies to study response to media as activity. In A. Watts Paillotet & P. Mosenthal (Eds.), *Reconceptualizing literacy in the media age* (pp. 3-39). Stamford, CT: JAI Press.

Cazden, C. (2000). Four innovative programs: A postscript from Alice Springs. In B. Cope & M. Kalantzis (Eds.), *Multiliteracies: Literacy learning and the design of social futures* (pp. 321-348). London: Routledge.

Chandler-Olcott, K., & Mahar, D. (2003). "Tech-savviness" meets multiliteracies: Exploring adolescent girls' technology-related literacy practices. *Reading Research Quarterly, 38*, 356–385. doi:10.1598/RRQ.38.3.3

Cole, M. (1996). *Cultural psychology: A once and future discipline.* Cambridge, MA: Harvard University Press.

Cope, B., & Kalantzis, M. (2000). *Multiliteracies: Literacy learning and the design of social futures.* New York: Routledge.

de Certeau, M. (1984). *The practice of everyday life.* Berkeley, CA: University of California Press.

Delpit, L. (1995). *Other people's children: Cultural conflict in the classroom.* New York: Free Press.

Dressman, M., O'Brien, D., Rogers, T., Ivey, G., Wilder, P., & Alvermann, D. (2005). Problematizing adolescent literacies: Four instances, multiple perspectives. In J.V. Hoffman, D.L. Shallert, C.M. Fairbanks, J. Worthy, & B. Maloch (Eds.), *55th yearbook of the National Reading Conference* (pp. 141-154). Oak Creek, WI: National Reading Conference.

Engestrom, Y., & Miettinen, R. (1999). Introduction. In Y. Engestrom, R. Miettinen, & R. Punamaki (Eds.), *Perspectives on activity theory* (pp. 1-16). Cambridge, UK: Cambridge University Press.

Freire, P., & Macedo, D. (1987). *Reading the word and world.* South Hadley, MA: Bergin & Garvey.

Gutierrez, K. D., Baquedano-Lopez, P., Alvarez, H., & Chiu, M. M. (1999). Building culture of collaboration through hybrid language practices. *Theory into Practice, 38*(2), 87–93.

Hagood, M. (2003). New media and online literacies: No age left behind. *Reading Research Quarterly, 38*, 387–391. doi:10.1598/RRQ.38.3.4

Holloway, S., & Valentine, G. (2001). "It's only as stupid as you are": Children's and adults' negotiation of ICT competence at home and at school. *Social & Cultural Geography, 2*, 25–42. doi:10.1080/14649360020028258

Jenkins, H., Clinton, K., Purushotma, R., Robinson, A. J., & Weigel, M. (2006). *Confronting the challenges of participatory culture: Media education for the 21st Century.* Chicago: The MacArthur Foundation.

Katz, J. (2000). *Geeks: How two lost boys rode the Internet of Idaho.* New York: Broadway Books.

Kirkland, D. E. (2008). "The Rose That Grew from Concrete": Postmodern blackness and new English education. *English Journal, 97*(5), 69–75.

Knobel, M., & Lankshear, C. (2002). Cut, paste, and publish: The production and consumptions of zines. In D. Alvermann (Ed.), *Adolescents and literacies in a digital world* (pp. 164-185). New York: Peter Lang.

Labbo, L. (2004). Seeking synergy between postmodern picture books and digital genres. *Language Arts, 81*, 202.

Lankshear, C., & Knobel, M. (2002). Do we have your attention? New literacies, digital technologies and the education of adolescents. In D. Alvermann (Ed.), *Adolescents and literacies in a digital world* (pp.19-39). New York: Peter Lang. Lapp, J., & Flood, D. (1995). Broadening the lens: Toward an expanded conceptualization of literacy. In K.A. Hinchman, D.J. Leu, & C.K. Kinzer (Eds.), *Perspectives on literacy research and practice* (pp. 1-16). Chicago: National.

Lave, J., & Wenger, E. (1991). *Situated learning: Legitimate peripheral participation.* Cambridge: Cambridge University Press.

Leander, K. M. (2003). Writing travelers' tales on new literacyscapes. *Reading Research Quarterly, 38*(3), 392–397.

Lewis, M. (2002). *Next: The future just happened.* New York: Norton.

Luke, C. (1997). Media literacy and cultural studies. In S. Muspratt, A. Luke, & P. Freebody (Eds.), *Constructing critical literacies: Teaching and learning textual practice* (pp. 19-50). Creskill, NJ: Hampton Press.

Moje, E. (2008). Youth cultures, literacies, and identities in and out of school. In Flood, J., Heath, S.B., & Lapp, D. (Eds.), *Handbook of research on teaching literacy through the communicative arts* (pp. 207-219). Newark, DE: International Reading Association.

Moje, E., Ciechanowski, K., Kramer, K., Ellis, L., Carrillo, R., & Collazo, T. (2004). Working toward third space in content area literacy: An examination of everyday funds of knowledge and Discourse. *Reading Research Quarterly, 39*, 38–70. doi:10.1598/RRQ.39.1.4

New London Group. (1996). A pedagogy of multiliteracies: Designing social futures. *Harvard Educational Review, 66*(1), 60–92.

Nussbaum, E. (2004, January 11). My so-called Blog. *The New York Times Magazine, 33*-37.

Oppenheimer, T. (2003). *The false promise of technology in the classroom and how learning can be saved.* New York: Random House.

Russell, D. R. (1997). Rethinking genre in school and society: An activity theory analysis. *Written Communication, 14*, 504–555. doi:10.1177/0741088397014004004

Skelton, T., & Valentine, G. (1998). *Cool places: Geographies of youth culture.* London: Routledge.

Valentine, G., Holloway, S., & Bingham, N. (2002). The digital generation: Children, ICT and the everyday nature of social exclusion. *Antipode, 34*, 296–315. doi:10.1111/1467-8330.00239

Vygotsky, L. S. (1978). *Mind in society: The development of higher psychological processes.* Cambridge, MA: Harvard University Press.

Wenger, E. (1998). *Communities of practice: Learning, meaning, and identity.* Cambridge, MA: Cambridge University Press.

Wertsch, J. (1998). *Mind as action.* New York: Oxford University Press.

Chapter 3
Hybrid Identity Design Online:
Glocal Appropriation as Multiliterate Practice for Civic Pluralism

Candance Doerr-Stevens
University of Minnesota, USA

ABSTRACT

The pedagogy of multiliteracies aims to push our understanding of literacy beyond that of traditional reading and writing practices to include multiple practices of designing meaning that are often multimodal in nature. This chapter explores one of these multiliterate practices, that of hybrid identity design online. This process examines how native English speakers intermix local and global resources in strategic ways in a process the author has termed glocal appropriation. The chapter reviews the growing body of research on English Language Learners who utilize local and global resources to construct hybrid identities, which in turn allow for participation in English language literacy practices. To shift the focus to native English speakers, she presents a case study of one native English speaker's use of local and global resources to design an online identity. She argues that through the hybrid identity practice of glocal appropriation, he is able to design new imaginaries of self, which promotes continued participation and, in turn, allows for literacy learning and spaces of civic pluralism.

INTRODUCTION

The Multiliteracies of digital electronic "texts" are based on notions of hybridity and intertextuality. Meaning-making from the multiple linguistic, audio, and symbolic visual graphics of hypertext means that the cyberspace navigator must draw on a range of knowledges about traditional and newly blended

DOI: 10.4018/978-1-60566-842-0.ch003

genres or representational conventions, cultural and symbolic codes, as well as linguistically coded and software-driven meanings. Luke (2000, p. 73)

Many studies document the expanding use of digital technologies by youth for purposes of personal expression and online sociality (cf. Ito, 2007; Jenkins, 2006; Lam, 2006a; Lankshear, 2007). As Luke (2000) states above, these "cyberspace navigators" must draw on various sets of knowledge in order to make meaning and forge relationships with others. Often shaping these online interactions are the performances of various online identities. These online identities are increasingly hybrid, in that they draw on diverse and often multimodal resources made available online at the click of a button. The consumption and production of these hybrid identities is often motivated by social relations forged and maintained by sharing content in specific new, and increasingly commercial, media spaces.

There are a growing number of researchers who view online participation as active cultural production, wherein media users take up social practices, identity construction included, to forge new routes of agency and participation through active appropriation or redesigning of cultural resources (Black, 2005, 2006; Ito, 2007; Jenkins, 1992, 2006; Lam, 2000, 2006a, 2006b; Lewis, 2007; Lewis & del Valle, 2008; New London Group, 1996, 2000; Willis, 2003). The "Designs of Meaning" framework, a meta-language of multiliteracies, forwarded by the New London Group (1996, 2000) is especially helpful for examining how media users produce culture anew through processes of design and redesign of cultural resources. This framework views semiotic activity as a creative process of design, composed of three elements: Available Designs, Designing, and The Redesigned (New London Group, 1996, 2000, p. 20). In other words, when interacting with a text through production or consumption, one designs a meaning for the text by drawing on his/her available designs, or available semiotic resources, and in the process creates new available designs. In this sense, the New London Group positions this process of Design and Redesign as highly productive in that transformed meanings are created through Redesign of old materials into new combinations and thus become new Available Designs for future meaning making (New London Group, 2000, p. 23). This process of design and redesign helps to explain how individuals, through a continuous process of design, are able to negotiate their

identities and in turn see new possibilities for their everyday practices.

The New London Group (2000) identifies two key practices of redesign, that of hybridity and intertextuality. They describe hybridity, which will be discussed in more detail later in this chapter, as the creation of new practices and conventions of meaning via mechanisms of creativity and "culture-as-process" (p. 29). As for intertextuality, they discuss how new meaning can be forged through relationships between texts, their similarities and differences, and how these connections construct histories or "intertextual chains" of meaning (p. 30). Whether it is described as hybridity or intertextuality, both practices highlight the commingling and appropriation of cultural resources to bring about new meaning and produce culture anew.

Among these multiple practices of Designing and Redesigning is the construction or designing of identities. Gee (2004, 2006) in particular, identifies this practice of identity design as "self-fashioning" or "shape-shifting," a design practice that is necessary for survival in today's "high-tech, global, fast-changing world" (Gee, 2004, 2006). In other words these Shape-Shifting Portfolio People, as he calls them, must be able to draw on hybridity and intertextuality in order to craft and re-craft themselves multiple times, using the available social and cultural resources at hand in order to prepare for multiple jobs and careers (2006, p. 166). Gee further claims that the modern economy desires these hybrid, diversified identities to fit consumer niches. As a result, the youth of today are summoned to take up these self-fashioning and shape-shifting practices not only for purposes of job security but also for social aspects of life, such as marriage and interaction with peers (Gee, 2006). In Gee's discussion of Shape-Shifting Portfolio People, multiple literacy practices and various social designs of identity converge to position fluid hybridity as a route to viability in today's global economy. In other words, the Designing and Redesigning of identities are among the various critical literacy practices proposed by the Pedagogy of Multiliteracies. These practices of identity design afford media users new routes to literacy learning whilst also promoting online spaces of civic pluralism, which according to the Multiliteracies Project, should be among the fundamental aims of 21st Century schooling (Cope & Kalantzis, 2000; Kalantzis & Cope, 2000; New London Group, 1996, 2000).

In terms of promoting new routes of participation and civic pluralism, the emerging body of research on English Language Learners' (ELL) participation online is especially convincing (Black, 2006; Lam, 2000, 2006a). ELL media users' participation online often involves the blending of local and global semiotic resources, which construct hybrid identities that facilitate their entry into these spaces. While there are a substantial and growing number of studies on the online practices of ELL participants forging new routes of participation, there are very few studies that address this same online identity practice with native English speakers, who also actively design hybrid identities using a variety of local and global semiotic resources. Given that we are all participants in the process of identity design, whether we knowingly choose so or not, this chapter will focus on the online identity practices of native English speakers, looking specifically at the design of hybrid identities via the process of what I call "glocal appropriation," asking how these hybrid identities through creative design and redesign of meaning might promote both literacy learning and civic pluralism. Before exploring how hybrid identity design promotes civic pluralism, we must first focus on how these hybrid identity practices occur online; how they challenge normative identities; and how they promote literacy learning.

To accomplish this task, I have organized this chapter into four sections. In the first section, I describe the Design and Redesign of hybrid identities as they occur online. Here, I pay special attention to the emerging body of research that addresses the online practices of English Language Learners (ELL) and how they participate in "transcultural spaces" (Lam, 2006b) for purposes of agency and language learning. Next, I move to an explanation of "glocal appropriation" as I use it to describe a specific type of hybrid identity practice. Here, I argue that glocal appropriation is a multiliterate practice of designing and redesigning identities, wherein new media users take up resources from both local and global contexts in specific ways for purposes of viability and prestige in online spaces. In the third section, I illustrate the multiliterate practice of glocal appropriation as shown by one online role-play participant. I then conclude the chapter with a critical discussion of the concept of glocal appropriation, asking what benefits and dilemmas it presents for a pedagogy of Multiliteracies in terms of promoting literacy learning and civic pluralism. This final section will also offer suggestions for future pedagogy and inquiry related to identity design in increasingly global spaces online.

Hybrid Identity Design Online

The notion of hybridity is not new. Viewing hybridity as a heterogeneous composition of semiotic elements, sometimes cultural other times social, scholars have found the concept to be generative in its ability to parse through the various literacy practices at work in the active negotiation of meaning and identity (Gutierrez, Baquedano-Lopez, & Alvarez, 2001; Kamberelis, 2001; Volk & Acosta, 2003). Beginning with Bakhtin's (1981) consideration of hybrid voices, or heteroglossia, we begin to see hybridity as more than a blending of different voices or elements but rather a dialogic interplay of conflicting voices and/or elements that accompany one's personal appropriation of meaning.

Kamberelis (2001) further extends Bakhtin's notion of heteroglossia with his focus on hybrid discourse practices and their transformative potential for rearticulating the power dynamics of a given space. As Kamberelis describes, "hybrid discourse practices foreground the power of improvisation and the potentially synergistic relations that can obtain between the planned and the improvised curriculum in teaching - learning interactions" (p. 121). Like Bakhtin (1981) and Kamberelis (2001), Gutierrez, Baquedano-Lopez, & Alvarez (2001) claim that this shifting and blending of competing voices is more than simple code switching but rather these practices are a strategic "sense making process" involved with identity construction (p. 128). As these studies suggest, the use of hybrid discourse practices, whether deliberate or improvisational, has the potential to revise identities and social relations, through production of new available designs for making meaning.

Others have further extended this examination of hybrid discourse practices as they occur online, arguing that online spaces are especially fruitful for hybrid textuality (Lewis, 2007), which in turn facilitates the design of hybrid identities. An emerging body of research has focused specifically on the hybrid identity practices of English Language Learners (ELL) online and how they relate to literacy and online literacy practices. Lam (2000, 2006a, 2006b) and Black (2005, 2006) have studied how English language learners (ELLs) use online resources to design and build identities that in turn promote literacy development. Black's (2005) study of ELL participation in online fanfiction spaces in particular, found that ELL fanfiction writers would use multimodal resources such as images and animation to design their "personal pages" on fanfiction websites. Building up their personal pages helped the writers to establish an online identity and "affiliation" with other fanfiction writers, which in turn granted them "access" to a community of writers. Once part of these communities, ELL writers interacted with other writers, often constructing hybrid texts and identities from various sets of resources: linguistic, literary, and popular culture. Through these online relationships, participants received

valuable feedback on their writing, a community practice that promoted development of English literacy practices.

These highly participatory spaces online often draw participants from all over the globe. Described by Lam as "transcultural spaces" (2006a, 2006b), these hybrid spaces online represent "the coming together of transnational capital, multicultural demographics, and media and communication technologies in the creation of new transcultural spaces within and across societies" (Lam, 2006b, p. 214). Similar to the New London Group's description of civic pluralism as a postnationalist space where differences are the norm and a "source of productive diversity" (New London Group, 2000, p. 15), these transcultural spaces have glocalized cultural flows, where local and global practices converge to create hybrid identities. Lam argues that ELL media users' participation online in transcultural spaces often provides more opportunity for literacy practice than at school. Besides being a source of pride for her study participants, Lam describes these transcultural identity practices as essential for success in a global economy where "semiotic workers" produce texts that must have cultural relevance for global audiences (2006b). Furthermore, Lam (2006b), like the New London Group, urges that we not view hybrid, transcultural identities as a problem of cultural deficiency in need of management, but instead that we see these intercultural resources as beneficial for strengthening international relations.

In the work of both Black and Lam, we see ELL writers drawing on various resources (multimodal, local, and global) to design hybrid identities, which not only increase their social capital in online spaces, in turn promoting literacy learning, but also forge transcultural spaces that promote civic pluralism. While these studies are fundamental in that they address the construction of transcultural spaces and hybrid identities for purposes of literacy learning, they do not address the ways in which these media users designed the hybrid identities in order to critique the systems in which they were participating and as a result open new routes for civic pluralism. Ito's (2007) study of Yugioh fans in Japan does address identity construction's potential for critique. Ito claims that through the converging of various digital technologies and the hypersociality of online spaces, participants are able to engage in critique of current social structures in ways that forge new "Available Designs", or what Ito calls, "technologies of the imagination" (p. 91). These new Available Designs for making meaning materialize not only in online practices but also offline in every-day interactions with peers.

Whether the participants are English Language Learners, Japanese speakers interacting with other Japanese speakers, or native English speakers, all media users engage in hybrid discourse practices to some extent in order to navigate the competing discourses of their daily interactions. Thus, it is important to understand how all learners, native English speakers included, might also design hybrid identities in order to build social capital, appropriate literacy practices, and/or critique social structures. To address this concern, I now turn to the concept of glocal appropriation, asking how it might help us to better identify and analyze the design and redesign of hybrid identities online.

Glocal Appropriation

I use the concept of *glocal appropriation* here to describe the hybrid identity practices that involve the combining of both local and global resources to design and redesign one's identity or relations with the world. The concept of glocal appropriation offers a specific type of hybrid discourse practice, one that allows for an understanding of hybrid identity that is active in its incorporation of resources from local situations and other larger, global conversations and contexts. Furthermore, glocal appropriation is often strategic in that it uses hybridity for purposes of prestige and/or critique. In focusing on this specific type of hybrid discourse practice, it is possible to identify and perhaps sup-

port media users' design of new identities. This current study therefore seeks to examine the hybrid identity practices of glocal appropriation, asking how it is that new media users intermix global and local resources to design identities that navigate across multiple contexts, while also engaging in critique and further literacy learning. To conduct this inquiry into glocal appropriation, I draw on the theoretical work of three disciplines. In other words, similarly to the media users addressed in my inquiry, I have designed a hybrid framework that serves to create new Available Designs for understanding online literacy practices.

First, I turn to socio-cultural theories of learning and literacy. Much like the approaches forwarded by the pedagogy of Multiliteracies, these socio-cultural theories view learning and literacy not as autonomous, discreet skills in need of acquisition, but rather as specific social practices that are appropriated over time through continuous participation in a situated context or community of practice (Lave & Wenger, 1991; Rogoff, 1995; Street, 2000; Lewis, 2007).

Second, I draw on work from the fields of cultural and communication studies to help me conceive of glocal appropriation as a form of hybrid identity design. To begin, I take up the notion of *appropriation* as discussed in terms of "cultural appropriation" by Rogers (2006) and more specifically in terms of popular culture by Jenkins (1992, 2006). Influenced by de Certeau's (1984) notion of "textual poaching," Jenkins (1992) uses the concept of appropriation to explain how fans and new media users remix existing cultural content in new ways. Rather than viewing the remixing as an act of piracy, Jenkins (2006) instead argues that this remixing is active appropriation of meaning, a process he calls "intelligent sampling" and "creative juxtaposition" wherein media users must critically engage with the content they remix (p. 33). This engagement involves analysis and critique of the content's meaning potential, its structure and materials. Thus, according to Jenkins, "fans actively assert their mastery over the mass-produced texts which provide the raw materials for their own cultural productions and the basis for their social interactions" (1992, p. 25). In this sense, the notion of appropriation provides researchers a lens to analyze how new media users design identities through an active sampling of cultural resources. Willis (2003) describes this process of active appropriation as one involving a "grounded aesthetics" which he describes as a process "whereby meanings are attributed to symbols and artifacts, now mostly commodities, in creative ways that produce new orders of symbolic meaning … [that] reset the possibilities for how every day is experienced and how the selection and appropriation of cultural materials will take place in the future" (p. 404).

Here Willis describes interaction with media content not only as active but productive in that it creates new resources for future redesign of identities and meaning. In other words, the ability to "reset the possibilities" through appropriation can also be strategic in that it builds in opportunity for critique and new modes of meaning.

De Certeau's (1984) distinction between "tactics" and "strategies" further delineates the ways in which appropriation can be purposeful. With "strategies" media users appropriate resources inline with the current power system, whereas with "tactics," media users appropriate in ways that oppose or challenge the power system. While the tactic form of appropriation may not dismantle a power system, it subverts it in some way, creating new resources and Available Designs for further tactic appropriation.

Cultural theorist George Lipsitz (1994) further examines the tactic form of appropriation that resists or critiques dominant power systems with his notion of "strategic anti-essentialism" (p. 63). Based on Gayatri Spivak's notion of strategic essentialism, Lipsitz posits his rendition, "strategic anti-essentialism," as a practice of cultural borrowing and cross-cultural identification that serves to "advance emancipatory ends" (p. 56). Lipsitz further explains that this cross-cultural

identification is sometimes more possible through temporary role play, a process that allows one to select and highlight certain aspects of one's identity. To illustrate this practice, Lipsitz describes the Maori youth in New Zealand who in the 1980's appropriated hip-hop to voice resistance and represent a common social struggle with "Black America" (p. 63). In this sense, by explicitly aligning themselves with African Americans and not traditional Maori notions of identity, the Maori youth chose to represent themselves as hybrid rather than pure, a strategic identity practice that offered them resources for further resistance of colonial structures still at work in New Zealand. However, Lipsitz does not see all cross-cultural appropriations as liberating. In fact, he claims that some forms of appropriation serve to reinforce existing power structures. To examine the consequences of cultural appropriations, Lipsitz (1994, p. 56) offers two key questions to consider when analyzing cultural appropriations.

1. Which kinds of cross-cultural identification advance freedom and which ones reinforce existing structures of power and domination?
2. When does identification with the culture of others serve escapist and irresponsible ends and when does it encourage an enhanced understanding of one's experiences and responsibilities?

In light of these questions, Lipsitz suggests that strategic anti-essentialism is legitimate and authentic when practiced by subordinate populations. While I agree with Lipsitz's claim that some forms of appropriation can serve to reify oppressive discourses, limiting the use of strategic anti-essentialism to only those of "subordinate" populations presents power as stable and centralized. Furthermore, it represents identity positions as fixed from one context to the next, even though different contexts, especially those online, have been shown to empower different identities. With online identity markets experiencing continual shift, the labels of "dominant" and "subordinate" also shift. Therefore, for the purpose of this chapter, I will utilize Lipsitz's concept of strategic anti-essentialism as a strategic form of hybrid appropriation that can be taken up by any online user or learner. I believe this rendering better allows us to envision new Available Designs for making meaning. That said, Lipsitz's two key questions mentioned above are integral for considering what appropriations serve to challenge and which serve to reify. It is this disruptive type of appropriation, which de Certeau (1984) and Lipsitz (1994) describe as challenging and/or critiquing the status quo, which the identity practice of glocal appropriation seeks to address. Thus, through Design and Redesign of identities that challenge dominant norms of national identity, glocal appropriation has the potential to forge new Available Designs for civic participation, and in turn promote civic pluralism.

Next, to further describe the practice of appropriation, I utilize the concept of "glocal" to make explicit that the process of hybrid identity construction that involves not only the appropriation of diverse resources, from both local and global contexts, but also the dialogic interplay of the competing discourses associated with these resources. The concept of "glocal" was originally used by sociologist Roland Robertson (1995) to foreground the spatiality of local and global relationships. While various scholars from literacy studies have also found the concept of "glocal" to be helpful for looking at how local and global forces intersect (cf. Leander & McKim, 2003; Lam, 2006b; Lewis, 2007; Lin, Wang, Akamatsu, & Riazi, 2002), I turn to the rendering of communication studies scholar, Kraidy (1999, 2005), who views glocalization as a dynamic process.

For Kraidy (1999, 2005), glocalization is a type of hybridity that is both product and process. Similar to Gee's (2004, 2006) description of shape-shifting in the new world order, Kraidy discusses how corporate interests within neo-liberal economic orders have co-opted hybridity as a "growth engine" for profit (p. 90). Yet, through focus on the dialogic struggle of the global and the local in his use of "glocalization," Kraidy (1999) is able to reposition hybridity as a process, one that can resist popular and corporate depictions of hybridity as commodity for corporate exploitation. In this light, Kraidy (1999) views glocalization as a hybrid space of transformation where symbolic codes and power relations are re-inscribed. Much in the same way that the New London Group positions civic pluralism as a space of productive diversity, Kraidy's presents "glocalization" as a heuristic to push beyond the global/local binary. This blurring of binaries allows for a focus on the transformative potential of local hybridity. For Kraidy (2005), local hybridity can be established through not only "transglobal" connections but also "translocal" connections made up of various localized network connections. This "translocal" approach, Kraidy argues, allows for an examination of the local-to-local power-shifts in everyday practices (Kraidy, 2005, p. 155). In this sense, Kraidy's focus on the translocal relations of glocalization, and their local-to-local power shifts offers a lens to analyze the Design and Redesign of identities and social relations as they occur through appropriation of different cultural resources from local, global or translocal contexts.

Thus, considered collectively, the work of Kraidy and Jenkins allow for a conception of glocal appropriation as hybrid identity practice, wherein new media users incorporate resources from multiple local and global contexts in order to negotiate the micro-politics of the contexts they move within and across. In focusing on both the local and the global and the moves both within and across, glocal appropriation becomes a specific type of multiliterate practice that, tactic like, has the potential to design identities that critique and resist dominant power structures.

Jacob's Practice of Glocal Appropriation

To illustrate the online practice of *glocal appropriation*, I turn to a case study of "Jacob", an online role-play participant and first-year college student who participated in an online role-play debate. The online role-play debate of focus in this chapter was part of a first-year writing course at a Midwestern University. Students in the writing course used a course blog throughout the semester to discuss issues related to globalization. The students then finished their semester course work with an online role-play debate, where they suggested and voted on topics to debate and created fictional personas for role-play interaction related to the selected debate topics. The two debate topics selected by the students were Debate #1: Should the US militarily intervene in North Korea? And Debate #2: Should the drinking age be lowered to 18? To begin the debate, students were required to post a biographical entry that gave some information about their role-play character. Then, for three weeks, students used these fictional personas as vehicles to discuss and debate the issues online with other students. After the three-week debate online, students closed the event with an in-class election of senator roles and a final vote on the debate issues. What follows is a selection of Jacob's blog postings from the debate related to lowering the drinking age.

I choose to focus on Jacob's online postings because of the noteworthy way in which his role-play identity continually shifts and exhibits a hybrid appropriation of online resources. Through multi-voiced shifts, Jacob takes up various semiotic resources, multimodal, local and global, in ways that allow him to perform multiple identities for various audiences. I argue that this practice of glocal appropriation allowed Jacob to critique normative male identities and produce new Available Designs for making meaning related to American, male identity. These new Available Designs forged a space of civic pluralism for

Jacob, which encouraged his continued participation and literacy learning in the role-play event. The questions guiding this analysis of Jacob's postings include:

1. What moves of glocal appropriation does Jacob take up to construct his online identity?
2. In particular, how and when does Jacob draw upon diverse resources to construct hybrid identities via glocal appropriation?
3. In what ways might glocal appropriation serve to establish social currency in online spaces through resistance and critique?

To begin, I will focus on Jacob's biography entry. This initial posting to the online role-play, while adhering to genre conventions presented by most of the other online, role-play participants, differs greatly in the way it constructs a distinctively ironic voice.

Either/Or*

Senator Victor Eremita has roamed the earth for many moons and was born in a manger sometime between 1950 and 1960, but his birthdate remains concealed by history. He attended college at the [MIDWESTERN UNIVERSITY]** simply because their mascot is a [RODENT].

He got a degree in women's studies and a minor in political science. he joined the latter-day black panthers right out of school, a division of the black panthers that allows for people of all races. after defeating the previous senator in a Tibetan gladiatorial contest to the death, he "won the election" to become Senator of Rhode Island. Some things you may not know about Mr. Eremita: he is a specialist in Chinese orthopedic massage. he was known as "Loc Dog" in the underground Wyoming rap scene. he is one of four people in the state of Rhode Island qualified to handle nuclear waste. the dalai lama wrote his college recommendation. he has a close affinity for fire and rodents. he has a teenage daughter for the sake of having a reason to care about the issue that he simply willed into existence. there was no mother.

If given the choice between going to some sports event, and traveling through the wilderness with some close friends looking for the famed fountain of youth, then he would chose the wilderness adventure because it sounds much more entertaining. This is the advertisement he requires local stations to run every hour on the hour that he suggests you watch simply to inspire yourself by himself:

http://www.Victor%20Eremita.youaremighty. com/

There is a clear hybridity at work in this posting, not only in terms of the different social languages present, that of a formal academic voice and a more informal irreverent voice, but also in terms of the presentation of his role as a Senator. To construct the fictional character, Jacob performs localizing moves as he reproduces the content and genre conventions of peers such as listing educational background, family information, etc. These localizing moves serve to mark him as part of the role-play literacy event. In doing so, however, he appropriates the genre convention for his own purposes. By interlacing his biography with the multiple allusions to an eclectic set of cultural icons, Jacob adds a critique of both the biography genre convention and the literacy event of the online role-play.

Jacob's main route of critique is through the design practice of intertextuality. In other words, Jacob alludes to several outside texts or external systems of meaning to add layers of interpretation to his writing. In the choice of "Either/Or" as the title of his posting, and in the naming of his role-play character "Victor Eremita," Jacob refers to the philosopher Soren Kierkegaard, who explores in his book *Either/Or* the dilemma

people face in choosing an ethical or hedonistic life. This direct reference to a philosopher's text in constructing his character may be in part due to another classmate's use of Socratic styles of writing in order to explore issues of globalization, a style Jacob revealed that he liked. In this sense, Jacob uses intertextuality to build relations between himself and Kierkegaard, a philosopher Jacob admires. Furthermore, Jacob builds a history for his role-play character by naming him after a character in *Either/Or.*

In addition to connections with extra-local texts through intertextuality, Jacob practices glocal appropriation through his contrasting references to political, cultural, and spiritual movements outside the local, role-play context of underage drinking. In representing his fictional character as a member of the latter day Black Panthers, and a rapper in a Wyoming hip hop scene, Jacob associates himself with African American culture yet suggests that he is not African American. This racial performance of identity is further complicated through his references to Eastern culture.

Jacob continues the hybridization of his character through his ironic representations of masculinity. At one point he states that his character has a degree in women's studies, a detail that suggests his character is sensitive to issues of female subordination. Yet, in the next sentence, he depicts his character as defeating the previous senator in gladiatorial contest to the death, in other words killing him, a detail that presents his character as highly aggressive and perhaps hyper-masculine. These conflicting representations of masculinity are further complicated by the mention of his character having a daughter, yet "there was no mother." This asexual representation of fatherhood challenges notions of the nuclear family and heterosexuality in that it explicitly omits narrative details that would present his father status as normative.

When asked in an interview why he decided to introduce his character in this way, Jacob replied:

I was just going to be goofy with that ... I saw some of the other people making their roles ... I thought first of all this would kind of give me something in the debate, tactic wise, people would recognize it a little more, because they'd be like, that is such a crazy... so if I said that I won the election by winning a knife fight in an underground Tibetan gladiator contest, or something like that, [laugh] that would be a little more recognizable because people would associate all this weirdness to that name and it is a weird kind of name.

Jacob goes on to describe how he named his character "Senator Victor Eremita" after a Soren Kierkegaard play, stating that he has a "man crush" on the philosopher and that he included the detail about having a daughter only to have "a back-up card" since everyone else was writing children into their biographies.

While some might argue that Jacob's cultural and gendered references are exploitative in that they reference these cultures for humorous effect alone, I argue that these conflicting details related to race and gender, juxtaposed within the same character, represent more than attempts at humor. They are an active Redesigning of his online identities, his fictional role and his real-life role, in order to build prestige among peers. In addition to boosting Jacob's "recognizability" these ironic practices were strategic in that they also performed a challenge to normative perceptions of white masculinity, using humor to critique and resist social norms. While not explicit challenges to social norms, these hybrid constructions do challenge white, heterosexual male dominance through mocking and calling into question the social norms that informed the identity practices that Jacob observed in the writings of his peers.

In this sense, Jacob practices glocal appropriation in that he draws not only on the resources of the situated context, the online role-play conventions set by his peers, but also performs translocal and transglobal moves by connecting his text to other texts and systems of signification. While

Jacob does this for purposes of prestige, or to be "recognizable" to his peers, he also takes up these moves for purposes of critique, to challenge what he perceives to be the local norms for white, male sexuality in the class. These critiques, in turn provide new Available Designs for future identity design and participation within the role-play, further forging a space of civic pluralism related to gender and nation-based identities.

It is not clear whether every detail in Jacob's writing was deliberate. While he did mention in his interview that he found other students' biography postings to be boring, relying too heavily on stereotypical depictions of the nuclear family, the conscious reasoning behind this critique is uncertain. Yet, as Kamberelis (2001) and Lipsitz (1994) argue, it is the improvisational and role-play aspects of the situation that free up one's ways of knowing to envision new designs of self and relations with others. In this sense, Jacob is able to envision new versions of his own identity through use of the fictional role-play identity along with the various multimodal online resources.

I close my focus on Jacob's glocal appropriation with his final role-play posting. In this posting we see Senator Eremita campaigning for re-election. Of interest in this posting are the multiple components and how they contrast in style and purpose. To begin, there is the prose component where Senator Eremita discusses his qualities as a senator and why he should be re-elected and not the other candidates. In the second component, the visual component, Senator Eremita is pictured amid a collage of contradictory and highly political images. These images are an unlikely pairing with the content discussed in the prose component. See excerpt below.

Eremita for Senator*

In the upcoming election an important decision regarding our nation's young people will take place. Vote for myself, Senator Victor Eremita, for the protection of our children. ...Please weigh

the facts and vote responsibly. My oppents have provided no concrete arguments or information to support their claims other then "feelings" that, contrary to years of behavior, significantly reduce their alcohol intake, and yet one of them owns a beer company. I have a daughter, and seek to gain the Congressional seat soley to prevent the lowering of the drinking age, unlike my oppoent, who would see his profits dramatically increase. Please vote for myself, I won't let you and our children down.

Thank you,

Senator Victor Eremita

In this posting we see a marked difference in voice from that of the initial biography posting. In cue with the writings of other senatorial roles in the online role-play, Jacob uses a formal and somewhat academic voice to perform his senator role's bid for re-election. Despite multiple spelling errors, Jacob uses what he calls a "sentence-by-sentence" rhetorical approach to break down the other candidates' arguments and show that he is the most qualified candidate for re-election. We also see him emphasizing his role as father to further support his platform of protecting children. In contrast to his initial biography, this entry makes no mention of the gladiatorial fights, or underground rap scenes. Instead he emphasizes his daughter and his desire to protect her as an emotional rationale for his position on the drinking age debate. In other words, we see Jacob using his "back-up card," the daughter, to build the credibility of his character according to what he perceives to be the values and genre conventions of his audience.

On the one hand, this shift to local conventions can be read as Jacob's active Redesign of identity to better appeal to his audience after not receiving the expected response from his initial entry. On the other hand, it could be a marketing attempt to attract audience members to view the attached campaign poster. In either case, we see Jacob shape-shifting his identity from that of eclectic and clever "that guy" to formal and senatorial "fellow American." Accompanying this entry, however, was also a visual text performing a very different senatorial identity (See Figure 1).

In sharp contrast to the prose text above,

Figure 1. Jacob's campaign poster

which performs a buy-in to the role-play event, this visual image, performs not only a critique but also a resistance to both local and global contexts within the role-play event. In terms of the local, this poster mocks the upcoming senatorial election. In terms of the global, the image expresses a strong critique of American politics and patriotism, issues that Jacob did not address in his role-play postings overall but did address frequently in course blog postings previous to the role-play event. Through a remixing of images, the Pope juxtaposed against the American flag, a group of African American athletes, nuclear explosions, and Senator Eremita foiled by a martini and women in bikinis, Jacob's identity design appropriates these divergent images and their intertextual meanings to present an image of himself as irreverent and skeptical of US Politics. Jacob describes this image remixing as "goofy and funny" a posting that would make him seem "more authentically awesome" because of the eye-patch and its symbolic reference to the gladiatorial knife fights mentioned in his initial biography posting. Yet, when probed to explain the political messages conveyed in these images, Jacob describes a different motivation for remixing the images, one that goes beyond appearing "cool" to his peers.

I am very cynical about America ... I have no problem making fun of America, I don't like America, I mean it has given us good things yes, but our entire foundation of our system where it is selling images and making money... it is so wrong and it is translated into so many bad things on so many levels and we don't even realize it, until oh my god, you know what I mean. There is a reason that the divorce rate and depression rates are so high in our country. There is something there that is wrong.

Jacob goes on to describe the US as overly patriotic and with a "dumb, testosterone-fueled misguidance." In this sense, the campaign poster serves a purpose beyond that of the role-play

related to underage drinking, in that it is a text that seeks an extra-local, perhaps even global audience. In the purposeful pairing of these two components Jacob exemplifies not only hybrid identity design but more specifically the hybrid identity practice of glocal appropriation wherein he juxtaposes multiple voices for purposes of critique. To begin, there is the academic, playing-by-the-rules voice of the prose piece that marks Jacob as insider and complicit with the debate goals of the online role-play. On the other hand, the visual piece, attempts to achieve multiple goals. The intermixing of various cultural icons serves to both build the fictional character of the Senator as "weird and goofy" in order to boost Jacob's prestige in the online role-play context, but also expresses an overall critique of the role-play event and the US political system. In other words, Jacob performs extra-local connections through utilizing the intertextual meaning of the cultural icons and remixing them for multiple purposes, both to build prestige among his role-play peers and to offer a critique of the US political system. This critique component could also be an attempt to participate in larger global conversations related to US politics, a practice Jacob does often online and at home with his father, who is an editorial columnist who writes about national and global issues.

In reading this image in light of Lipsitz's key questions related to cultural appropriation one could argue that, similar to Jacob's initial biography posting, this posting is also exploitative in its cross-cultural connections, and that it serves to mask more than enhance Jacob's understanding of self. While the heavy use of humor could be seen as a masking element, I argue that humor is being used as a way to examine social constructs of self. To do this I draw on Lipsitz's notion of "strategic anti-essentialism" to better understand Jacob's remixing of resources in this image. This image, along with his initial biography posting, appropriate cultural resources for the purposes of "strategic anti-essentialism" in order to mark himself as white, male other. I use "other" here in a local sense, in that Jacob is trying to distinguish himself as different from his peers in the class, whom he views as somewhat provincial, pro-globalization and blindly patriotic. In an interview with Jacob, he describes how he views his classmates.

I don't mean to sound like arrogant city kid, but I feel like a lot of kids here [at MIDWESTERN university] have come from like small towns and they haven't really seen the bad aspects [of society] I mean like I'm from [LARGE URBAN CITY IN THE SOUTH] and there's a whole, uh, all I have to do is drive 20 minutes and I see the difference, I mean up here there are the white rich people... where people have made their own city so they don't have to pay their taxes to the rest of [SOUTHERN CITY] because the rest of [SOUTHERN CITY] is poor black. You see how stupid this system is. It is letting everyone down... I've met kids here from small towns of less than a hundred, and then I come from a city of several million.

In this sense, Jacob draws on hybrid practices of glocal appropriation to construct an identity of outsider. He uses this outsider identity to critique global depictions of white male Americans as hyper-masculine, chauvinistic, and pro-globalization, all qualities he does not want to associate with himself. This glocal appropriation is tactical in that he uses the resources of the given contexts, local and global, to disrupt and challenge local systems, such as the classroom role-play debate and larger, global systems such as US foreign policies and cultural norms. He does so in a way that allows him to continue participation and buy-in to the online role-play event, yet at the same time allows him to negotiate contradictions he sees at work in both the local and global contexts. Thus through a specific type of hybrid identity design, that of glocal appropriation, Jacob is able to engage in critique of local and global contexts. This critique led to continued participation within the

local context, which in the end promotes literacy learning and production of new Available Designs that have the potential for forging spaces of civic pluralism.

Glocal Appropriation: Implications for Pedagogy and Inquiry

The above description of Jacob's online identity construction, illustrates the hybrid identity practice of glocal appropriation, allowing us to see ways in which Jacob intermixed various semiotic resources from local and global contexts to perform multiple identities that shifted according to their audience and also critiqued the local and global contexts within the role-play event. This critique-based practice facilitated Jacob's continued participation, which allowed him to negotiate the micro politics of the situation through construction of an identity that Jacob could buy into, that of the eclectic cynic of American policy. Through continued participation, Jacob designed multiple new Available Designs for meaning related to masculine, American identities and in this process forged an online space of civic pluralism related to gendered and nationalized identities. In addition to promoting civic pluralism, Jacob performed multiple persuasive writing tasks, which served to support his development of persuasive literacy practices. In this sense, glocal appropriation as a specific multiliterate practice allows both researchers and educators an avenue to examine hybrid identity practices that perform critique, while also promoting literacy learning through continued participation and civic pluralism.

Continued Participation and Literacy Learning

How does glocal appropriation promote hybrid identity design in a way that promotes continued participation with the simultaneous result of literacy learning? For Jacob, the identity practice of glocal appropriation allowed him to create hybrid identities that coincided with his perception of himself as clever and funny, while at the same time performing the tasks required for class participation. In other words, Jacob positioned himself as both compliant and resistant in ways that worked for multiple audiences. It is here that I find helpful Guerra's (2004) notion of "transcultural repositioning," wherein hybrid identities, or what Guerra calls "border dwellers," those who move about in multiple worlds simultaneously, use peripheral positions for rhetorical purposes. In this light, Jacob is able to take up glocal appropriations to design identities that dwell in the realm of both the "good student," who participates in class activities, and the "irreverent student," who uses participation to critique and resist.

For Jacob's glocal appropriations to be recognized as routes to continued participation, however, researchers and educators must be able to recognize these identity practices as productive and supportive of literacy learning. To address this need, some researchers suggest an incorporation of "intercultural capital" into definitions of knowledge (Lam, 2006b; Luke, 2004a; Luke & Goldstein, 2006). Having intercultural capital would involve the ability of both youth and educators to negotiate meaning across a variety of local and global communities (Luke, 2004b). Lam (2006b) advocates that we consider agency as intercultural capital due to cross-cultural understandings that allow mobility and viability across online and offline contexts (p. 229). This development of intercultural capital as agency would involve participation on the part of educators and curriculum, two powerful forces that shape learners' access to knowledge.

For educators, it would be essential that notions of knowledge and literacy be pluralistic in ways that acknowledge learners as drawing upon multiple funds of knowledge to produce meaning. Youth in particular, often draw on popular culture metaphors and narratives for appropriation through hybridity and intertextuality. Moreover, popular culture continues to be the cultural currency of

choice for circulation and production online, an important vehicle for intercultural navigation. In addition to participation on the part of educators, curriculum would also need to provide opportunities for students to build repertoires of semiotic systems of meaning in order to develop intercultural capital. Lam (2006b) suggests production of intercultural capital through learning in global contexts that involve "intercultural navigation" of diverse semiotic resources: images, ideas, and designs of meaning (p. 228). Participation online brings global contexts within close proximity.

It is here that we must consider the potential of online participation, and role-play in particular, as curricular possibilities for development of intercultural capital. In many ways role-play provides opportunities to experiment with new identities through perspective taking. The potential for experimentation of identities is further enhanced by online participation with increased sociality and easy access to various resources for hybrid identity construction. The possibility for engagement with intercultural resources is further enhanced if the practice involves participants from across the globe, who, in bringing forth their worldviews, help to forge cross-border connections. Thus, combining online participation with role-playing activities offers a rich space for appropriation of intercultural capital.

Yet in thinking about the curricular possibilities of online role-play, we must consider thoughtful design of role-play events to account for the disrespect of online textual bodies. Some scholars suggest the need to build in critical reflection. This critical reflection can help students understand not only the rhetorical impact of their participation (Salibrici, 1999) but also the ethical and interpersonal implications (Edmiston, 2000; Thomas, 2007).

Thomas (2007) in particular, suggests that online identity construction develops toward "accountability." To explain how media users practice accountability, Thomas (2007) offers a progression of stages for online identity development.

She describes the first stage as "Ego" in which the user sees his/her online identity as free, "all about me, me, me." It is in this stage that users see everything online as a game and thus not to be taken seriously. It is perhaps here where media users may practice cultural appropriation that may be exploitative or offensive.

The next stage, "Original Choice" is where users grapple with issues of whether to represent their online identities as realistic or fantasy. The final stage of "Refining" is a process where users continually travel back and forth between different identities selecting qualities they want to keep and others they want to discard. The final stage in Thomas's identity model is that of "accountability," a time when users start to feel responsible for their online actions and develop a sense of impact in their virtual interactions.

Critique and Civic Pluralism

In addition to exploring ways to support learners' continued participation through the production of intercultural capital and critical reflection of identity design, it is paramount that we also support learners' continued critique of the social structures that surround them. It is through the embracing of critique and resistance that the full potential of glocal appropriation is realized. That said, for critique to be nurtured we need not only schools, but also larger cultures and societies that value difference, or spaces of "civic pluralism" (New London Group, 1996, 2000). Spaces of civic pluralism promote a plurality of knowledge practices and ways of being. Rather than promoting a singular cultural or linguistic standard, advocates of civic pluralism "arbitrate difference," grant access, power, and symbolic capital to all learners regardless of their identity markers (New London Group, 2000, p. 15). To support the practice of critique and in turn promote spaces of civic pluralism, the Pedagogy of Multiliteracies suggests four pedagogical practices: situated practice, overt instruction, critical framing, and transformed prac-

tice (New London Group, 2000, p. 31). While all four practices are interrelated, working together to promote multiliteracies, the practices of critical framing and transformed practice relate most to glocal appropriation's potential for promoting critique and civic pluralism.

The New London Group defines critical framing as a practice of "interpreting the social and cultural contexts of particular Designs of Meaning" (2000, p. 35). In this sense, media users take up skills of critical literacy to analyze the audience and purpose of a given situation online. This critical framing of the situation and context would then inform decisions related to appropriation. In other words, which cultural resources should/should not be appropriated when designing his or her identity. One possible suggestion for fostering practices of critical framing would be an engagement with hybrid texts, such as music, film, painting, and literature that represent cultural appropriation of various cultural genres and styles. Dimitriadis and McCarthy (2001) claim that this critical engagement with hybrid texts would nurture development of a "postcolonial imagination," an analytical mindset that emphasizes the hybrid as potent and generative in its ability to see new possibilities for identity formation and social interactions. In repositioning hybrid from that of abnormal, impure, and deficient to intercultural capital and empowering, we open new spaces for thinking, questioning, and authoring what Luke (2004a) calls "redressive texts," texts that challenge social ways of being and structures of interaction. It is through design of redressive texts that glocal appropriation addresses the practice of transformed practice.

Described as the production of new texts from transformed meaning, transformed practice involves the Redesign of identities that challenge and re-create discourses through direct engagement and innovative use of resources (New London Group, 2000, p. 35). In many ways, Jacob's appropriation and purposeful juxtaposition of various cultural resources represents transformed practice in that he used hybridity to offer an alternative narrative for masculinity. The practice of transformed practice in the classroom might involve explorations into how hybrid texts, paintings, music, and literature, might be presented as redressive texts. Having learners engage with and design their own hybrid texts might forge new imaginaries for how they view themselves and the social structures around them. These hybrid texts might then, in turn, lead to the production of new redressive texts, like they did for Jacob, that serve as available resources for future media production and further participation. The continual analysis and production of hybrid texts, especially those that are redressive, could forge new spaces of plurality, wherein difference is embraced and new designs of self are possible.

The above explorations of intercultural capital, critical framing, and transformed practice raise important questions for considering the pedagogical implications and future research of glocal appropriation as hybrid identity practice. First of all, how does the intercultural capital produced through participation in global contexts promote new routes of participation in ways similar and different to that of glocal appropriation? How do the practices of hybrid identity design, glocal appropriation in particular, differ according to the different developmental stages offered by Thomas (2007), and how might these differences be helpful in light of Lipsitz's key questions for cultural appropriation? In other words, how does glocal appropriation in the Ego stage differ from that of the glocal appropriation in the Accountability stage, and do these differences impact on one's participation, literacy learning, and contributions to civic pluralism? What is the potential of redressive texts as vehicles for production of intercultural capital? These questions are important for considering how we study identity design in global contexts and for how we support learners' literacy learning through curriculum that promotes continued participation and critique.

Whether to promote participation or critique,

it is paramount that we consider how these translocal, transglobal and glocal designs of identity, whether online or off, serve to build social futures that value pluralism. This pluralism, it is hoped, would extend beyond school walls to online spaces of social interaction, where cyberspace navigators negotiate multiple sets of knowledge and modality in order to design meaning. Yet with this hope, we must also realize that macro change occurs over time and through continued participation, a practice that Jacob took up through one blog posting at a time.

CONCLUSION

This chapter explores hybrid identity design online, specifically the practice of glocal appropriation. The concept of glocal appropriation is conceptualized through the convergence of theories of socio-cultural learning and literacy, cultural studies, and communication studies to present an identity practice that views online identity design as an active process of making meaning. In examining how one online role-play participant appropriates various semiotic resources from local and global contexts, I illustrate how the hybrid components of glocal appropriation allows for continued participation and critique; processes of cultural production that have the potential of producing new routes for participation online and possibly offline. For these new structures of participation to be possible a recasting of knowledge and schooling as intercultural and civic pluralism must be considered.

REFERENCES

Bakhtin, M. M. (1981). *The dialogic imagination: Four essays by M. M. Bakhtin.* Austin: University of Texas Press.

Black, R. (2005). Access and affiliation: The literacy and composition practices of English language learners in an online fanfiction community. *Journal of Adolescent & Adult Literacy, 49*, 118–128. doi:10.1598/JAAL.49.2.4

Black, R. (2006). Language, culture, and identity in online fanfiction. *E-Learning, 3*, 170–184. doi:10.2304/elea.2006.3.2.170

Cope, B., & Kalantzis, M. (2000). Designs for social futures. In B. Cope & M. Kalantzis (Eds.), *Multiliteracies: Literacy learning and the design of social futures* (pp. 203-238). London: Routledge.

de Certeau, M. (1984). *The practice of everyday life*. Berkeley, CA: University of California Press.

Dimitriadis, G., & McCarthy, C. (2001). *Reading and teaching the postcolonial: From Baldwin to Basquiat and beyond*. New York: Teachers College Press.

Edmiston, B. (2000). Drama as ethical education. *Research in Drama Education, 5*, 63–84. doi:10.1080/135697800114203

Gee, J. P. (2004). *Situated language in learning: A critique of traditional schooling*. London: Routledge.

Gee, J. P. (2006). Self-fashioning and shape-shifting: Language, identity, and social class. In D. Alvermann, K. Hinchman, D. Moore, S. F. Phelps & D. R. Waff (Eds.), *Reconceptualizing the literacies in adolescents' lives* (2nd ed., pp. 165-185). Mahwah, NJ: Lawrence Erlbaum Associates.

Guerra, J. C. (2004). Emerging representations, situated literacies, and the practice of transcultural repositioning. In M.H. Kells, V. Balester & V. Villanueva (Eds.), *Latino/a discourses: On language, identity and literacy in education* (pp. 7 – 23). Portsmouth, NH: Heinemann.

Gutiérrez, K. D., Baquedano-López, P., & Alvarez, H. H. (2001). Literacy as hybridity: Moving beyond bilingualism in urban classrooms. *The best for our children: Critical perspectives on literacy for Latino students* (pp. 122-141). Columbia University: Teachers College.

Ito, M. (2007). Technologies of the childhood imagination: Yugioh, media mixes, and everyday cultural production. In J. Karanagis (Ed.), *Structures of participation in digital culture* (pp. 88-110). New York: Columbia University Press.

Jenkins, H. (1992). *Textual poachers: Television fans & participatory culture*. New York: Routledge.

Jenkins, H. (2006). *Confronting the challenges of participatory culture: Media education for the 21st century*. MacArthur Foundation White Paper.

Kalantzis, M., & Cope, B. (2000). A multiliteracies pedagogy: A pedagogical supplement. In Cope, B. & Kalantzis M. (Eds.), *Multiliteracies: Literacy learning and the design of social futures* (pp. 239-248). London: Routledge.

Kamberelis, G. (2001). Producing heteroglossic classroom (micro) cultures through hybrid discourse practice. *Linguistics and Education, 12*, 85–125. doi:10.1016/S0898-5898(00)00044-9

Kraidy, M. (1999). The global, the local, and the hybrid: A native ethnography of glocalization. *Critical Studies in Mass Communication, 16*, 456–476. doi:10.1080/15295039909367111

Kraidy, M. (2005). *Hybridity or the cultural logic of globalization*. Philadelphia: Temple University.

Lam, E. (2000). L2 literacy and the design of the self: A case study of a teenager writing on the Internet. *TESOL Quarterly, 34*, 457–483. doi:10.2307/3587739

Lam, E. (2006a). Re-envisioning language, literacy, and the immigrant subject in new mediascapes. *Pedagogies: An International Journal, 1*, 171–195. doi:10.1207/s15544818ped0103_2

Lam, E. (2006b). Culture and learning in the context of globalization: Research directions. *Review of Research in Education, 30*, 213–237. doi:10.3102/0091732X030001213

Lankshear, C. (2007). Introduction. In M. Knobel & C. Lankshear (Eds.), *A new literacies sampler*. New York: Peter Lang.

Lave, J., & Wenger, E. (1991). *Legitimate peripheral participation*. New York: Cambridge University Press.

Leander, K., & McKim, K. (2003). Tracing the everyday 'sittings' of adolescents on the internet: A strategic adaptation of ethnography across online and offline spaces. *Education Communication and Information, 3*(2), 211–240. doi:10.1080/14636310303140

Lewis, C. (2007). Internet communication among youth: New practices and epistemologies. In J. Flood, D. Lapp & S.B. Heath (Eds.), *Handbook on teaching literacy through the communicative, visual and performing arts*. Mahwah, NJ: Lawrence Erlbaum Associates.

Lewis, C., & del Valle, A. (2008). Literacy and identity. In L. Christenbury, R., Bomer & P. Smagorinsky (Eds.), *Handbook of adolescent literacy research*. New York: Guilford Press.

Lin, A., Wang, W., Akamatsu, N., & Riazi, A. M. (2002). Appropriating English, expanding identities and re-visioning the field: From TESOL to teaching English for glocalized communication (TEGCOM). *Journal of Language, Identity, and Education, 1*(4), 295–316. doi:10.1207/S15327701JLIE0104_4

Lipsitz, G. (1994). *Dangerous crossroads: Popular music, postmodernism and the poetics of place*. New York: Verso.

Luke, A. (2004a). Notes on the future of critical discourse studies. *Critical Discourse Studies, 1*(1), 149–152. doi:10.1080/17405900410001674551

Luke, A. (2004b). Teaching after the marketplace: From commodity to cosmopolitanism. *Teachers College Record, 106*, 1422–1443. doi:10.1111/j.1467-9620.2004.00384.x

Luke, A., & Goldstein, T. (2006). Building intercultural capital: [Online supplement to Rogers, T., Marshall, E., & Tyson, C.A. (2006). Dialogic narratives of literacy, teaching, and schooling: Preparing literacy teachers for diverse settings. *Reading Research Quarterly, 41*(2), 202–224. Available at http://dx.doi.org/10.1598/RRQ.41.2.3. doi:10.1598/RRQ.41.2.3

Luke, C. (2000). Cyber-schooling and technological change: Multiliteracies for new times. In B. Cope & M. Kalantzis (Eds.), *Multiliteracies: Literacy learning and the design of social futures* (pp. 69-91). London: Routledge.

New London Group. (1996). A pedagogy of multiliteracies: Designing social futures. *Harvard Educational Review, 66*, 1–28.

New London Group. (2000). A pedagogy of multiliteracies: Designing social futures. In B. Cope & M. Kalantzis (Eds.), *Multiliteracies: Literacy learning and the design of social futures* (pp. 9-37). London: Routledge.

Robertson, R. (1995). Glocalization: Time-space and homogeneity-heterogeneity. In M. Featherstone, S. Lash & R. Robertson (Eds.), *Global modernities*. London: Sage.

Rogers, R. (2006). From cultural exchange to transculturation: A review and reconceptualization of cultural appropriation. *Communication Theory, 15*, 474–503. doi:10.1111/j.1468-2885.2006.00277.x

Rogoff, B. (1995). Observing sociocultural activity on three planes: Participatory appropriation, guided participation, and apprenticeship. In J.V. Wertsch, P. Delrio & A. Alvarez (Eds.), *Sociocultural studies of mind*. Boston: Cambridge University Press.

Salibrici, M. (1999). Dissonance and rhetorical inquiry: A Burkean model for critical reading and writing. *Journal of Adolescent & Adult Literacy, 48*, 628–637.

Street, B. (2000). Literacy events and literacy practices: Theory and practice in the New Literacy Studies. In M. Martin-Jones (Ed.), *Mutilingual matters*. Philadelphia, PA: J. Benjamins.

Thomas, A. (2007, February). *Avatar as new literacy*. Paper presented at National Council of Teacher of English Assembly of Research. Nashville TN.

Volk, D., & de Acosta, M. (2003). Reinventing texts and contexts: Syncretic literacy events in young Puerto Rican children's homes. *Research in the Teaching of English, 38*(1), 8–48.

Willis, P. (2003). Foot soldiers of modernity: The dialectics of cultural consumption and the 21st century school. *Harvard Educational Review, 73*(3), 390–415.

ENDNOTES

*   All spelling and punctuation are reproduced here as they were originally published on the blog.

** Bracketed content is used to protect the identity of Jacob.

Chapter 4
Unpacking Social Inequalities:
How a Lack of Technology Integration may Impede the Development of Multiliteracies among Middle School Students in the United States

Laurie A. Henry
University of Kentucky, USA

ABSTRACT

This chapter is based on a comparative, qualitative study that explored social equity issues related to technology integration among middle schools located in the United States of America. Differences between economically privileged and economically disadvantaged school districts were explored to determine if inequalities related to technology integration generally, and the development of multiliteracies specifically, exist. Participants included middle school students from grades 5 to 8, and teachers and administrators from nine schools located in four different school districts. Data included transcripts from interviews and focus groups, observational field notes, and various school artifacts collected from the research sites. Using these data, an exploration of the contextual factors that might influence the inclusion of instruction for new literacies directly related to literacy activities on the Internet was conducted. The results suggest that a disparity does exist along economic lines and several contextual factors were identified that may impede the development of the new literacies including the use of the Internet as an information resource among middle school students in the United States.

INTRODUCTION

Over the past decade an upsurge of attention focused on technology integration in K-12 schools has inundated teachers everywhere. The Internet has become widely accepted as an information resource critical to teaching and learning in all subjects and at all levels of education (Forsyth, 1998; Pickering, 1995). Many argue that the Internet is the defining technology among our youth (Fallows, 2004; Hay, 2000; Leu, Kinzer, Coiro, & Cammack, 2004; Levin & Arafeh, 2002) and developing proficient skills for using the many digital technologies that the Internet has introduced are essential for success in a global, knowledge-based economy (Friedman, 2005; New Literacies Research Team, 2007; Partnership for

DOI: 10.4018/978-1-60566-842-0.ch004

21st Skills, 2004). As teachers struggle to keep up with the constant emergence of new technologies to motivate and engage their students, school districts are faced with the issue of where these skills fit within their curricula. As we shift our attention from reading and writing with book, paper, and pencil technologies to reading and writing in digital, multimodal, networked, and social information spaces, we need to rethink what skills and strategies are required of our students to successfully engage in Internet-based literacy activities and how best to address these skills as part of the curricula.

In this chapter, the development of multi-literacies, or new literacies, specific to reading and writing required when using the Internet are explored. The chapter:

- Provides an overview of the new literacies of Internet-based reading and writing and reviews the body of research in this area.
- Identifies contextual factors that may impact the development of new literacies and, in turn, raises questions about social equity.
- Provides suggestions to advance our thinking about new literacies, new directions for literacy pedagogy, and further research in this area.

BACKGROUND

This chapter is framed by an emerging theoretical perspective referred to as multiliteracies or *new literacies* (Coiro, 2003; Coiro, Knobel, Lankshear, & Leu, 2008; Lankshear & Knobel, 2003; Leu, 2000, 2002; Leu et al., 2004). A new literacies perspective seeks to include the multiple text formats and multimodal environments associated with the complex literacy demands of the Internet and other networked technologies (Cope & Kalantzis, 2000; Lankshear & Knobel, 2003; Leu et al., 2004). Leu and colleagues (2004)

define these new literacies as skills and strategies required when using the Internet and other information communication technologies (ICTs) that "allow us to identify important questions, locate information, critically evaluate the usefulness of that information, synthesize information to answer questions, and then communicate the answers to others" (p. 1572). This view of multiliteracies focuses specifically on new literacies in relation to school-based literacy activities for learning, whereas other views of multiliteracies include a more encompassing perspective that address out of school literacy engagements (Gee, 2000; Lankshear & Knobel, 2003) and a pedagogy that fosters literacy development for work and community that help shape an individual's social future (The New London Group, 1996). However, many researchers agree that Internet-based literacy is different than traditional print-based literacy, which necessitates a broadened definition of literacy to include the multimodal texts found in the digital environments of the Internet and other ICTs (e.g. Alvermann, 2002; Gee, 2000; International Reading Association [IRA], 2001; Kress, 2003; Leu, 2000; RAND Reading Study Group, 2002; Snyder, 1996; Tyner, 1998).

A New Definition of Literacy

The introduction of the Internet into school classrooms has been met with an array of new research, new curricula, new instructional approaches, and new definitions of what it means to be literate. A barrage of new terms has erupted concerning literacy over the past decade, including Internet literacy (Tyner, 1998), network literacy (McClure, 1997), information literacy (Spitzer, Eisenberg & Lowe, 1998), media literacy (Alvermann, Moon, & Hagood, 1999; Hobbs, 1998), and digital literacy (Gilster, 1997) to name a few. These definitions and others can all be viewed as part of a *New Literacies* or *Multiliteracies* perspective (Castek, Coiro, Hartman, Henry, Leu, & Zawilinski, 2007;

Cope & Kalantzis, 2000; Lankshear & Knobel, 2003; Leu et al., 2004; The New London Group, 2000), which focuses on the new Internet-based reading and writing skills that are essential for success in the 21st century.

Many agree that the Internet requires unique applications of traditional literacy skills as well as novel literacy skills to address the large cognitive demands that Internet-based literacy activities place on the individual (Coiro, 2003; IRA, 2001; Leu et al., 2004; RAND Reading Study Group, 2002). Eagleton and Dobler (2007) argue that reading on the Internet introduces an additional layer of complexity that is not found in traditional, print-based texts. This added complexity can produce cognitive overload and increased frustration, especially among struggling readers, when individuals do not possess the new literacies required when interacting with the multimodal, digital texts of the Internet (Coiro, 2003). With the onset of new definitions of literacy comes a need to specifically identify the new literacies skills and strategies that are required for Internet-based literacy activities as well as how to address these new literacies during classroom instruction.

Recent work (e.g. Coiro et al., 2008; Eagleton & Dobler, 2007; Henry, 2005, 2006a, 2006b, 2006c; Leu, Castek, Hartman, Coiro, Henry, & Lyver, 2005; Leu, Coiro, Castek, Hartman, Henry, & Reinking, 2008) has started to explore these new literacies and the specific skills and strategies that Internet-based literacy activities require. It has been discovered that simply providing access to technology and the Internet does not ensure that individuals are acquiring these new literacies nor does it mean that these skills are taught in our schools (Dewan & Riggins, 2005; Henry, 2006c; Powell, 2007). In order for our youth to become successful citizens in an information-driven, technological world, it is increasingly important for our schools to provide rich learning experiences that include instruction in the new literacies of the Internet and other ICTs. Without these experiences, our students will be ill prepared for their futures in

the 21st century and beyond (Gates, 2007; Mack, 2001; Paige, 2002).

Issues of Social Equity

A new literacies perspective also addresses issues of social equity. According to Leu and colleagues (2004), it is ever more important to "avoid societies in which economic advantage is sustained by the wealthy and denied to the poor" (p. 1598) thus creating an economic gap. This gap is a critical social problem not only in the United States but worldwide and is "one of the most important social equity issues facing the information society" (Eastin & LaRose, 2000, p. 54; see also Lievrouw & Farb, 2003; Martin, 2005; Parayil, 2005). The New London Group (2000) concurs that "an authentically democratic new vision of schools [which] must include a vision of meaningful success for all; a vision of success that is not defined exclusively in economic terms" (p. 13) is paramount. Furthermore, Gee (2000) argues for "a 'Bill of Rights' for all children, but most especially for minority and poor children" (p. 67) to ensure all children receive equality of education. Yet, research shows that there has been little change in this social equity issue over time. Parayil (2005) substantiates earlier claims of this issue, "the divide between the income rich and the income poor, the technology haves and the technology have nots, the information rich and the information poor, has become the most serious political economic problem facing the world today" (p. 42). By turning our attention to a theory of new literacies, we can confront one of the most critical issues facing the education system, which may be a catalyst for increases in the achievement gap. A central question needs to be addressed: How do we ensure all children receive the highest level of quality instruction regardless of socioeconomic status or ethnicity?

One of the most important national issues in the United States is to ensure all our students are able to read and write at high levels (RAND

Reading Study Group, 2002). Regardless of our efforts, we are increasingly becoming a nation divided by literacy ability into two groups, one predominantly white and affluent with proficient reading and writing skills and the other primarily students of color, economically underprivileged, and who possess low proficiency in reading and writing (Kleiner & Lewis, 2003). At the center of this issue is the contrast between economically privileged and economically disadvantaged school districts where academic inequalities have been a prominent problem for more than a decade and result in an academic achievement gap (Anderson, 1993; Kozol, 1991). For instance, economically privileged students consistently score higher on the National Assessment of Educational Progress (NAEP) compared to economically disadvantaged students (Kleiner & Lewis, 2003). Students with Limited English Proficiency (LEP) and minority students often experience much lower levels of reading comprehension compared to white students (Connecticut Alliance for Great Schools [CTAGS], 2006). Research has also shown that students who have parents with low levels of education are more apt to struggle academically (Henderson & Berla, 1994). The root of this problem in the United States is related to the manner in which public schools are primarily funded. Although federal dollars are distributed to all public schools, the majority of the funding for schools is tied to local property taxes (Hoxby, 1997). Schools in affluent neighborhoods have a higher tax base that results in more funding for the school. Those located in low socioeconomic areas where property values tend to be lower have a much lower tax base. As we look toward a new definition of literacy that incorporates the new literacies of the Internet, we may see further divisions between these two groups thus intensifying the already widening achievement gap.

It is true that more and more classrooms are indeed connected to the Internet, however there is a difference between students' access to the Internet at school when comparing economically

privileged and economically disadvantaged school districts as described by Mack (2001):

While all public schools are equally likely to have Internet access in at least one room, getting access at the classroom level where it can be incorporated into daily instruction has been more of a challenge. As might be expected, the percentage of classrooms with access is divided along wealth lines, with 74 percent of the wealthiest schools likely to have classroom access while only 39 percent of the poorest schools have similar capabilities (p. 78).

Similarly, Lazarus and colleagues (2005) found that "only 36 percent of children aged 7 to 17 from households earning less than $15,000 annually say they use the Internet at school compared to 63 percent from households earning more than $75,000 annually" (p. 8). Schools that serve students in economically disadvantaged districts have fewer computers and slower Internet connections than schools serving students in communities that are more affluent, thus issues of inequality already exist (Attewell, 2001; Goslee & Conte, 1998; Warschauer, 2002; Warschauer, Knobel, & Stone, 2004; Williams, Coles, Wilson, Richardson, & Tuson, 2000). An additional layer of this inequality is shown when we begin looking at the level and type of technology integration that is occurring in economically disadvantaged schools compared to economically privileged schools. Simply placing computers in classrooms does not mean that effective technology integration is the result (Kleiman, 2000; Malone, 2007). The CEO Forum on Education and Technology report (1999) showed that only one-fourth of the schools in the United States were effectively using technology and half (50 percent) were identified as being in the "Low Tech readiness" category. Although 96 percent of the states in this country have developed technology standards, a mere 8 percent evaluate students based on those standards (Editorial Projects in Education [EPE] Research Center, 2007).

Until we have widespread assessments in place to evaluate students' abilities with using technology, these patterns are likely to continue.

Today, public schools report Internet access in the majority of instructional classrooms (Parsad & Jones, 2005; EPE Research Center, 2007). However, differences still exist along economic lines. Schools with the highest concentration of students living in poverty have a much larger student to computer ratio than those schools with the lowest numbers of students living in poverty (Parsad & Jones, 2005). Unless schools are held accountable for helping students develop the skills that are required to be successful in the 21st century, inequities will continue to grow and the social stratification within the United States will be emphasized even further as students in economically disadvantaged schools are left further and further behind in an international, information-based economy.

Study Design

This research was a comparative qualitative study that sought to explore the contextual factors that enhance and/or impede the development of new literacies among middle school students enrolled in economically privileged and economically disadvantaged public schools in the United States. For the purpose of this study, economically privileged and economically disadvantaged school districts were operationally defined in terms of several socioeconomic factors, such as family income, education levels, and home language. Research has shown that these social factors are commonly associated with gaps in academic achievement (Lee & Croninger, 1994). Those schools that are identified as economically privileged typically have little diversity, a high tax base, higher levels of median household income, and higher levels of academic achievement (Lee & Croninger, 1994; Rothstein, 2004). Economically disadvantaged school districts are distinguished by diverse populations, a low tax base, lower levels of median household

income, and reduced levels of academic achievement (Rothstein, 2004). Participants from middle schools were selected because research shows that Internet usage among school-age children in the United States surges at the seventh grade level (Lenhart, Madden, & Hitlin, 2005) and that older students report more varied Internet usage habits than younger students (Levin & Arafeh, 2002). The purpose of this study was to obtain a rich understanding of school contexts in order to answer the central research question: *How do elements of a school context appear to contribute to factors that affect technology integration and the development of new literacies among middle school students?*

Data consisted of transcripts from interviews and focus groups, observational field notes, and various school artifacts collected from the research sites. Analyses included a multilevel conceptual content analysis and semantic mapping techniques (Carley, 1990; Krippendorf, 1980; Mayring, 2000; Miles & Huberman, 1994). Through these data, an exploration of the contextual factors that might influence the inclusion of instruction for new literacies or multiliteracies directly related to literacy activities on the Internet was conducted.

Participants and Settings

The participants in this study included 57 middle school students, 13 teachers, and 13 administrators from nine schools located in four different school districts in the northeast region of the United States. Two school districts were identified as economically privileged and two were identified as economically disadvantaged. Table 1 provides an overview of the participants involved in this study.

Data Collection and Analysis

This study combined several qualitative data collection and analysis techniques to identify what school factors might enhance and/or impede the

Table 1. Study participants by district

	Economically privileged districts	Economically disadvantaged districts
Students	36	21
Teachers	8	5
Administrators	7	6

development of new literacies among middle school students. In order to obtain a better understanding of literacy instruction, Pressley (2006) argued for a multilevel and multidimensional research agenda that would encompass foci both within individual classrooms as well as the outside contexts at the district and state levels. Since teaching and learning does not occur in isolation but as part of a larger, complex learning context, this study sought to gain insights regarding the broader contextual factors within school districts that impact attainment of new literacies at the lowest level, with individual students.

Interviews

A total of 41 semi-structured, individual interviews were conducted with the adult participants, which included principals, assistant principals, English/ Language Arts teachers, library media specialists, and computer teachers. The interview questions were developed to obtain information about the school context that would identify variables that influence the development of multiliteracies. More specifically, participants were asked questions focused on the following constructs of interest: (a) visionary goals related to technology and Internet integration (e.g. Can you tell me about the school's vision in regard to technology and Internet integration?), (b) Internet access inside school (e.g. What is the accessibility of technology and the Internet in your building?), (c) use of technology and the Internet during instruction (e.g. Can you tell me about your use of the Internet during classroom instruction?), (d) specific skills related to Internet-based reading and writing activities (e.g. Do you

think your students have good skills when using the Internet?), (e) professional development opportunities focused on technology integration (e.g. What types of professional development opportunities have been provided by the district for technology integration?), and (f) contextual factors that might impede or enhance technology integration (e.g. What do you think some of the biggest challenges are when it comes to Internet and technology integration?). Dependent upon the participants' responses, additional probes were used to obtain a thorough description of the factors associated with the stated constructs of interest. Each individual interview session was approximately 30 minutes in length. All interviews were audio recorded and transcribed to make certain that the content was documented correctly.

Three common elements of content analysis were used to organize and reduce the interview transcripts into meaningful units (Miles & Huberman, 1994). First, a combined deductive and inductive coding process (Mayring, 2000) was used to reduce data into useable excerpts that corresponded with the research question. Second, a matrix was assembled to organize the data and identify response patterns (Miles & Huberman, 1994). Table 2 shows a partial data display matrix that illustrates patterns of responses related to new literacies. As seen in this matrix, responses were sorted by economically privileged and economically disadvantaged school districts for comparison purposes.

Lastly, the final element of content analysis described by Miles and Huberman (1994) centered on the processes of conclusion drawing and verification. These procedures were used to test

Table 2. Data matrix for interview question: What specific skills and strategies are taught in relation to Internet use?

Deductive coding themes		Inductive coding themes	
Locating information	Critical evaluation	Internet safety	Software use
Economically privileged districts			
• Advanced search options • Locating information • Learning Internet searches • How to find what they're looking for • Searching on the Internet, different skills with that	• Critical evaluation • A lot of website evaluation • How to evaluate what they're looking for • The difference between .com, .org, .edu and what it means	• Places not to go (Internet Safety)	
Economically disadvantaged districts			
• Goes over with students what they're looking for			• I don't think there are many • Mostly skill oriented, Word, PowerPoint, Publisher, Excel • Using Print Shop—how to create a pamphlet or folder • It's more of "how to" right now

the plausibility of the researcher's hypotheses to ensure credible and defensible conclusions were drawn (Neuendorf, 2002).

Focus Groups

Student participants engaged in focus group discussions at each of the research sites. These groups combined students across grade levels that met with the researcher on two separate occasions. The topics of discussion focused on descriptions of students' experiences with the use of the Internet and other ICTs inside the school environment. The researcher probed the students to talk about the following constructs of interest: (a) Internet access inside school, (b) use of the Internet inside school, and (c) specific skills related to Internet-based reading and writing activities. Based on the conversations, the researcher used questions to guide the discussions and maintain attention on the topics of interest in order to obtain useable data. Examples of these guiding questions include:

1. What kinds of things do you do on the Internet at school?
2. What types of school assignments do you have that require the use of the Internet?
3. How often do your teachers use the Internet during instruction?
4. Have any of your teachers taught you strategies for locating information on the Internet?

Focus group discussions were videotaped and transcribed for analyses.

The same three elements of content analysis were employed to analyze the transcript data from the focus group discussions. First, data reduction using deductive and inductive coding (Mayring, 2000) helped organize the data into meaningful units (Miles & Huberman, 1994). Then, a matrix display was assembled to organize the data for cross comparisons between economically privileged and economically disadvantaged school districts. Finally, conclusion drawing and verification techniques ensured the stated hypotheses were valid (Miles & Huberman, 1994).

Observations

Field notes were collected at each participating school to identify and describe technology and Internet integration during a "typical" school day. Observations were conducted on a drop in basis without prior notification to ensure the data was documented in a natural setting and not as part of a contrived lesson. During the observation period, the researcher visited all areas of the school building in which computers were housed to document specific lessons and activities related to technology integration. These areas included computer labs, library media centers, and instructional classrooms. Field notes were written in an open format that included a general description of the technology available within the school and the manner in which it was being used. More specifically, the location and numbers of computers were documented, the activities students were engaged in were described, and the supervising teacher involved was noted.

A formal analysis of the field note data was not utilized. Instead, the recorded field notes served as a source to inform, validate, and provide additional insight into the contextual factors identified by alternate data points. These data primarily served as a source for the triangulation of the data that was collected by the other methods in this study and as a way to validate the researcher's conclusions.

Textual Artifacts

Several textual artifacts were collected from each research site to enhance the description of the school contexts portrayed by the interviews, focus groups, and observations. These artifacts included two curricula documents, three technology plans, and two school improvement plans. Content analyses were used to determine how technology was integrated within each school context. Two different analysis techniques, a conceptual analysis and a semantic analysis (see Krippendorf, 1980), were completed in two distinct stages.

During the first stage, a conceptual analysis was conducted to look at the frequency of concepts in the documents that related to the broad themes of (a) literacy and (b) technology. This analysis identified single words or sets of words (e.g. "computer" or "computer technology") as one concept. Translation rules were created to ensure consistency of concepts across documents (Carley, 1993). Irrelevant information was omitted. Interactive coding was conducted (Northcutt & McCoy, 2004) and a two-column list of concepts was created for the two identified themes of interest (i.e. literacy and technology). The researcher made two complete passes through each of the textual artifacts to ensure thoroughness in identifying the lists of relevant concepts. Frequency counts were tabulated for each concept in order to make comparisons between economically privileged and economically disadvantaged school districts.

In the second stage, a semantic analysis was completed that looked at associations between the two broad themes (i.e. literacy and technology). This technique looked specifically at where concepts appeared in relation to each other within the documents (Palmquist, Carley, & Dale, 1997). Semantic analysis allows for the comparison of semantic connections across texts through a proximity map analysis (Carley & Palmquist, 1992). The coding of text from the first stage of this analysis was used to conduct a proximity map analysis that focused on a specific question of interest (Carley, 1993): *How is technology being integrated into reading/language arts curriculum?* The use of a map analysis technique was desirable because the researcher was interested in the explicit concepts within the textual artifacts and not emotional considerations or interpretations (Carley & Palmquist, 1992). A graphic representation of the relationships between the concepts of interest was produced to assist with the interpretation of the associations.

Evidence and Discoveries

This study investigated the contextual factors that appear to enhance and/or inhibit the development of new literacies among middle school students. The results suggest that several contextual factors found in economically disadvantaged schools may in fact impede the development of the new literacies required to use the Internet as an information resource among this group of students. These factors include: (a) access and availability of technology, (b) effective technology integration during instruction, (c) instruction specific to the development of new literacies, and (d) public policy and legislation. These results are presented and discussed according to these main factors of impact.

Access and Availability of Technology

Results showed that access to computers and the Internet was the most critical factor inhibiting the integration of technology in classroom instruction. This is especially true for teachers working in economically disadvantaged school districts where Internet access in the classroom is sometimes non-existent. Schools in economically privileged school districts showed increased availability and access to technology, and the Internet specifically, compared to schools in economically disadvantaged school districts. In economically privileged school districts, computers with Internet access were found in every classroom. In contrast, schools in economically disadvantaged districts reported that not all classrooms have a computer, and the computers that they did have were reportedly slow and outdated. The following interview excerpts illustrate this contrast:

(Transcript 7: Economically privileged school): Every classroom has Internet access. We have a seventh and eighth grade building where there are certain teams there that are exploratory. They have a 36-day exploratory in the computer room.

The students regularly go to one of our two computer labs in their Science and Social Studies or Language Arts class; and those are also Internet accessible. I have observed many classes in those labs that are not only using the computer but they are using the Internet for research to complete their projects.

(Transcript 17: Economically privileged school): In the classrooms, teachers do have access, too, based on the design of the classrooms that we have. Everyone has the widescreen TV and it interconnects with the one or two classroom computers there in each room. The teacher can work with the kids from the computer and frequently will draw upon the Internet either for research-based things, or we also are, um, we have a subscription to streaming video that we access through the Internet. Teachers will frequently access video snippets to use to support instruction in the classroom.

As is described by these two participants, classrooms in economically privileged districts are well equipped with Internet-connected computers. In addition, teachers in these schools reported at least two computer labs that were available to them for whole-class instruction. Access to computers and the Internet do not appear to be an issue. In stark contrast, teachers in economically disadvantaged districts reported access to technology as a huge issue, which is made apparent in the following interview excerpt:

(Transcript 30: Economically disadvantaged school): I think we would like to see at least a computer for each one of our teachers, because we don't even have that yet. Our, our…server is sometimes slow and, um, the…I think that there's such, not really with our server as much as…but the computers that the teachers use are so slow. I mean…they're hand-me-downs. [pause] I definitely think the technology in this building…just what the teachers have to work with. The comput-

ers are very old and very slow. The computer lab, I mean, three labs with 75 computers for 1100 kids. I think that the teachers are very willing to learn but I think that they get frustrated with what's available and...they're just trying to sign up for things and get things done and not have it be a complete hassle using the technology and the Internet.

Not only did participants in economically privileged districts report much more access to technology, but they also seemed content with the technology they had in place as none of them commented or complained about the age or speed of the technology available in their school building. This seems to be an additional layer of the issue of inaccessibility. Not only is it critical to provide access to technology, but also it is important to ensure the technology is adequate for the instructional needs of the teachers.

Data from the focus group discussions confirmed this imbalance related to the accessibility of technology. Students from economically privileged schools indicated that they have ready access to computers and the Internet at school. These students also reported that teachers often use a projection device in the classroom as well as a portable laptop cart. Additionally, students from economically privileged school districts reported greater numbers of computers in their homes that are connected to the Internet compared to those in economically disadvantaged school districts. Conversely, students from economically disadvantaged schools reported issues with accessing certain websites, exceptionally slow download speeds, and minimal use of computers by their teachers.

These findings are supported by earlier research that identifies Internet access as one of the biggest challenges facing teachers who want to integrate technology into their classrooms (Attewell, 2001; Goslee & Conte, 1998; Mack, 2001). Although 90 percent of schools in the United States report an Internet connection in every instructional classroom (Kleiner & Lewis, 2003), teachers report access to computers and the Internet as the most inhibiting factor for technology integration (Henry, 2005; Lazarus et al., 2005; Williams et al., 2000). Lazarus and colleagues (2005) also argue that differences between having access to a fast Internet connection speed (e.g. broadband) versus a slow Internet connection speed (e.g. dial-up modem) may be greater than the difference between whether an individual has Internet access at all, which was an issue raised by participants in this study. The results herein show that accessibility to technology is a major factor that serves as an impediment to the development of multiliteracies, particularly for individuals in economically disadvantaged schools.

Effective Technology Integration During Instruction

The effective use of technology appeared to vary greatly between schools where some schools, those in economically privileged districts, focused on meaningful Internet activities as part of the curriculum while others, those located in economically disadvantaged districts, used technology primarily for skill and drill type activities. Data from the interviews indicated that teachers in economically privileged schools effectively integrate the Internet using activities that they themselves created for their students, including Internet web quests and scavenger hunts. Data from the classroom observations confirmed these reports. For example, observational data in economically privileged schools documented a social studies teacher using a webquest to engage students in a lesson about women's suffrage and a science teacher was observed conducting a lesson about the evaluation of websites to determine good Internet resources for a research project. In contrast, observations in economically disadvantaged schools showed students using computers to play math games located on a publisher's website for a popular math series, and one entire computer lab

Table 3. Comparison table of technology use by district type

Type of activities	Economically disadvantaged districts	Economically privileged districts
Computer-based	-Assessments (math/reading) -Educational games	-Assessments (math) -Create video games -Educational games -Video editing -Website development
Internet-based	-Email -Look up information -Reference resources -Research projects -Textbook websites -Watch videos (educational)	-Blog (teacher created) -Citation makers -Databases (library) -Email -Find pictures -Internet publishing -Key pals (French class) -Language translators -Look up information -Quiz site (Quia.com) -Read specific websites -Reference resources -Research projects -Teacher websites -Textbook websites -Watch videos (educational) -Webquest -Website development -YouTube

was dedicated to the use of Accelerated Reader, a software program used to develop traditional reading comprehension skills.

Data from the focus group discussions showed students in economically privileged schools discussing specific lessons that were taught in relation to Internet safety, cyberbullying, and plagiarism. Although the students in economically disadvantaged schools reported an awareness of the same themes, they reported that they did not receive specific instruction, examples, or ways to avoid any of these issues. As was expected, students reported the majority of Internet use inside school was for educational purposes. However, there was a large difference between the numbers and types of activities that students in economically privileged districts reported compared to what was reported by students in economically disadvantaged districts. Table 3 highlights these differences.

As can be seen from this table, there are some similarities in how computers and the Internet are being used in schools, but there are many more uses for technology reported by the students in economically privileged districts. For example, these students reported more than twice as many computer-based activities and more than three times as many Internet-based activities compared to students in economically disadvantaged districts.

An analysis of the textual artifacts confirmed the differences noted by the interview and focus group data. Initially, a pattern was discovered in the textual artifacts that were reviewed. Curricula documents from economically privileged schools showed high levels of technology integration across the curriculum. In one such school, a separate technology curriculum did not exist. All of the technology standards were fully integrated into other content areas. For example, the science curriculum included student objectives related to the critical evaluation of websites. Suggested instructional activities were included to help guide the teachers. In one of these activities, a popular hoax website was referenced (i.e. *Save the Pacific*

Table 4. Conceptual content analysis of technology plans by district type

Concepts	Economically privileged districts		Economically disadvantaged districts	
	Unique	Total	Unique	Total
Literacy terms	15	24	5	10
Technology terms	402	1449	187	524

Northwest Tree Octopus from Extinction, http://zapatopi.net/treeoctopus/) with guidelines on how to teach students skills for checking Internet-based information for accuracy and validity. The curricula documents collected from economically disadvantaged school districts had little or no integration of technology into the content areas and a stand-alone technology curriculum was the norm.

The results of the conceptual analyses of the textual artifacts further illustrate these differences. A comparison of the technology plan documents between economically privileged and economically disadvantaged school districts showed an imbalance in frequency counts of concepts related to *literacy* and *technology*. The result of this conceptual content analysis is shown in Table 4 and indicates that the technology plans appear to be similar in content. However, one distinct difference was identified when comparing these documents. The total number of technology concepts was much greater for economically privileged districts, which was nearly three times the number of concepts found in the documents from economically disadvantaged districts as outlined in Table 4.

These results indicate that schools located in economically privileged districts have a greater emphasis on technology integration related to literacy instruction than do schools located in economically disadvantaged districts as shown by the appearance of unique literacy terms within the technology plan documents. This discovery was fleshed out further through the use of proximal map analyses.

Following the conceptual content analysis, proximal map analyses were completed for the technology plans. Figure 1 displays the results of the map analysis for economically disadvantaged districts. This analysis indicates only one out of nine (11.1 percent) concepts related to literacy were present with a proximal relationship to 12 out of 15 (80.0 percent) of the concepts related to technology. Additionally, there are only 12 occurrences of cross-category proximal relationships between the generalized concept literacy and generalized technology related concepts.

Figure 2 displays the results of the map analysis of the technology plan for economically privileged districts. This map illustrates a much richer integration between literacy and technology. As can be seen from this analysis, 5 out of 9 (55.5 percent) of the concepts related to literacy show a relationship to 13 out of 15 (86.7 percent) of the concepts related to technology. Additionally, there are 35 occurrences of cross-category proximal relationships between literacy and technology concepts, nearly three times as may as the previous document showed.

The results of the analyses of the textual artifacts show that documents from economically disadvantaged districts are very dense in technology content but lack integration between literacy and technology concepts. In contrast, the documents from economically privileged districts indicated a much higher rate of literacy and technology integration. Another specific difference between the documents from these districts is related to the technology concept for *Internet*. This concept was absent from the documents associated with economically disadvantaged districts but not so with documents from economically privileged districts. In addition, looking at the relationship between

Figure 1. Relational map of technology plan for economically disadvantaged districts

the term *Internet* and the five different literacy concepts where connections were identified (e.g. *critical reading, curriculum, literacy, texts,* and *thinking strategies*) validates the results of the interviews and focus group discussions regarding technology integration and instruction related to developing the new literacies of the Internet as presented in the following section.

Research indicates that there are significant inequalities related to Internet use between economically privileged and economically disadvantaged students that stem from several different variables (Attewell, 2001; Livingstone, 2003; Rice, 2002). First, it has been discovered that students in economically disadvantaged schools are more likely to use computers for drill and practice type activities when compared to their more privileged counterparts. The results from

the current study confirm these earlier reports regarding inequalities specific to the effective use of technology when comparing students along economic lines. But, this factor may actually be a consequence related to the skill level of teachers, a second variable to consider. Since the integration of technology is largely driven by the activities and assignments that teachers use during instruction (Levin & Arafeh, 2002), it is important to ensure that teachers are skilled in using technology. Poor and minority students are more likely to have teachers with lower levels of computer training (Attewell, 2001). In addition, one study that looked specifically at school and classroom variables that contribute to effective technology integration found that the teacher is the most influential variable (Collis & Lai, 1996). Until schools make technology integration

Figure 2. Relational map of technology plan for economically privileged districts

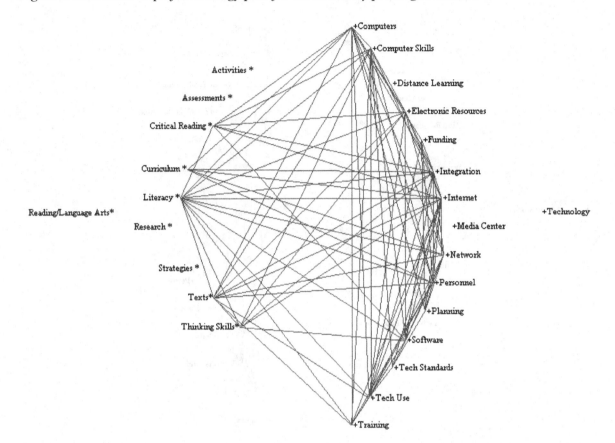

a priority and provide the necessary training for teachers to become skilled, it is likely that an even larger economic gap will result in relation to the skills that our youth require to be successful in an increasingly digital workplace.

Instruction Specific to the Development of New Literacies

Instruction specific to the development of new literacies was an additional factor identified in both the interviews and focus groups that showed differences between economically privileged and economically disadvantaged schools. Skills and strategies associated with the development of new literacies were much more prevalent in economically privileged schools compared to economically disadvantaged schools. Teachers

and students in economically privileged schools reported and described lessons specific to the new literacies needed for using the Internet as an information resource as outlined in Table 5. These new literacies included critically evaluating websites and the development of specific search strategies to help students become more proficient information searchers. Conversely, teachers and students in economically disadvantaged schools indicated that no specific skills were taught in relation to the use of the Internet. Finally, schools in economically privileged school districts have a more integrative approach for teaching literacy and technology skills that has resulted in an increase in the development of multiliteracies among students.

As can be seen from the table above, once again, there was a difference shown between economi-

Table 5. Comparison table of instruction specific to new literacies by district type

Economically disadvantaged districts	Economically privileged districts
-Accuracy of information -Scroll and skim for information -Read search engine results -Search strategies	-Accuracy of information -Authorship of websites -Big 6 research skills -Currency of information -Different sources (compare) -Evaluating websites -Fake images and photos -Look at address bar (URL) -No Wikipedia (not reliable) -Read search engine results -Reliability of information -Scroll and skim for information -Search strategies -URL characteristics -Website features -Website links history

cally privileged and economically disadvantaged school districts in relation to the development of new literacies skills and strategies. Students in economically privileged districts had more in-depth knowledge about the new literacies of using the Internet. These students identified four times as many skills and strategies they acquired for Internet-based reading and writing activities compared to students in economically disadvantaged districts. Another trend that this data shows is that the specific skills and strategies identified by students in economically disadvantaged districts are all related to conducting an information search on the Internet. Although these are critical skills for reading on the Internet, they are of a more rudimentary level than the critical reading skills that are required to evaluate information for accuracy, currency, and reliability that were identified by students in economically privileged districts.

During focus group discussions, students in economically privileged districts spoke at great length about lessons specific to the critical evaluation of Internet-based information and websites. The following transcript excerpt from a focus group discussion provides an example of what these students have learned:

R: Do your teachers ever give you hints for searching or talk about the information you find on the Internet?

S1: We got taught to put the quotation marks

S4: Quotation marks and stuff

S1: and then like splashes and dashes

S2: "not" and don't like use "and" or something like that because there's half

S1: because they're like, if you go on Google they'll like look for all the words you're looking for and it's really hard to figure out

[pause]

S3: One time we had to like evaluate websites

S4: Right, yeah

S2: Yeah, that wasn't fun.

R: Okay. Tell me a little bit about evaluating websites.

S3: Um...

S2: I hate it.

S3: Um, we had to go on a website

S4: and it's kind of like going through the works cited process

S2: yeah

S3: The website was on evaluating websites so it was like, first it like, it like

S4: URL

S3: Yeah, it gave suggestions like you could do, like you could look at the URL. What else? Is there an author and you can contact them and stuff.

S2: Or like an organization

S3: Yeah

S1: We talked about stuff

S4: Um, they, there was different sites, like she gave us a section on like made up ones like the tree octopus or something and then she, um, she would show us and we had to get a piece of paper and like find ideas of why it was wrong like spelling or grammar was off. And, like, uh, there…it wasn't organized. So, she gave us specific details like that.

R: Okay. Any other web sites she showed you besides the tree octopus?

S4: Yeah, there was like a whole section. There was like the anatomy of Barney and there was like some made up dog that was, uh, posted and then,

S1: Don't go to wikipedia

S2: Mrs., our teacher, she went on it and she changed like the birth date of some really important person in history

S3: Then she changed it back

S2: And then she changed it back but it like shows that you can change

S1: You can hack on it

S2: And change all the stuff and she wasn't happy, I don't know

S1: You can change it

S3: Like, it's not reliable because people can make up like a random person and like make them president

S2: Yeah

S1: That's actually not a bad idea

Group: (laughing)

S1: [Student's name removed], president of the United States

Group: (Laughing)

(School C, Focus Group 5)

In contrast, students in economically disadvantaged districts only reported one element of critical evaluation (i.e. accuracy of information). They did not share any additional elements of new literacies for using the Internet and other ICTs that they had learned from their teachers.

Making the Internet accessible and integrating technology into the curriculum does not guarantee that students are developing new literacies. Most often, technology integration centers around *computer literacy* with a focus on the use of computer applications (Goodson & Mangan, 1996; Halpin, 1999; Williams, 2003) and not the new literacies of the Internet (Coiro, 2003, 2007; Eagleton & Dobler, 2007; Henry, 2005; Leu et al., 2004). Gibson and Oberg (2004) found "teachers, even experienced Internet users, appeared to have little knowledge of the search engines and search strategies to make efficient use of Internet resources" (p. 571). Carvin (2002) argues, "unless people can read and understand what they find online, Internet access isn't very meaningful" (p. 9). Since research has shown that only one-third of teachers feel adequately prepared to integrate technology into classroom instruction (Smerdon, Cronen, Lanahan, Anderson, Iannotti, & Angeles, 2000), this is an important factor for schools to pay attention to.

Public Policy and Legislation in the United States

While No Child Left Behind legislation (U.S. Department of Education [DOE], 2002) does not seem to affect technology integration in economically privileged districts, it may cause economically disadvantaged districts to use technology primarily for the assessment of basic reading and math skill development, not the higher level, critical reading skills needed to use the Internet successfully as an information source. Interviews with both administrators and teachers in economically disadvantaged schools indicated that NCLB legislation required them to focus wholly on meeting adequate yearly progress (AYP), which left them in a situation where they were unable to look at technology integration in the curriculum. Data from the interviews and observations also showed that computers in these districts are often dedicated to the evaluation of traditional math and reading skills through the use of specific software programs, which provide summary reports to inform instruction and remediation. In contrast, administrators and teachers from economically privileged schools indicated that NCLB had no impact whatsoever on their ability to integrate technology into classroom instruction. In fact, none of the participants from economically privileged schools reported the use of computer-based assessments for the same purposes as described by participants in economically disadvantaged schools.

It could be argued that federal legislation, which was designed to close the achievement gap, may actually be contributing to this equity issue. Research shows that urban, largely minority districts face greater pressure to achieve AYP on tests that focus on traditional literacy skills; hence, they must abandon instruction focused on new literacies (Leu, Ataya, & Coiro, 2002). As such, "it may be the cruelest irony of NCLB that students who need to be prepared the most for an online age of information are precisely those who are being prepared the least" (NLRT, 2006, p. 21). Hargittai (2002) has illustrated that the frequency of Internet use is positively correlated with proficiency in using the Internet. Unless changes are made to public policy that provide all schools with the opportunity to include the new literacies required when using the Internet and other ICTs, a newly defined gap related to academic achievement and school success is likely to emerge between those students who are skilled with using the Internet and those who are not.

Implications for Future Research

Many studies have focused on measuring elements of Internet access among various populations as an indicator of the presence of a digital divide (e.g. Barzilai-Nahon, 2006; Cooper, 2002; Fairlie, 2005; Norris, 2001). Additional studies have looked at differential patterns of Internet use among different populations (e.g. Attewell, 2001; Dewan & Riggins, 2005; Hargittai, 2002). Numerous studies have also focused on the use of digital technologies within schools (e.g. Anderson & Ronnkvist, 1999; Becker, 1999; Bronack, 2006; Kleiner & Lewis, 2003; Levin & Arafeh, 2002;

Rowand, 2000). Still others have looked at the implications for teachers' use of computers in the classroom (Collis & Lai, 1996; Kleiner & Lewis, 2003; Lenhart et al., 2005; Levin & Arafeh, 2002). Finally, a new group of studies looks specifically at the new literacies of online reading amongst middle school students (Coiro, 2007; Coiro & Dobler, 2007; Leu et al., 2005; Leu & Reinking, 2005). However, there are no studies to date that look specifically at the contextual factors that impact upon the development of new literacies between students from economically privileged and economically disadvantaged school districts. This study sought to fill that void and provide a springboard for additional research in this area.

This qualitative study was designed to provide insights regarding contextual factors that might enhance or impede the development of new literacies for using the Internet and other ICTs among middle school students. However, this study provides a mere snapshot of the contextual factors that appear to have an effect on the acquisition of these important skills. Research that would provide a more in-depth understanding of these factors would be beneficial. A case study approach that focuses more intensely on comparisons between an economically privileged school and economically disadvantaged school may provide additional insights into the contextual factors that contribute to or impede technology integration and the development of new literacies. This type of study would allow further documentation of teacher skill level with technology integration to better understand the role of the teacher as well as additional contextual factors that appear to create differences in the acquisition of new literacies among students.

Implications for Classroom Practice

The results of this qualitative study have important implications for classroom practice and literacy pedagogy. First of all, we need to address the issues of unequal access to the Internet. Without access,

classroom teachers will continue to struggle in providing instruction in the new literacies that our young people need for success in the 21st century. If we continue on the current trajectory in which the rich get richer and the poor get poorer, the academic achievement gap is certain to grow. Schools located in economically disadvantaged districts can look for funding opportunities and programs that provide refurbished computers to schools (e.g. Computers for School and Free Surplus Computer Program). This will help put more computers in the hands of teachers and students and begin to equalize the disparities in access to technology that currently exist in the United States.

Secondly, classroom teachers need to be trained to effectively integrate technology during instruction. Without adequate training for teachers, current pedagogical methods will continue with an emphasis on traditional literacy skills that do not transfer to the new, multimodal texts found on the Internet. Administrators should provide professional development opportunities for teachers that emphasize new literacies and better prepare their teachers to integrate technology during classroom instruction.

Third, the data presented herein suggest that school districts should thoroughly review curricula documents in relation to the new literacies of Internet-based reading and writing. This would allow schools to identify particular content areas in which technology integration is weak (e.g. using the Internet to read about and investigate science or math topics), and then revise the curricula to include student objectives related to the development of new literacies. Additionally, content areas with higher levels of Internet integration in the curriculum could be paired with content areas showing lower levels of integration to develop focused, interdisciplinary units of instruction that include new literacies.

Finally, literacy pedagogy needs to expand to include the new literacies to better prepare our students for success in a global economy. Just as we teach students strategies for reading and writing poetry or informational texts, we need to teach students how to read and write with Internet-based texts. Instruction should include: a) strategies for searching for and locating information; b) critically evaluating information for accuracy, relevancy, and bias; c) considering how information may be shaped based on authorship or sponsorship of a web page; and d) effectively communicating information using both informal and formal Internet-based tools (e.g. email, instant messages, blogs, wikis, etc.). Until we include these new literacy skills and strategies as part of classroom instruction in all our schools, we will continue to see the discrepancies outlined in the results of this study. The impact will be an additional layer added to the social equity issues that plague the United States as a critical problem for our education system to address.

CONCLUDING REMARKS

It is clear that the Internet can be used to change learning and transform our classrooms into a global conurbation. However, our education systems are not evolving at the same rate as businesses. When it comes to providing our young people with the skills they need to be successful in today's workplace and the workplaces of tomorrow, education falls flat and fails to adequately prepare them for a global, knowledge-based economy (Gates, 2007; Paige, 2002). Thus, a better understanding of these new literacies and a broadened definition of literacy is required to address the needs of the present workplaces as well as the workplaces of the future. Results from this study indicate several contextual factors that impede the development of multiliteracies among middle school students. Among the most prominent factors may be the structure of school curricula and literacy pedagogy. One solution may be a more integrative approach to instruction. By integrating technology across the curricula and abandoning a stand-alone technology

curriculum model, the impact of other contextual factors may decline. This is especially true for the factors related to effective technology integration and instruction specific to the development of new literacies. In so doing, we as a society can support our young people to compete in a quickly changing economy and prepare them for the futures they deserve.

REFERENCES

Alvermann, D. E. (2002). Effective literacy instruction for adolescents. *Journal of Literacy Research, 34*(2), 189–208. doi:10.1207/s15548430jlr3402_4

Alvermann, D. E., Moon, J. S., & Hagood, M. C. (1999). *Popular culture in the classroom: Teaching and researching critical media literacy.* Newark, DE: International Reading Association.

Anderson, J. D. (1993). Power, privilege, and public education: Reflections on savage inequalities. *Educational Theory, 43*(1), 1–10. doi:10.1111/j.1741-5446.1993.00001.x

Anderson, R. E., & Ronnkvist, A. (1999). The presence of computers in American schools. *Teaching, learning and computing: 1998 national survey.* (Center for Research on Information Technology and Organizations Report No. 2). Retrieved April 25, 2006, from http://www.crito.uci.edu/tlc/findings/Computers_in_American_Schools/reprot2_text_tables.pdf

Attewell, P. (2001). The first and second digital divides. *Sociology of Education, 74*(3), 252–259. doi:10.2307/2673277

Becker, H. J. (1999). Internet use by teachers: Conditions of professional use and teacher-directed student use. *Teaching, learning and computing: 1998 national survey.* (Center for Research on Information Technology and Organizations Report No. 1). Retrieved April 14, 2006, from http://www.vermontinstitutes.org/tech/research/i-use-teach.pdf

Brazilai-Nahon, K. (2006). Gaps and bits: Conceptualizing measurement for digital divide/s. *The Information Society, 22*(5), 269–278. doi:10.1080/01972240600903953

Bronack, S. (2006, Spring). Learning unplugged: The Internet divide in American schools. *Electronic Magazine of Multicultural Education, 8*(1). Retrieved August 22, 2006, from http://www.eastern.edu/publications/emme/2006spring/bronack.html

Carley, K. (1990). Content analysis. In R. E. Asher (Ed.), *The encyclopedia of language and linguistics* (pp. 725-730). Edinburgh: Pergamon Press.

Carley, K. (1993). Coding choices for textual analysis: A comparison of content analysis and map analysis. *Sociological Methodology, 23,* 75–126. doi:10.2307/271007

Carley, K., & Palmquist, M. (1992). Extracting, representing, and analyzing mental models. *Social Forces, 70*(3), 601–636. doi:10.2307/2579746

Carvin, A. (2002, April 1). Digital divide still very real. *Cnet News.* Retrieved April 17, 2007, from http://news.com.com.Digital+divide+still+very+real/2010-1071_3-872138.html

Castek, J., Coiro, J., Hartman, D. K., Henry, L. A., Leu, D. J., & Zawilinski, L. (2007). New literacies, new challenges, and new opportunities. In M. B. Sampson, P. E. Linder, F. Falk-Ross, M. M. Foote, & S. Szabo (Eds.), *Multiple literacies in the 21ˢᵗ century: The twenty-eighth yearbook of the college reading association (pp. 31-50).* Logan, UT: College Reading Association.

CEO Forum on Education & Technology. (1999, February). *Professional development: A link to better learning* (Year 2 STaR report). Washington, DC: Author.

Coiro, J. (2003). Reading comprehension on the Internet: Expanding our understanding of reading comprehension to encompass new literacies. *The Reading Teacher, 56*(6), 458–465.

Coiro, J. (2007). *Exploring changes to reading comprehension on the Internet: Paradoxes and possibilities for diverse adolescent readers.* Unpublished doctoral dissertation. University of Connecticut, Storrs.

Coiro, J., & Dobler, B. (2007). Exploring the comprehension strategies used by sixth-grade skilled readers as they search for and locate information on the Internet. *Reading Research Quarterly, 42*(2), 214–257. doi:10.1598/RRQ.42.2.2

Coiro, J., Knobel, M., Lankshear, C., & Leu, D. J. (Eds.). (2008). *Handbook of research on new literacies.* Mahwah, NJ: Erlbaum.

Collis, B. A., & Lai, K. W. (1996). Information technology and children from a classroom perspective. In B. A. Collis, G. A. Knezek, K. W. Lai, K. T. Miyashita, W. J. Pelgrum, T. Plomp, & T. Sakamoto (Eds.), *Children and computers in school* (pp. 43-68). Mahwah, NJ: Erlbaum.

Connecticut Alliance for Great Schools (CTAGS). (n.d.). *The achievement gap.* Retrieved August 26, 2006 from http://www.ctags.org/gap.php

Cooper, M. (2002). *Does the digital divide still exist? Bush administration shrugs, but evidence says "Yes"*. Washington, DC: Consumer Federation of America. Retrieved April 15, 2007, from http://www.comsumerfed.org/DigitalDivideReport20020530.pdf

Cope, B., & Kalantzis, M. (Eds.). (2000). *Multiliteracies: Literacy learning and the design of social futures*. New York: Routledge.

Dewan, S., & Riggins, F. J. (2005). The digital divide: Current and future research directions. *Journal of Association for Information Systems*, 6(2), 298–337.

Eagleton, M. B., & Dobler, E. (2007). *Reading the web: Strategies for Internet inquiry*. New York: The Guilford Press.

Eastin, M. S., & LaRose, R. (2000). Internet self-efficacy and the psychology of the digital divide. *Journal of Computer-Mediated Communication*, 6(1), 25–56.

Editorial Projects in Education (EPE) Research Center. (2007, March). *Technology counts 2007: A digital decade*. Bethesda, MD: Education Week.

Fairlie, R. W. (2005, September 20). Are we really a notion online? Ethnic and racial disparities in access to technology and their consequences. *FreePress*. Retrieved September 3, 2006, from http://www.freepress.net/docs/lccrdigitaldivide.pdf

Fallows, D. (2004). The Internet and daily life. *Pew Internet and American Life Project*. Retrieved August 17, 2006, from http://www.pewinternet.org/pdfs/PIP_Internet_and_Daily_Life.pdf

Forsyth, I. (1998). *Teaching and learning materials and the Internet*. New York: Routledge.

Friedman, T. L. (2005). *The world is flat: A brief history of the twenty-first century*. New York: Farrar, Straus, & Giroux.

Gates, W. H. (2007, March). Written testimony of William H. Gates, Chairman, Microsoft Corporation: Before the committee on Health, Education, Labor and Pensions, U.S. Senate. *Business Week*. Retrieved March 14, 2007, from http://www.businessweek.com/bwdaily/dnflash/content/mar2007/db20070307_617500.htm

Gee, J. P. (2000). New people in new worlds: Networks, the new capitalism and schools. In B. Cope & M. Kalantzis (Eds.), *Multiliteracies: Literacy learning and the design of social futures* (pp. 43-68). New York: Routledge.

Gibson, S., & Oberg, D. (2004). Visions and realities of Internet use in schools: Canadian perspectives. *British Journal of Educational Technology*, 35(5), 569–585. doi:10.1111/j.0007-1013.2004.00414.x

Gilster, P. (1997). *Digital literacy*. New York: John Wiley.

Goodson, I. F., & Mangan, J. M. (1996). Computer literacy as ideology. *British Journal of Sociology of Education*, 17(1), 65–79. doi:10.1080/0142569960170105

Goslee, S., & Conte, C. (1998). *Losing ground bit by bit: Low-income communities in the information age*. Retrieved August 12, 2006, from the Benton Foundation Web site: http://www.benton.org/PUBLIBRARY/losing-ground/home.html

Halpin, R. (1999). A model of constructivist learning in practice: Computer literacy integrated into elementary mathematics and science teacher education. *Journal of Research on Computing in Education*, 32(1), 128–138.

Hargittai, E. (2002). Second-level digital divide: Differences in people's online skills. [from http://www.markle.org/downloadable_assets/hargittai-secondleveldd.pdf]. *First Monday*, 7, ▪▪▪. Retrieved October 14, 2005.

Hay, L. E. (2000). Educating the net generation. *School Administrator*, *57*(54), 6–10.

Henderson, A. T., & Berla, N. (Eds.). *A new generation of evidence: The family is critical to student achievement*. Boston: Center for Law & Education. (ERIC Document Reproduction Service No. ED375968).

Henry, L. A. (2005). Information search strategies on the Internet: A critical component of new literacies. *Webology, 2*. Available at http://www.webology.ir/2005/v2n1/a9.html

Henry, L. A. (2006a). SEARCHing for an answer: The critical role of new literacies while reading on the Internet. *The Reading Teacher*, *59*(7), 614–627. doi:10.1598/RT.59.7.1

Henry, L. A. (2006b, December). *What reading demands does searching on the Internet require? A review of the literature*. Paper presented at the annual meeting of the National Reading Conference. Los Angeles, CA.

Henry, L. A. (2006c, May). *Investigation of literacy skills and strategies used while searching for information on the Internet: A comprehensive review and synthesis of research*. Paper presented at the annual convention of the International Reading Association, Chicago, IL.

Hobbs, R. (1998). The seven great debates in the media literacy movement. *The Journal of Communication*, *48*(1), 6–32. doi:10.1111/j.1460-2466.1998.tb02734.x

Hoxby, C. M. (1997). *Local property tax-based funding of public schools*. Heartland Policy Study No. 82. Retrieved September 18, 2008 from http://www.heartland.org/

International Reading Association (IRA). (2001). *Integrating literacy and technology in the curriculum* (Position statement). Retrieved December 15, 2005, from http://www.reading.org/downloads/positions/ps1048_technology.pdf

Kleiman, G. M. (2000). *The digital classroom: Myths and realities about technology in K-12 schools*. Cambridge, MA: Harvard Education Press.

Kleiner, A., & Lewis, L. (2003, October). *Internet access in U.S. public schools and classrooms: 1994-2002*. (NCES 2004-011). Retrieved September 3, 2006, from the National Center for Education Statistics Web site http:/nces.ed.gov/pubs2004/2004-011.pdf

Kozol, J. (1991). *Savage inequalities*. New York: Crown Publishers.

Kress, G. (2003). *Literacy in the new media age*. London: Routledge.

Krippendorf, K. (1980). *Content analysis: An introduction to its methodology*. Beverly Hills, CA: Sage Publications.

Lankshear, C., & Knobel, M. (2003). *New literacies: Changing knowledge and classroom learning*. Philadelphia: Open University Press.

Lazarus, W., Biemans, H. J. A., & Wopereis, I. (2005). Differences between novice and experienced users in searching information on the World Wide Web. *Journal of the American Society for Information Science American Society for Information Science*, *51*(6), 576–581.

Lee, V. E., & Croninger, R. G. (1994). The relative importance of home and school in the development of literacy skills for middle-grade students. *American Journal of Education*, *102*(3), 286–329. doi:10.1086/444071

Lenhart, A., Madden, M., & Hitlin, P. (2005). *Teens and technology: Youth are leading the transition to a fully wired and mobile nation*. Pew Internet and American Life Project. Retrieved May 8, 2006, from http://www.pewinternet.org/pdfs/PIP_Teens_Tech_July2005web.pdf

Leu, D. J. (2000). Our children's future: Changing the focus of literacy and literacy instruction. *The Reading Teacher, 53*(5), 424–429.

Leu, D. J. (2002). The new literacies: Research on reading instruction with the Internet and other digital technologies. In A. E. Farstrup & S. J. Samuels (Eds.), *What research has to say about reading instruction* (3rd ed., pp. 310-337). Newark, DE: International Reading Association.

Leu, D. J., Ataya, R., & Coiro, J. (2002, December). *Assessing assessment strategies among the 50 states: Evaluating the literacies of our past or our future?* Paper presented at the annual meeting of the National Reading Conference, Miami, FL.

Leu, D. J., Castek, J., Hartman, D. K., Coiro, J., Henry, L. A., & Lyver, S. (2005). Evaluating the development of scientific knowledge and new forms of reading comprehension during online learning. In R. Smith, T. Clark & R. L. Blomeyer, *A synthesis of new research on K-12 online learning* (pp. 30-34). Naperville, IL: Learning Point Associates, North Central Regional Educational Laboratory.

Leu, D. J., Coiro, J., Castek, J., Hartman, D. K., Henry, L. A., & Reinking, D. (2008). Research on instruction and assessment in the new literacies of online reading comprehension. In C. C. Block & S. R. Parris (Eds.), *Comprehension instruction: Research-based best practices* (2nd ed., pp. 321-346). New York: The Guilford Press.

Leu, D. J., Kinzer, C. K., Coiro, J., & Cammack, D. (2004). Toward a theory of new literacies emerging from the Internet and other information and communication technologies. In R. B. Ruddell & N. Unrau (Eds.), *Theoretical models and processes of reading* (5th ed., pp. 1568–1611). Newark, DE: International Reading Association.

Leu, D. J., & Reinking, D. (2005). Developing Internet comprehension strategies among poor, adolescent students at risk to become dropouts [Grant proposal]. Grant funded by Institute of Educational Sciences.

Levin, D., & Arafeh, S. (2002). *The digital disconnect: The widening gap between Internet-savvy students and their schools.* Pew Internet & American Life Project. Retrieved May 8, 2006, from http://www.pewinternet.org/PPF/r/67/report_display.asp

Lievrouw, L. A., & Farb, S. E. (2003). Information and equity. *Annual Review of Information Science & Technology, 37,* 499–540. doi:10.1002/aris.1440370112

Livingstone, S. (2003). Children's use of the Internet: Reflections on the emerging research agenda. *New Media & Society, 5*(2), 147–166. doi:10.1177/1461444803005002001

Mack, R. L. (2001). *The digital divide: Standing at the intersection of race & technology.* Durham, NC: Carolina Academic Press.

Malone, T. (2007, February). Educators face new technological challenge. *Daily Herald,* February 22, 2007. Retrieved March 22, 2007, from http://www.dailyherald.com/search /printstory.asp?id=284007

Martin, B. (2005). Information society revisited: From vision to reality. *Journal of Information Science, 31*(1), 3–11. doi:10.1177/0165551505049254

Mayring, P. (2000). Qualitative content analysis. *Forum: Qualitative Social Research, 1.* Retrieved August 28, 2006, from http://www.qualitative-research.net/fqqs-teste/2-00mayring-e.htm

McClure, C. R. (1997). Network literacy in an electronic society: An educational disconnect? In R. Kubey (Ed.), *Media literacy in the information age. Current perspectives: Information and behavior* (pp. 403-439). New Brunswick, NJ: Transaction.

Miles, M. B., & Huberman, A. M. (1994). *Qualitative data analysis* (2nd ed.). Newbury Park, CA: Sage.

Neuendorf, K. A. (2002). *The content analysis guidebook*. Thousand Oaks, CA: Sage Publications.

New Literacies Research Team. (2006). Thinking about our future as researchers: New literacies, new challenges, and new opportunities. In M.B. Sampson, S. Szabo, F. Falk-Ross, M. Foote, & P.E. Linder (Eds.), *Multiple Literacies in the 21st Century: The twenty-eighth yearbook of the college reading association* (pp. 31-50). Logan, UT: College Reading Association.

New London Group, The. (1996). A pedagogy of multiliteracies: Designing social futures. *Harvard Educational Review, 66*(1), 60–92.

New London Group. The. (2000). A pedagogy of multiliteracies. In B. Cope & M. Kalantzis (Eds.), *Multiliteracies: Literacy learning and the design of social futures* (pp. 9-38). New York: Routledge.

Norris, P. (2001). *Digital divide: Civic engagement, information poverty, and the Internet worldwide*. Cambridge, UK: Cambridge University Press.

Northcutt, N., & McCoy, D. (2004). *Interactive qualitative analysis: A systems method for qualitative research*. Thousand Oaks, CA: Sage Publications.

Paige, R. (2002, September). *Introductory letter*. Visions 2020: Transforming education and training through advanced technologies. Retrieved April 15, 2007, from the National Science and Technology council Website, http://www.visions2020.gov/Papers.htm

Palmquist, M. E., Carley, K. M., & Dale, T. A. (1997). Two applications of automated text analysis: Analyzing literary and non-literary texts. In C. Roberts (Ed.), *Text analysis for the social science: Methods for drawing statistical inferences from texts and transcripts*. Hillsdale, NJ: Lawrence Erlbaum Associates.

Parayil, G. (2005). The digital divide and increasing returns: Contradictions of information capitalism. *The Information Society, 21*(1), 41–51. doi:10.1080/01972240590895900

Parsad, B., & Jones, J. (2005). *Internet access in U.S. public schools and classrooms: 1994–2003* (NCES 2005-015). Retrieved August, 18, 2006, from the National Center for Education Statistics Website, http://nces.ed.gov/pubs2005/2005015.pdf

Partnership for 21st Century Skills. (2004). Learning for the 21st century. Retrieved August 15, 2006, from http://www.21stcenturyskills.org/reports/learning.asp

Pickering, J. (1995). Teaching on the Internet is learning. *Active Learning, 2*, 9–12.

Powell, A. H. (2007). Access(ing), habits, attitudes, and engagements: Re-thinking access as practice. *Computers and Composition, 24*(1), 16–35. doi:10.1016/j.compcom.2006.12.006

Pressley, M. (2006). *What the future of reading research could be*. Paper presented at the Reading Research Conference at the annual meeting of the International Reading Association, Chicago, Illinois.

RAND Reading Study Group. (2002). *Reading for understanding: Toward an R&D program in reading comprehension*. Retrieved March 3, 2004 from the RAND Corporation Web site: http://www.rand.org/multi/achievementforall/reading/readreport.html

Rice, R. (2002). Primary issues in Internet use: Access, civic and community involvement, and social interaction and expression. In L. Lievrouw & S. Livingstone (Eds.), *The Handbook of New Media: Social shaping and consequences of ICTs* (pp. 105-129). London: Sage.

Rothstein, R. (2004). *Class and schools: Using social, economic, and educational reform to close the black-white achievement gap*. New York: Teachers College Press.

Rowand, C. (2000, April). *Teacher use of computers and the Internet in public schools*. (NCES 2000-090). Retrieved August 18, 2006, from the National Center for Educational Statistics Website, http://nces.ed.gov/programs/quarterly/Vol_2/2_2/q3-2.asp

Smerdon, B., Cronen, S., Lanahan, L., Anderson, J., Iannotti, N., & Angeles, J. (2000). *Teachers' tools for the 21st century: A report on teachers' use of technology*. (NCES 2000-102). Retrieved August 18, 2006, from the National Center for Education Statistics Website, http://nces.ed.gov/pubs2000/2000102A.pdf

Snyder, I. (1996). *Hypertext: The electronic labyrinth*. New York: New York University Press.

Spitzer, K. L., Eisenberg, M. B., & Lowe, C. A. (1998). *Information literacy: Essential skills for the information age*. ERIC Clearinghouse on Information and Technology: Syracuse, NY.

Tyner, K. (1998). *Literacy in a digital world: Teaching and learning in the age of information*. Mahwah, NJ: Erlbaum.

U.S. Department of Education (DOE). (2002). *No Child Left Behind Act of 2001*. Washington DC: Author. Retrieved September 22, 2005, from http://www.ed.gov/policy/elsec/leg/esea02/index.html

Warschauer, M. (2002). *Technology and social inclusion: Rethinking the digital divide*. Cambridge, MA: MIT Press.

Warschauer, M., Knobel, M., & Stone, L. (2004). Technology and equity in schooling: Deconstructing the digital divide. *Educational Policy, 18*(4), 562–588. doi:10.1177/0895904804266469

Williams, D., Coles, L., Wilson, K., Richardson, A., & Tuson, J. (2000). Teachers and ICT: current use and future needs. *British Journal of Educational Technology, 31*(4), 307–320. doi:10.1111/1467-8535.00164

Williams, K. (2003). Literacy and computer literacy: Analyzing the NRC's "Being fluent with information technology" [Electronic version]. *The Journal of Literacy and Technology, 3*. Retrieved July 1, 2006, from http://www.literacyandtechnology.org/v3n1/williams.htm

Chapter 5

Information Technology:
A Critical Discourse Analysis Perspective

Thao Lê
University of Tasmania, Australia

Quynh Lê
University of Tasmania, Australia

ABSTRACT

Information technology (IT) has permeated many fields and aspects of modern society such as education, business, health and entertainment. It provides users with innovative and powerful products which were unimagined decades ago. The Internet is one of the most powerful IT developments. The introduction of the Internet has brought in new areas such as e-commerce, e-health and e-learning. Thus the instrumental role of IT is unquestionable in this digital age. However, from a Critical Discourse Analysis (CDA) perspective, IT is socially situated and its role and impacts cannot be divorced from its socio-cultural context. CDA is an interdisciplinary approach which studies linguistic and social issues in relation to social discourse with a main aim to examine how social power permeates and controls discourses and consequently creates social inequality and injustice. As IT is closely linked to its social discourse, its use and value are embedded in social structures and processes which are organized through institutions and practices such as political systems, business, education and the media, each of which is located in and structured by a particular discursive field. There are different social groups with competing discourses and they can exert power to use IT to their advantage. The challenge to IT experts, educators and IT users is not about the instrumental power that IT has brought to them. The real challenge is how to use it wisely to enhance humanity.

INTRODUCTION

The presence of information technology (IT) in various aspects of society strongly confirms that we

DOI: 10.4018/978-1-60566-842-0.ch005

are firmly situated in the information age. A small technical problem or breakdown in a local network can create a huge problem for its user community. One could not imagine the devastating impacts on society if there were a crash involving computer networks around the world. Thus, industrialized societies are at the mercy of information technology as our destiny is strongly tied to it. It appears that IT, like many other technologies, exists for a utilitarian purpose. Its presence is fundamentally instrumental in the sense that its nature intrinsically is neither good nor bad. In other words, it is value-free. IT itself is not the master who exerts powerful control over people. It is the human and social factors within the IT discourse which cause social disunity, social injustice, and ideological imposition to society. This chapter attempts to examine IT from a Critical Discourse Analysis (CDA) perspective as the discussion is based on the tenet that as IT is embedded in social discourses, its function is not ideologically free. The chapter will first discuss what CDA is and will examine how IT is viewed from a CDA perspective.

What is Critical Discourse Analysis?

According to Fairclough (2003), CDA is fundamentally critical social research aimed at achieving a better understanding of how societies work, both in terms of beneficial and detrimental effects, and particularly how to end or mitigate detrimental effects. For Fairclough the following questions are considered:

- How do existing societies provide people with the possibilities and resources for rich and fulfilling lives?
- On the other hand, how do these societies deny people the possibilities and resources?
- What is it about existing societies that produce poverty, deprivation, misery, and insecurity in people's lives?
- What possibilities are there for social change which would reduce these problems and enhance the quality of the lives of human beings? (Fairclough, 2003, p. 202).

Critical Discourse Analysis is an interdisciplinary approach which studies linguistic and social

issues in relation to social discourse with a main aim to examine how social power permeates and controls discourses and consequently creates social inequality and injustice. Thus it provides evidence against social and cultural injustice such as racism, social abuse, discrimination and cultural imperialism. Thus, the term 'critical' is vital here as the aim of CDA is not merely to describe a discourse but fundamentally it is against unfair hegemonic practices of social discourses which need social solutions for improving human life. 'Critical' does not mean being 'negative' in disagreement due to conflict of personal views and worldviews, it means that CDA research takes a stance against social injustice by contributing its research vigour to providing important insights into selected social issues.

CDA is interdisciplinary in the sense that it does not belong to one single academic discipline or rely on a single research method. CDA research is undertaken in different areas such as linguistics, management, health, psychology and sociology. Though CDA is an interdisciplinary approach, its development has been strongly influenced by linguistics, postmodernism and modern sociology. CDA often utilises concepts and ideas derived from linguistics such as 'text', 'intertexuality', 'nominalization' and 'metaphor'. Fairclough (1992) who is renowned for his contribution to CDA, has incorporated Systemic Functional Linguistics (SFL) into CDA. While traditional linguistic theories have a common focus on syntax and discourse is restricted to sentence structure, SFL deals with a much wider scope involving semantics, genres, pragmatics and sociolinguistics. Thus SFL is seen by Fairclough as a powerful tool for CDA in its analysis of discourses. The term 'discourse' itself can be problematic for some readers. Depending on the academic context, the term 'discourse' can be used to mean a number of things such as 'text', 'phenomenon', 'ways with power and ideology'.

The focus of CDA is emancipation and empowerment which has inspired researchers to adopt a critical stance in educational research against social inequality, injustice and ideological imposition. However, the question of ideology is problematic and controversial. It is impossible to expect a human discourse free from ideology. Ideology is about one's beliefs and values which reflect one's social background and worldviews. For example, Ellsworth (1989) mounted a course against discrimination in her university but encountered the ideological problem of her background against the students with whom she was allied with. She explained: "My understanding and experience of racism will always be constrained by my white skin and middle-class privilege. Indeed, it is impossible for anyone to be free from these oppressive formations at this historical moment" (Ellsworth, 1989, p.308).

Thus, the main interests of CDA analysts are social issues which reveal power distribution, social control, inequity and social injustice. The following themes are widely examined in CDA in relation to social issues: text, hegemony, social control, distribution of power, social and cultural imposition and interference. It first appears that these concepts and issues have little or nothing to do with IT. However, IT cannot be divorced from the human discourse in which it is situated. The following discussion will focus on IT from a CDA perspective.

Critical Information Technology

Discourse analysis has been a popular research focus in education, sociology and linguistics. As stated, CDA has emerged as a new interdisciplinary research paradigm which argues strongly that a discourse can empower some people and discriminate against others. CDA is a type of an analytical discourse that primarily studies the way in which social power abuse, dominance and inequality are enacted, reproduced and resisted by text and talk in the social and political context. CDA faces a challenging task to understand, expose and ultimately to resist social inequality.

The interesting question to ask here is: Why is CDA interested in IT?

The Critical Theory of Technology argues that the real issue is not technology or progress per se but the variety of possible technologies and paths of progress among which we must choose. Modern technology is no more neutral than medieval cathedrals or The Great Wall of China; it embodies the values of a particular industrial civilization and especially of its elites, which rest their claims to hegemony on technical mastery. We must articulate and judge these values in a cultural critique of technology. By so doing, we can begin to grasp the outlines of another possible industrial civilization based on other values. (Feenberg, 1991, p. 3)

As technology exists for people to benefit, it is important to examine technology in the discourse of humanity. Technology is the implementation of science to serve human beings. Science has little use to human beings if it does not provide us with technologies to achieve better things in life. Thus technologies provide people with tools, resources and systems to improve the conditions of their living. A bridge is built to facilitate the interaction of people living on two different sides of a river. A jet plane is developed to help people to conquer time and space, and computers act as a tool for multi-dimensional functions such as communication, problem solving and entertainment. We often think of technology in terms of concrete artefacts. However, they are only the instrumental products of technology. In a broader sense, technology includes creative scientific processes and skills in problem solving.

We are now living in a modern discourse of technology in which the computer is the mind of Information Technology. However, IT, like any other technology, is socially situated. Its use and value are embedded in social structures and processes which are organized through institutions and practices such as the political system, business world, education system, media and religion, each of which is located in and structured by a particular discursive field. Discursive fields consist of competing ways of giving meaning to the world and of organizing social institutions and processes. They represent hegemonic realities which can enhance the wellbeing of certain groups and disadvantage others. They offer individuals a range of modes of subjectivity. Some will account for and justify the appropriateness of the status quo and can create false consciousness even among those who are disadvantaged. Discourse participants can also give rise to challenges to existing practices from within or will contest the very basis of current organization and the selective interests which it represents. In the view expressed by The New London Group (1996), the changing technological and organizational shape of working life provides some with access to lifestyles of unprecedented affluence, while excluding others in ways that are increasingly related to the outcomes of education and training.

The Internet has been hailed as one of the greatest developments of IT. It is a superhighway which travels around the world in just seconds. In a metaphorical sense, it turns the world into a global village. It is normally accepted that the power of the Internet has increased rapidly. It is very powerful as it can perform huge tasks with great speed. It empowers many institutions to revolutionize their old practices. The Internet and globalization walk merrily together. However, emancipation through the Internet is perceived differently. It can create disempowerment as the Internet creates a gap between the e-people and those who cannot afford the Internet or those whose cultural values are not ready for radical changes that technology motivates.

In many countries there has recently been an upsurge in the extension of the market to new areas of social life: sectors such as education, health care and the arts have been required to restructure and reconceptualise their activities

as the production and marketing of commodities for consumers. These changes have profoundly affected the activities, social relations, and social and professional identities of people working in such sectors. (Fairclough 1992, p. 6)

In an industrialized society, the Internet is the darling of professional institutions. Without it, their functioning is greatly affected. In the fields of business and education, for instance, the Internet is not just a tool, it has permeated so deeply into the central services of these sectors that their existence would be in great doubt if they were deprived of the Internet. Internet banking and on-line learning depend exclusively on the Internet. The prefix 'e' in e-banking, e-health, e-learning clearly indicates the penetration of the Internet into many aspects of modern society. While the contribution of the Internet to humanity is undoubtedly enormous, there are also issues and problems which are associated with or caused by the Internet.

A good society should enlarge the personal freedom of its members while enabling them to participate effectively in a widening range of public activities. At the highest level, public life involves choices about what it means to be human. Today these choices are increasingly mediated by technical decisions. What human beings are and will become is decided in the shade of our tools no less than in the action of statesmen and political movement. The design of technology is thus an ontological decision fraught with political consequences. The exclusion of the vast majority from participation in this decision is the underlying cause of many our problems. (Feenberg, 1991, p. 3)

The Internet is not just a tool. It is an extremely powerful tool in a social discourse and this factor is also a cause for concern as power can be mismanaged or destructive. Metaphorically, the image of the Internet as a wonderful superhighway can be placed by an image of a bad wolf. The Internet is not a free superhighway which belongs to no social institutions. Instrumentally, it appears neutral in terms of ideology, power control and social justice. However, it is situated in a social context and is subject to power control and abuse. There are questions which need to be examined such as: Who are those who have influential control over the Internet? Can the Internet be manipulated to serve the interests of some privileged powerful groups and disadvantage others? What are the social problems associated with the Internet?

To answer these questions, the mass media can be used as an example of the close link between IT and social discourse. A piece of news taking place in a remote land can reach the whole world in just a matter of seconds due to the innovation of IT. International conflicts do not only happen on battlefields but more so in the mass media. Though we expect absolute neutrality in the handling of information in the mass media, there are different 'realities' presented to the public depending on the choice of texts manipulated by the controller. This is a manifestation of power control over public discourse. As Van Dijk (2008, p. 55) points out, "much work on news production has shown that these processes are not arbitrary and not simply determined by intuitive, journalistic notion of interestingness". He argues that journalists learn how to portray the power of others and at the same time learn how to contribute to the power of their own organizations. It is hard for IT-dependent workers not to reproduce the dominant ideologies of their organizations.

Another feature that has often been found to characterize western news discourse is the ethnocentric, stereotypical portrayal of Third World nations and peoples. Although not all news about the Third World is of the 'coup and earthquakes' brand, it certainly focuses on only a few types of events and actors, which are generally stereotypical if not negative: poverty, lack of democracy, dictatorship, violence and civil war, and technological and cultural 'backwardness' (Van Dijk, 1008, p. 58).

It has been emphasized in this discussion that IT cannot be divorced from its social and cultural context. Thus it cannot be immune from problems due to social and cultural interference. For instance, in the field of health informatics which relies entirely on computer technology, culture plays an important part in its implementation. According to Le (2007) security is an essential factor in health informatics. The loss of or unauthorised access to personal and sensitive data can result in financial and legal costs and personal trauma. From an intercultural perspective, there are two issues involved. Health workers and patients of different cultural backgrounds may treat data security differently. Security risk and privacy in health informatics needs absolute commitment from those who are privileged to have authorised access. However, such commitment can vary due to different cultural attitudes towards data security and the cultural discourse in which security is reinforced.

Instances of 'information leak' from computer files in some public services show that human factors influence the effectiveness of IT. One of the most common IT security problems is the management of passwords. Though technical security can be very effective, it is the user's handling of passwords which can make computer security vulnerable. It first appears that culture has nothing to do with password security. Human errors reflect cultural influence on users' attitudes and behaviours in dealing with computer security. In a culture which emphasizes collectivism and mutual responsibility, sharing is a common feature in daily interaction, particularly among family members and close friends. Ownership does not belong to individuals but it can be extended to close others. Friendship and kinship are based on mutual trust. In this cultural context, sharing security passwords is not an offence but can be treated as a symbol of trust and loyalty.

In summary, there are two perspectives about IT: neutrality of instrumentality and Critical IT. The instrumentality perspective holds the view that technologies are tools to serve their users. Technology is value free and indifferent to social variations. Whereas Critical IT argues that IT cannot be divorced from its socio-cultural context. In relation to the Internet, as Zurawski (1998, para. 1) points out, culture and identity are two of the foremost subjects when speaking about the Internet and its social aspects. But there seem to be two opposing views when it comes to the relationship between technology, society and culture at large: the Internet then is either bad or good for society and culture in general. Both views, obviously both sides of the same coin, reinforce Zurawski's (1998) deterministic view of technology.

Implications for Education

The traditional focus on print literacy may not prepare students for a fast changing world driven by the rapid growth and strong dominance of information technology. Children are not only exposed to books but also to e-texts in various forms. As The New London Group (1996) argues, new communications media are reshaping the way we use language. When technologies of meaning are changing so rapidly, there cannot be one set of standards or skills that constitute the ends of literacy learning, however taught. Thus education must prepare to accept that the new discourse requires people to interact effectively using multiple languages, multiple 'Englishes' and communication patterns that more frequently cross cultural, community and national boundaries. The term 'multiliteracies' is introduced to signal a way to focus on the realities of increasing local diversity and global connectedness. Thus, The New London Group (1996) believe that the use of a multiliteracies approaches to pedagogy will enable students to achieve the twin goals for literacy learning: creating access to the evolving language of work, power and community, and fostering the critical engagement necessary for them to design their social futures and achieve success through fulfilling employment.

In education, people find themselves under pressure to engage in new activities which are largely defined by new discourse practices (such as marketing), and to adopt new discourse practices within existing activities (such as teaching). This includes 'rewordings' of activities and relationships. It also includes a more subtle restructuring of the discourse practices of education – the types of discourse (genres, styles, etc.) which are used in it – and a 'colonization' of education by the types of discourse from outside. (Fairclough, 1992, p. 7)

While the attraction of technology in educational practice is strong, it is important to ensure that it is the pedagogy which serves humanity, not the technology that is essential. The emergence of IT has introduced to education many advantages but also brings along great challenges. There are many issues which need to be addressed. We need to raise issues about the effectiveness of IT in teaching and learning in different socio-cultural contexts to ensure that IT is not a means to exert power control and to impose foreign ideologies. Apart from the problems caused by an inappropriate use of technology, attention should also be on student learning in different cultural discourses.

CONCLUSION

This chapter has discussed IT in relation to its human discourse. It has argued that Critical Discourse Analysis can contribute to the understanding of IT due to the fact that IT is socially situated. Computers, like many other products of different technologies, are a physical entity which can be subjected to good use or abuse by social agencies. It is a product and an instrument which cannot be divorced from its historical background and functioning. It can be exploited by some social institutions to serve their growing needs and to reinforce their power control over others. IT, particularly the Internet, does not exist in a harmonious global village. There are different social groups with competing discourses and they can exert power through the use of IT to their advantage. The challenge to IT experts, educators and IT users is not about the power that IT has brought to them. The real challenge is how to use it wisely to enhance mankind.

REFERENCES

Ellsworth, E. (1989). Why doesn't this feel empowering? Working through the repressive myths of critical pedagogy. *Harvard Educational Review*, *59*(3), 303–314.

Fairclough, N. (1992). *Discourse and social change*. Cambridge, UK: Polity Press.

Fairclough, N. (2003). *Analyzing discourse*. London: Routledge.

Feeberg, A. (1991). *Critical theory of technology*. New York: Oxford University Press.

Lê, Q. (2007). 'Health informatics: An intercultural perspective'. *Proceedings of MEDINFO 2007 - Building Sustainable Health Systems*, 20 – 24 August 2007, Brisbane, Australia, (pp. 1194-1198).

The New London Group. (1996). A pedagogy of multiliteracies: Designing social features. *Harvard Educational Review*, *66*(1), 66–92.

Van Dijk, T. (2008). *Discourse and power*. New York: Palgrave Macmillan.

Zurawski, N. (1998). *Culture, identity and the Internet*. Retrieved January 20, 2009 from http://www.uni-muenster.de/PeaCon/zurawski/Identity.html

Section 2
Technoliteracy in Practice

Chapter 6
CALL Course Design for Second Language Learning:
A Case Study of Arab EFL Learners

Abbad Alabbad
The University of Queensland, Australia

Christina Gitsaki
The University of Queensland, Australia

Peter White
The University of Queensland, Australia

ABSTRACT

The study presented in this chapter investigated the impact of computers and the Internet on both the achievement of learners of English as a foreign language (EFL) and their attitudes toward learning EFL. The field study took place at a University in Riyadh, Saudi Arabia, where first year students study English 101, a compulsory English language course. Thirty students were randomly selected to study in an alternative EFL course using computers, the Internet and collaborative activities within a constructivist framework. Another group of 38 students was also randomly selected to be the control group. These students attended English 101 taught using traditional teaching aids and the grammar-translation teaching method. The study was 13 weeks long. The findings of the study indicate a strong positive shift in the subjects' attitude and motivation toward learning EFL after using the new technology-based approach. As to the subjects' language achievement, the treatment group outperformed the control group by 30%. These findings provide strong support for the effectiveness of a technology-enhanced learning environment for second language teaching and learning.

INTRODUCTION

In recent years, the question of what it means to know and learn and its implications on how we should teach have inspired various academic disciplines,

e.g. mathematics, science, and language teaching, to undergo a significant change in the epistemology which underlies their pedagogical practice (Reagan, 1999). In order to address the limitations of the commonly practised teacher-based instructional pedagogy, scholars turned to constructivism as a

DOI: 10.4018/978-1-60566-842-0.ch006

theory of learning that gives more attention to the learner, as learners become active and engaged in the learning process (Schcolnik, Kol, & Abarbanel, 2006). Among the core principles of constructivism is the rejection of the behaviorist model of learning, e.g. the teacher-centered approach, which is the linear transmission of knowledge from teacher to student with the student in a passive role. Instead, constructivism focuses on the learners as active participants in constructing their own knowledge. According to constructivists, learners construct their knowledge with the help of the teacher by means of various types of interaction, including interaction with their learning environment (Fosnot, 1996; Gagnon & Collay, 2001; Meunier, 1994). Students' active participation in creating learning materials has been associated with higher levels of achievement, as shown in early and more recent research (see for example Clarke, 2007; Hunter & Harman, 1985). It is important, however, that the tasks are challenging, authentic, and multidisciplinary in order for the learners to be engaged (Wang & Kang, 2005). Such tasks are often collaboratively performed by the students and their peers. Therefore, in addition to active learning, constructivism is also associated with collaborative and project-based learning as essential and integral components of the learning process (Herrington, Reeves, Oliver, & Woo, 2004; Neo, Neo, & Xiao-Lian, 2007). Unlike the traditional teacher-centered classroom, where each student works alone and is assessed individually, in the constructivist classroom students engage in the investigation of real life problems (Barron, 1998) and create meaningful collaborative learning projects. Although the study of collaborative learning has a relatively brief history (Littleton & Hakkinen, 1999), there are empirical studies that have shown positive results when investigating group work (see Meunier, 1994). In the language learning classroom, when the learners are actively engaged with other learners to express meaning this can promote the language skills needed for effective communication in the target language

(Chen, 2005; Rust, Price, & O'Donovan, 2003). Seliger (1983) found that the learning rate among students who were interacting with their peers was faster than the students who were passively receiving their knowledge from the lecturer. Pica and Doughty (1985) also observed that ESL students showed more expertise in negotiating meaning when working in groups rather than through the teacher-centered model. Similarly, Green (1993) found that students who work together showed a higher degree of achievement and better attitude toward the language they were learning.

Equally important, though, in a constructivist learning environment are the resources and tools used in teaching and learning. The use of computers and the Internet has long been advocated by educators who seek to apply a learner-centered constructivist model through the use of technology (Newhouse, 2001). In a computer-supported environment where time and space are no longer constraints to learning, students can work collaboratively on projects either synchronously or asynchronously, whether in the classroom, at home, or anywhere else as long as they have access to the Internet (Roberts, 2005). Furthermore, as the Net-generation grows up in a world dominated by digital devices, electronic communications, constant multimedia exposure, and the Internet, the expectation is that these tools and resources would be employed in teaching and learning as well. With the advent of multimedia, and new technologies, teachers could enable their students to learn in more productive ways (Zheng & Zhou, 2006). This is particularly important when it is revealed that people remember 75% better when they receive information through audiovisual media than through hearing or seeing separately (see Lindstrom, 1994). Other researchers (see Fulford, 2001; Mayer & Moreno, 2003; Zheng & Zhou, 2006) have also suggested that computer technology and multimedia in particular can enhance different aspects of learning including motivating students to learn, promoting deep understanding, and engaging them in problem solving. This chapter presents a course design model for second language learning that is distinct from the traditional instructional model. It creates a constructivist and collaborative learning environment that focuses on the learner as the center of the learning process where active learning takes place with the aid of computer technologies and web-based learning materials and resources.

BACKGROUND

The context of this study is Saudi Arabia. In this country there is a well established tradition of English language learning at the school and university level. For many years, the dominant language teaching approaches in Saudi Arabia have been the audio-lingual and the grammar translation method (Al-Kamookh, 1983; Al-Mazroou, 1988; Zaid, 1993). The inadequacy and the shortcomings of these language teaching methodologies have been widely acknowledged in the literature in general (Savignon, 1991), and in the Saudi context in particular, where learners have been found to be unable to use English even after attending six or more years of EFL instruction (Al-Ahaydib, 1986; AL-Mazroou, 1988; Zaid, 1993). In addition to low language performance, Saudi EFL students exhibit a negative attitude towards studying EFL and low motivation for further or independent study. Given the ineffectiveness of the current teaching methodologies, in recent years there has been a growing realization among Saudi educators of the value of technology, such as the use of computers and the Internet, in the improvement of EFL teaching and learning. Utilizing computers for language learning is relatively new in Saudi Arabia (Al-Kahtani, 2004) with only a few studies conducted in the field of Computer-Assisted Language Learning (CALL) (Abalhassan, 2002; Al-Juhani, 1991; Al-Kahtani, 2001). In an effort to remedy the unsatisfactory achievement level of the Saudi EFL students, Al-Juhani (1991) investigated the effectiveness of computer-assisted instruction

in teaching English as a foreign language in Saudi secondary schools suggesting that the traditional method that was used in the English curriculum (i.e. the grammar translation method) was no longer serving the needs of Saudi EFL learners. Al-Juhani's hypothesis was that if CALL could be implemented in the core curriculum of secondary schools, students would achieve greater results in grasping the English language. The results of his study confirmed the positive effects of computer-assisted instruction in teaching English as a foreign language in Saudi secondary schools. Ten years later Al-Kahtani (2001) investigated the extent to which computer-based resources are utilized in EFL instruction in Saudi Arabia. The attitudes of the instructors towards using computer resources to teach EFL were studied as well. The results revealed that the majority of the Saudi EFL instructors held positive attitudes towards CALL, but the use of computers in EFL teaching was both minimal and superficial, while a range of social factors (such as the cultural and religious attitudes held by EFL faculty, administrators, and students) affected this limited use of computer-based resources. A year later, Abalhassan (2002) conducted a qualitative study in order to examine the pedagogical methods teachers used in EFL technology-equipped classrooms in private schools in Saudi Arabia and the beliefs of Saudi teachers toward the use of technology in EFL classrooms. The findings showed that the use of computer-based multimedia in Saudi private schools lacked a theoretical background and an adequate understanding of the computer-enhanced learning environment. Administrative and contextual factors were found to be having adverse effects on the use of technology and technology-based resources. Even though the teachers' beliefs about the role of technology in EFL education were positive, their understanding and conceptualization of computer-assisted instruction was inadequate, inaccurate, and misleading.

Given the low second language achievement of Saudi students and the underpinning reasons for it, such as the outdated didactic teaching methodology and the lack of an effective, theoretically-grounded framework for CALL, the goal of the study was to design a course that would apply constructivist principles in a second language setting through the use of computers and the Internet. In this setting, fluency and the ability to communicate effectively has prior significance over accuracy, and the learners are expected to be active and engaged in the learning process. After all, students' engagement is an essential foundation in second language learning (Batstone, 2002). While active learning and student engagement are important parts of an effective learning environment, there is little research investigating the relationship between classroom activities, learners' engagement and positive learning outcomes (Bulger, Mayer, & Almeroth, 2008; Fredricks, Blumenfeld, & Paris, 2004). It is one of the current study's intentions, therefore, to contribute to the investigation of this important issue.

While the current study emphasizes the development of effective communication skills as the goal of language teaching, it is also important to highlight that there are communicative skills, as Canale and Swain (1980) pointed out, that are beyond grammatical competence. Among the important types of knowledge the learner should construct while learning a foreign language is to develop an understanding about the culture of the target language and its social dimensions, such as family and kinship relations, marriage and gender roles, and how people use it to communicate with each other (Celce-Murcia, 2007). Therefore intercultural competence is also an important objective of foreign language teaching (Sercue, 2004; Thorne, 2006), particularly if the target language culture is widely different from the learners' own culture (as is the case with Saudi students). In order to allow exposure to the target culture and how its people communicate in real life, learners need to be provided with the appropriate learning materials that allow them to have a deeper insight into the target language and its people. Computers

and the Internet are among the various tools and materials that could be integrated in the design of language courses for the development of intercultural language skills.

Based on the constructivist theoretical premises and the language goals discussed above, the following prototype model for a CALL course was developed (see Figure 1). The model shows how constructivism and its overarching principle of learner-centeredness would be applied in the CALL course design. The active learner premise would be realized through resources and activities that would engage and motivate learners while allowing them to have direct access to the learning materials, direct their learning into the areas they are interested in, and the opportunity to manage their learning at their own pace. The use of Internet-based resources would make this possible. The premise of collaborative learning would be put into action through project-based learning and group work activities that require learners to work with their peers on real-life projects and simulations that would increase their opportunities to use the target language with their peers. Finally the use of authentic materials would ensure exposure to the target culture and real life language use in an effort to increase the learners' intercultural knowledge and skills.

THE STUDY

There were two groups of participants: a treatment group (30 participants) and a control group (38 participants). All subjects were students of English at a University in Saudi Arabia, aged 18-20 years, and their native tongue was Arabic. All subjects were of low to intermediate English proficiency. Each group enrolled in a 13-week course (namely *English 101*) and attended three 50-minute lessons a week. The control group completed their course using the University prescribed textbook (*American Kernel Lessons* by O'Neil, Kingsbury, & Yeadon, 1978) which focuses mainly on gram-

Figure 1. CALL design model

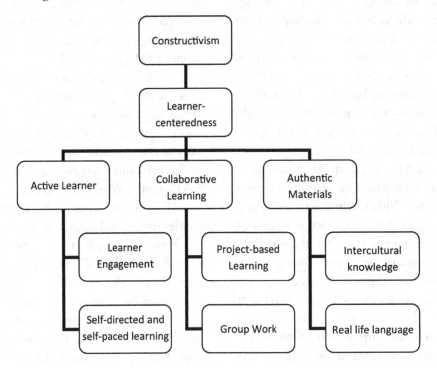

mar, while the treatment group attended a CALL course that focused on general English skills. At the completion of the course both groups participated in the final University exam which was based on the grammar included in the *American Kernel Lessons* textbook.

The CALL Course

Based on the model designed for the study (see Figure 1 above), the CALL course consisted of three major components: a multimedia resource, three collaborative web-based projects, and *PowerPoint* lessons covering grammar topics. The broad objectives of the CALL courseware were to enable the learner to communicate effectively in the target language, receive and deliver messages easily, recognize the sociocultural aspects of the target language, and learn a foreign language in realistic learning situations.

Multimedia Resource: English for All (EFA)

50% of the CALL course was comprised of the on-line program *English for All* (EFA) which targets pre-intermediate learners of English. It was developed by the Division of Adult and Career Education of the Los Angeles Unified School District (Pedroza, 2003). EFA, www.myefa.org, is a web-based courseware package that requires access to the Internet for both the instructor and the student to access all the features that the package offers. The EFA courseware consists of five distinct stories, and each story is carefully divided into four theme-related episodes (a total of 20 episodes). The stories are presented by a humorous wizard who guides the learner through the episodes and provides simple explanations of the basic grammar points presented in the 15-minute video clip that features in each episode. During each episode the learner is engaged in real-life conflicts inviting the character to decide between two opposing courses of action. Each episode of the EFA courseware contains the following sections:

- **An introduction:** The wizard introduces the lesson, the theme of the story, and the characters to the student in the introductory video clip.
- **Objectives:** What the student is going to learn in this episode.
- **Vocabulary:** A list of the important words that are going to be used throughout the episode and their pronunciation.
- **Vocabulary activities:** Exercises to identify the sound and the meaning of each of the new words.
- **Comprehension:** A video clip with or without text.
- **Comprehension activity:** An exercise related to the video clip.
- **Life skills:** The part of the story that focuses on everyday life skills, such as finding an apartment or finding a job.
- **Life skills activity:** An exercise associated with the life skills video clip.
- **Grammar:** The part of the story that highlights how the featured language structures and forms are used in real life situations.
- **Grammar lesson:** A brief explanation of the language forms used in the episode.
- **Grammar activity:** A grammar exercise.
- **Special skills:** The part of the story where the student becomes involved in the story and makes a decision.
- **Special skills activity:** A listening exercise linked to the special skills video clip.
- **Conclusion:** The wizard highlights the important topics explored throughout the episode.
- **Test:** A quiz that covers all the sections of the episode.

Collaborative Web-Based Projects

The second major resource in the CALL course was a set of collaborative task-based projects. During the course there were three such projects, which comprised 40% of the course design. Two of these (*Famous People* and *Vacation Abroad*) were based on the *Internet English* textbook (Gitsaki & Taylor, 2000). The third project (*Grand Canyon Imaginative Voyage*) was an online collaborative travel simulation activity developed by the Intensive English Institute at the University of Illinois at Urbana-Champaign.

For the *Famous People* and *Vacation Abroad* projects, the students used the Internet as a resource to search for pictures, audio, video clips and relevant information to complete their projects. Students performed these projects in four steps: a) identified key vocabulary items related to the topic; b) prepared their research question; c) searched the Internet for information; and d) shared the information they found with their classmates using presentations or pair interviews. The *Grand Canyon Imaginative Voyage* was a travel simulation activity and students worked in pairs or groups. At the end of the project, each group was required to submit a detailed report to the instructor, describing their trip, including transportation, accommodation, and the activities they (virtually) undertook throughout their trip.

PowerPoint Grammar Lessons

Ten percent of the CALL course was assigned to cover the mandatory grammar lessons which were required by the course curriculum and which were central in the final University examination. *PowerPoint* was used for these lessons, which also had hyperlinks to Internet websites, which the students could use for further interactive exercises and games related to the grammar lesson. The *PowerPoint* grammar lessons, as well as all the materials used with the treatment group, were uploaded to a website specially designed for the CALL course.

Additional Resources: Easy Lingo

For the CALL group, each of the computers in the laboratory had an English-Arabic dictionary, *Easy Lingo* (Text-to-Speech, 1998). This dictionary not only translates words and phrases into Arabic, but it also pronounces any word in a selection of male or female voices in English or Arabic. The role of the dictionary was to facilitate learning new vocabulary and to improve the students' understanding of the instructions in the other resources.

Teaching the CALL Course

The first step was to make all the subjects familiar with using the embedded English-Arabic dictionary on the computer, and with using the interface of the EFA program and its features. The subjects were led step by step through the registration process online at the *EFA* website. They also learnt how to use the embedded communication system in the *EFA* program. Table 1 presents the 13-week schedule of the CALL lessons.

Data Collection Instruments

The study employed both quantitative and qualitative data collection methods. Quantitative data were collected through the *Quick Placement Test* (QPT), the *Key English Test* (KET), the *Final Examination* (FE), and the *Evaluation Questionnaire* (EQ). Qualitative data were obtained through student interviews.

Quick Placement Test (QPT)

Prior to the start of the treatment, the *Quick Placement Test* (QPT), a computer-based multiple choice test of English language proficiency, was administered to all the subjects in the treatment and in the control group. The test included grammar, reading and listening comprehension questions.

Key English Test (KET)

The first post-treatment performance measurement instrument was the *Key English Test* (KET), a general language proficiency test which is the first level Cambridge ESOL examination. KET tests the learner's ability to cope with everyday communication at a basic level. The KET was administered to both groups of subjects at the end of the *English 101* course.

Final Examination (FE)

The second measure of performance was the *Final Examination* (FE). The test was designed by selected faculty members of the University where the study took place. The test targeted the language skills taught in the textbook (AKL), which focused mainly on grammar. This test consisted of multiple choice questions on reading, vocabulary, and grammar. The grammar section comprised 80% of the test. Both the treatment and the control groups took the same final test at the end of the course.

Evaluation Questionnaire (EQ)

The *Evaluation Questionnaire* was designed for the treatment group. The questionnaire included three sections: a) students' attitudes regarding learning English as a foreign language using computers and the Internet (10 items); b) students' perceptions regarding their performance throughout the treatment (11 items); and c) students' attitudes regarding the collaborative activities (10 items). Subjects responded to the thirty one statements using a Likert scale ranging from 1 (*strongly disagree*) to 5 (*strongly agree*). There were also seven open-ended questions at the end of the questionnaire. The *Evaluation Questionnaire* was written and administered in Arabic in order ensure that all subjects clearly understood and responded to the entire questionnaire.

Table 1. Week by week activities for the treatment group

Week	Activities
1	• Introduction to *EFA* courseware. • Introduction to the online dictionary.
2	• Episode 1 at *EFA* website: Verbs of like and dislike in the present simple tense. • *PowerPoint* lesson: simple present tense.
3	• Episode 2 at *EFA* website: Going to/ will to express the future. • *PowerPoint* lesson: Verb *Be* • The first web-based *(Internet English)* project, *Famous People,* was introduced in class using examples from the Internet.
4	• *PowerPoint* lesson: simple past tense. • Episode 3 at *EFA* website: simple past tense of regular and irregular verbs. • Episode 5 at *EFA* website: verbs of necessity (have to/must).
5	• Collaborative group work in the classroom to perform the first web-based project *Famous people.* • Episode 6 at *EFA* website: Can, could, to express ability in the present and past. • Episode 8 at *EFA* website: Make vs. Do.
6	• *PowerPoint* lesson: present continuous tense. • *PowerPoint* lesson: countable and the non-countable nouns. • Subjects' presentations of their first project *Famous People* in the classroom using either the *PowerPoint* on the projector or in pair-interviews.
7	• Episode 9 at *EFA* website: count and non-count nouns; plurals. • Episode 10 at *EFA* website: Quantifiers: much, many, some, a few, any, a lot of, a little. • Subjects' presentations the *Famous People* project using either the *PowerPoint* on the projector or in interviews.
8	• *PowerPoint* lesson: adjectives and adverbs. • Episode 13 at *EFA* website: adjectives. • Subjects' presentations of the *Famous People* project using either the *PowerPoint* on the projector or pair-interviews.
9	• The second web-based *(Internet English)* project *Vacation Abroad* was introduced in class using examples from the Internet. • Episode 14 at *EFA* website: adverbs of frequency. • Episode 15 at *EFA* website: adverbs of manner.
10	• *PowerPoint* lesson: comparisons using adjectives and adverbs. • Episode 16 at *EFA* website: comparative and superlative forms of adjectives. • Collaborative group work in the classroom to perform the second web-based project *Vacation Abroad.*
11	• Episode 17 at *EFA* website: asking questions with *"wh"* words. • Subjects' presentations of the *Vacation Abroad* project using either the *PowerPoint* or pair interviews. • Episode 19 at *EFA* website: use of *"did"* in the simple past questions.
12	• Episode 20 at *EFA* website: past tense forms of verbs. • Subjects' presentations of the *Vacation Abroad* project using either the *PowerPoint* or pair-interviews.
13	• The third collaborative web-based project was introduced in class using the webpage designed for the project in the Internet. • The subjects worked on *The Grand Canyon Trip* project in groups of 2-4.

Student Interviews

There were individual semi-structured interviews with all the subjects in the treatment group. The interviews were performed in Arabic and they were digitally recorded. The interviews were between 10 and 20 minutes long, depending on the responses provided by each subject.

Findings and Discussion

The statistical analysis of the QPT administered at the start of the treatment study showed that the two groups (the control and the treatment) were similar in terms of their English proficiency level (i.e. no significant differences were found between the two groups of students). After the 13-week course subjects in both groups were tested using the FE and the KET. The results of the FE showed that there was no significant difference between the two groups of subjects (control and treatment), t(58) = 0.117, p=0.907, even though the final exam was based on the textbook used only by the subjects in the control group. In other words, the treatment group performed in the final university examination as well as the control group even though they were not taught the designated textbook which was the basis for designing the final examination. The other language performance measurement, the KET, showed that there was a significant difference in the performance between the control and the treatment groups, with the treatment group outperforming the control group (t(60) =5.19, p=0.000). Despite the fact that neither of the two groups had received any special training in taking the KET test, the results show that the students in the treatment group performed significantly better than the students in the control group in terms of their general English ability. In other words, the CALL course enhanced students' English language skills more than the traditional textbook-based EFL course.

In order to find out what the treatment group thought about the CALL course, the *Evaluation Questionnaire* was administered at the end of the course. The results showed highly positive attitudes among subjects toward using CALL in learning EFL. Subjects favored the CALL method over the traditional method for studying English in the future and 96% felt that they liked and enjoyed learning English more than before the treatment. Nearly all subjects (96%) agreed that computers and the Internet made learning interesting, while most of the subjects (81%) reported that because of the treatment course they were thinking of using the Internet and English programs to learn English on their own. 92% of the subjects thought that the assignments using CALL were more interesting than the activities in the textbook. In addition, all the subjects believed that the materials used during the treatment helped them to learn how native speakers of English used their language

in real situations and positively motivated them to put more effort into learning English. 85% of the subjects were satisfied with the assessment method in the course that included task based projects and online interactive assignments. They believed it was more preferable than the traditional methods of assessment. A considerable number of subjects (77%) reported that working in groups to perform collaborative projects was more enjoyable than working individually, while 73% believed that group work positively affected their language performance. Most of the subjects (69%) believed that one of the positive outcomes of group work was giving them the opportunity to practise speaking the target language in the group, while 73% reported that working in groups enhanced their relationships among group members during the course.

After responding to the Likert-scale items of the *Evaluation Questionnaire*, all the subjects in the treatment group were asked to comment on the open-ended questions. The students' responses were classified into a set of themes and sub-themes under three categories: resources and materials; learner-related factors; and teaching methodology. The subjects valued the role of the resources and materials and 38% mentioned the collaborative projects, in particular. Another 27% of the students considered the learning of other skills, such as using the computer and searching the web, which were beyond learning the language itself, as motivational. The content of the materials was also found to be motivating by the students. 19% thought that the audiovisual aids enhanced their attitudes toward the new method through the use of colours, graphics and their interactive design. A student reported that "The graphics and colors linked the words with the figures in my mind". The subjects also saw more chance in the new teaching method for self-learning. 23% of the students pointed out that they could study at their own pace and repeat the lessons at any time. With respect to the learner role, 19% thought that they had an active learning role in the new method. Subjects

(42%) highlighted the advantages using the target language in real-life situations, e.g. emailing the teacher, speaking and listening in their groups, watching the video-clip incidents. About 31% of the subjects believed that the new method, including the collaborative projects in particular, enabled them to have more speaking practice with their classmates. One of the subjects pointed out that one of the advantages of the CALL course was that it focused on all language skills and not only on grammar as the AKL textbook did. Another subject reported that learning about the culture of the target language was equally important as studying the language. By and large, the questionnaire showed that students in the treatment group had a positive attitude towards learning English using the CALL-based materials and perceived the use of these materials as instrumental in enhancing their English language skills.

Finally, the subjects in the treatment group were interviewed individually for about 15 minutes each. During the interviews the subjects discussed their experiences in learning English with a teaching method and learning resources that were different from those they were used to. The students also gave feedback regarding their use of computers and the Internet in a communicative and group work learning environment. A large number of the issues the students mentioned in the interviews were similar to those reported in the *Evaluation Questionnaire*. Students talked about the active learner role in the course, the opportunities to practise learning and use the target language in context, and the enjoyment while learning. To the students, the chance to see and use the target language in real life situations was a valuable experience in this course.

The significant change in the learner's role was one of the important advantages the students discussed during the interviews. They explained how their role had shifted from being merely receptive to the information delivered by their teacher to being active in the classroom. Furthermore, the students also mentioned other positive consequences of being active in the classroom, such as having more opportunities for self-directed learning and having more control over the learning content. As one of the subjects stated: "The new teaching method gave me a chance to choose what to study. I was not merely receiving rules and information any more. I had a greater role in the learning process. It also allowed for self learning" [Student 18, I-2, 4-6].

The subjects expressed their pleasure that the new CALL course provided a motivating learning atmosphere in the classroom. To one of the subjects, learning English in this course was nothing like being in a traditional English classroom. It was a fun session: "I don't feel like I am in a regular classroom. I feel that I come to an entertaining learning session which has video and interactive computer programs." [Student 19, I-2, 4-6].

Through the interviews it became apparent that enjoying the new method of teaching was among the most important issues for the subjects, as it was mentioned 36 times in the interviews.

Besides allowing for a more active role for the students in the learning process, the CALL-based teaching method also provided the students with the opportunity to learn in a comfortable environment. Almost one half of the subjects found the CALL course to be less stressful than the traditional textbook-based course, mainly due to the variety of the learning options the CALL course provided, such as the different teaching aids, and several assessment options. The students described the CALL method as being an easier way to learn English because in addition to using English as a medium of communication it also gave attention to language skills, not only to grammar. Another important feature mentioned by six subjects was that the CALL teaching method allowed for longer retention of the learning content in their memory. According to the subjects, this was due to the fact that the students learnt, practised and used the learning materials, which made remembering what they learnt more effective. As subject 13 noted: "The stuff I learnt stays longer in memory because

I learn by practising and searching" [Student 13, I-2, 4-5].

With regard to the teaching resources, students found them to be motivating. The subjects found that using computers and the Internet was very useful for learning as it provided them with learning opportunities and control over learning that would not be possible otherwise. According to the students, these tools were exciting and enjoyable and enhanced their learning outcomes. Students mentioned that learning with computers was less difficult and much faster than the traditional textbook-based mode of learning. As one of them said: "Using the technology made it faster to learn and find the information we needed" [Student 5, I-2, 3-4]. Another student commented on how easy it was to edit the written work on the computers. Not only finding information was quicker with the aid of computers, but also looking up new words in the electronic dictionary was seen to be one of the advantages of the CALL course. More than one half of the subjects mentioned that the computers and the Internet supplied them with the resources to learn things beyond the regular curriculum. Another good feature about the CALL resources, according to the subjects, was that the grammar was embedded in the activities so the learners could see how the grammar forms were used in context. Subject 8 affirmed: "I learned not only grammar in theory but also how it is used in real situations" [Student 8, I-2, 12-13]. The subjects also stressed their satisfaction with the technical features of the CALL course, such as the flexibility and control it provided the learners to access the resources from anywhere and repeat the lessons at their own pace; the ability for the learners to have instant feedback on their tasks and assignments; and finally the design of the program, the exercises, the quizzes, and the embedded communication system between the instructor and the students. The subjects also believed that the collaborative projects enhanced their language skills. More than one third of the subjects confirmed that working in groups provided them with the opportunity to

practise within the same working group. A large number of the subjects also indicated that working in their projects required them to do extensive reading, which they believed had enhanced their reading skills and made them learn new vocabulary. Likewise the projects were also useful in enhancing their listening, writing, and spelling skills. "As to learning outcomes, I feel that I learnt more while doing the projects in reading, listening, translating new words, and speaking. It was difficult for me to speak in front of the others before this experience, which positively changed" [Student 6, I-2, 47-51].

Although the students generally felt very positive about the CALL course, there were some concerns regarding the design of the course. Most of the students' concerns were related to technical issues during the course, such as the difficulty that some of the students had at the beginning of the course enrolling in the EFA program. The subjects also suggested having a better communication system with more features than the one embedded in the EFA program, which could allow them, for instance, to send attachments and communicate with their classmates. Another complaint that a few students had about the course was the language difficulties they had while browsing some websites.

Despite these concerns, the interviews showed that all of the subjects where happy with the new CALL course in general and with their choice to study *English 101* using the CALL course instead of the traditional textbook-based course. From the analysis of the students' responses it is apparent that the CALL course had a positive influence on the students' attitudes toward learning English. The students reported a range of advantages they saw during the course that had an effect on both their attitudes and language learning outcomes. They highlighted the opportunities they were given during the course to experience and practise the target language in real-life situations and to learn effectively in an enjoyable learning environment. Some of them even suggested generalizing this teaching method in other schools and universities.

CONCLUSION

The study discussed in this chapter adapted constructivism as its broad theoretical framework and therefore it was an important objective to engage the learners into meaningful learning activities and encourage them to construct their new knowledge about the target language. In terms of the CALL course design the students were provided with learning activities that were aimed at promoting learner engagement in and out of the classroom. These activities included web-based resources that gave learners a substantial amount of control over the learning materials. Students were doing more exercises and games related to language learning that were not part of the lesson. Through the course website, (www.geocities.com/al3abbad), students were offered further opportunities for self-directed learning and by the end of the CALL course students realized that language learning did not require traditional textbooks and teachers for learning to take place. The study showed that student engagement and learning are highly correlated, as students' active role in the classroom led to significant language learning outcomes. The embedded tracking system in the EFA program as well as the computer laboratory's monitoring program (*Netsupport*) were valuable tools that assisted the researcher to observe how the students interacted with the course components and their engagement in learning. The EFA tracking system showed the progress of the students in watching the different lesson sections as well as how they dealt with the exercises and quizzes. The computer laboratory's monitoring program also provided the researcher with an insight into how the students were interacting with the course activities. Replaying the video clips, focusing on the pronunciation section more than the other skills, and repeating the grammar and comprehension exercises were

some of the learning strategies the students employed. Throughout the study it was apparent that the CALL course motivated the students to work harder and employ different learning strategies to enhance their performance.

Another valuable feature of the course was the collaborative learning activities where the learners got the opportunity to interact with one another in a communicative way, share their own ideas and views on a regular basis. As one of the students stated: "It was more enjoyable to work with my classmates as we helped each other and got more excited to do the job. It was also useful as we exchanged what each of us knew and learned from each other. [Student 19, I-P2, 25-27].

In the literature, collaborative learning is often associated with the constructivist approach that perceives collaboration as an essential principle in the learning process which involves collaborative projects, task-based and problem-based learning (see Land & Hannafin, 1996; Neo et al., 2007; Newby, Stepich, Lehman, & Russell, 2000; Yildirim, 2005). In this study the web-based collaborative projects gave the students a significant amount of control over what and how to learn, while the teacher's role was limited to offering assistance. In this respect, the collaborative projects were a practical implementation of self-directed learning while the opportunity to personalise the activities had a positive impact on the students and their engagement in the learning process (see Benigno, Bocconi, & Ott, 2007; Koper & Manderveld, 2004). As one of the students put it, "The projects were very enjoyable because we had the option to choose the topics that we would like to research" [Student 2, I-P2, 47-48].

Another objective of the CALL course design was to expose learners to the culture of the target language in order to facilitate effective communication. As Magnan (2007) pointed out, there are multiple goals for language learning including: the ability to communicate with peoples of other cultures, to understand and be sensitive to other cultural differences, and to analyse critically content and ideas from other nations (p. 249). The video clips in the EFA program, the selection of the web-based reading texts, and the websites the students browsed for their projects, helped them develop an understanding of the target culture. Even though the students in the treatment group did not have the chance to communicate with native speakers of the target language, they still developed an understanding of the cultural differences between their culture and the target culture and started to critically analyse their perceptions of the target culture. The authentic computer-based materials served as a practical vehicle to deliver the intercultural understanding to the learners in the treatment group. As the following quote from one of the students in the treatment group illustrates: "During the course I learned not only the language but more importantly about the people and the culture of the language we are learning. They have different ideologies and their way of thinking is very different from ours, they are more frank and direct" [Student 5, I-2, 16-19].

Finally, all of the students in the treatment group confirmed that their attitudes and motivation positively changed due to the CALL course. They credited this attitudinal shift to the web-based resources and materials, the collaborative activities, and the teaching methodology. Together, the constructive orientation of the course that put the student at the centre of the learning process in a communicative language teaching setting and the computer-based materials and resources used in the CALL course enhanced the students' motivation and attitude to learn English. However, the outcomes of the study were not limited only to the enhancement of the students' attitudes and language performance. It extended to include other advantages as well, such as presenting the students with literacies that are beyond the linguistic knowledge of the target language. The CALL course allowed the students to develop a range of multiliteracies as they encountered knowledge in multiple forms - in print, in images, in video, in combinations of forms in digital contexts - and

they were asked to represent their knowledge in an equally complex manner. Technology, according to Stevens (2005), has a considerable impact on how we formulate meaning and represent it in interaction with others, and how the teachers must prepare their students to cope with these developments. It was a necessity, therefore, to design a course that would help students develop multiliteracies that are consistent with the daily life discourse which is nowadays not limited to printed literacy but rather employs all types of multimedia literacies. As constructivism stresses, learners should understand how the resources of language, including image and digital rhetoric can be used interactively to construct different kinds of meanings. As one of the students noted: "I learned other skills in addition to the language like using the computer and searching the web" [Student 2, EQ-P2, 3-4]. As educators of the net-generation we should look at the tools embedded in the multimedia literacies, as Daley (2002) said, as approaches to learning that place production technology in the hands of the learner, which makes different forms of technology an instrumental part of the learning process.

REFERENCES

Abalhassan, K. M. I. (2002). *English as a foreign language instruction with CALL multimedia in Saudi Arabian private schools: A multi-case and multi-site study of CALL instruction.* Unpublished PhD, Indiana University of Pennsylvania.

Al-Ahaydib, M. E. A. (1986). *Teaching English as a foreign language in the intermediate and secondary schools of Saudi Arabia: A diagnostic study.* Unpublished PhD, University of Kansas.

Al-Juhani, S. O. (1991). *The effectiveness of computer-assisted instruction in teaching English as a foreign language in Saudi secondary schools.* Unpublished PhD, University of Denver.

Al-Kahtani, S. (2004). Deterrents to CALL in Saudi Arabia. *Essential Teacher, 1*(3), 26–30.

Al-Kahtani, S. A. (2001). *Computer-assisted language learning in EFL instruction at selected Saudi Arabian universities: Profiles of faculty.* Indiana University of Pennsylvania, PA.

Al-Kamookh, A. (1983). *A survey of the English language teachers' perceptions of the English language teaching methods in the intermediate and secondary schools of the eastern province in Saudi Arabia.* Kansas: University of Kansas.

Al-Mazroou, R. A. Y. (1988). *An evaluative study of teaching English as a foreign language in secondary schools in Saudi Arabia as perceived by Saudi EFL teachers.* Unpublished M.A, Southern Illinois University, Carbondale.

Barron, B. J. S. (1998). Doing with understanding: Lessons from research on problem and project-based learning. *Journal of the Learning Sciences, 7*(3/4), 1179–1187.

Batstone, R. (2002). Making sense of new language: A discourse perspective. *Language Awareness, 11*(1), 14–29. doi:10.1080/09658410208667043

Benigno, V., Bocconi, S., & Ott, M. (2007). Inclusive education: Helping teachers to choose ICT resources and to use them effectively. *eLearning Papers, 6*, 1-13.

Bulger, M., Mayer, R. E., & Almeroth, K. C. (2008). Measuring learner engagement in computer-equipped college classrooms. *Journal of Educational Multimedia and Hypermedia, 17*(2), 129–144.

Canale, M., & Swain, M. (1980). Theoretical bases of communicative approaches to second language teaching and testing. *Applied Linguistics, 1*(1), 1–47. doi:10.1093/applin/1.1.1

Celce-Murcia, M. (2007). Rethinking the role of communicative competence in language teaching. In E. A. N. Soler & M. P. S. Jordà (Eds.), *Intercultural language use and language learning.* Netherlands: Springer Netherlands.

Chen, Y. H. (2005). Computer mediated communication: The use of CMC to develop EFL learners' communicative competence. *Asian EFL Journal, 7*(1), 167–182.

Clarke, M. A. (2007). *Creativity in modern foreign languages teaching and learning.* Higher Education Academy Report.

Daley, E. (2002). *Multimedia literacy.* Retrieved 22/11/2008, from http://www.si.umich.edu/about-SI/news-detail.htm?NewsItemID=136

Easy Lingo. (2006). Instant translator English-Arabic. Aramedia.

Fosnot, C. (1996). *Constructivism: Theory, perspectives, and practice.* New York: Teachers College Press.

Fredricks, J. A., Blumenfeld, P. C., & Paris, A. H. (2004). School engagement: Potential of the concept, state of the evidence. *Review of Educational Research, 74*(1), 59–109. doi:10.3102/00346543074001059

Fulford, C. P. (2001). A model of cognitive speed. *International Journal of Instructional Media, 28*(1), 31–42.

Gagnon, G., & Collay, M. (2001). *Constructivist learning design.* Retrieved 06/02/2006, from http://www.prainbow.com/cld/cldp.html

Gitsaki, C., & Taylor, R. P. (2000). *Internet English: WWW-based communication activities.* Oxford: Oxford University Press.

Green, J. M. (1993). Student attitudes toward communicative and non-communicative activities: Do enjoyment and effectiveness go together? *Modern Language Journal, 77*(1), 1–10. doi:10.2307/329552

Herrington, J., Reeves, T. C., Oliver, R., & Woo, Y. (2004). Designing authentic activities in web-based courses. *Journal of Computing in Higher Education, 16*(1), 3–29. doi:10.1007/BF02960280

Hunter, C. S. J., & Harman, D. (1985). *Adult illiteracy in the United States.* New York, NY: McGraw Hill.

Koper, R., & Manderveld, J. (2004). Educational modelling language: Modelling reusable, interoperable, rich and personalised units of learning. *British Journal of Educational Technology, 35*(5), 537–551. doi:10.1111/j.0007-1013.2004.00412.x

Land, S. M., & Hannafin, M. J. (1996). *Student-centred learning environments: Foundations, assumptions and implications.* Paper presented at the National Convention of the Association for Educational Communications and Technology, Indianapolis: IN.

Lindstrom, R. (1994). *The Business Week guide to multimedia presentations: Create dynamic presentations that inspire.* New York: McGraw-Hill.

Littleton, K., & Hakkinen, P. (1999). Learning together: Understanding the process of computer-based collaborative learning. In P. Dillenbourg (Ed.), *Collaborative-learning: Cognitive and computational approaches* (pp. 1-19). Oxford: Elsevier.

Magnan, S. S. (2007). Reconsidering communicative language teaching for national goals. *Modern Language Journal, 91*(2), 249–252. doi:10.1111/j.1540-4781.2007.00543_3.x

Mayer, R. E., & Moreno, R. (2003). Nine ways to reduce cognitive load in multimedia learning. *Educational Psychologist, 38*(1), 42–52. doi:10.1207/S15326985EP3801_6

Meunier, L. E. (1994). Computer-assisted language instruction in cooperative learning. *Applied Language Learning, 5*(2), 31–56.

Neo, M., Neo, T. K., & Xiao-Lian, G. T. (2007). A constructivist approach to learning an interactive multimedia course: Malaysian students' perspectives. *Australasian Journal of Educational Technology, 23*(4), 470–489.

Newby, T. J., Stepich, D. A., Lehman, J. D., & Russell, J. D. (2000). *Instructional technology for teaching and learning: Designing instruction, integrating computers, and using media* (2nd ed.). New Jersey: Merrill/Prentice Hall.

Newhouse, P. (2001). A follow-up study of students using portable computers at a secondary school. *British Journal of Educational Technology, 32*(2), 209–219. doi:10.1111/1467-8535.00191

O'Neil, R., Kingsbury, R., & Yeadon, T. (1978). *American Kernel Lessons.* White Plains, N.Y: Longman.

Pedroza, H. A. (2003). *English for All (EFA).* Los Angeles: Sacramento County Office of Education and the Division of Adult Career Education (DACE).

Pica, T., & Doughty, C. (1985). Input and interaction in the communicative language classroom: A comparison of teacher-fronted and group activities. In S. M. Gass & C. Madden, (Eds.), *Input in Second Language Acquisition.* Rowley, MA: Newbury House.

Reagan, T. (1999). Constructivist epistemology and second/foreign language pedagogy. *Foreign Language Annals, 32*(4), 413–425. doi:10.1111/j.1944-9720.1999.tb00872.x

Roberts, T. S. (2005). *Computer-supported collaborative learning in higher education.* Hershey, PA: Idea Group Pub.

Rust, C., Price, M., & O'Donovan, B. (2003). Improving students' learning by developing their understanding of assessment criteria and processes. *Assessment & Evaluation in Higher Education, 28*(2), 147–164. doi:10.1080/02602930301671

Savignon, S. J. (1991). Communicative language teaching. *TESOL Quarterly, 25*(2), 261–277. doi:10.2307/3587463

Schcolnik, M., Kol, S., & Abarbanel, J. (2006). Constructivism in theory and in practice. *English Teaching Forum, 4,* 12–20.

Seliger, H. W. (1983). Learner interaction in the classroom and its effect on language acquisition. In H. W. Seliger & M. H. Long, (Eds.), *Classroom oriented research in second language acquisition* (pp. xi, 305 p). Rowley, MA: Newbury House.

Sercue, L. (2004). Intercultural communicative competence in foreign language education: Integrating theory and practice. In O. St.John, K. V. Esch, & E. Schalkwijk (Eds.), *New insights into foreign language learning and teaching.* Frankfurt: Peter Lang.

Stevens, V. (2005). Multiliteracies for collaborative learning environments. *TESL-EJ, 9*(2).

Thorne, S. L. (2006). Pedagogical and praxiological lessons from Internet-mediated intercultural foreign language education research. In J. A. Belz & S. L. Thorne (Eds.), *Internet-mediated intercultural foreign language education.* Boston, MA: Thomson Heinle.

Wang, M., & Kang, M. (2005). Cybergogy for engaged learning: A framework for creating learner engagement through information and communication technology. In M. S. Khine (Ed.), *Engaged learning with emerging technologies.* Amsterdam: Springer Netherlands.

Yildirim, Z. (2005). Hypermedia as a cognitive tool: Student teachers' experiences in learning by doing. *Educational Technology & Society, 8*(2), 107–118.

Zaid, M. A. (1993). *Comprehensive analysis of the current system of teaching English as a foreign language in the Saudi Arabian intermediate schools.* Unpublished Ph.D., University of Colorado at Boulder, Boulder.

Zheng, R., & Zhou, B. (2006). Recency effect on problem solving in interactive multimedia learning. *Educational Technology & Society, 9*(2), 107–118.

KEY TERMS AND DEFINITIONS

Second/Foreign Language Teaching: The teaching of a language to non-native speakers.

Computer-Assisted Language Learning (CALL): Using computer-based resources for the teaching and learning of a second/foreign language.

Constructivism: A theory of learning.

Active Learner: The basic principle of constructivism that stipulates that the learner is active in the classroom and constructs his/her own knowledge.

Course Design: Designing a course based on a theoretical framework and pedagogical principles.

Chapter 7
ICT in Malay Language Learning:
Lessons Learned from Two Case Studies

Abduyah Ya'akub
The University of Queensland, Australia

Christina Gitsaki
The University of Queensland, Australia

Eileen Honan
The University of Queensland, Australia

ABSTRACT

With digital communications and technological media becoming an integral part of the new professional workplace and everyday lives of the younger generation (especially in post-industrial societies), comes the clarion call for educators to develop a more complex understanding of language and literacy and how to go about designing pedagogies that equip students with 21st Century skills. This chapter presents two case studies that examine the complex interaction of teachers, students, writing pedagogies, language curriculum and Information and Communication Technologies (ICT). The study explored students' experiences of using ICT in second language writing and the impact of ICT on writing pedagogy and the curriculum, producing in-depth descriptions and interpretations to answer a set of focused research questions.

INTRODUCTION

The use of ICT for education is not just about technologies. It is important to think of ICT as practice – as ways of doing things – albeit by adopting a particular and sophisticated sense of practice that involves communities of learners. What schools teach and how they should respond to change and changing circumstances can be represented as a gap that exists between what key agents in the larger cultural context (e.g., the ministry and policymakers) and key agents concerned with classroom curriculum (e.g., teachers and students) see as important in social, cultural and historical terms (Lankshear & Knobel, 2003). This gap can largely be defined by reference to practices in, approaches to and understandings of technologies and literacy.

DOI: 10.4018/978-1-60566-842-0.ch007

The setting for this study is Singapore. Singapore has a unique linguistic background because of its multi-racial society. While all classes are taught in English, it is compulsory for all students to learn a second language in Singaporean schools. Knowing a second language enables Singaporeans to preserve their values and also gives them an identity as an Asian society (Shepherd, 2005). This second language for most students may be the language spoken at home (e.g., students of Malay cultural heritage choosing to study Malay as a second language at school); while for others it may be a foreign language (e.g., students of Chinese or Tamil descent choosing to learn Malay at school). Students are required to learn a second language from Primary 1 (Year 2). The time allocated in the curriculum is 3.45 hours per week or six to seven periods of 30 to 45 minutes duration. During these language classes students learn the four language skills of listening, speaking, reading and writing (MOE, 2004).

In the latest Malay Language Curriculum Review conducted in 2005, it was noted that there was a shift in home language use. In the Malay community, the proportion of Primary One students (aged 6 to 7) who use English as their main language at home increased from 17% in 1996 to 28% in 2005. This means that Malay language teachers now face the challenge of further developing innovative and creative teaching methods to stimulate learners, given that more parents and students appear to perceive that learning English is vital whereas the Malay language is considered less important. Thus, the use of ICT in Malay language classrooms is seen as a necessary method in order to empower learners through customised technology-enhanced teaching and learning (MOE, 2005).

BACKGROUND

Planning for ICT in education in Singapore provides a blueprint for the use of ICT in schools and access to an ICT-enriched school environment for teaching and learning for every student. The first ICT Masterplan (1997-2002) or MP1 laid the foundation for integrating ICT into education. The mission of MP1 was to harness ICT for instructional purposes and to provide directions to schools for integrating up-to-date technologies into the educational process. The following actions were carried out to achieve the MP1 objectives:

- Training school teachers in the use of technology for classroom teaching that could enhance learning;
- Providing hardware and software to schools;
- Supporting schools in the ICT implementation;
- Initiating special projects to engage teachers and students in the continual and active exploitation of ICT use; and
- Collaborating with the ICT industry.

The Ministry of Education (MOE) launched the second Masterplan (MP2) for ICT in Education in 2002. This was to ensure that schools continued to integrate ICT into their curriculum so as to develop a culture of thinking, lifelong learning and social responsibility (MOE, 2002). To meet these goals, four key dimensions of the ICT Masterplan were identified: curriculum and assessment; learning resources; teacher development; and physical and technological infrastructure. The Masterplans clearly spelt out how ICT was to be used and integrated into the curriculum as a strategy to meet the challenges of the future and envisaged that by 2002 students would spend 30% of curriculum time using ICT (MOE, 2002).

By 2004 there were changes in the teaching and learning approaches adopted by schools. Evidence of these changes was reflected on school websites where teachers uploaded and shared their teaching resources using ICT with other teachers in the same zonal areas (MOE, 2004). Additionally, an increasing number of students uploaded their ICT projects onto school websites to showcase learning in Mathematics and Science (MOE, 2004). More recently and in line with MP2, *FutureSchools@Singapore* was initiated in 2007. This project focuses on innovative teaching approaches that leverage ICT and novel school infrastructure designs to bring about greater student engagement.

THE MALAY LANGUAGE CURRICULUM

In Singapore, the Malay Language (ML) Curriculum aims to help students become independent lifelong learners, creative thinkers and problem solvers who can communicate effectively in Malay Language. According to the curriculum (MOE, 2003), to achieve this, students need to read widely, learn how to analyse and evaluate language and the media, and respond creatively to issues concerning writing problems and new technology. The aims of the writing pedagogy are such that students will be able to read, view and write with understanding, accuracy and critical appreciation, using a wide range of fiction and non-fiction texts from print, non-print and electronic sources.

The teaching and learning of writing using the process writing model is reflected in the ML syllabus. For example, the principles of process orientation, learner-centredness, and contextualisation form part of the pedagogical framework used in the syllabus. The process orientation is illustrated through the use of the stages of writing, planning, modelling, drafting, editing, and revising, being used in the syllabus as the basis for conducting lessons in writing classrooms. The learner-centeredness principle is promoted through the encouragement of minimal teacher-led instruction in the teaching of writing, with teachers bearing in mind that students are accountable for their own learning of writing. With regard to the principle of contextualisation, teachers are expected to help students unfold the multi-layered contextualisation aspects of writing through text samples. Students learn about the nature and purpose of a text. Also consistent with the process writing model is the indication in the Malay Language curriculum that writing is not a one-off activity and that reviewing and editing students' own writing is an activity that needs to be done consistently throughout the writing process.

Given the emphasis in the ML curriculum on the three principles of process orientation, learner-centeredness and contextualisation, it was expected that these would be observed in operation in the ML writing classrooms. In addition, the use of ICT is widespread in Singapore schools and the ML curriculum emphasises that teachers should use ICT in their teaching and learning, therefore the study also investigated the influence of ICT on the use of these principles.

THE STUDY

The present study focused on ICT, Malay Language Curriculum and pedagogy. It aimed to explore how teachers integrated ICT as integral or mediated tools to accomplish instructional objectives in the classrooms. From a theoretical perspective, this study is guided by a transformative view of literacy as it converges with ICT and curriculum in the socio-cultural context of the classrooms (Lim & Chai, 2007a; 2007b). Kapitze and Bruce (2006) identify four ways in which literacy and technology might be associated: technology for literacy, literacy for technology, literacy as technology; and technology as literacy. This study is situated within the field of technology for literacy and, in particular, examines how various ICTs are applied to writing pedagogy.

Two schools were selected for the case studies. A Malay language teacher and students in each school were invited to participate in the study. Data were collected using classroom observations (five lessons from each classroom on one unit of work), student questionnaires and reflective journals, and teacher and student interviews (10 students from each class and their teacher).

Case Study 1

School A is an elite private girls' secondary school located in an inner-city area of Singapore and it is well-resourced and famous for its academic and sports excellence. The school has two computer labs and a special classroom where students attend the Malay Language lessons unless otherwise requested by the teachers, who may also choose to conduct lessons in the computer lab. Mrs Aminah, the Malay Language teacher who participated in the study, taught two years of primary school before transferring to this secondary school where she has taught for the past 8 years. The students involved in this study are in Secondary 3 (Year 10). There are 25 girls in this class; 21 Malay, 2 Chinese and 2 Indian. The students are high achievers, task-oriented and motivated to excel academically. The following section discusses the observations of writing lessons in Classroom A.

Analysis of Lessons and Discussions

Table 1 summarises the lesson structure of a unit of work in Mrs Aminah's writing classroom and indicates how different stages in the process writing model, namely planning, modelling, drafting, editing and publishing are aligned in each lesson. Five lessons of Mrs Aminah's unit of work on speech writing were observed. Only the first lesson was conducted in the special Malay Language classroom with the remainder of the lessons conducted in the computer lab.

In Lesson 1, Mrs Aminah gave an overview of the new unit of work. Students were told to imagine themselves to be a famous person who is invited to give a speech to commemorate the opening of a school. In the speech, they were to highlight the leadership qualities of the famous person that they

have chosen to be, with the theme for the speech being *Noble Leadership*. Mrs Aminah wrote some English website addresses about famous people on the board that the students could browse for homework. For homework, students were required to search the Internet for samples of speeches given by locally and internationally famous people and bring them for the next lesson. To illustrate this point, Mrs Aminah mentioned the Honourable Mr Yusof Ishak, the first President of Singapore, while Mahatma Gandhi was offered as an example of an internationally- renowned figure.

Lesson 1 reflects a well-planned flow of activities, with evident teacher preparation. Through the writer approach, Mrs Aminah was able to provide her students with clear goals and a manageable writing task as recommended by scholars (Noor, 2001; Dornan, Rosea, & Wilson, 2003). Students were aware of the teacher's expectations and what was expected of them in the next few lessons. The teacher checked her students' attentiveness by asking questions of two students about the topic and the venue for the next lesson. Mrs Aminah's interaction with her students suggests that she believes that a trusting and comfortable relationship between herself and her students allows her to guide her students successfully to understand expectations and motivates them to write better.

The student questionnaires showed that 100% of the students agree that Mrs Aminah lessons are always clearly and carefully planned. 92% of the students indicated that they knew what the task was about and 96% agreed that their Malay Language class is always well organised. From the interview with Mrs Aminah, it became apparent that she assumes that all her students were equipped with research skills. However, in essence, though she wanted students to gather information at the planning stage of the writing process, her scaffolding in this introductory lesson was lacking. She could have added more details in scaffolding the lesson to help students generate and organize ideas in this planning stage of the process writing model. Since the students were new to the use of

Table 1. Summary of the unit of work in Classroom A and the process writing model

Lesson	Classroom A	Process Writing Model
1 (30 mins)	*Overview of Unit* • Teacher introduced students to topic and task. • Writing task: Speech writing (A speech of a famous person to commemorate the opening of a school.) • Teacher suggested popular website addresses of famous persons to students. • Homework: - Students choose a famous person that they imagine themselves to be. - Students search for the leadership qualities and characteristics of the chosen famous person. • ICT tools: Not used in this lesson.	
2 (60 mins)	*PowerPoint slide presentation* • Teacher asked students to download PowerPoint from the school portal. • Teacher provided a genre model of a speech • ICT tools: PowerPoint, School portal.	
3 (60 mins)	*Searching and Writing draft one* • Students searched for information from the Internet. • In pairs, students discussed the materials and sources to help them in planning. • Students saved their draft and some emailed text to their own email addresses. • Homework: Students completed first draft. • ICT tools: PowerPoint, School portal, The Internet, Word Processor.	
4 (60 mins)	*Peer Editing* • Teacher taught students how to use the Track Changes tool available from the word processor to insert comments. • Teacher gave students a checklist to use for peer editing. • ICT tools: Word Processor.	
5 (30 mins)	*Revising and Writing draft two* • Students to finish editing their friends' work. • Students to discuss their writing with the checker. • Teacher asked the students to refer to her if there are any issues concerning the language or context of speech writing should there be any disagreements between the writers and the checker. • Students to submit the corrected speech writing text next lesson. • Homework: Students reviewed and completed final draft. • ICT tools: Word Processor.	

the Internet to search for information in Malay, in this lesson she could have allocated some time to demonstrating how to use a range of tools available from the Internet to help students perform effective searches as recommended by some scholars (Holdich & Chung, 2003; Lordusamy, Hu, & Wong, 2001; Sutherland, Armstrong, Facer, & Fulong, 2004). In the reflective journals, some students suggested that Mrs Aminah should have taught them how to narrow their search when using the search engines. Some literacy scholars (Jones, Garralda, Li, & Lock, 2006; Lockard & Pegrum, 2006; Loretta, 2002; Vanithamani, 2005) propose teaching students to use key words, bookmarking

to find relevant materials and information from the Internet and creating and transforming the text in the context of their writing task. This would definitely help to unfold the steps of conducting an effective search for relevant resources before students could progress further in their writing process. It was observed in the following lessons that many students encountered difficulty in sourcing relevant materials for the topic and this could be attributed to a lack of scaffolding in lesson 1.

Lesson 2 was a presentation of the PowerPoint slides, conducted in the computer lab. Mrs Aminah wrote specific instructions on the board in Malay.

The translation of these instructions into English is as follows:

- Browse the school website.
- Download the PowerPoint slides from the portal.
- Read the slides.
- At the end of the slides, answer the 6 questions without referring to the previous slides.
- Write your answers on a piece of paper and I will collect the answer sheet.
- Wait for my further instructions.

The PowerPoint slides included some notes on the characteristics of speech writing and a model speech. The students were given about 10 minutes to read through the slides and answer the questions. Students worked individually to download the PowerPoint slides file, however, the computers were slow. While the students downloaded the slides, Mrs Aminah invited students to share any information they had gathered from the Internet about famous people (the homework she assigned in the previous lesson). Less than half of the total number of students managed to gather some information about the topic. The majority of the students told Mrs Aminah that they found it difficult to find good websites that provided relevant and appropriate information about the famous person they had chosen. Mrs Aminah gave feedback that some of the materials were irrelevant and inappropriate to use in speech writing. For instance, one of her students mentioned a famous person's personal food preference. There were a few students who found tips on how to write an effective speech instead of gathering information regarding the famous person. Mrs Aminah did not explore these students' findings further. While the students were reading the slides, Mrs Aminah walked around checking on her students and stopped to answer questions from two of them. In the final slide, students were required to answer some comprehension questions about

how to construct a speech and were permitted to discuss the answers with their peers sitting next to them. However, they were not allowed to scroll back to the previous slides viewed. Some students who downloaded their files quickly and had read answered the questions from the slides used the excess time available to search for additional information regarding models of good speeches.

Mrs Aminah's use of PowerPoint slides in Lesson 2 seemed to provide a model of the genre, as required at the planning stage of the process writing model. She reiterated the importance of using standard Malay Language in speech writing and reminded her students to avoid colloquial terms to achieve the purpose of writing. However, the students' engagement with the model was limited. Mrs Aminah assumed that through reading the model text, her students would gather knowledge about the language and structure. However, there was no elaboration given on the structure, language features or vocabulary that was required to suit the purpose, context and target audience in a speech. Mrs Aminah could have highlighted the syntax and vocabulary that were particular to the historical period and created scripts that used period language. Students were seen merely to read the genre without any follow up activities or discussion to stimulate their thoughts on how the text was structured, the impact that specific language has and the publication and presentation aspects of the speech to a real audience. It could be expected that more time was invested in deeply immersing students in the writing process of the modelled genre given that it was available and easily accessible by the students. For instance, when a few students found websites on tips for writing effective speeches and models of good speeches, Mrs Aminah could have directed the whole class to these particular websites. However, she ignored the students' findings and, instead, continued to focus on the content rather than the structure of the genre.

Kinchin and Alias (2005) argue that the use of PowerPoint to scaffold lessons is more effective if teachers provide a concept map in an early slide to show students the different stages of the writing process. This could facilitate an effective dialogue between the teacher and the students as the students could visualise and understand the writing process (Belle & Soetaert, 2001). Instead, Mrs Aminah provided the model but not an explanation of the structure and key to writing good speeches. She could have elaborated further by showing some interactive slides demonstrating how the text writer weaves the speech by giving examples of the use of meaningful word combinations (Atkinson, C., 2005), specific terms and conjunctions to produce a continuous coherent text, as well as the use of quotations to influence the target audience (Adams, T., 2006). Power-Point is able to stimulate students' thinking and promote an active classroom culture (Adams, C., 2007) and can be used as a tool to further enhance and extend learning. Also, as one of her students wrote in the student' reflection journal, Mrs Aminah could have inserted a video clip of a famous person giving a speech as this would definitely have helped students to listen to and understand the lexicon and appropriate terms used.

Lesson 3 involved searching for information and writing a first draft. It was a 60-minute lesson and again the lesson was conducted in the computer lab. Mrs Aminah wrote instructions on the white board. While the teacher went through the step-by-step instructions, a few students were seen opening the PowerPoint slides about speech writing from the school portal. First, students were allotted 10 minutes of pair-discussion on the famous person that they had chosen and those leadership qualities and charismatic characteristics that warranted them being seen as remarkable figures. Second, students were given 30 minutes to type their first draft using *MS Word* and were told to save their work on their USB memory sticks. Third, students were asked to bring their completed draft to the next lesson. Students who had sufficient materials and sources started to write their draft after discussing with a peer. Mrs Aminah reminded the

students to contextualise their speech according to the time period of the life of the prominent person. The students made use of the information they had gathered from the Internet at home and brought these additional notes to school as hard copies. Some students were given permission to continue their search for a further 10 minutes as they found the material they had gathered earlier was insufficient. Others wrote additional notes while in discussion with their peers.

During this lesson, some students were observed asking Mrs Aminah questions about the information they had gathered. One of the Chinese students showed Mrs Aminah some speech writing models in English available online that she had discovered. Mrs Aminah did not comment on the models. Another Chinese girl asked the teacher for some feedback on her introductory paragraph and looked satisfied after Mrs Aminah helped her with her writing problem. Mrs Aminah checked her students' progress by moving around the classroom. Another Malay student asked her about a few statements within a speech made by another famous person and she clarified that in this particular case it was actually a quote from another prominent person integrated into the speech. Those students who had forgotten to bring their USB stick were told to save their writing on the hard disk and e-mail their work to their e-mail address. By doing this, the students would be able to continue writing their draft as homework if they were not able to finish it in class. Almost at the end of the lesson, one student was observed moving to another computer after writing about half of her composition because she was unable to save her work and e-mail her writing due to technical problems. She looked frustrated. Mrs Aminah asked for those who had finished writing their drafts, as she wanted to scan their writing and see that they had answered the questions correctly. Two students had finished writing their draft ahead of the others and Mrs Aminah was seen giving them samples of printed speech text in Malay that she had prepared earlier. Mrs Aminah then told all the students that they would be peer editing during the next lesson. Mrs Aminah assured the students that a checklist would be provided to help them review their friend's draft. Before the bell rang, students were reminded again to bring the USB stick containing the completed draft and meet her at the computer lab for the next lesson.

In Lesson 3, Mrs Aminah taught her students that writing is a nonlinear, recursive and interactive process in which they needed to move back and forth from accumulating information and resources to writing their speeches. For instance, she provided ample opportunities for students to develop their thoughts and ideas before writing by referring to the materials they have gathered, discussing with a peer and then drafting the speech. Mrs Aminah was prompt in answering her students' queries. She encouraged students' understanding about the topic by providing specific instructions so that her students knew what was expected of them. However, it wasn't clear why Mrs Aminah distributed speech writing samples to the students who had already finished their drafts, rather than distributing them in Lesson 1. The students would then have been able to study and understand the structure, forms and the language used so that they could apply the knowledge they had then acquired to assist them in writing the draft. Through students' prewriting discussion, Mrs Aminah encouraged peer interaction as proposed by Fearn & Farnan (2001) to help students engage with the writing task. Mrs Aminah helped students contextualise the writing according to the time period of the famous person they have chosen. However, she could have asked those students who had chosen the same famous person to work in pairs for the first draft. Bruton (2005) recommends that it is more effective in the drafting phase for teachers to include collaborative pair writing rather than limit peer interaction to pair-oral interaction and individual drafting. Wesche and Skehan (2002) and Ellis (2003) argue that pair-collaborative writing clearly helps students to write independently at a later stage.

Lesson 4 was based on peer editing and was also a 60-minute lesson conducted in a computer lab. Mrs Aminah wrote specific instructions on the board and reminded students to read these instructions whenever they were in doubt. She anticipated that there would be students coming late for class, but given the whiteboard instructions they would still be able to follow her lesson outline. She emphasized that she would not repeat the instructions given at the beginning of the lesson. First, Mrs Aminah asked students to open their draft word document file from the USB memory stick. All of the students were told to pay attention as she demonstrated how to use the Track Changes tool available in the word processing software. She also showed the students how to insert comments when checking their friend's work. These demonstrations were projected on a wide screen. Then she asked her students to type their name at the end of the text after they have checked and edited their friend's writing. Almost all students were on task and engaged with the activities as instructed, except for two students who had forgotten to bring their drafts and who were asked to rewrite the speech within 30 minutes. Mrs Aminah appeared to be very disappointed with these two girls. Before the rest of the students began their peer editing session, Mrs Aminah gave students the prepared checklist. The students were not taught explicitly how to use the checklist as it was quite detailed, self-explanatory and in accordance with the Malay Language Curriculum assessment guidelines. Some students had difficulty inserting their comments and asked the teacher for help, while others who were unsure about aspects of their friend's writing asked Mrs Aminah how to correct grammatical errors. Mrs Aminah reminded students to indicate their names as the editors and then save the edited text with a different filename. At the end of the lesson, those students who experienced difficulty saving their work to their USB memory stick, were instructed to e-mail the edited text to their own e-mail addresses.

Chandler (2003) argues that it is important for teachers to highlight whether the students had written an attractive introduction which would invite audience attention when giving feedback in order to improve their fluency. This aspect was not observable in Mrs Aminah's class. She did not discuss whether the ideas in the speech writing were organized so that the overall content of the speech was easily understood. While checking, the student writers did not focus on whether their peers concluded their speech creatively by inserting popular quotations to create an impact. It was expected that some students and Mrs Aminah would suggest ideas during this session that would benefit other students and be incorporated into their writing. Had Mrs Aminah gone through this process with her students, the peer editing session could have been proactive with students fully engaged, thus enriching their learning experiences. Instead, Mrs Aminah's editing checklist and feedback focused on mistakes in grammar, spelling and punctuation. Mrs Aminah could have showed her students how certain words could be used to demand attention from the audience to suit the purpose of the speech. An emphasis on structure and adherence to genre were lacking in this lesson. As Warschauer and Ware (2006) argue, while feedback regarding grammar and spelling is necessary, the real learning occurs when the reviewer asks thought-provoking questions about how the material is presented. Another issue was that Mrs Aminah did not fully exploit the capabilities of the word processing software. For instance, Perry and Smithmier (2005) suggest that teachers use the 'verbal comments' choice available on the Insert menu, which then enables students to vocalise their comments into an audio file and save their ideas as part of the word processed file.

Lesson 5 was a 30-minute revision. Students were told to revise their first draft according to the comments and suggestions made by their peers and to focus on grammatical errors and spelling. Mrs Aminah highlighted to her students that the major weakness in their writing was the frequent use of English words. She reminded her students that marks would be taken away if they used English instead of Malay in their writing. The majority of the students used their time productively and were engaged with their writing task. Students revised and wrote the second draft and Mrs Aminah asked them to check with her whenever they were in doubt about their peers' comments. They could not finish their work in time and were told to finish the second draft at home and save their writing under a different filename. In addition, Mrs Aminah emphasised the importance of referencing in their final draft.

In this lesson, Mrs Aminah took her students through a process of reading and analysing reader comments and evaluations. The students responded to the comments and feedback expressed by the peer editor. During the teacher interview, Mrs Aminah explained that the students revised and attempted to produce a good piece of writing by factoring in the comments offered by their peers. Three students indicated during the interviews that responding to peer writing was one of the most challenging aspects of the writing process. Two students wrote in the journals that reading comments from their peers filled them with anxiety because they felt that some of the comments not only did not help, they added to their confusion. Nevertheless, by and large, the majority of the students wrote in their journals that the feedback they received from their peers and their teacher helped them in their writing. These responses coincide with research (Ferris, 2004, 2007; Turbill, 2003; Yi, 2007) which demonstrates that audience feedback is valued highly.

Case Study 1 - Summary of the Unit of Work

Generally, the five lessons that were observed and analysed indicate that although Mrs Aminah shows great interest in and motivation to teach Malay Language writing with ICT, in practice, the use of ICT in this classroom was relatively low and focused on a narrow range of applications, with Word Processing, PowerPoint, the Internet and e-mail all being underutilised. This echoes findings from research into ICT and second language writing that ICT as a tool to promote learning is not generally well embedded in teachers' practice (Cox & Abbot, 2004; Warschauer & Ware, 2006; Zhao & Cziko, 2001) and that "ICT in the classroom is used in an ineffective way and has proven difficult to integrate within traditional curriculum settings" (Belle & Soetaert, 2001, p. 38). In the Malay Language classroom context of School A, the evidence suggests a similar picture. Mrs Aminah recognises a range of benefits for the students and for her in using ICT, but more often than not failed (within the parameters of this study) to integrate ICT meaningfully into the teaching and learning of Malay Language writing.

Mrs Aminah's failure to use ICT effectively in the observed lessons could be due to three factors: lack of resources and support; lack of knowledge and skills; and, pedagogical difficulties in integrating ICT into instruction. In terms of the lack of resources and support, Mrs Aminah could have uploaded available software such as English to Malay translation and spelling and grammar check software into the school computer's word processor programme to help students with their writing. However, according to Mrs Aminah, the technical assistants in her school were always busy and often unavailable to help her configure software packages to support her computer-mediated lessons. Cuban (2004) as well as Lim (2004) and Lordusamy et al., (2001) argue that the ineffective use of technology is often caused by the lack of an environment that is conducive to technological integration. The second factor that impacts on this teacher's ability to use ICT effectively is a lack of knowledge and skills to manipulate resources available from the Internet in order to scaffold the lessons effectively. In lesson 2, for instance, Mrs Aminah could have inserted video files in the PowerPoint slides to help students view speeches given by prominent

leaders to real audiences. Tardy (2005) argues that extending the use of PowerPoint to include the verbal and visual modes of expression allows for a richer understanding of a genre and can help multilingual writers to produce their texts. In that way, there is a clear sense of purpose in using PowerPoint in the classroom. Mrs Aminah did not have the overall skills to integrate ICT fully into her lesson for scaffolding and, thus, PowerPoint used in this classroom was limited in purpose. In this instance, it was used only to provide notes about speech writing - a similar process to that which occurs in a traditional classroom where the teacher gives students a printed handout. The third factor could be categorized as pedagogical difficulties integrating ICT into instruction. Mrs Aminah could have responded instantly when her students suggested websites that contained tips for writing effective speeches and good models of speeches as she has this facility in the computer lab. However, she did not take advantage of the opportunities initiated by her motivated students to do a follow up and further explore the websites and share them with other students in the classroom. Instead, she continued to focus on gathering information about famous people. She disregarded the actual needs of her students who required samples of good speeches even though she claimed that she was using the writing process modelling the genre. As well, she did not fully utilise the available tools. For instance, she used e-mail only as a student-to-student file forwarding device, but could have used this tool to enable her collect and give feedback to students' essays more efficiently and without the concern of inadvertently missing a student.

The underutilisation of ICT in Mrs Aminah's class may not have happened if she believed that she had the capability to use the available tools and that these tools could help her perform her teaching task efficiently. She did not make use of ICT to give a meaningful and effective task to her students, such as guiding them to create a multimodal text (Kress, 2003; Shetzer & Warschauer, 2000). Instead, the students wrote the same plain text normally produced by students in a traditional classroom. The students did not make use of ICT tools to publish and present their prepared speeches to wider audiences by, for example, uploading those written and oral speeches to the school website so that other students in the school could view their work. This could have added a sense of accomplishment and motivated students as their speech writing task would have been more meaningful.

Case Study 2

School B is a co-educational secondary school located on the outskirts of Singapore. The class that participated in the study comprised of two girls and eight boys (eight Malay, one Chinese and one Indian) in Secondary 3 (Year 10). They are of average ability but motivated to learn and explore new challenges. The school believes in curriculum innovation and it is strongly oriented towards showcasing teachers' use of ICT in the classroom. The school has three computer labs. However, the resources and support are markedly inconsistent with the school's mission and aspirations to integrate ICT into the curriculum. One of the computer labs is rarely used as it has no Internet access and, in addition, most of the computers are old and faulty. Only one of the three computer labs in the school is accessible. Mr Muhammad, the teacher in this study, commented that access to facilities was opportunistic and problematic in the school, although the school leaders encouraged teachers to use computers in their teaching. As in School A, School B also has a special Malay Language room with lessons sometimes conducted in the school computer lab. Mr Muhammad is very passionate about computers and believes the use of ICT in Malay Language classroom may improve students' learning. He is an enthusiastic, young teacher and has been teaching Malay Language in the school for three years and is also actively involved in conducting free workshops for the Teachers' Network at the Ministry of Education training centre. In these workshops, Mr Muhammad shares his knowledge on how to use computers to help Malay Language teachers in their day-to-day classroom teaching.

Analysis of Lessons and Discussions

Table 2 provides a summary of the lesson structure of a unit of work on recycled water in Mr Muhammad's writing classroom and shows how each lesson aligns with the different stages in the process writing model. Note that Mr Muhammad focuses on the planning stage, but not on other stages of the process writing model such as modelling, drafting, reviewing and revising. Mr Muhammad indicated during the interview that the argumentative topic on recycled water was chosen because at that time it was a heated topic of discussion in Singapore.

In Lesson 1 which was of 30 minutes' duration, Mr Muhammad provided the students with the unit overview. He distributed the worksheet with the following guided questions to be discussed in pairs.

- Why do we need to conserve water?
- How can we conserve water?
- How can you as students help to conserve water?
- What are some cost-effective methods for sewerage treatment?
- List the advantages or disadvantages of using recycled water.

There was no discussion about writing with the students. At the end of the lesson, students were reminded to complete the worksheet for homework and bring it to the next lesson that would be conducted in the computer lab.

In this lesson, Mr Muhammad familiarised students with the planning stage of the process writing model. The use of the worksheet was

Table 2. Summary of the unit of work in Classroom B and the process writing model

Lesson	Classroom B	Process Writing Model
1 (30 mins)	*Overview of Unit* • Worksheet was distributed. • Writing Task: Argumentative writing (Recycled water – the way of the future?) • Homework: Complete worksheet. • ICT tools: No ICT tools were used in this lesson.	
2 (30 mins)	*Searching for Information* • Teacher shared reliable and good local websites. • Students searched and retrieved information from the Internet. • ICT tools: Internet.	
3 (60 mins)	*Blogging* • Students used weblog. • Homework: Students made postings on the blogs. • ICT tools: Internet, Weblog.	
4 (60 mins)	*Debating* • Student debate on topic of recycling water. • ICT tools: No ICT tools were used.	
5 (30 mins)	*Writing Essay* • Students write essay using word processor. • Homework: Finish essay and email the teacher. • ICT tools: Word Processor and Email.	

deemed to play an important part in structuring the discussion and generating ideas for writing. Mr Muhammad could have provided more help with the writing task. Instead, he focused on the content rather than the form of writing. In terms of form, he could have described to his students the genre in which they would be expected to write at the end of the series of lessons. This information should have been given priority so that students were aware of the genre, language and structure of the writing task (Hyland, 2003; 2007). As scholars (Bruton, 2005; Martin, 2007; Storch, 2005) argue, students must be told the purpose, audience and context of writing clearly at the beginning of the lesson to engage them in the writing activities.

Additionally, Mr Muhammad could have provided a sample of argumentative writing and have students read an exemplary piece. Using the inquiry method of instruction, Mr Muhammad could have had students debrief the elements or characteristics of the genre by going back to the model essay (Hyland, 2003). Scholars (Archibald,

2004; Bruton, 2005; Ferris, 2007) suggest realistic strategies for generating plans and researching topic information, while second language writing experts (Hyland, 2007; Kobayashi & Rinnert, 2007, Yi, 2007) encourage teachers to furnish students with a genre model as a method of exposing them to the required form of writing. Feez (2002) argues that students need to be given explicit teaching in the structure of target text types. Mr Muhammad's students were of average ability and needed constant support and guidance from their teacher before they could write independently. While genre modelling would definitely have benefited these students, their teacher overlooked its importance. Scaffolding from the introductory lesson did not seem to carry over to later lessons in terms of good practice that would have supported learners to carry out their task successfully. In terms of content, although Mr Muhammad did scaffold the content of writing, it is vital that teachers demonstrate both orally and in writing the language of argument. It is also essential that students are taught how to incorporate evidence into their writing to strengthen their position when writing argumentative essays (Thompson, G., 2002). Mr Muhammad could have also asked the students to identify reasons for alternate perspectives on the issue of water recycling as this would have helped them to formulate their argument in defence of their position. As a result of being taught how to reflect on what had been written, students would be in a better position to write a well constructed, argumentative essay (Laurinen & Marttunen, 2007; Sime & Priestley, 2005).

Lesson 2 was a 30 minute lesson conducted in the computer lab. The purpose of this lesson was to gather information from the Internet on water recycling. Mr Muhammad asked the students to perform an Internet search. However, no demonstration on the wide screen was provided by the teacher and no writing was discussed. The students conducted their searches individually to find relevant resources and materials on recycled water from the Internet. A few students were seen using Yahoo and Alta Vista search engines, with the most popular search engine used being Google. Mr Muhammad recommended English website addresses that the students could browse through. According to Mr Muhammad, these websites provided accurate information about water conservation as they were published by the Singapore Ministry of Environment. Mr Muhammad reminded the students to take out the worksheet on water conservation discussed during the previous lesson. The overall atmosphere in the classroom was noisy but purposeful. Even though the Internet connection was slow, the majority of students were engaged with the search task. The students took some time to scroll up and down the text as they skimmed and scanned, clicked on links to see what was there and searched for relevant materials for their essay. In deciding how to allocate their increasingly limited time, most of the students were observed prioritising the use of those recommended websites as their teacher had led them to believe that these sites were important in meeting the assessment demands for

this unit of work. Towards the end of the lesson, three students were still trying to connect their computers to the Internet.

Deaney, Ruthven and Hennessy (2004) suggest that few students have been taught to search effectively and critically and this accurately reflects the situation in Mr Muhammad's writing class. The majority of the students in this class claimed that one of the challenges they face in using the web as language learners was in finding the resources appropriate to their needs and, in this case, relevant to the topic of recycled water. Closer examination of the students' search for information revealed fascinating insights into the writing process and the contribution that ICT can make to the development of reading - but not writing - skills. The students had to choose how much and in what depth to read and explore. Given the information density of a screen full of text, students have to learn to search for information on their topic by scrolling up and down the text. It seems like an obvious requirement for anyone familiar with reading on computer screens (Kress, 2003), but it is an important additional reading skill that students need to have to cope with digital texts (Kress, 2005). Thus, Mr Muhammad could have taught the students a range of reading strategies, including the deployment of distinctive reading skills such as visualising, locating, selecting and evaluating information, organising and reasoning suitable for the purpose of writing, as these skills are critical in helping students with writing. In this way, the teacher could have assisted his students to identify arguments available in the digital texts. Some students thought it would be easier to find information on the screen rather than to borrow books from the library, while others thought that researching topic information would be more effective if they were given scope to search for information by themselves. A few students wrote that they had difficulty accessing the vast web resources without specific guidance from the teacher. In addition to providing some website addresses, Mr Muhammad could have referred students to portals which could have enabled them to access, browse and search a smaller range of deliberately assembled material (Ruthven, Hennnesy, & Deaney, 2004). Mr Muhammad indicated in the interview that he was aware of a wealth of information on the web that includes authentic samples of argumentative texts in English, online communities of student writers and practitioners, wonderfully inviting websites spotlighting conservation practices, vibrant exchanges of views on the subject on recycled water and plenty of opportunities for reading and writing. Even though Mr Muhammad reiterated in the interview that the Internet enhanced lesson resources by providing a rich source of information and illustration, he did not demonstrate how to harvest the vast potential of rich text and visual sources of this medium.

A general concern for both teachers and the students in this study is one which is articulated in research by Pelgrum (2001), that is, the potential and actual malfunctioning of computer facilities. Poor access to computer lab and technical dysfunctions disrupted a few lessons during this study. Research indicates that technical malfunctions can be a great obstacle to teachers and students as, clearly, they disrupt the flow of the lesson (Redd, 2003). Mr Muhammad sometimes encountered "technical hitches" when conducting computer mediated lessons in the lab and had recommended to the Head of Department of Technology that the computers be upgraded. Likewise, some students agreed that the school needed to replace slow, old and obsolete computers. Mr Muhammad strongly believed that technical problems posed a major problem for him in conducting effective, computer mediated lessons in the school. This view echoes that of Cuban, Kirkpatrick and Peck's (2001) whose research findings report that the inconveniences and unreliability of new technologies under school conditions constitute important barriers to their use. In other local studies (Lordusamy et al., 2001), it was reported that the slowness of school Internet connection was rampant and, as a result, posed major problems to the effectiveness of computer-mediated lessons (Hennessy, Deaney & Ruthven, 2003).

The focus of Lesson 3 was based on blogging. A few students brought to Mr Muhammad's attention that they still needed time to conduct searches for more information about water recycling from the Internet. Mr Muhammad then agreed to allow students to conduct further searches for another 10 minutes. While the students conducted their search, Mr Muhammad walked around the lab helping students who were having problems. Ten minutes later, Mr Muhammad asked his students to stop the search activity. He informed them that the focus of the lesson was blogging. Mr Muhammad asked the students to listen attentively as this was their first time blogging in the writing classroom and he then demonstrated how to log in using their username and password. He later gave the students their usernames and passwords. Mr Muhammad used Blogger24, a facility that hosts a weblog for free and restricts access to registered members only, in this case, Mr Muhammad as the administrator, and the students. Mr Muhammad demonstrated step-by-step how to create a new post. He pointed out that the Compose tab on the top right of the box should be selected as this would give the students space to post a title, enter content, format and create links by using the fairly standard icons along the top. As the blog administrator, Mr Muhammad had complete control over the blog. He reinforced positive social and communication skills to ensure that students post with respect and not ridicule each other's ideas and opinions. He asked the students to save all posts as drafts. He would then activate the Publish button and the post would be published on the weblog. In this way, nothing could go online without Mr Muhammad's consent. The students listened attentively while the technical aspects of logging in and posting were demonstrated. Mr Muhammad also informed the students that there is a Blogger for Word tool that allows the students to post directly to the blog from Microsoft Word and that they would have the ability to spell or grammar check their post before publishing it. This provided them with an easy way to save their work locally. Subsequently, students tried to log in on their own. Some students were looking at the screen while others were chatting away. 3 students had difficulty logging in and Mr Muhammad was fast and knowledgeable in handling students' queries regarding technical issues.

For their writing task, students were asked to reflect on the use of recycled water in Singapore based on their own experiences and observations in school and public areas. While the students were composing their texts, Mr Muhammad sat at his desk. During this time, there was very little interaction between the teacher and the students. At the end of the lesson, Mr Muhammad encouraged his students to post and support their arguments with statistical evidence. They were also told to read the contributions made by their classmates in the blogs and reminded to use appropriate language when posting their comments and critically evaluating other classmates' postings. He told the students that the blogging would last about one week. The students were informed that there was a compulsory dimension to the blogging, in that they had to make at least five meaningful postings based on the information they had gathered which were supported by ideas from readings and built on issues raised by other classmates.

To evaluate the effectiveness of the writing pedagogy in the use of asynchronous CMC, Swan (2003) suggests reviewing how the teacher organised learning in five areas: the learners' interactions with the writing task, the teacher and each other, and with the computer and their virtual interactions. In this lesson, Mr Muhammad emphasised the computer and the learners' virtual interactions. There was, however, a lack of emphasis on pedagogical aspects as few interactions were observed between teacher and students and among classmates. No aspect of writing was discussed or taught. Mr Muhammad could have made this lesson more effective by explicitly teaching the

students how to transfer their knowledge gained from reading the digital text and the ideas generated from the discussion to writing paragraphs in the blog (Chesher, 2005; Laurinen & Marttunen, 2007). Scholars (Bloch, 2004, 2006; Jones et al., 2006) point out that it is critically important for students to identify salient points, to extract information, summarize this in key words and then to include it in their postings (Lamb & Johnson, 2006). This, of course, involves teaching the fundamental skills of analysis, contextualization and conceptualization (Jones et al., 2006), all of which was lacking in Mr Muhammad's lesson scaffolding. During the interview, Mr Muhammad stressed that, beyond traditional applications, blogging allows a new type of writing that forces his students to read carefully and critically, demands clarity in construction and links to the sources of ideas. Mr Muhammad appeared to assume the students would acquire these skills automatically. A few students said that blogging served as a platform for them to discuss the writing topic, build arguments and collaborate with other students. What Mr Muhammad called "writing with connection" is closely aligned with Vygotsky's (1978) view that one of the difficulties a learner has in writing is that he or she addresses an absent or an imaginary person and thus has no motivation or feels no need to write, whereas in oral conversation every sentence is prompted by a motive. The dialectic and complex relationships between visualization and conceptualization as well as between spoken and written languages discussed by Vygotsky (1978) provides us with food for thought when we look at how students learn through online asynchronous written dialogue.

A few students wrote that blogging helped them in their writing as sometimes they found it difficult to start a writing assignment because it did not mean anything to them or to anybody else. The presence of an online audience thus acted as a motivating factor for these students to write. The writing became a tool for exchanging information and challenging opinions among a group of learners. The students' interaction in cyberspace during the observed lessons allowed them to interact based on sharing beliefs and thoughts over the issue of recycled water in a local context. Indeed, many of the social norms that usually restrict interaction are either absent or become greatly reduced in significance in cyberspace. The students were more eager to learn and to pursue their thoughts as well as to challenge and discuss relevant issues with a group of peers who share similar goals and interests in cyberspace rather than in the classroom. The students felt less threatened to socialise as they need not use 'perfect' Malay Language sentence structure to communicate with peers as compared to face-to-face interaction in the classroom. There was some evidence in this classroom that students had the freedom to express their thoughts, as students wrote in their reflections. Mr Muhammad believed that this could have a positive effect in the Malay Language classroom. Smith (2003) argues that CMC in general can increase the amount and quality of classroom participation, while Sullivan and Pratt (1996) claim that technology can affect traditional power structures within the classroom, which, in turn, can reduce the level of anxiety for second language writers. Other researchers (Lin, Cranton, & Bridglall, 2005; Yoon, 2003) claim that asynchronous written dialogue allows the student writers to clarify thoughts before stating his or her points in a posting.

In this study, a few students stated that the use of asynchronous CMC helped them to perceive writing as a recursive process, in that they could always go back to revise what they had written as a result of their peers' comments in the postings. This medium allows students to review previous postings, examine what has been said, make new discoveries and share their meanings in a deeper and clearer way. Also, the asynchronous written dialogue allowed time for students to support a point of view with new or compelling information through various resources including the Internet (Sime & Priestley, 2005). The results of this study support findings from other research

(Bloch, 2004; 2006) which argue that text based and time-delayed communication in blogs support the argumentation process by allowing learners more time to reflect and carefully select evidence, support the students' contentions or question and challenge claims in the arguments (Laurinen & Marttunen, 2007). The potential of using asynchronous computer-mediated practices to provide students with authentic opportunities to use the language and support the development of a social network of Malay Language speakers was evident in Classroom B. Students reported that the deviant language forms found in e-text enabled them to engage in online interactions without the pressures of having to spell the words correctly. However, the students also expressed their frustration in not being able to distinguish between correct and non-standard forms of the language when writing, which appeared to have affected their offline language use in Malay Language writing.

Lesson 4 was a 60-minute lesson allocated to debate on the topic, conducted orally in the classroom. There was no writing taught nor was any post-discussion conducted after the debate. Mr Muhammad divided students into affirmative and negative groups to debate the topic: *Recycled sewage drinking water is the way of the future*. Students were told to be specific and clear in their arguments. They supported their claims with reliable evidence and statistics from the Singapore Ministry of Environment. The most heated issue focused on whether treated wastewater could be considered clean enough to drink and free from viruses and hazardous substances. Economic issues were also a concern with one of the debaters posing the question: "Is it cheaper to treat wastewater to replenish aquifers or import water from other sources?" At the end of the lesson, the teacher gave his verdict on the debate.

In the interview, Mr Muhammad implied that developing his students' rebuttal skills would indirectly help them in their writing. He believed that the use of persuasive words and the opportunity to establish solid arguments to convince opponents definitely helped his students to write a well-argued essay. He argued that students learn argumentative writing through plunging into actual discussions and debates by trying out different modes of response and, in this way, gain a sense of what works and what does not work to persuade different audiences. However, scholars (Hirsch, Saeedi, Cornillon, & Litosseliti, 2004; Oh & Jonassen, 2007) argue that students need elaboration and stronger links to apply the skills gathered from the debate and transfer them into writing. It was expected that Mr Muhammad would identify the inductive or deductive reasoning in the debate and structure these arguments into a post-debate discussion. This would have helped his average ability students to write an argumentative essay. Although the debate was supposed to help students develop their arguments to build and structure the paragraphs in their essays, the teacher drew no explicit connection between the debate and the writing task to follow. Another issue is that the use of informal language in the debate affected the language used in writing the argumentative text. In fact, Mr Muhammad also raised concerns about some of his students' use of an Indonesian accent and of colloquialisms and non-standard Malay. He noted: "Whilst the local accent adds vigour and structure to the debate and asynchronous dialogue writing, when it impinges on the writing style it can damage a student's potential for academic success". This comment shows that the students learning Malay Language in Mr Muhammad's class require guidance on how to use the Malay Language effectively as well as acquire knowledge of the difference between its spoken and written form. Clearly, this is important to establishing and maintaining good writing skills that take into account purpose, audience and context.

Lesson 5 was a 30-minute lesson conducted in the computer lab and, as usual, the computers were already switched on when the students came into the lab. The students were told to use the word processing software to write an argumentative essay from a variety of sources such as the class discussion notes, pointers from the debate, blogs as well as information they had collected from the Internet. The students worked individually at their terminals with a couple of the students referring to additional notes they had gathered from the online discussion and the debate. As time was very limited, the students were told to complete their writing task at home. Students were reminded to save their work on the USB memory sticks. None of the students had any difficulty saving their writing. At the end of the lesson, the students were told to e-mail the completed argumentative text to Mr Muhammad.

In this lesson, it seems that Mr Muhammad attempted to expose the students to the idea of composing as a non-linear process. The students were required to go back and forth from their notes to their screen-based writing (Bruton, 2005). However, the writing task appeared to have no real purpose or audience. Mr Muhammad could have extended the blogs to allow other students in the school or parents or local community members (or perhaps a global audience) to be the target reader or audience and participate in the discussion instead of limiting it just to his writing classroom (Biesenbach & Weasenforth, 2001). It is also important to note that Mr Muhammad did not explicitly explain the form and structure of an argumentative text.

Students were not taught clearly how to transfer their knowledge and skills from the asynchronous written dialogue to the argumentative text. Mr Muhammad made a lot of assumptions and gave minimal guidance to his students. He could have demonstrated virtually in the lesson how to transfer an argument from the blog to the writing text (Belle & Soetaert, 2001). He appeared to assume that his students had the knowledge to complete the task without much problem. Mr Muhammad's students were not given opportunities to draft, edit and publish the argumentative text. It was surprising that Mr Muhammad did not conduct any peer editing sessions or conferences with the students to discuss their writing, as it is one of the critical stages of the process writing model. The lessons looked very much like a typical, old style writing activity in which students read, answer questions and are required to write about what they have read in their own words. E-mail was also used with a limited purpose. Scholars (Biesenbach & Weasenforth, 2001; Redd, 2003; Tuzi, 2004) point out that when e-mail is used critically in second language classrooms, it may have positive effects as it develops collaborative writing which will then improve on students' written language.

Case Study 2 - Summary of the Unit of Work

While it is reasonable to assume that students would have at least basic technical proficiency, Mr Muhammad assumed that the students were equipped with higher ICT skills than was actually the case. He assumed that his students would have the knowledge to search for reliable and accurate information from the Internet; however, from the lesson observations and the students' testimonies, gathering useful, relevant materials and incorporating the Internet resources into their writing were some of the major obstacles faced in generating solid ideas for writing. Also, the students were not seen to use the available digital resources creatively and needed teacher scaffolding to make these resources useful in the real context of writing (Goodyear & Jones, 2003). Mr Muhammad attempted to provide students with reading and writing as well as oral argumentative skills, which he believed to be important in educating and preparing his students for the Information Age. However, although the students were challenged to think critically, they struggled to get to the core of the topic - to put forward different points of view, claims, arguments and counterarguments that would be convincing as a result of exploring all avenues deeply and critically.

The worksheet given to students in the introductory lesson did not highlight the fact that students would need to know how to access the necessary texts from the Internet. In addition, students were not guided to consider relevant information. This supports findings from another local study (Abu Bakar & Abdul Rahim, 2005) which noted minimal student teacher interactions when computers were used in Malay Language classrooms. It would seem that Mr Muhammad's articulated sets of assumptions about his students' capabilities in conducting independent research did not correspond to reality.

It was also observed that the process writing model outlined in the Malay Language syllabus was not followed in the lessons. Mr Muhammad focussed predominately on the planning stage but not on genre modelling, shared writing, drafting, editing and publishing. He seemed to view the other stages in the process writing model as insignificant. However, it is clear that students exposed to good models and conventions of writing can gain confidence in writing independently and produce better writing (Turbill & Bean, 2006). Scholars (Dornan, et al., 2003; Fearn & Farnan, 2001) suggest that shared writing is a powerful approach for developing writing practice. These scholars argue that the ultimate goal of teaching writing is for students to use what they have learned in shared and guided writing and take responsibility for the writing process, thus becoming independent writers.

Mr Muhammad did not focus on forms of writing and ignored the linguistic features of writing. In contrast, Lin et al., (2005) argue that students need to be explicitly taught how ICT can help them make linguistic choices to suit purpose, audience and context, culturally, locally and internationally. The students in Mr Muhammad's class did not have the opportunity to write multiple drafts and do peer-editing. Instead, the students submitted the first draft of their completed argumentative writing directly to him. After writing the argumentative essay, there was no follow-up activity where Mr

Muhammad could have discussed with his students what they had learnt from the series of lessons. This series of lessons was not seen as sequential, as it should be in the process writing model. Instead the lessons seemed disconnected and not a series of planned activities to help students in writing a good argumentative essay.

It was also observed that Mr Muhammad seemed to overemphasise the use of ICT tools. Many scholars (Bloch, 2004, 2006; Richardson, 2006) report the use of blogging results in positive learning outcomes. However, Mr Muhammad failed to use the tool purposefully. Blogging can help students writing at paragraph level because they need to produce an argument and post it as written dialogue. At the end of the blogging session a series of arguments does, therefore, develop with the medium providing avenues for collaborative writing (Noel & Robert, 2003; 2004) where each participant contributes his/her ideas and opinions about the topic. Even though students appeared to be motivated to learn writing through blogging, there was no follow up by the teacher to take the arguments outlined in the blog and translate them into a coherent text as part of an argumentative essay (Salvo, 2002). Mr Muhammad assumed that his students would automatically acquire the skills of transferring those arguments without first teaching them how to do it.

Warlick (2005) claims that there should be connective writing that is closely aligned with the information inquiry activities performed by the students. Will (2006) suggests that rather than viewing blogging as a series of content-area writing activities, the teacher should consider the specific critical and creative thinking that occurs in this learning environment. Lamb and Johnson (2006) recommend that blogs could be used as a means to increase the students' awareness as they see themselves as authors with a purpose to write or to generate ideas for writing. Teachers could use blogs to share and develop a variety of writing strategies and inform students about the strengths and weaknesses of their writing (Lamb

& Johnson, 2006). Blogs could also be used as a low cost medium for students to publish and distribute their work to a wider audience. However, as a result of using blogs superficially in Classroom B, there was little impact on writing pedagogy. The use of ICT was supposed to support writing but what happened in this classroom was that the tools impeded the students' progress. Mr Muhammad became so focussed on the use of ICT that he did not critically consider the pedagogical aspect of the writing lesson. There was very little teaching of writing and minimal interaction between the teacher and the students; indeed, most of the interactions observed were between the students and their computer screens.

CONCLUSION

Despite the pedagogical potential of computer-mediated instructions (Adams, T., 2006; Cox & Abbot, 2004; Strenski, Feagin, & Singer, 2005; Wellington, 2005), there seemed to be little pedagogical value in using ICT in the two writing classrooms observed in this study. These two teachers' specific management of the role of ICT in teaching writing has significance in terms of illuminating key ideas and issues associated with ICT integration into second language classrooms.

There were some attempts by the two participating teachers to integrate ICT into classroom practices, but their attempts were far from what was expected. Both teachers displayed deficiencies in following the process writing model as stipulated in the Malay Language syllabus. Mrs Aminah and Mr Muhammad did not conduct shared writing and the publishing of multimodal texts as proposed by Kress (2003). Mrs Aminah did provide opportunities for students to experience a sequential series of lessons that contained planning, drafting, editing and reviewing, but in Mr Muhammad's case, planning predominated, with little attention given to drafting and editing of the complete argumentative essay. Based on the process writing model, the expectation was that students of Mr Muhammad would prepare multiple drafts. Instead, they wrote only one argumentative essay and submitted it upon completion. Even the paragraph which students constructed while blogging was undertaken without their teacher's input.

The themes emerging from these two classrooms provide evidence for the underutilisation of ICT in the teaching and learning of Malay Language writing. Successful teaching of Malay Language writing in the 21st Century depends on the realization by teachers that it takes more planning and scaffolding than in the pre-ICT era to teach a 'wired' generation. Also, teachers need to be sensitive to the needs of students in the computer- mediated learning environment. The teachers must not allow technology to control them and the classroom culture; rather, it should be the reverse.

Pedagogical change needs to be far more penetrating than just the use of the Internet, PowerPoint, Word Processing or Asynchronous Computer-Mediated Communication. The question is how teachers manage these available tools to help their students explore innovative ways to produce creative and objective texts in the Malay Language. The observations in this study also suggest that Malay Language teachers' facilitation of their students' learning plays a key important role in making the use of ICT purposeful, productive and meaningful.

However, using available ICT tools to transform Malay writing pedagogies is not straightforward. This is because new ICT tools often challenge an existing practice of teaching and threaten a well-established knowledge domain. Malay Language teachers require time and support: time to allow them to reflect on how they might infuse ICT productively into their everyday classroom practice, as well as support from the school administrators and the Ministry of Education in terms of providing resources and flexibility. This will allow teachers opportunities to explore,

experiment and discover productive pedagogies to stimulate students' thinking through the use of ICT tools in learning.

In addition, the lack of computer infrastructure and technical support in both schools in this study had a demonstrable impact on the Malay Language writing classrooms. The overall reliability of Internet access is crucial to ensure that teachers are able to incorporate the use of the Internet effectively into their lessons. As ICT has become an integral part of the Malay Language Curriculum, there is a need to overcome these obstacles by upgrading computers and labs.

These findings help present a broader and more complex view of ICT used in the second language writing context. It reflects the challenge second language students and teachers face in learning and teaching writing amidst the backdrop of keeping up with advancements in technology (Kubota, 1997; 1998). As Wellington (2005) argues, the rise of the Internet and other computer mediated technologies force educators to reflect further on the role of ICT in transforming pedagogy and in mediating the changing needs and nature of both print and technological literacies.

REFERENCES

Abu Bakar, M., & Abdul Rahim, R. (2005). *A preliminary report on teaching of Malay as a second language in Singapore schools: An analysis of initial data from the Singapore pedagogy Coding Schema.* Retrieved December 7, 2007, from http://crpp.nie.edu.sg/file.php/337/ RRS05-003 final version.pdf

Adams, C. (2007). On the 'informed use' of PowerPoint: Rejoining Vallance and Towndrow. *Journal of Curriculum Studies, 39*(2), 229–233. doi:10.1080/00220270601175246

Adams, T. (2006). PowerPoint, habits of mind, and classroom culture. *Journal of Curriculum Studies, 38*(4), 389–411. doi:10.1080/00220270600579141

Archibald, A. (2004). *Writing in a second language.* Retrieved February 13, 2008, from http://llas.ac.uk/resources/goodpractice.aspx 157

Atkinson, C. (2005). *Beyond bullets: People communicating with people.* Retrieved March 29, 2008, from http://socialble media.typepad.com/beyond-bullets/

Belle, G. G., & Soetaert, R. (2001). Breakdown into the virtual user-involved design and learning. *Journal of Technology and Teacher Education, 9*, 31–42.

Biesenbach, L. S., & Weasenforth, D. (2001). E-mail and word processing in the ESL classroom: How the medium affects the message. *Language Learning & Technology, 5*(1), 135–165.

Bloch, J. (2004). Second language cyber rhetoric: A study of Chinese second language writers in an online usenet group. *Language Learning & Technology, 8*(3), 66–82.

Bloch, J. (2006). Abdullah's blogging: A generation 1.5 student enters the blogosphere. *Language Learning & Technology, 11*(2), 128–141.

Bruton, A. (2005). Process writing and communicative-task-based instruction: Many common features, but more common limitations? *Teaching English as a Second or Foreign Language, 9*(3), 1–31.

Chandler, J. (2003). The efficacy of various kinds of error feedback for improvement in the accuracy and fluency of second language student writing. *Journal of Second Language Writing, 12*, 267–296. doi:10.1016/S1060-3743(03)00038-9

Chesher, C. (2005). *Blogs and the crisis of authorship.* Retrieved May 29, 2008, from http://incsub.org/blogtalk/?page_id=40.

Cox, M., & Abbot, C. (Eds.). (2004). *A review of research literature relating to ICT and attainment.* Coventry, Becta/London: Deparment of Children, School and Families.

Cuban, L. (2004). Meeting challenges in urban schools. *Educational Leadership, 61*(7), 64–69.

Cuban, L., Kirkpatrick, H., & Peck, C. (2001). High access and low use of technologies in high school classrooms: Explaining an apparent paradox. *American Educational Research Journal, 38*(4), 813–834. doi:10.3102/00028312038004813

Deaney, R., Ruthven, K., & Hennessy, S. (2004). *Teachers developing practical theories of the contribution of ICT to subject teaching and learning: An analysis of cases from English Secondary School.* Cambridge, UK: University of Cambridge.

Dornan, R., Rosea, L., & Wilson, M. (2003). *Within and beyond writing process in the Secondary English classroom.* Upper Saddle River, NJ: Allyn and Bacon, Pearson Education.

Ellis, R. (2003). *Task-based language learning and teaching.* Oxford, UK: Oxford University Press.

Fearn, L., & Farnan, N. (2001). *Interactions: Teaching writing and the language arts.* Boston: Houghton Mifflin Company.

Feez, S. (2002). Heritage and innovation in second language education. In A. M. Johns (Ed.), *Genre in the classroom* (pp. 47-68). Mahwah, NJ: Lawrence Erlbaum Associates.

Ferris, D. (2004). The "Grammar Correction" Debate in second language writing: Where are we, and where do we go from here? (and what do we do in the meantime…?). *Journal of Second Language Writing, 13*, 49–62. doi:10.1016/j.jslw.2004.04.005

Ferris, D. (2007). Preparing teachers to respond to students' writing. *Journal of Second Language Writing, 16,* 165–193. doi:10.1016/j.jslw.2007.07.003

Goodyear, P., & Jones, C. (2003). Implicit theories of learning and change: Their role in the development environments for higher education. In S. Naidu (Ed.), *Learning and teaching with technological practices.* London: Kogan Page.

Hennessy, S., Deaney, R., & Ruthven, K. (2003). *Pedagogic strategies for using ICT to support subject teaching and learning: An analysis across 15 case studies.* Cambridge, UK: University of Cambridge.

Hirsch, L., Saeedi, M., Cornillon, J., & Litosseliti, L. (2004). A structured dialogue tool for argumentative learning. *Journal of Computer Assisted Learning, 20,* 72–80. doi:10.1111/j.1365-2729.2004.00068.x

Holdich, C., & Chung, P. (2003). A 'computer tutor' to assist children to develop their narrative writing skills: Conferencing with HARRY. *International Journal of Human-Computer Studies, 59,* 631–669. doi:10.1016/S1071-5819(03)00086-7

Hyland, K. (2003). Genre-based pedagogies: A social response to process. *Journal of Second Language Writing, 12,* 17–29. doi:10.1016/S1060-3743(02)00124-8

Hyland, K. (2007). Genre pedagogy: Language, literacy and second language writing instruction. *Journal of Second Language Writing, 12,* 3–15.

Jones, R. H., Garralda, A., Li, D., & Lock, G. (2006). Interactional dynamics in online and face-to-face peer-tutoring sessions for second language writers. *Journal of Second Language Writing, 15,* 1–23. doi:10.1016/j.jslw.2005.12.001

Kapitzke, C., & Bruce, B. C. (2006). *Libr@ries: Changing information space and practice.* Mahwah, NJ: Lawrence Erlbaum Associates.

Kinchin, I. M., & Alias, M. (2005). Exploiting variations in concept map morphology as a lesson-planning tool for trainee teachers in Higher Education. *Journal of In-service Education, 31*(2), 569–592. doi:10.1080/13674580500200366

Kobayashi, H., & Rinnert, C. (2007). Task response and text construction across first and second language writing. *Journal of Second Language Writing, 7,* 1–23.

Kress, G. (2003). *Literacy in the New Media Age.* London: Routledge.

Kress, G. (2005). Gains and losses: New forms of text, knowledge, and learning. *Computers and Composition, 22,* 5–22. doi:10.1016/j.compcom.2004.12.004

Kubota, R. (1997). A reevaluation of the uniqueness of Japanese written discourse. *Written Communication, 14,* 460–480. doi:10.1177/0741088397014004002

Kubota, R. (1998). An investigation of first to second language transfer in writing among Japanese university students: Implications for contrastive rhetoric. *Journal of Second Language Writing, 7,* 69–100. doi:10.1016/S1060-3743(98)90006-6

Lamb, A., & Johnson, L. (2006). Key words in Instruction, Blogs and Blogging Part II. *School Library Media Activities, 22*(9), 40–44.

Lankshear, C., & Knobel, M. (2003). *New Literacies Changing Knowledge and Classroom Learning.* Philadelphia: Open University Press.

Laurinen, L., & Marttunen, M. (2007). Written arguments and collaborative speech acts in practicing the argumentative power of language through chat debates. *Computers and Composition, 24,* 230–246. doi:10.1016/j.compcom.2007.05.002

Lim, C. P. (2004). Learning technology in transition. *British Journal of Educational Technology, 35*(6), 754–755. doi:10.1111/j.1467-8535.2004.00432_11.x

Lim, C. P., & Chai, C. S. (2007a). An activity-theoretical approach to research of ICT integration in Singapore schools: Orienting activities and learner autonomy. *Computers & Education, 43*(3), 215–236. doi:10.1016/j.compedu.2003.10.005

Lim, C. P., & Chai, C. S. (2007b). *Teachers' pedagogical beliefs and their planning and conduct of computer-mediated classroom lessons.* Retrieved December 4, 2008, from http://www.blackwellsynergy.com.ezproxy.library.uq.edu.au/doi/pdf/10.1111/j.1467-8535.2007.00774.x

Lin, L., Cranton, P., & Bridglall, B. (2005). *Psychological type and asynchronous written dialogue in adult learning.* Ann Arbor, MI: The University of Michigan Press.

Lockard, J., & Pegrum, M. (Eds.). (2006). *Brave new classrooms: Democratic education and the Internet.* New York: Peter Lang.

Lordusamy, A., Hu, C., & Wong, P. (2001). *Perceived Benefits of EduPAD in enhancing learning.* Paper presented at the AARE Conference. Perth, Australia: Fremantle.

Loretta, K. (2002). Technology as a tool for literacy in the age of information: Implications for the ESL classroom. *Teaching English in the Two-Year College, 30*(2), 129–145.

Martin, R. (2007). *Teaching problem-solving skills in writing rather than rules.* Paper presented at the IFTEALEA National Conference, Melbourne.

MOE. (2002). *IT Masterplan.* Retrieved June 9, 2004 from http//www1.moe.gov.sg/iteducation

MOE. (2003). *Malay Language Curriculum.* Retrieved February 21, 2005, from http//www.moe.gov.sg/cpdd/syllabuses.htm

MOE. (2004). *IT in Education.* Retrieved May 21, 2005, from http//www1.moe.edu.sg/iteducation/masterplan/brochure.htm

MOE. (2005). *ICT projects.* Retrieved December 29, 2004, from http//www.moe.gov.sg/schools

Noel, S., & Robert, J. M. (2003). How the web is used to support collaborative writing. *Behaviour & Information Technology, 22*(4), 245–262. doi:10.1080/0144929031000120860

Noel, S., & Robert, J. M. (2004). Empirical study on collaborative writing: What do coauthors do, use and like? *Computer Supported Cooperative Work: The Journal of Collaborative Computing, 13*(1), 63–89. doi:10.1023/B:COSU.0000014876.96003.be

Noor, R. (2001). Contrastive rhetoric in expository prose: Approaches and achievements. *Journal of Pragmatics, 33,* 255–269. doi:10.1016/S0378-2166(99)00136-8

Oh, S., & Jonassen, D. H. (2007). Scaffolding online argumentation during problem solving. *Journal of Computer Assisted Learning, 23,* 95–110. doi:10.1111/j.1365-2729.2006.00206.x

Pelgrum, W. J. (2001). Obstacles to the integration of ICT in education: Results from a worldwide educational assessment. *Computers & Education, 37,* 163–178. doi:10.1016/S0360-1315(01)00045-8

Perry, D., & Smithmier, M. (2005). Peer-editing with technology: Using the computer to create interactive feedback. *English Journal, 94*(6), 23–24.

Redd, T. (2003). "Tryin to make a dolla outa fifteen cent": Teaching composition with the Internet at an HBCU. *Computers and Composition, 20,* 359–373. doi:10.1016/j.compcom.2003.08.012

Richardson, W. (2006). *Blogs, Wikis, Podcasts, and other powerful web tools for classrooms.* Thousand Oaks, CA: Corwin Press.

Ruthven, K., Hennnesy, S., & Deaney, R. (2004). *Incorporating Internet resources into classroom practice: Pedagogical perspectives and strategies for secondary school subject teachers.* Retrieved May 21, 2004 from http://www.tcrecord.org.

Salvo, M. (2002). Critical engagement with technology in the computer classroom. *Technical Communication Quarterly, 11*(3), 317–337. doi:10.1207/s15427625tcq1103_5

Shepherd, J. (2005). *Striking a balance: The management of language in Singapore.* New York: Peter Lang.

Shetzer, H., & Warschauer, M. (2000). An electronic literacy approach to network – based language teaching. In W.M. Warschauer, & R. Kern (Eds.), *Networked-based language learning: Concepts and practice* (pp. 171-185). Cambridge, UK: Cambridge University Press.

Sime, D., & Priestley, M. (2005). Student teachers' first reflections on information and communications technology and classroom learning: Implications for initial teacher education. *Journal of Computer Assisted Learning, 21*, 130–142. doi:10.1111/j.1365-2729.2005.00120.x

Smith, B. (2003). Computer-mediated negotiated interaction: An expanded model. *Modern Language Journal, 87*(1), 38–57. doi:10.1111/1540-4781.00177

Storch, N. (2005). Collaborative writing: Product, process and students' reflections. *Journal of Second Language Writing, 14*, 153–173. doi:10.1016/j.jslw.2005.05.002

Strenski, E., Feagin, C., & Singer, J. (2005). E-mail small group peer view revisited. *Computers and Composition, 22*(2), 191–208. doi:10.1016/j.compcom.2005.02.005

Sullivan, K., & Pratt, E. (1996). A comparative study of two ESL writing environments: A computer-assisted classroom and a traditional oral classroom. *System, 24*, 491–501. doi:10.1016/S0346-251X(96)00044-9

Sutherland, R., Armstrong, V., Facer, K., & Fulong, R. (2004). Transforming teaching and learning: Embedding ICT into everyday classroom practices. *Journal of Computer Assisted Learning, 20*(6), 4–13.

Swan, K. (2003). Learning effectiveness: What the research tell us. In J. Bourne & J. C. Moore (Eds.), *Elements of quality online education: Practice and direction* (pp. 13-45). Needham, MA: Sloan Center for Online Education.

Tardy, C. (2005). Expressions of disciplinarity and individuality in a multimodal genre. *Computers and Composition, 22*(3), 319–336. doi:10.1016/j.compcom.2005.05.004

Thompson, G. (2002). Interaction in academic writing: Learning to argue with the reader. *Applied Linguistics, 22*, 58–78. doi:10.1093/applin/22.1.58

Turbill, J. (2003). Exploring the potential of the digital language experience approach in Australian classrooms. *Reading Online, 6*(7), Retrieved February 7, 2008, from http://www.readingonline.org/international/inter_index.asp?HREF=turbill7.

Turbill, J., & Bean, W. (2006). *Writing Instruction K-6: Understanding process, purpose, audience.* New York: Richard Owen Publishers.

Tuzi, F. (2004). The impact of e-feedback on the revisions of second language writers in an academic writing course. *Computers and Composition, 21*, 217–235. doi:10.1016/j.compcom.2004.02.003

Vanithamani, S. (2005). 'Thinking Schools, Learning Nations': Implementation of curriculum review in Singapore. *Educational Research for Policy and Practice, 4*(2-3), 97–113. doi:10.1007/s10671-005-1543-x

Vygotsky, L. S. (1978). *Mind in society: The development of higher psychological processes.* Cambridge, MA: Harvard University Press.

Warlick, D. (2005). *Classroom Blogging: A teacher's guide to the blogosphere.* Raleigh, NC: Lulu.

Warschauer, M., & Ware, P. (2006). Automated writing evaluation: Defining classroom research agenda. *Language Teaching Research, 10*(2), 157–180. doi:10.1191/1362168806lr190oa

Wellington, J. (2005). Has ICT come of age? Recurring debates on the role of ICT in education, 1982-2004. *Research in Science & Technological Education, 23*(1), 25–39. doi:10.1080/02635140500068419

Wesche, M. B., & Skehan, P. (2002). Writing in the secondary classroom: The effects of prompts and tasks on novice learners of French. *Modern Language Journal, 84,* 171–184.

Will, R. (2006). *Blogs, wikis, podcasts and other powerful web tools for classrooms.* Thousand Oaks, CA: Corwin Press.

Yi, Y. (2007). Engaging literacy: A biliterate student's composing practices beyond school. *Journal of Second Language Writing, 16*(1), 23–39. doi:10.1016/j.jslw.2007.03.001

Zhao, Y., & Cziko, G. A. (2001). Teacher adoption of technology: A perceptual control theory perspective. *Journal of Technology and Teacher Education, 9,* 5–30.

KEY TERMS AND DEFINITIONS

Information Communication and Technologies (ICT): Technologies such as computers and the Internet that enhance communication and the retrieval of information.

Writing Pedagogy: Philosophy of teaching of writing to achieve learning outcomes.

Second Language Teaching: The teaching of a language to non-native speakers.

Language Education: Pedagogies related to the teaching of language.

Blogging: Posting a message on a web-based log (diary).

Chapter 8

A Snapshot View of how Senior Visual Arts Students Encounter and Engage with Technology in Their Arts Practice

Martin Kerby
St. Joseph's Nudgee College, Australia

Margaret Baguley
University of Southern Queensland, Australia

ABSTRACT

This chapter reports the findings of a pilot research project that investigated how senior visual arts students engage with and utilise technology in the creation of art works during their program of study. During the course of a year, six students from two schools were interviewed and their work was visually documented to ascertain whether technology played a predominant part in their practice. Analysis of the interview data was framed within a social constructivist perspective and drew on notions of skills and expertise, support, access, awareness and inspiration. The findings revealed that the senior visual arts students regularly used technology as part of their process but often reverted to using traditional media with some technological aspects in the creation of their final work.

INTRODUCTION

Within the Australian senior visual art classroom young people engage in an intensive two year personal journey of exploration and expression. During this period they utilise higher order learning and thinking skills evidenced in their ability to articulate the process they have undertaken to create works of art which are informed, innovative and unique.

However, this journey is complex and undertaken with varying degrees of expertise and exposure to a range of media and current/emerging technologies (Davis, 2008; Queensland Studies Authority, 2007). Additionally, students are under increasing pressure in their final years before potentially joining the workforce to choose subjects which are considered to provide as many opportunities as possible for career choice. There are many factors which can affect these decisions including issues related to

DOI: 10.4018/978-1-60566-842-0.ch008

gender, socio-economic factors and motivation (Kniveton, 2004; Lapan, Hinkelman, Adams, & Turner, 1999; Tringali, 1993; Morgan, 1986).

There is extensive literature regarding the value of the arts in engaging students in higher order thinking processes and the benefits the arts have in promoting creative and lateral thinking (Bamford, 2006; Davis, 2008; Gardner, 1993; Sawyer, 2006; Wright, 2003, 2004). The arts reflect issues which are occurring in society such as the impact of technology on everyday life. The recent Australian National Review of Visual Education (Davis, 2008) proposed that information which was formerly represented through words or numbers is increasingly being depicted by visual images and therefore an extensive amount of technology relies on the ability of the participant to be visually literate. Many students are already 'connected' with one another through various types of technology including email, instant messaging and chat rooms. They utilise the Web to search for information, play games in virtual environments, use their mobile phone to record and send images and manipulate images on the computer. Visual arts education endeavours to prepare students to read, analyse and create visual images in an informed and discriminating way; however the influences on young people are many and varied. According to the UK body, National Advisory Committee on Creative and Cultural Education (NACCCE):

... young people now live in a complex web of interacting cultures and sub-cultures: of families, gender, peer groups, ideological convictions, political communities and of ethnic and local traditions. They also live in a global culture that is driven by the interplay of commercial interests, the creative energies of young people themselves, and the enveloping influence of information technologies. (NACCCE, 1999, p. 23)

This article seeks to enhance our understanding of how senior visual arts students utilise technology in their arts practice and what fac-

tors encourage or discourage the use of this medium.

CONTEXT

In Australia the subject Senior Visual Art is undertaken during the final two years of high school prior to students moving into university studies. The results students gain from this subject, contribute towards their overall score to be considered for university entrance. Two schools, from different states in Australia, were chosen for this study. The first, known in this study as School A, was a co-educational independent school from early learning (aged three years) to Year 12 catering for approximately 1100 students including boarders. It has a purpose-built building for sole use by Year 11 and 12 students which contains the visual arts department. The second school, known in this study as School B, is a private school for boys, which caters for approximately 1400 students including boarders from Years 5 – 12. The second school also has a purpose-built centre for visual arts education.

Both schools were chosen for their high commitment to the arts evidenced in a rigorous and robust visual arts program, the enthusiasm and passion of the teachers and high profile events such as exhibitions which occur on a regular basis. In addition, both schools are able to effectively resource their art departments and students have access to a range of equipment and media to develop their arts practice. During this study there was one female and two male participants from School A and three male participants from School B. One of the participants from School A was an English Second Language (ESL) student. Another participant from School A was the only person in this study who had not taken art through junior school (Years 8 – 10). One of the participants from School B was the only student at the school who was enrolled in three arts subjects: Visual Arts, Drama and Music. The other two participants from School B had achieved the highest academic achievement, also known as Dux, in a number of their subjects. School A was located in a regional area with access to one major art gallery, an alternative art space and a school art gallery. School B was located in a capital centre with access to a major state gallery attached to a modern art centre, and a range of commercial and alternative art galleries.

This research project began in the first semester and was concluded towards the end of the year for both schools. Four of the participants were in the first year and two participants were in their final year of their senior art course.

THEORETICAL BACKGROUND

In the contemporary world creativity is seen as being the new economic driver for international competitiveness (Davis, 2008; Robinson, 2001; Sawyer, 2006; Wind, 2006). In addition, recent international research also reveals a focus on the connection between the arts and their ability to foster creative and lateral thinking (Bamford, 2006; European University Association, 2007; Oakley, 2007). Davis (2008, p. 10) proposes that "the curriculum stalwarts of literacy and numeracy are no longer sufficient to equip students with the basics they need to operate in the innovation oriented, digitally wired twenty first century." The Australia Council for Education and the Arts (ACEA) note that technology skills and the ability to access and exert influence within the 'knowledge society' is a capacity which 21st students should possess.

The value of the arts in developing creative and lateral thinking is also espoused by Robinson (2001). He proposed that all national systems of education are based on two underlying models: economic and intellectual, and that these are now inadequate due to the rapid and extraordinary nature of technological and economic change. The concept of rapid change and the ability of people to cope were also examined in Alvin Tof-

fler's *Future Shock* (1974). Researchers have been investigating the phenomenon of technology and its effect on education creating new terminology such as "digital native" in the process. The term "digital native" describes anyone born after 1980 that has grown up in a world saturated with digital technology (Palfrey & Gasser, 2008; Prensky, 2001). However, as the "digital natives" website hosted by the Berkman Centre for Internet and Society at Harvard University and the Research Centre for Information Law at the University of St. Gallen notes, those who were not "born digital" could be just as connected, if not more so, as their younger counterparts (www.digitalnative. org/#about). Prensky (2001) describes teachers as "immigrants" in this new world because of the perception that they are struggling to teach a group of people a new language using the outdated language they already use.

Bamford's (2006) *The Wow Factor* provided a global research perspective on the impact of the arts in education. In relation to arts education and technology she found that in schools where computers were readily available to arts educators and students, arts education contributed significantly to computer and technology skills. In Australia, Bamford found arts education was seen as being a key part of ICT literacy programs with high computer usage in schools. However, her findings also revealed that arts teachers need access to computers and the opportunity to gain competence in their use in order to enhance the innovative use of ICT in the arts classroom. Aland's (2004) investigation into the impact of digital technologies on contemporary visual arts education concluded that "teachers need to know about, understand and appreciate the ways in which technology has changed, and is changing artistic practice; to become informed about the attributes and features which characterise such works, and to reflect these understandings in their approach to teaching visual arts (p. 7).

There have been numerous texts which seek to assist teachers to integrate technology in their classrooms (Ivers, 2003; Roblyer, Edwards & Havriluk, 1997; Ross & Bailey, 1996; Twombey, Shamburg, & Zieger, 2006), however the rapid pace of technological change often renders such materials redundant after a short period of time. Therefore it appears that the existing technical expertise of the senior visual arts teacher, in combination with the levels of individual expertise of their students, affects whether technology is incorporated as a medium into the students' art practice (Bamford, 2006; Davis, 2008; Robyler, Edwards & Havriluk).

METHODS AND TECHNIQUES

In order to examine how senior students encounter and engage with technology in their arts practice, we utilised both qualitative and quantitative inquiry methods to investigate the students' experience. The qualitative method was able to provide a 'deeper' understanding of this phenomenon and created richer connections with the participants. Visual data was also obtained regarding the process the students documented in their visual diaries. Both the interview and visual data were utilised in this pilot study to investigate the use of technology in the senior visual arts students' practice. The quantitative method was utilised to ascertain the number of times thematic statements were made during the interviews. This method is underpinned by precision and control and is usually reliant on numerical data (Burns, 2000). Therefore, the use of both qualitative and quantitative methods in this study to see whether they corroborate one another provides additional validity to the research (Silverman, 2001). In order to proceed with the study the researchers sought and were granted ethics approval from the Tasmania Social Sciences Human Research Ethics Committee.

A semi-structured interview schedule was utilised with all of the participants and was conducted for approximately one hour in duration at the beginning, middle and end of the year. The questions sought information on the type of work and process the students were undertaking to create their art works, without specific reference to technology. In this way the researchers were able to gather data about the how students were using technology without the inference that they should be incorporating it in their arts practice.

During the interview sessions the participants referred to their visual diaries as they explained the motivation and inspiration behind the creation of their art works. Key images from the diaries were documented to record the progress students had made in their work. In particular, instances of technological exploration were documented to ascertain the extent to which it was evidenced in the final art works.

The trustworthiness of this research has been achieved by ensuring the research procedures are coherent and visible (Kvale, 1996). The thematic analysis undertaken of the interviews provides further perspectives on how senior visual arts students encounter and engage with technology in their arts practice. There is strong reliability within the interview responses as all subjects were presented with a standardised semi-structured interview schedule which provides consistency in responses and eliminates unreliability in the researcher's observations (Baruch, 1999).

ANALYSIS

The analysis of the interviews focussed on emergent themes and recurrent patterns which were grouped into similar categories. The categories were then identified, coded and analysed to allow for meaningful interpretation and reporting of the data. The researchers undertook the analysis independently to determine the themes they identified as emerging from the data. These findings were then shared to ascertain the final categories. A statement in this pilot study is referred to as a sentence from the interview narrative relevant to the theme. Therefore two statements refer to two sentences of data. The statements were analysed to determine the number of times similar thematic statements were made from the participants in each school.

The main focus in the analysis of the interview data was to determine how and to what extent the participants used technology in their arts practice to create major pieces for their senior visual arts course. Due to the fact that participants bring a range of different perspectives to the research process (Burns, 2000; Denzin & Lincoln, 2000; Lincoln & Guba, 2000), the researchers looked beyond the themes the participants were exploring to seek similarities in the data.

FINDINGS

Three participants from School A and three participants from School B agreed to take part in the study. All of the participants attended three interviews throughout the year. Most of the interviews were conducted in a quiet area away from the distraction of the senior secondary art studio.

The researchers collaboratively agreed upon the following common themes arising from the interview data: technological expertise, skills and expertise, support, access, awareness, and inspiration. These are explained as follows:

*   **Technological Expertise** – statements where the participant referred to their expertise with a range of technologies.
*   **Skills and Expertise** – statements where the participant referred to existing skills and expertise in traditional media or techniques.
*   **Support** – statements where the participant acknowledged the emotional and/or physical support of their teacher, relatives or friends in the completion of their artwork.
*   **Access** – statements where the participant

referred to digital media they had access to or other sources such as galleries to view these types of works.

*   **Awareness** – statements where the participant demonstrated their awareness of where their arts practice positioned them in terms of future careers.
*   **Inspiration** – statements where the participant referred to digital media as providing inspiration for their artworks.

A numerical analysis of the written responses against the six themes revealed fairly evenly balanced responses between School A and School B in relation to technological expertise. There were distinct differences however between both schools in relation to: Skills and Expertise, Support, Access, Awareness and Inspiration. The comparative analysis between both School A and School B is shown below (see Table 1).

These themes will be discussed in the following section in context with the thematic analysis.

TECHNOLOGICAL EXPERTISE

Muffoletto (1994, p. 25) notes that technology is commonly considered to be "gadgets, instruments, machines and devices" including computers. However, Saettler (1990) argues the historical function of educational technology was as a process rather than a product and therefore any useful definition of educational technology must focus on the process of applying tools for educational purposes, as well as the tools and materials that are used.

In this study the participants referred to technological expertise as both process and product. There were a fairly even number of statements to this theme (School A = 49; School B = 47). Participants from School A described technologies they utilised at home such as the use of digitiser tablets, programs which mimic brushstrokes, and their expertise in computer aided design (CAD).

Table 1. Theme count

	School A	School B	
	n = 3	n = 3	Total
Theme			
Technological Expertise	49	47	96
Skills and Expertise	51	111	162
Support	48	106	154
Access	18	43	61
Awareness	54	101	155
Inspiration	21	12	33

I love digital art. I have like a graphics tablet that you can draw on. It's like a digitiser tablet. You can draw on it and it goes on the computer. It's really cool. I actually also have a program that mimics like brush strokes. Like when you brush it, it will go to brush strokes and it's got this stuff called real bristle technology. Each time you stroke it it's got different bristle indents and you can see all of it. (School A)

Participants from School B discussed a number of ways they engaged with technology including completing their visual diary on the computer, producing films and manipulating digital images.

We had to pick out a topic that was controversial in the media so I looked at girls who were really materialistic. So I got a picture of Nicole Ritchie and we had to edit them on Photoshop ... so I made her look incredibly skinny just like an absolute stick – then I put a Louis Vuitton bag except I cropped out some of the symbols on the bag and put drugs on it. Then above that I wrote 'Obsession' for her as in like the perfume title. It turned out really well. (School B)

It was evident that a number of the participants were comfortable with a range of technologies including using digital cameras, accessing the internet, manipulating digital images and playing electronic games. Some of the participants had also been introduced to a range of technologies in their junior classes, such as filmmaking, which they had drawn on to support their senior visual arts studies. One of the participants remarked that their senior art teacher advised them to build on their existing expertise rather than try to learn a new medium in their final year. The breakdown between the participants thematic responses revealed another fairly even response with two participants from each school only mentioning technological expertise a limited number of times (School A = 7; School B = 5). Their final pieces also reflected a more traditional approach to media and techniques. Each school also had a participant who was very comfortable with technological expertise (School A = 27; School B = 29). These participants' expertise with technology complemented their passion for, and interest in, pursuing the arts beyond their final year of schooling.

SKILLS AND EXPERTISE

The participants had a wide range of skills and expertise in traditional media which were also informed by a range of technologies such as animated cartoons, films, computer tutorials for different software programs and computer aided design.

... he said [teacher] I could have some completely free standing thing and I immediately thought 'oh what if I had the characters cut out completely' like out of MDF. Because I've been working next door which is computer aided design and they have the big routing machine. (School A)

The participants at School B each noted that they have a class of 26 students which impacts on their ability to develop their skills and expertise with their teacher's assistance. Participants at School A have a lesser teacher to student ratio and therefore limited time with their teacher was not raised as any issue in any of their interviews. The issues raised by participants in School B in relation to skills and expertise were having the opportunity to experiment with a range of media and techniques at the school before commencing senior art and learning new skills as required. However, the participants also were aware of their limitations and how this would affect their major artworks.

For my next project I want to make a short film. I think that's where my strengths are – in shots. I can do painting but I don't think I have the skill yet to paint a magnificent painting. I can do it but it's not my strength ... I think my strength is looking at things from different angles and so forth. So the camera will be really good and I'll be able to present a story that I want to tell. (School B)

It was evident that participants from both schools were supported to extend their existing repertoire of skills; however the participants placed restrictions on themselves through their realisation that limited amounts of time affected the type of work they could produce. There was quite a divergence between the thematic responses for skills and expertise (School A: 51; School B: 111). An analysis of the responses revealed that this was directly attributable to the large number of senior art students in the class which resulted in one participant stating "... [name of teacher]

hates having a big class and I can see why – it's not physically possible for him to move around the classroom to see everyone in half an hour – like not even for a minute each. You can't really teach art, especially in senior like that" (School B). For these participants it meant seeking the support of their teacher outside of designated class time. The participants at School A were able to use spare periods to work in the senior secondary art studio with one boarding school student admitting that they did not really work on their arts practice outside of school hours.

I always stay in here at recess on that day because I've got art first thing, study and then I stay in. I come here in period one and two because I've got art. Then I stay here normally in recess. Then period three and four I've got study. So I stay in here for that and then I stay in for five which I'm technically not supposed to do but I do anyway. (School A)

SUPPORT

All of the participants felt supported by their teachers in the approaches they wished to take in their arts practice. In many cases these support structures had been built up in previous grades resulting in an easier transition into senior art. However, one participant had not completed art in the junior grades but felt strongly supported by his senior art teacher who he described as firm and encouraging. The participants who also had strong family support tended to push the boundaries of their arts practice and were able to ask for assistance when required.

I think he's a pretty good teacher ... I haven't done art for two years ... I thought as soon as I started the subject they're going to use a whole bunch of technical terms and I'm going to sit there going what? The first two lessons I just stayed back to talk to him ... he didn't just go on

with a whole bunch of art stuff I can't understand.
(School A)

Issues raised by participants from School B concerned their overall grade for admission to university. It appears that parents/guardians had discussed at some length the viability of senior art as a career choice. In some cases the direct intervention of the senior art teacher persuaded the participants to reconsider the passion they felt for the subject and enabled them to pursue it as a recognised subject for consideration into university. This support has evidently been ongoing evidenced by the following statement from one of the participants who had been dealing with a number of issues which had distracted him from his work:

He said he was really concerned ... because he had watched everything I've done and then to see me sitting in class and not doing anything. He said he was worried about my performance and whether or not I would even pass this unit. I went away and thought I've really got to step it up ... I probably wouldn't have cared about the grade at that point I was probably most worried about disappointing him ... I would have absolutely died if I had, in any kind of way, just given up. And it could have easily been the case. (School B)

There were less references to supportive thematic statements from School A (48) with a strong contrast to School B (106). These figures may have been affected due to the fact that the Senior Art Teacher at School A had only started at the school the year before and two of the participants had no contact with him prior to this. The three participants at School A had known their Senior Art teacher for at least three years prior to this study. However, each of the participants from School A spoke very highly of their teacher and it was evident he had provided extensive support for each of them.

ACCESS

The participants referred to access as the range of websites, television shows, networking forums, street art and art galleries they were able to view. Other aspects related to access included notable artists' works that a participant from each school had in their family art collection, including the famous contemporary Australian artists Gary Greenwood and Howard Arkley.

... [we own] Gary Greenwood's leather artwork as well. We're collectors. We've got five pieces and the museum only has four. (School A)

We used to own a Howard Arkley original. We flew to Melbourne at the end of 2006 for the retrospective. We've sold the work now – I think we sold it to renovate the kitchen and I'm sure that killed my parents but I guess we couldn't really hang on to it forever. (School B)

Another issue with access involved convincing their teacher that they should be allowed particular kinds of materials such as spray cans to use in their art work.

... he'll allow you to use those sorts of materials. Like so if you want to use spray cans for instance, you've got to be pretty, you've got to have it pretty well set out and you've got to encourage them that you're not going to go tagging. (School B)

Once again there was a strong contrast between thematic responses from School A (18) compared to School B (43). Due to the location of the school in a large metropolitan city and its proximity to galleries and street culture, participants from School B have greater exposure to a wider range of visual culture opportunities. Participants from School A are located in a smaller regional centre with limited opportunities to visit galleries and engage in street culture which may have affected this result.

AWARENESS

Thematic statements which were relevant to this theme included the way the participants felt their artworks could be interpreted by the viewer in the same way that artists can imbue their artworks with subversive messages. Some of the participants were also aware of how the combination of technology with their art could give their folio an edge over other students' artworks during assessment and ultimately for consideration into university.

[in reference to application for University] ... I've got to send twelve different pictures of my work. So I'm sending them a diversity, just a diverse amount of my stuff ... You have to print them out and send them like twelve hard copies of your work. Yeah I'm sending two digital pieces, two life drawings, three from my journal, two from my comic, three different paintings as well ... The digital also includes like 3D stuff that I've been doing which is so much fun. I hope they see that I want to do digital art. So if they see that I'm capable with a computer then they'll be like "oh cool" hopefully. (School A)

Another aspect was enhanced aesthetic awareness particularly in regards to how technology can be used indiscriminately and be called art.

So for this theory assignment we had a statement that said 'artists have to use their artworks to challenge rather than reflect society' and then you have to state whether it is true or not ... So this theory assignment has the technological explosion of the 1950s and 1960s and how that has altered the way artists do art and a lot of that has to do with the camera, because it's technology, it's art, someone takes a picture. But I was trying to argue that it shouldn't really be considered that because anyone with half a brain can press a button then go on the computer, do things with Photoshop and now its art. (School B)

There were less thematic statements concerning the theme of Awareness from the participants at School A (54) compared to the participants at School B (101). Two of the participants from School B were extremely passionate about their arts practice and wished to continue it after they had finished their schooling. One of the participants from School A intended to pursue his arts practice after Year 12 which may have contributed to the lower response rate from School A.

INSPIRATION

Thematic statements related to inspiration included electronic sources such as the internet, television, music or other similar types of resources. References to the theme of inspiration from School A included descriptions of particular cartoons such as "Samurai Shampoo", musical bands such as "Justice", documentaries about the stencil revolution in Melbourne and images from books and DVDs.

Because I've got the DVD you see, that's how I went about it. It's just amazing ... Like you see this along here how it's dark. What they did to do that they called them a trim and there's six of them going around the entire building and the way they've done that is they have grabbed every floor and rotated it like five degrees around. It's 40 stories high and every floor is five degrees difference to the other one. That's helping with ventilation as well which is making the building look just amazing. (School A)

Participants from School B discussed the inspiration they derived from graffiti artists which they saw on trains and in the city and also through books. One participant made direct reference to the contemporary Australian artist Howard Arkley's work which his family owned and linked it to his skills in airbrushing.

Another participant described how his sixties style poster art work and film making also complemented the band he was involved with.

I really like Banksy's work – he's a London graffiti artist. He does lots of street art around London like politics and all that sort of thing. He released a book about two years ago called "Banksy" with all these pictures taken of the work. It's like vandalism really but it's like done with art. It really, really makes you think. (School B)

Even though the responses were lower for the theme of Inspiration (School A = 21; School B = 12), it was evident through the participants' visual diaries that they had included a large amount of information from the internet to draw upon as inspiration for their work. One of the participants from School A admitted that he had put together three journals of other artists' work from images downloaded off the internet. It is a requirement for senior visual arts students to illustrate the process of their thinking through their visual diaries, therefore the participants' diaries were filled with a range of visual inspiration which had been annotated to describe the process they were undertaking.

DISCUSSION

In this pilot study we have examined how senior art students encounter and engage with technology in their arts practice. The small sample size limits broad generalisations from a study of this nature, however naturalistic generalisations are achievable. Stake (1995, p. 85) describes these as " ... conclusions that are arrived at through personal engagement ... by vicarious experience so well constructed that the person feels as if it happened to themselves." The extracts from the interviews supplied in the section of the findings provides the reader with descriptive data in order to create naturalistic generalisations. The assur-

ance of anonymity to the participants enabled them to provide an honest and reliable response regarding their engagement with technology in their arts practice. In addition, the subject matter was not ostensibly of a personal nature which also assisted the participants in providing reliable and non-emotive data.

The relationship the two participants' groups had with their senior art teacher appeared to have had an effect on the interview responses. Participants from School A had a shorter term relationship with their senior art teacher as opposed to participants from School B. "Often the jokes he made I never got in Year 10. I thought he was just being really mean but obviously he's joking around and stuff and I never quite got that sort of thing until like Year 11 where everything he does is a challenge to bring you up further" (School B). In addition, the exposure the participants had to a diverse range of media and techniques, and the opportunity to experiment during their years in junior art, appeared to have a significant impact on the risks they took in creating their works. "I chose art at [name of school] and it was a fairly good course. It basically taught us to do skills and things like that so that set you up fairly well for the senior art syllabus" (School B).

The support the students had from their senior art teacher and the exposure they had to a range of different artworks in different media enabled them to combine different concepts, media and approaches to produce artworks which enabled them to define and solve problems with flexibility and creativity. The participants also demonstrated that they were able to explore, appreciate and embrace contemporary visual arts practices and emerging technologies in the creation of their artworks (Queensland Studies Authority, 2007).

One of the participants, an ESL student from Korea, combined eastern and western influences and relied on her drawing skills to complete her major works. Her senior art teacher recognised her high standard of drawing skills and encouraged her to pursue this as the primary medium for her artworks. During the interviews the participant revealed that her visual arts education consisted of copying traditional works and "didn't really teach different kinds of art". She enjoyed learning about photography and designing at her new school as opposed to solely learning about drawing and painting. Yi and Sook (2005, p. 21) state that "the characteristics of traditional Korean paintings are mysteriousness, quietness, emptiness, calmness, vitality and lifelikeness". These features were evident in this participant's major art works which combined "eastern and western culture together ... so I can show the English and Korean difference in cultures." Her work examined the concept of angels with a combination of Buddhist inspired and Western angels and Korean text in the background. Her use of an overhead projector to enlarge images and the internet to source images was important to her process. It was evident however that drawing was her primary medium of expression. She admitted that it was difficult for her when she has difficulty understanding spoken English, however "[my teacher] is really good – he tries to understand what I'm saying and he's helping out what I want to find with some of the images ... he's really nice to me." This support and encouragement was instrumental in her approach to her final art works which challenged her traditional art education.

The other participants all used technology to a lesser or greater degree. Two participants developed their manual skills with using Perspex, bamboo and metal in one case to construct a series of cubes, and the other to make a plinth from Perspex within which were placed Ninja weapons. Another participant used the computer aided router to cut out figures from MDF board which were then painted with the aid of an overhead projector. The use of digital photographs which were manipulated and exhibited in conjunction with a series of photographs, in transition on a computer with a sound background, was created by another participant. One of the participants drew on his existing skills in stencil making and

filmmaking to create two significant bodies of work during the year using these as his primary mediums. It appears that most of the participants were comfortable in using technology – including older technologies such as overhead projectors – as part of their process and as a complement to their existing skills as evidenced in these descriptions of two of the participants' major artwork:

My next artwork is a reflection of a journey. It was more the physical sense of a journey. I had collected 2000 bus tickets – and I thought I'll use them in my artwork. So I added a picture and I zoomed in and zoomed out images in the exact shape of a bus ticket and put them on a scene. So it's kind of a bit like a puzzle except looking at it from a distance you can clearly see it and some are detailed, it's kind of meant to mean that some things are more important in a journey as opposed to others. There's tickets all through it, tickets over the whole thing and it's a street, the whole thing is a street, the picture, and I had to buy a toy bus which I ended up cutting in half, sticking it through the canvas, wrapping it in bus tickets so it kind of looked like a papier mache of a bus and it's coming out of the street. (School B)

I've made stencils of every five years of a person's life. At twenty they're getting their first job and wearing headphones, which is the connection to communication. My view or thing I was trying to say was that the headphones don't have a negative or positive impact on our communication. They just change the way we communicate. So if you're on a train and everyone's wearing headphones, they're not just talking to each other but they're talking to the artist who's playing music to them. So it's still communication, just changed differently, ... so the whole way through their life their wearing headphones. So there's somebody at their wedding and they're still wearing headphones and it finishes off with a gravestone and that's got the headphones falling off it. (School B)

It is interesting to note that in addition to utilising technology to some extent in the production of these pieces, the participants concurrently investigated the theme of technology in their major artworks. The participants demonstrated that they are critical consumers of technology with well developed analytical skills to critically evaluate diverse forms of information, including that which exists in technological environments. This was evidenced in the participants' ability to digitally manipulate images to parody material culture. As Robyler, Edwards and Havriluk (1997) note, it is important to understand that the communicative language of new technologies such as sound, animation, music, drama, video, graphics, text and voice, is also the language that the arts use. In this study it was evident that in addition to the existing skills with the technologies they were using, the participants also had critical analytical skills which allowed them to experiment with, refine and combine different media to create informed artworks. Technology in this study was not used indiscriminately or for its novelty value by the participants.

CONCLUSION

In this study we have examined how senior visual arts students encounter and engage with technology in their arts practice. Analysis of the interview data identified a number of themes that were consistently found within both participant groups. These included references to technological expertise, skills and expertise with traditional artistic media such as drawing and painting, support from their teacher, family and peers and access to and awareness of the inspiration that can be gained from a range of resources such as galleries, websites and computer programs. What was not investigated was the teachers' perceptions of how senior visual arts students encounter and engage with technology in their arts practice. However, the participants' discussion of the relationship

they had with their teacher inadvertently provided some insight into this area.

The purpose of this study sought only to investigate the extent to which senior visual arts students utilise technology in their arts practice. The researchers believe, however, that this study has highlighted a number of areas which may need to be investigated before the assumption can be made that all senior visual arts students have the ability to engage with and utilise technology effectively in their practice. These include: the cultural background and level of technological skills of senior art students; the socio-economic background of the home and school environment; the ratio of teacher to student; the teacher's expertise and confidence with technology; the support given to senior art students in their choice of the subject; the senior art students relationship with their teacher and lastly the scope within the senior art program for students to pursue self-directed study.

REFERENCES

Aland, J. (2004). The impact of digital technologies on contemporary visual arts education. *Australian Art Education*, *27*(2), 4–21.

Bamford, A. (2006). *The Wow Factor: Global research compendium of the arts in education*. Berlin: Waxmann.

Baruch, Y. (1999). Response rates in academic studies: A comparative analysis. *Human Relations*, *52*(4), 421–438.

Burns, R. (2000). *Introduction to Research Methods*. (4th ed.). Frenchs Forest, Australia: Pearson Education.

Davis, D. (2008). *First we see: The national review of visual education*. Australian Government.

European University Association. (2007). *Creativity in Higher Education*. Report on the EUA Creativity Project 2006 – 2007. Retrieved on January 15th 2007 from <www.eua.be/fileadmin/user_upload/files/Publications/Creativity_in_higher_education.pdf>

Gardner, H. (1993). *Frames of mind: the theory of multiple intelligences*. New York: Basic Books.

Ivers, K. (2003). *A teacher's guide to using technology in the classroom*. Westport, CT: Libraries Unlimited.

Kniveton, B. (2004). The influences and motivations on which students base their choice of career. *Research in Higher Education, 72*, 47–59.

Kvale, S. (1996). *InterViews: An introduction to qualitative research interviewing*. Thousand Oaks, CA: Sage.

Lapan, T., Hinkelman, J., Adams, A., & Turner, S. (1999). Understanding rural adolescents' interests, values and efficacy expectations. *Journal of Career Development, 26*(2), 107–124.

Morgan, D. (1986). *Girls' education and career choice: What the research says*. Sydney: NSW Joint Non-Government Schools' P.E.P. Committee.

Muffoletto, R. (1994). Technology and restructuring education: Constructing a context. *Educational Technology, 34*(2), 24–28.

Oakley, K. (2007). *Educating for the creative workforce: Rethinking Arts and Education*. Australia Council for the Arts. Retrieved 14 March, 2008 from <www.australiacouncil.gov.au/publications/education_and_the_arts/creative_workforce_re-thinking_arts_and_education>

Palfrey, J., & Gasser, U. (2008). *Born digital: Understanding the first generation of digital natives*. New York: Basic Books.

Prensky, M. (2001). Digital natives, digital immigrants. *On the Horizon, 9*(5). Retrieved on 20 January, 2009 from http://www.marcprensky.com/writing/Prensky%20-%20Digital%20Natives%20Digital%20Immigrants%20-%20Part1.pdf

Queensland Studies Authority. (2007). *Senior visual art 2007*. Spring Hill, Queensland: Queensland Government.

Robinson, K. (2001). *Out of our minds: Learning to be creative*. Chichester, UK: Capstone.

Robyler, M., Edwards, J., & Havriluk, M. (1997). *Integrating educational technology into teaching*. Upper Saddle River, NJ: Prentice-Hall Inc.

Ross, T., & Bailey, G. (1996). *Technology-based learning: A handbook for teachers and technology leaders*. Australia: IRI/Skylight Training and Publishing, Inc.

Saettler, P. (1990). *The evolution of American educational technology*. Englewood, CO: Libraries Unlimited.

Sawyer, R. K. (2006). *Explaining creativity*. New York: Oxford University Press.

Silverman, D. (2001). *Interpreting qualitative data*. (2nd ed.). London: Sage Publications.

Stake, R. (1995). *The art of case study research*. Thousand Oaks, CA: Sage.

Toffler, A. (1971). *Future shock*. London: Pan Books.

Tringali, D. (1993). *Success not stereotyping: Gender perceptions in a low socio-economic school and the effects this has on subject selection and career choice*. Dissertation, The University of Queensland, Australia.

Twombey, C., Shamburg, C., & Zieger, L. (2006). *Teachers as technology leaders*. Washington, DC: International Society for Technology in Education.

Wind, Y. (2006). Managing creativity. *Rotman Magazine*, Spring/Summer, 20-23.

Wright, S. (2003). *The arts, young children, and learning*. Boston: Allyn & Bacon.

Wright, S. (2004). *Children, meaning-making and the arts*. Frenchs Forest, Australia: Pearson, Prentice Hall.

Yi, S. D., & Kim, H. S. (2005). The value of Korean art and cultural heritage. *Art Education*, *58*(5), 18–24.

Chapter 9
The Bard and the Web:
Using Vodcasting to Enhance Teaching of Shakespeare to Pre-Service English Teachers

Anita Jetnikoff
Queensland University of Technology, Australia

ABSTRACT

In a multiliterate age we are teaching through technology, even in erstwhile conservative subjects such as English. Once teacher preparation involved only print based texts which preservice teachers read. English has always occupied the territory of the printed word, but is there room for technology in the study of the bard? Multiliteracies involve the mastery of a repertoire of literacy practices, including those deploying technology. This chapter describes a research project, which explores the challenges and concerns preservice teachers face when teaching complex literature such as Shakespeare. The chapter describes and evaluates the effectiveness of preservice students' interactions with a set of digital vodcasts featuring an 'expert teacher' teaching Shakespeare's Hamlet. This is an exploratory study deploying mostly qualitative analysis of survey data and focus group discussions with preservice teachers in their final year of undergraduate study at an Australian university. The use of vodcast resources allowed preservice teachers to effectively access 'expert performance,' to critically problem-solve specific issues around teaching Shakespeare, detailed in the project's design. In deploying this technology, the preservice teachers effectively engage in a 'cognitive apprenticeship' through a repertoire of literacy practices on their way to becoming reflective practitioners.

TEACHING HOW TO TEACH SHAKESPEARE: WHICH APPROACH?

Is complex literature such as Shakespearean plays now being taught using technology or does it rely mostly on the printed word of the original play texts alongside articles about pedagogical approaches? A multiliteracies approach to literature study means that students need to master a 'repertoire of literacy practices', become researchers themselves and to encourage their own students to research texts analytically. The multiliteracies 'four resources model'

DOI: 10.4018/978-1-60566-842-0.ch009

for reading can be applied at tertiary level (Luke & Freebody, 2000) and I will refer to this framework in reviewing the relevant literature on pedagogical approaches to Shakespeare. Each model of English teaching approaches the teaching of Shakespeare in different ways, so some of this literature needs to be canvassed here. The 'cultural heritage' approach was in favour when I was at school and University. This favoured 'cracking the code' of Shakespearean language, through close, heavily glossed study of the written text. As students, we were asked to respond by writing an unseen, expository, literary essay with an audience of one examiner; the teacher. This formulaic approach falls short of how Luke and Freebody (2000) described the reader role of the 'text analyst', even though the final task was analytical in its broadest sense. It was somewhat surprising then that much of the current online content on Shakespeare, especially web sites devised in the United States still has this cultural heritage approach at its heart. Recent online Study Guides such as 'Sparknotes,' (Barnes & Noble, 2006) provide author-centred text guides to canonical texts which do little more than the print based ones do, except perhaps allow greater access to a wider audience. The suggested student assessment in these online environments often takes the form of analytical exposition, with some option for performance or film related tasks (Littauer, 2006). Performance approaches which depend on reading and acting from the original written text before viewing professionals are advocated by some teachers (Kissler, 1997). Performance approaches depend on students 'participating' in the text or 'using' it, in terms of the four reader roles.

More current and relevant approaches both in online and offline environments ask students to study various versions of the play in text, film or performance and to respond in ways which recreate 'known' texts with wider imagined audiences (Davis, 2003; Farabaugh, 2007; Kliman, 2001; Plasse, 2004). These can still work at developing arguments deploying the language of persua-

sion in the same way that a literary exposition can; a feature article or comment can do much the same linguistic work. The latter however, envisage a wider audience and call on students' knowledge of the mediated world in which they live. I take the position that critical literacy and technology must have a place in the classroom if it is to make the canon digestible and relevant (Freesmith, 2006; Jetnikoff, 2006; Kliman, 2001; Snyder, 2008). Some teachers have used online technology such as wikis to establish a discourse community to enhance students' learning about Shakespeare in relation to written assignments (Farabaugh, 2007). There is much research evidence to support the view that Shakespeare must be taught alongside popular and contemporary texts (Hulbert, Wetmore, & York, 2006; Plasse, 2004) to prepare students to operate in a multiliterate world (Franks, Durran, & Burn, 2006). If the clever, satirical animation series, *The Simpsons,* helps students to understand and enjoy *Hamlet,* then why wouldn't we use it? It is certainly part of my students' reading/viewing repertoires.

Reviewing the extant literature reveals a plethora of pedagogical approaches and teachers do their best to update new techniques and teaching strategies on top of their old ones. For instance the critical literacy elements of the current Queensland Syllabus means that students are asked to engage 'critically' with these 'classical' Elizabethan texts, both as literary works and through available contemporary 'readings,' such as film versions (QBSSS, 2002)[1]. This approach assumes that students read Shakespeare through their own historical lenses, and teachers are using combined approaches of performance, cultural heritage elements, in terms of reading the plays as poetry and as narrative, and also through critical literacy, as text which mobilises discourses (Mellor, 1989; Strickland, 1993). The text-based approach is still used, where students read around the class from the text and combine this with filmed modernised film adaptations versions, such as *Ten Things I Hate About You* (Junger, 1999) alongside the text of

Shakespeare's *The Taming of the Shrew* (Jetnikoff, 2003). This textual juxtaposition involves readers as 'text analysts' (Luke & Freebody, 2000) within the parameters of the four resources model in a much more applied way then the literary essay described earlier.

With this plethora of approaches and given the heavy demands of an English Curriculum unit needing to cover all aspects of the senior syllabus, theories of language, texts and learners, how do we best prepare our students to confidently teach the bard? Prior to this vodcast project our preservice English teachers had previously been prepared by print- based, 'set readings,' including secondary teaching units and films based on Shakespeare. For my pre-service teachers to be multiliterate and critically literate readers I make the following assumptions. They can read and/or view a wide range of texts with critical lenses. That means they can question the underlying assumptions made by the text, whether that text is a Shakespearean play or a reading *about* the teaching of Shakespeare, rather than read it at face value. That they can engage in 'dialogue' or conversations with the text (whether print- based or digital). This process should empower and enable preservice English teachers to become powerful readers who ask questions both of the texts they read, and the culture within which they have been created and read, and ultimately encourage this of their students.

The pre-service teachers studying English Curriculum were offered a diverse set of readings which covered different pedagogical approaches, which they were asked to engage critically with. These readings comprised a range of models, teaching methods and strategies familiar to English teachers in Australia. For instance semiotics might be deployed to investigate the opening scene of Baz Luhrman's *Romeo and Juliet*, (1996). Personal reactions may be sought in response to a vivid scene involving young lovers in *Romeo and Juliet* or revenge in *Hamlet*. Rather than slipping back into a personal growth or 'reader response' model

(Karolides, 2000), these approaches encourage an intertextual reading of the play, so that students can relate to the characters and events of the play to texts with which they are more familiar. This can lead into an effective and critical discussion of the discourses of the play, for instance by investigating discourses of madness in *Hamlet*, or through comparing historically constructed representations of characters in different filmed versions as described above. I asked the students when they were completing the previous curriculum unit at third year level, to read or watch one or two video versions of *Hamlet* in their semester break in preparation for their final curriculum unit.

The set of readings the pre-service teachers were given were mostly written by other teachers and included teaching strategies framed both as broad approaches and as specific lesson and unit ideas. One of the set readings covered a performance approach to *Romeo and Juliet*, (Robinson, 1999). Students were also asked to read a film based teaching approach (Lusted, 1991) and an article on using film adaptations in Senior English, (Jetnikoff, 2005). An extract from Mellor's (1989) critical literacy approach to *Hamlet*, was also set. Another reading intertextually combined film, literature, pop culture and text-based approach to *Romeo and Juliet* (Miller & Colwill, 2003). This pedagogical approach combining critical readings of film, pop culture and the original play text of *Hamlet* was the one demonstrated by the expert teacher with her senior classes in the vodcast lessons. The set readings were also accessed from an online 'Course Materials' data base. Even to access course readings, tertiary students must now be computer literate. If we argue that 'print based' literacy is necessary, but no longer sufficient, (Luke & Freebody, 2000) then other technologies also needed to be taken into account in my own teaching and in my students' teaching and learning. Thus the vodcasting project was born.

BACKGROUND

In a multiliterate age English teachers now must master digital technologies both in their learning and teaching. When the Education Queensland 'Literate Futures' (Luke & Freebody, 2000) document was published, the millennial way of the future encompassed students' mastery of digital technologies as an integral part of teaching in 'new times.' Current debates, especially recent, reactionary press reports (Donnelly, 2006; Snyder, 2008) reflect considerable confusion about technology's vital place in the English Curriculum. Cries of the 'dumbing down' of English by including media study, has been given considerable press coverage and academics involved in pre-service teaching preparation have been blamed for an ostensible demise in literacy standards (Snyder, 2008). Uninformed conservative critics (Donnelly, 2006) would have us return to the kind of 'one true way of reading' that they were exposed to in their own schooling decades ago. Tertiary students' familiarity with technologies means that if we do not use them in our own teaching, we are not deploying a set of skills and knowledge with which they are already confident (Baelstri, Ehrman, & Ferguson, 1992; Buckingham, 1993; Chambers & Stacey, 2005; Kress, 2003). Furthermore 'critical literacy', which underpins the multiliteracies project represents a 'threshold concept,' after which there is no turning back to regressive methods of teaching literature.

The vodcasting project builds on the findings of another preservice study using 'stimulated video recall' (Ethell & McMeniman, 2000). The researchers first filmed an effective teacher teaching secondary classes. They then used a 'video recall,' technique to record this 'expert practitioner' reflecting on his teaching in workshops with preservice teachers. Ethell and McMeniman discussed the teacher's critical self-reflections on his own practice, with preservice teachers with very positive results. The workshops revealed 'expert-to-novice' principles (Sternberg & Horvath, 1995)

were at work as the teacher reflected on the intentions behind his classroom strategies. These were then discussed with the pre-service teachers who found this to be very effective in building their own approaches to classroom teaching. Other than this, their only experience had been the often mimetic practices derived from observational experiences on practicum with supervising teachers. As Ethell and McMeniman (2000) note, this experience contributed significantly to preservice teachers' understandings of good teaching.

STUDY DESIGN

The vodcasting project involved seventy final year preservice teachers responding to 'situated, problem-based, learning' (Savery & Duffy, 2001) through five video streams of an expert teacher in action. Twenty-two of these were surveyed at the end of the unit, using a voluntary, anonymous Likert style questionnaire, to determine how effective their preparation to teach Shakespeare had been. The questionnaire canvassed opinions on whether or not Shakespeare should be mandatory in the curriculum, their prior experience of Shakespeare, the effectiveness of print- based readings and the vodcasts for determining their pedagogical approaches, including assessing Shakespeare in schools. Following this, the same twenty-two participants were invited to engage in three separate focus groups, where further discussions centred on the effectiveness of the vodcasts and the other materials in preparing them to become confident teachers of Shakespeare.

My approach to the vodcasting project was slightly different to the Ethell and McMeniman study (2003). The video resources were created through a small Teaching and Learning Grant. Rather than following the teaching episodes with the teacher's reflections, I began with an 'up-front' interview with the expert teacher, Chris Poulsen. Chris Poulsen teaches English at an inner city state school. I asked the students to look for the particular strategies Chris spoke about in her classes in the subsequent videoed lessons. The interview video was titled, "What does English teaching mean to me?" In this vodcast the expert teacher responded to my questions about her teaching practice, philosophy, and how current theory underpins her English teaching practices. In this interview Chris touched on pertinent issues relating to current 'literature' debates, such as the need to balance the critical with the aesthetic, notions of pleasure and displeasure in the text. The aim of the interview was to establish how an experienced teachers' pedagogy reflects her understanding of theory along with her values, attitudes and beliefs about learning, language, and text. These reflections were then illustrated and realised in the edited videos of a term's work in her classroom, teaching two different, Year 12 English cohorts. One class was highly academic and the other a class of 'excellence in dance' students. Chris explained in the interview that she would teach the same text, *Hamlet*, quite differently with the two classes, using more kinaesthetic strategies with the dancers. One preservice teacher noted, "Chris taught some things in ways I would never have thought to, like lining the students up with the narrative structure and placing them [plot events] in the correct order." Filming and editing and uploading of teaching episodes as vodcasts allowed the preservice teachers not only the face-to-face workshopping and discussion of the classroom events, but also to access these again in their own time.

The DVD version of the interview was played to all the students in a tutorial at the beginning of the English Curriculum unit. I asked the preservice teachers to return to it at the end of the nine week unit, after they had watched Chris teach the *Hamlet* unit to see if and how her philosophy had infused her teaching. The participating students saw a clear connection between her pedagogical *intentions*, her *approach* and her pedagogical *practice*. This demonstrates how acquired knowledge is enhanced by practice, and illustrates the expert

teacher's ability to engage in 'reflection-in-action' and 'reflection-on-action' (Schon, 1983). Vodcasting expert teaching episodes, viewed in conjunction with what Schon (1983) termed, 'coaching', by university tutors who are also experienced secondary English teachers, makes the expert teacher's thinking transparent to the novice.

I envisaged this approach combined with more traditional ones, including wide, critical reading around the topic of teaching Shakespeare, would be an effective method to help preservice teachers see how experienced teachers apply current language and literary theory to practice. The preservice teachers could then use this information, as part of a 'cognitive apprenticeship' (Ethell & McMeniman, 2000) to reflect on their own pedagogical practices and identities as future English teachers. Thus although the process was preparative rather than based on recall, the streamed video resources and associated materials were designed to capture 'expert knowledge' of experienced English teachers in action (Ethell & McMeniman, 2000; Schon, 1983). In doing so the preservice teachers engaged in all four reader roles (Luke & Freebody, 2000).

THE CONTENT OF THE VODCASTS

There were five vodcasts in all, which were viewed formally across the nine-week tertiary English Curriculum unit. Some involved several combined lessons. Each videostream was edited into teaching episodes mostly between 15 and 20 minutes long. Most 'lessons' were interspersed with appropriate segments of interview material, where 'expert' teacher, Chris, explained specific strategies and aspects of her teaching and described her learners. The videostreams were uploaded to the University unit website, numbered and titled and covered the following content and processes:

1. 'What English teaching means to me,' contained the opening interview, where the

expert teacher spoke about her philosophy of English teaching and approaches to text, language, unit planning assessment, learners, and teaching strategies.

2. 'Unit planning' interspersed interview questions and responses about Chris's approach to unit planning with examples of these strategies appearing as actual teaching segments in the classroom. In both this and the previous vodcast, the preservice teachers were engaging in the reader roles of text analyst and text participant, in that they were generating information from one text and relating it to their own use and production and design of their Shakespeare teaching units.

3. 'Focussed learning episode' showed Chris doing very close textual analysis of the printed Shakespearean text interspersed with a filmed version of the same text. Her Year 12 students read around the class and they discussed in detail the meaning of the text and different readings and interpretations of the filmed versions. This vodcast in particular, showed the teacher's 'expert knowledge' of the play and her secondary students engaging in 'Shakespearean 'code cracking.' The preservice teachers were being 'text participants' and 'text users' in deploying 'lesson planning' and curriculum specific metalanguage to discuss the learning activities.

4. 'Processing assessment' entailed interview responses about current assessment principles and the actual tasks set by the teacher and the school interspersed with teaching episodes of Chris processing the assessment task and criteria with her students. These were supplemented by soft copies of the task sheets and other materials constructed by the teacher and used in the lesson clips of the final vodcasts. This vodcast showed the teacher's expertise and knowledge of current theory and pedagogical approaches. It also

demonstrated the Year 12 students' ability to take on the role of 'text analyst' or reader as researcher as wide research informed their final summative tasks in response to *Hamlet.*

5. 'Student Assessment samples' was the longest video stream of 45 minutes where the Year 12 students were filmed performing their spoken assessment tasks. Some of the comments of the expert teacher were left on the video to model her thinking about evaluating the spoken tasks. Others were left without comment so that the preservice teachers could use the school-designed, 'authentic' criteria sheets to evaluate the students' orals. This vodcast showed the teachers expertise and knowledge of current approaches to holistic, authentic and contextualised assessment. Interacting with this vodcast saw the preservice teachers 'using' the available texts (downloaded written criteria) by participating in the assessment of the secondary students.

TEACHING APPROACHES TO SHAKESPEARE

To determine the effectiveness of the set readings, the twenty-two preservice teachers participated in a voluntary, anonymous questionnaire. They were asked to indicate which readings they had read and if these had helped with their teaching approaches to Shakespeare.

Of the twenty-two participants, nineteen said the readings had been very helpful in assisting their pedagogical approaches to teaching Shakespeare. Of the three who said the readings had not helped them, two had done virtually no reading at all and one, who said the readings had "not [helped] greatly," had read nothing. One said, "Not really [helpful] - would prefer to have more in-class examples." In spite of this response, the readings had been explicitly examined, analysed and compared with one another for their strategies and approaches, each student becoming an 'expert' on one approach and teaching it to others, in the manner of an "expert jigsaw". No matter how well a course is prepared, no one can actually make students read. Many had found the readings quite helpful as one respondent said, "...they've given me new ideas". Another said, "They have put some teaching activities into perspective". One participant, "...would have liked more". Some of the other responses are recorded below:

"I loved the article on the performance/ drama approach, great ideas for teaching, because I don't have a drama background".

"I like the practicality of performance and breaking down scenes/pivotal moments into kinaesthetic focussed activities."

"...it's useful seeing that there is more than one way to approach the text."

"They were most helpful- lots of good ideas for adapting into your own classroom."

"Yes, but perhaps more examples."

"They gave me great ideas of performance in the classroom."

"They have given me some lesson ideas."

"They are fantastic."

"...[the readings] opened entirely new ways of approaching these texts".

I interpret these findings as indicating that the preservice teachers who engaged with the readings found them beneficial in helping them to develop ideas for teaching Shakespeare. They were clearly demonstrating here the reader role of 'text users'. I also wanted to know however, if

these 'apprentices' thought that the bard should be a mandatory part of the curriculum, since 'cracking the codes' of Shakespeare is seen as a daunting challenge.

SHOULD SHAKESPEARE BE MANDATORY?

The Queensland Syllabus indicates that senior students should have access to and study, "2-4 drama texts (in most cases one Shakespearean play)," which leaves the decision largely to the individual school (QBSSS, 2002). Of the 22 preservice teachers involved in this research project, 12 thought that Shakespeare should be a mandatory aspect of the English curriculum. This was in spite of some participants expressing apprehension about teaching it well. One student echoed many others in the focus group saying, "Shakespeare is an example of how beautiful and powerful language can be". Another wrote, "I believe all students should have the opportunity to engage with Shakespeare" and, "Shakespeare was written for 'the people'. Students should be able to enjoy it as much as they did years ago," and, "...it has influenced so many other texts." This refutes the critics who have argued that MacDonalds has supplanted *Macbeth* in the English classroom and that English teachers no longer teach Shakespeare. This hardly sounds like a group of prospective English teachers who are denouncing the canon. Another said, "Shakespeare is an important part of English and can demonstrate language themes over time," and one defended their inclusion in a more 'critical' way in saying, Shakespeare should be a mandatory part of the curriculum, "as it is completely relevant to today's society and contemporary ideologies and discourses". This was echoed by the idea that, "you can address many of today's issues with a Shakespearean play," and, "I think including Shakespeare should be mandatory as it offers so many benefits for students – they should be given the opportunity [to study it]... although it may not suit all classes/contexts."

Six preservice teachers with misgivings about *mandatory* teaching of Shakespeare circled the option, "it depends on the teacher and/ or the class." Some did not include a comment, however, one respondent wrote, "it should be mandatory if it can be done well. It can show students how beautiful language can be and how far we have come... understanding Shakespearean texts leads to a higher understanding of our own cultural development and discourse." Another said that Shakespeare, "needs to be taught properly, therefore if teachers aren't comfortable with it/ capable of teaching it properly maybe it should be passed over. Otherwise students might end up hating it through no fault of their own." Four participants circled, 'it depends on...' with the option to include their reason. One said, "I don't think texts should be forced upon classes so teacher should use it as a part of study so students are familiar... Shakespeare is 'cultured' and there is an underlying classicist [sic] knowledge... I don't really like the fact that it is valued over other texts." And, "...this is a chicken/ egg question- students should 'do' Shakespeare, however, if it's done badly- students may well be scarred for life- so it is dependant on how well the teacher is presenting the material." Another said, "...It should be up to the teacher, as if the teacher does not feel comfortable teaching it they won't teach it well." This position of needing to teach it well was reinforced by many other respondents. One said, while it should not be, "... mandatory, the use of language and ubiquity of Shakespeare in our modern culture means that Shakespeare would definitely be taught to most classes. However, only the teacher can gauge the benefits such a topic may have to their class." To summarise these comments, the preservice teachers were in favour of teaching Shakespeare as long as it could be taught well. These responses are interesting in their focus on pedagogy.

PRIOR EXPERIENCE AND PERFORMANCE

Since this study is premised on the concept of a 'cognitive apprenticeship', the notion of experience is significant. Viewing the vodcasts of an expert teacher in action and reflection constitutes a vicarious experience. This engaging 'from the edge,' of a, 'community of practice' is what Lave and Wenger (1991) call, 'legitimate peripheral participation'. The preservice teachers also bring lived experience to their study of Shakespeare. Their prior knowledge and experience of Shakespearean works is therefore important. This constituted previous study, viewed or acted performance through theatre and/or film, and prior teaching practicum. Such prior experience probably had a bearing on how confident the participants were as prospective teachers.

All of the twenty-two participants had studied Shakespeare at school. Those whose only exposure was the secondary school experience, can probably be summed up by this response, "...it does not prepare me confidently to teach as my experience was very dry." This was echoed in the focus group discussion. Some of the participants in the survey had attended professional performances, seen films, tutored and had exposure to teaching methods during their previous practicum. Others had attended professional performances, or seen films. The list of plays they had collective experience of was vast, although the figures in parentheses indicate how many had studied each play in an educational context: *Romeo and Juliet (14), Macbeth (8), Hamlet (8), Julius Caesar (2) Taming of the Shrew (3) Much Ado about Nothing (3), King Lear (1), Othello (1)*. The following plays had been seen in performance or film versions: *Othello, King Lear, a Midsummer Night's Dream (3), The Merchant of Venice (2), Twelfth Night (2), Comedy of Errors (1), Richard II (1), Richard III (1), The Tempest (1), and Titus Andronicus (1)*.

Some participants in the survey had also studied the Sonnets. About 50 per cent of the responding cohort had undertaken a semester-long discipline unit at undergraduate level focusing exclusively on Shakespeare. Students who had taken this unit reported mixed responses, such as, "[I]...studied at uni at a cursory level. Definitely [I am] more confident- especially from the practicum." A different response indicated, "...my difficulty in '[Shakespeare:] Then and Now,' kind of shattered my confidence in my own ability". Another suggested, "[I'm] definitely more confident about teaching it and looking at how cultural values from the past and present affect the way we read the texts. The "Redressing the Canon Course" was most useful".

Their prior experience had various effects on their confidence, for some it increased while others still felt daunted by the task ahead of them. One said, "I know a little bit so I'm not scared of teaching Shakespeare, but I'm not confident". The overriding theme of the discussion suggested that those displaying the most confidence had actual *experience* of teaching as well as the theoretical preparation of having studied it themselves at school and at the university. This shows that they were reflecting-on-action, in describing themselves as practitioners (Schon, 1983).

The focus group discussion revealed fears about the challenges of "obscurity of the language." The focus group also commonly identified the following as specific challenges: 'getting students beyond the fear of the language,' 'coming up with dynamic teaching ideas' and 'student engagement'. One pre-service teacher said, her biggest challenge about teaching Shakespeare was, "...making it fun, interesting and engaging. Understanding the language well enough yourself to feel comfortable teaching it." Most of the preservice teachers saw the greatest challenge as, "...keeping students engaged"... and "coming up with dynamic teaching ideas." Others expressed a wish that their students operate on the affective as well as the knowledge domain in suggesting they want to, "make it fun as well as breaking down the barriers of the language" and another

was aware of, "...help[ing] students to overcome the fear of Elizabethan language ... and...helping students to enjoy Shakespeare as much as I do." Another suggested that, "some students have a fear of the language and this can block their affective filter to prevent their appreciation of the text." Such honest responses suggested to me that these future teachers in their final semester of Curriculum Studies were certainly seriously reflecting on their own performance as teachers. This is indicated by their concern for 'engaging' the learners who would soon be in their charge. This signals their growing desire to perform as 'dynamic' and interesting teachers. It also signals a desire to get students beyond the 'code cracking' phase of reading Shakespeare to the point where they can participate in the texts, use them and respond to them in creative ways.

The nervousness expressed by the preservice teachers who described themselves as unconfident, related largely to their lack of teaching experience. For instance, one said, s/he was confident, "...to some degree. Having not had the opportunity to teach it yet, I would feel somewhat apprehensive". One wrote:

Before I saw Romeo and Juliet on prac the only experience I had with Shakespeare was very limited ... small amount at school and personal enjoyment watching film versions... So this lack of experience made me very nervous about teaching Shakespeare.

The notion of experience here relates to the concept of performance. Even those students who had witnessed teachers teaching on practicum felt better prepared than those who had not. It is supposed then that the exposure to an expert teacher actually teaching her classes across a unit on *Hamlet*, might allow these 'apprentice' teachers to peripherally participate in those classroom events, taking on some of the characteristics of that expert.

THE CONTENT AND PROBLEM-SOLVING RELATING TO THE VODCASTS

The form which such 'peripheral participation' took in our tertiary classrooms was problem-based learning in a virtual community. The preservice teachers were posed questions to reflect on what was being taught and how this married both with Chris's approach in the videostreams and with current theoretical approaches to learning and teaching English and assessment. By engaging with the vodcast materials, the preservice teachers could define their own particular cognitive problematics, investigating relevant pedagogical issues.

The Effects of the Vodcasts Streams on Preservice Teachers

So although the set print based readings were helpful, and applying the multiliteracies maxim, that 'print based text is necessary but no longer sufficient,' (Luke & Freebody, 2000) I wondered if the vodcasts of an expert teacher in action could substantively add to their experience and /or confidence? I asked in the questionnaire: "Were the video streams showing an experienced teacher actually teaching a unit on *Hamlet,* useful in shaping your approach to teaching Shakespeare at school?" The analysis of the responses to the vodcasts focussed around two areas of interest for me as a researcher. The first was the effect they had on preservice teachers' pedagogy and the second focus was on assessment. The following responses were recorded and classified into three themes relating to pedagogy: *creative teaching strategies and ideas*; *theory to practice*; and *active learner engagement*. These correspond to some of the fears and challenges about teaching Shakespeare the preservice teachers identified earlier. In all of these categories, the preservice teachers showed themselves to be participating in all four reader roles: text code cracker, text participant, text user

and text analyst (Luke & Freebody, 2000) while reading or viewing these vodcast texts. Firstly they were 'cracking the codes' of Shakespearean language as well as the language components of teaching units and lessons. Readers use the 'text participant' role as they brought theoretical information to the practices in the vodcast texts. In drawing information from the text and relating the ideas in the vodcasts to their own practice these preservice teachers were clearly *using* the text for their own specific purposes. In using the ideas from the vodcasts to influence the design of their own units and lessons they were engaging in the role of the 'text analyst'.

Creative Teaching Strategies and Ideas

The students responded positively to the expert teacher's lessons as a springboard for their own teaching ideas. One said, "They showed me more ways to be creative in my teaching," and another said, the vodcast lessons were, "... full of ideas." Another participant validated the concept of 'situated learning,' by suggesting that the vodcasts, "... showed a real teaching context, teaching strategies and resources." Another was able to see that they were valuable in offering, "useful suggestions and ideas." This was echoed in the response, "...Some very good ideas, especially for that particular class." This shows the participant was thinking about the need to tailor learning experiences for specific cohorts of students, including those potentially resistant to Shakespeare, like the less academic class in the vodcasts. One preservice teacher said the series of vodcasts, "... demonstrated how an articulate and experienced teacher can explain the design, structuring and implementation of a unit with thoughtful teaching advice and recommendations. Very useful." This is clearly a demonstration of reflection-in-action.

THEORY TO PRACTICE

Other pedagogical responses to the vodcasts related to the translation of linguistic and literary theory to teaching practice. Preservice teachers must master fairly complex language and literary theories specific to the discipline of subject English. These theories make deeper sense if they are applied and demonstrated through specific unit and lesson design. At fourth year level, these preservice teachers have already imbibed many of the complexities and intricacies of lesson and unit planning, and the nature of different learners, but they must also implement these at an appropriate senior stage of learning, using a range of literature and media. The gap between designing a unit and actually teaching it can be quite wide.

Of the participants surveyed the most confident were the few who had actually *experienced* or *witnessed* effective teaching of Shakespeare on practicum as explained above. The vodcasts were intended not just to replicate this practicum experience for *all* the preservice teachers in the study, but to also provide insights into *why* an expert teacher's chosen strategies were effective in the classroom. After watching Chris describe her approach and then perform it, one preservice teacher remarked, "The video streams helped me to see that it could be done. It has also given me some lesson ideas." Another said, "Yes, I think it is always more beneficial to see theory in practice." One said, the vodcast series of lessons, "... shows us what can work in the classroom. It scaffolds our ideas." Two qualitative comments that really demonstrate reflection-on-action are these: the vodcasting was effective, "... because she [Chris] told you what she was going to do and how to do it,"... and..."it is always useful to see other teachers in action." This last response shows the preservice teacher casting herself as a teacher and the 'expert teacher' as a fellow practitioner. Other respondents described engaging with particular theoretical problems by gleaning the following from the viewing of the vodcasts. One said, "...

the aesthetic/critical argument was informative." Another suggested that the vodcasts, "put into focus the critical and cultural analysis of teaching Shakespeare." In this the preservice teachers also demonstrate the role of the 'text user', since the vodcast texts prompted the reader to take action for their own purposes or learning outcomes (Luke & Freebody, 2000) .

Active Engagement

When describing fears and challenges about teaching Shakespeare, "engaging learners" was a common concern amongst the surveyed preservice teachers. After viewing the vodcasts, one responded with, "...it was great getting to watch a teacher actively engaging a class with Shakespeare." Another said, "...it was very helpful to see it taught so explicitly and to see how if taught effectively, kids will enjoy it." Another preservice teacher noted that it was, "good to see texts that were used...would like to see lesson plans also." This last comment reflects the experience gap between the 'apprentice' and the 'expert practitioner', whose vast experience means that she no longer needs to write detailed lesson plans of the type that we ask preservice teachers to write, to theoretically evaluate their prospective competence in the classroom.

Only one student reported a negative response to the videostreams, which related to not having experience of the Shakespearean and associated texts under study. "Not having read the texts spoken about in the video streams I did not always connect." This respondent admitted to only watching one of the streams. This also meant the student was a non-attendee, since all the streams were viewed and workshopped in tutorials.

THE VODCASTS' EFFECTS ON UNDERSTANDING ASSESSMENT

Two of the longer videostreams focussed particularly on assessment and on preparing students for the tasks. Because we do not teach to an external examination in Queensland, potential assessment tasks are open to wide variation within the mandated and 'verified' aspects of the Syllabus (QBSSS, 2002). In particular, the preservice teachers found the videostreams useful in learning about current assessment tasks and strategies. As described above in the content of the vodcasts, soft copies of assessment instruments, such as tasks and conditions, accompanying criteria sheets, and handouts to assist 'negotiated tasks' were uploaded to the English Curriculum Studies unit website to accompany the streams. Prior to introducing the vodcast initiative, these were always previously provided in print form, to model how assessment is shaped, designed and implemented. Our students were able to assess written work using these matrices. With the vodcasts, however, the process of teaching these tasks became explicit.

One respondent said, the vodcasts and assessment instruments showed, "...the way in which tasks can be multimodal, cater for a range of different interests." The difference between the printed materials and the vodcasts is that the former presented a hypothetical context but with the latter they could actually see an expert teacher teaching texts and tasks in a real context. They could also evaluate her effectiveness as a teacher by viewing her senior students effectively performing their oral assessment as a result of her exceptional teaching. In terms of the reader roles this is 'text participation' at its best as the preservice teachers scaffolded their own pedagogical strategies from the material in the vodcast texts. The preservice teachers could also interact with each other and their own tutors, about the teacher's performance of the task and her students' responses to the teaching approach and to the actual assessment design and evaluation. Schon (1983) describes

this process as 'coaching.' They could also, as 'apprentices' learn to use the teacher's assessment instruments (detailed criteria and standards matrices) to evaluate the students' work in the same way that the expert teacher could in the classroom. In tutorials we watched the students perform 8-10 minute speeches. Using these complex criteria sheets proved to be quite difficult for these 'novice' teachers. We discussed the nature of holistic assessment, subjective responses and marking explicitly to the criteria. The discussion surrounding the assessment tasks and marking was very fruitful in also modelling the process of writing these standards which the preservice teachers had to undertake in their final work program and unit development assignment. This 'peripheral participation,' (Lave & Wenger, 1991) through observing and absorbing the performance of an expert from the edge, assisted them enormously in learning about the processes surrounding assessment. As readers and writers, this process also mobilises the reader roles of 'text users' and 'text analysts' as the preservice teachers apply the knowledge from the vodcast texts to the new texts they produce. One participant wrote, "...it's great to be able to make a Shakespearean unit before implementing it in the school. It's so great to have an experienced person like Anita give us feedback so we have a better chance of teaching properly". This comment not only acknowledges the usefulness of the performance in the videostreams but reflects the 'problem-solving' we undertook together relating to the design of Shakespearean units, focussed learning tasks and assessment. It also acknowledges the role of the 'coach', or tutor, in helping the preservice teachers develop as 'reflective practitioners'.

The following responses were recorded to the question, "Did you find the assessment tasks useful in shaping your approach to teaching/ assessing Shakespeare at school?" One student responded, "The videostreams were great to see how Shakespeare can be assessed... because I have to do it." The respondent here seems to be projecting her identity into her future role as a teacher, who will then have to perform assessment. The 'expert' knowledge builds the students towards performance, as a preservice teacher remarked, "The way they have scaffolded the task has helped my understanding." Another response was, "they [vodcasts and assessment tasks] gave me an understanding of how to give students the opportunity to negotiate their assessment as they could focus on areas which interest them". Another participant stated that "...modelling is a critical component of my learning. I can do it without the model, but explicit teaching is very important...[and] ...it's always good to have new ideas for tasks and assessments... It gave me an understanding of how to approach Shakespeare." This response shows a preservice teacher projecting her own approach to Shakespeare by focusing on the need for assessment about Shakespeare to be engaging and relevant to secondary students. As one respondent remarked, the vodcasts show:

...just how the assessment can be tapered to accommodate for contemporary/modern examples. This allows students to be able to relate and understand concepts that may not necessarily be understood if not distanced from the context of Shakespearean language and historical context.

Such insightful comments illustrate the effectiveness of the videostreams and accompanying materials in assisting pre-service teachers to think about their future roles as English teachers. Clearly the 'apprentices' are reflecting deeply and critically on becoming 'performers.'

In conjunction with other more traditional methods, such as set readings these vodcasts and resources seemed to be quite effective in helping students see effective teaching ideas and strategies in action. The written response survey revealed that not all students did all the readings, but that those who had generally found them to be useful. The expert teacher's insights into her pedagogical practice along with the 'coaching' in

tutorials about approaches to Shakespeare proved to be a fruitful way of supplementing these more traditional approaches. The focus discussion about Chris's methods, ideas and beliefs about teaching English and how these related to what actually happened in her lessons built a useful framework around which the students could think about their own ways of teaching: their methods, strategies and techniques and why things were done as they were done in the classroom.

LIMITATIONS OF THE RESEARCH

The next time I teach this unit I will return to the original interview in the last class instead of leaving it up to the preservice teachers. I would like to follow up by filming the teacher's reflections on the entire series of videos to see if she would have done anything differently. When I showed Chris the series of videos to ensure she approved of what was going to be uploaded onto a closed web site, she remarked that they were, "all a bit clean and beautiful, as if nothing ever goes wrong in the classroom." She suggested it could be useful to make a video of outtakes, which I did. This was the first video I showed in class after the interview, to demonstrate that even an experienced teacher may have bad days. This however, was not the point of the series, which was to demonstrate excellent English teaching in action and have our students reflect on that in the light of their own teaching. In reading and viewing the texts the preservice teachers engaged in all four multiliteracies reader roles and also witnessed the secondary students doing the same. Overall I think it has also been very useful in this instance to deploy current web based technologies *to demonstrate how to teach* Shakespeare in a lively way in schools. The streamed video resources and associated materials developed and evaluated in this project were designed to capture 'expert knowledge' of experienced English teachers in action. The data here shows that they were able to peripherally participate in the vodcast classroom events, and effectively reflect on the expert performance in relation to their prospective roles as English teachers.

REFERENCES

Baelstri, D., Ehrman, S., & Ferguson, D. (Eds.). (1992). *Learning to design, designing to learn: Using technology to transform the curriculum.* New York: Taylor and Francis.

Barnes & Noble. (2006). *SparkNotes LLC.* Retrieved 26 May, 2008, from http://www.sparknotes.com/lit/

Buckingham, D. (1993). English and media studies: Making the difference. *English Quarterly, 25*(4), 8.

Chambers, D. P., & Stacey, K. (2005). Developing and using multimedia effectively for undergraduate teacher education. *Australasian Journal of Educational Technology, 21*(2), 211–221.

Davis, L. (Ed.). (2003). *Shakespeare matters: History, teaching, performance.* Newark, DE: University of Delaware Press.

Donnelly, K. (2006). The Muffled Canon. *The Weekend Australian*, May 5th, 2006, 20. Ethell, R. G., & McMeniman, M. (2000). Unlocking the knowledge in action of an expert practitioner. *Journal of Teacher Education, 51*(2), 87–101.

Farabaugh, R. (2007). "The Isle Is Full of Noises": Using wiki software to establish a discourse community in a Shakespeare classroom. *Multilingual Matters, 16*(1), 41–56.

Franks, A., Durran, J., & Burn, A. (2006). Stories of the three-legged stool: English, media, drama, from critique to production. *English Education, 40*(1), 63–78.

Freesmith, D. (2006). The politics of the English curriculum: Ideology in the campaign against critical literacy in The Australian. *Engineers Australia, 41*(1), 25–30.

Hulbert, J., & Wetmore, J. K., & York, R. (2006). *Shakespeare and youth culture.* New York: Palgrave Macmillan.

Jetnikoff, A. (2003). Expanding our literacy repertoires: Using film in senior English Classrooms in Queensland. *Australian Screen Education, 33*, 78–82.

Jetnikoff, A. (2005). Adaption: A case in point about adapting films from books. *Engineers Australia, 143*, 88–94.

Jetnikoff, A. (2006). Combating cyclops: Critical approaches to media literacy and popular culture in senior English. *English in Australia, 41*(1), 37.45.

Junger, G. (1999). *Ten Things I Hate About You.* Screen Writers: Mc Cullah Lutz, K. & Smith, K. Produced by Jeffrey Chernov, Touchstone Pictures.

Karolides, N. J. (Ed.). (2000). *Reader response in secondary and college classrooms.* Mahwah, NJ: L. Erlbaum.

Kissler, L. (1997). Beyond the text. In R. Salome & J. Davis (Eds.), *Teaching Shakespeare into the twenty-first century.* Athens, OH: Ohio UP.

Kliman, B. W. (Ed.). (2001). *Approaches to teaching Shakespeare's Hamlet.* New York: Modern Language Association.

Kress, G. (2003). *Literacy in the new media age.* London: Routledge.

Lave, J., & Wenger, E. (1991). *Situated learning: Legitimate peripheral participation.* Cambridge: Cambridge University Press.

Littauer, J. S. (2006). *Hamlet: Teacher's guide and student activities.* Retrieved 25 May, 2008, from http://www.sdcoe.k12.ca.us/score/ham/hamtg.html

Luke, A., & Freebody, P. (2000). Literate futures: The teacher summary version [of the] report of the Literacy Review for Queensland State Schools.

Lusted, D. (Ed.). (1991). *The media studies book.* London: Routledge.

Mellor, B. (1989). *Reading Hamlet.* Perth, Australia: Chalkface Press.

Miller, M., & Colwill, R. (2003). *Queensland senior English.* South Yarra, Austalia: Macmillan Education Australia.

Plasse, M. (2004). Crossover dreams: Reflections on Shakespeareans and popular culture. *College Literature, 31*(4), 12–18. doi:10.1353/lit.2004.0061

QBSSS. (2002). *English: Senior syllabus.* Brisbane, Australia: Queensland Board of Senior Secondary Studies.

Robinson, S. (1999). Exploring Shakespeare: Dynamic drama conventions in teaching "Romeo and Juliet". *Engineers Australia, 125*, 88–91.

Savery, J. R., & Duffy, T. M. (2001). *Problem based learning: An instructional model and its constructivist framework.* Indiana University, IN.

Schon, D. A. (1983). *The reflective practitioner: How professionals think in action.* New York: Basic Books.

Snyder, I. (2008). *The Literacy Wars.* Sydney: Allen and Unwin.

Sternberg, R. J., & Horvath, J. A. (1995). A prototype view of expert teaching. *Educational Researcher, 24*(6), 9–17.

Strickland, R. (1993). Teaching Shakespeare against the grain. In *Teaching Shakespeare today: Practical approaches and productive strategies.* Urbana, IL: National Council of Teachers of English.

ENDNOTE

[1] The Queensland Board of secondary Studies, which published the Queensland 2002 Senior English Syllabus has since become known as the QSA or the Queensland Studies Authority.

Chapter 10
Developing Literate Practices in Design and Technology Education

Mike Brown
University of Ballarat, Australia

ABSTRACT

This chapter reports on research that details the emerging literacy demands faced by both the teachers, and the students who are participating in Design and Technology education within secondary schools across Victoria, Australia. The processes of design are at the centre of the curriculum for Design and Technology education and they are the main content focus of both the teacher's work of developing curriculum and teaching, and for the learner's engagement. In this chapter the field of Design and Technology education is presented and discussed as a site where communication, interpretation and articulation of learning and understanding are inexplicably bound up with texts and literacies. In order to ground the discussion in the specifics of an authentic program, the curriculum and pedagogical practices associated with the current Year 12 Design and Technology program are analysed to illustrate the development and use, (production and consumption) of texts, particularly multimodal texts, within new, emerging and multi-literacies. In this way the chapter acknowledges the significance of literacy development across the school curriculum. This chapter also takes up a point made by Unsworth (2001) that literacy as a social practice takes up numerous and different forms in the various fields across the curriculum, therefore this research analyses explicitly what the development of literate practices specifically look like in the field of Design and Technology education.

INTRODUCTION

This chapter reports on research which looks at the development and use of literate practices by both the teachers and the students as they engage in Design and Technology education within secondary schools across Victoria, Australia. Design and technology education is conceptualised within Victorian secondary schools as using a curriculum and pedagogical approach to learning that can be summarised as

DOI: 10.4018/978-1-60566-842-0.ch010

designing, making and evaluating. The field uses the mediums of resistant and non-resistant materials, such as metals, wood, textiles, plastics, ceramics, and glass, but in its broadest conception also includes food, electronics, mechanical structures, and electro-mechanical systems. Students learn to use these materials and related processes to solve design problems and issues. Most often these take the form of projects.

As the researcher is also a teacher educator, this study was designed to explore both the teacher and learner experiences and perspectives. To teacher educators, these viewpoints are considered to be complimentary like two sides of the same coin and are represented here as two broad and generic narratives. This first narrative outlines the work of teachers as they design, develop and implement the curriculum and involves teachers producing and consuming texts. This narrative can be further sub-divided into two parts. The first part of this first narrative explains the designing of the official curriculum document. This involves a relatively small and select number of expert teachers utilising literate practices to research, negotiate and produce curriculum documents for broad public consumption. While the second part of the first narrative explains how all the teachers in the field are required to develop curriculum for their own teaching – as they interpret and transform the previously developed curriculum documents, transforming these into enacted teaching programs.

The second generic narrative derives from the learners' engagement with the teaching program. This second narrative is about the students' experience and learning. Like the teachers in the first narrative, this involves students in the consumption and production of texts. While, together these two narratives represent two different viewpoints and two ways of experiencing engagement within this subject area it needs to be acknowledged that each of these narratives represents a generic and idealised form for which there are many further variations. The diversity within each of these

narratives is currently being analysed further by the author elsewhere.

Running through both of these narratives, and fundamental to this field of study, is the development of understanding, and proficiency with the processes of design. These processes offer numerous possibilities of working through a design problem, yet they are often referred to in the singular as 'the design process'. Likewise, for pedagogical reasons a generic design process is often presented to students with the caveat to deviate from this generic process when the working with a specific situation or design brief is enhanced or requires such action. Any model representing the design process is intended to be used as a starting point and allowing for deviation and flexibility.

BACKGROUND TO THE STUDY

In recent times there has been recognition that literacy and numeracy are not restricted to English and Maths classes but rather are embedded in all subject areas across the curriculum. In Victoria the authority responsible for Teacher Registration (Victorian Institute of Teaching – VIT) require all teachers to undertake courses in the teaching of literacy and numeracy within their pre-service teacher education programs. In this way literacy has become every teacher's business. However as Unsworth (2001) notes literacy practices do not appear in the same guise in each and ever subject area but instead are subject to variation within each different field of educational study. Hence, there has been the emergence of the notion of subject specific literacies. This research analyses how literacies are involved in the teaching and learning of one specific area across the curriculum – that of Design and Technology education. With a few notable exceptions such as Williams (2009) there is a dearth of research literature on the use of literacies within Australian secondary Design and Technology education programs. Yet, as this study shows, this subject area is a site where literate practices are developed and where further research is required. A complication to further research is that the language and terminology of literacies and multiliteracies are not generally familiar to or well understood by many Design and Technology teachers.

In part because the researcher is also a teacher educator he is very much interested in the learning that occurs in and for the classroom, by both the teachers and the students. The research question that guided this study was framed as 'how are literate practices developed and used within Design and Technology education in secondary schools across Victoria, Australia? This question leads to a series of sub-questions, foremost amongst these are:

- What literate practices are the teachers developing as they teach design and technology education? And how are they developing these practices?
- What literate practices are the students developing as they learn through design and technology education? And how are they developing these practices?

A further question focused specifically upon how students utilise literate practices as they create, design and develop their ideas.

In pursuing these questions the researcher, visited classrooms, observed teacher and student interaction and engagement, interviewed teachers, students and curriculum writers, reviewed teaching programs, visited exhibitions of students' work and conducted in-depth analysis of student portfolios and their artefacts.

The four key findings from the study that are discussed in this chapter include the following:

1. A clear nexus is identified between pedagogy, curriculum and literacies in this field of study, in fact, the development of particular literate practices were found to be integrally bound up with building deep understanding within Design and Technology education;

2. Teachers and students are required to develop and utilise a broad range of literate practices;

3. These practices are developed and honed through engagement with the processes of design; and

4. The literate abilities of these teachers and students are often understated and can even go unrecognised.

An essential aspect of highly developed literate practices is proficiency with a broad range of texts. Texts can take numerous forms, and as this study found, are present in these numerous forms within the curriculum development, the pedagogy, and the learning that occurs within Design and Technology education. This chapter presents a three staged model of curriculum development and loosely uses the three stages as a framework to organise the discussion. The chapter works through the various phases of the curriculum development process in order to locate the various actors and their activities and to identify, locate and explain different texts. Importantly, the diversity of text forms serves different but related purposes. Finally, the multiliterate citizens of the twenty-first century need to understand and develop literate practices to use and apply these with a diverse range of texts. They need to know how these texts work and therefore, in turn, how they can use them (Cope & Kalantzis, 2000). Multiliterate citizens need to be able to access literal and implied meanings of these texts and know how to critically analyse them.

The discussion that follows is presented in four sections. The first section provides an explanation of texts and semiotic systems. These are presented as part of new and emerging literacies located within a context of 'new times'. The second section provides a general explanation of curriculum and describes a three phase model that summarises the curriculum development process.

This model depicts how curriculum is designed, developed and enacted in Victorian secondary schools and is used to identify, explain and locate the main texts associated with the curriculum development process. While the later part of this section focuses specifically on the curriculum context within Victoria, similar programs operate in all other states throughout Australia. The third section presents the generic narrative of the teachers' work and the literate practices that teachers use as they produce and consume the texts associated with the design and development of the teaching program. The work of the teachers in designing and developing the Year 12 (Units 3 and 4), Victorian Certificate of Education (VCE), Design and Technology program is described in order to provide an authentic program to illustrate the argument being presented. The fourth section provides a working through of the Year 12 program to show what products, artefacts and multi-modal texts learners need to complete. In particular, the Year 12 School-Assessed Task (SAT) is used to ground this discussion. The SAT is a year long project requirement undertaken by each student and specific to each. The SAT contributes 50% of the students' final Year 12 grade. The working through of the SAT develops a narrative of the students' engagement in learning and is the means by which students can demonstrate their understanding and proficiency with the design process. A brief discussion and some final comments round off the chapter.

Section 1: Texts and Emerging Literacies within 'New Times'

This first section explains what constitutes a text and provides an introduction to the concepts of multimodal texts, modes and semiotic systems, placing each of these in the context of a developing world, changing work demands and emerging literacies. Anstey and Bull (2006) summarise the findings of a number of literacy researchers when they explain that texts can be presented in a num-

ber of forms. Texts can be written down on paper, they can be electronic or digital, or they can be live. Kress (2003) explains, 'in the era of the new technologies of information and communication, mode and choice of mode is a significant issue. *Mode* is the name for a culturally and socially fashioned resource for representation and communication' (p. 45). Importantly, each mode has its own resources and conventions. Anstey and Bull (2006), in their explanation of the visual semiotic system which includes still images, list the codes associated with this mode as colour, texture, line, shape and form. Significantly, a Design and Technology teacher would describe these not as 'codes' but as 'elements of design'. Anstey and Bull (2006) explain that these codes are combined through conventions which, in the case of still images, are balance, layout and vectorality. Again, a Design and Technology teacher would not use the terminology of 'conventions' but would explain these same concepts as 'principles of design' (Guthrie 2003).

Texts can comprise one or more modes from different semiotic systems. Texts that utilise more than one semiotic system to derive meaning are classified as multimodal. Texts are consciously constructed, though they can have several possible meanings. A text can be constructed to make meaning through associations with other existing texts. In addition, texts can be interactive, linear and nonlinear (Anstey & Bull, 2006, p. 24). These features are very useful for understanding, first, what constitutes a text, and second, the range of texts that exist and what is possible.

The argument has been put elsewhere, by researchers such as Cope and Kalantzis (2000), Freebody and Luke (2003), Lankshear and Knobel (2003), and Anstey and Bull (2006), that members of the developed world are experiencing life and their world differently due mainly to the introduction and take-up of new and developing technologies. Some say metaphorically that the world is shrinking, as travel and digital communications are being taken up by more people than in previous times. These same technologies are seeing changes to the experience of work (Billett, 2006). Whole sectors of Australian manufacturing are moving offshore to countries with lower labour costs. This leads to a changing domestic labour market with new occupations emerging and a rise in the service, information and knowledge economies. Relations at work are also changing, with some workers experiencing flatter work structures and a rise in peer management and teamwork. Changing workplaces are also said to be becoming more flexible, collaborative and more techno centric (Gee, Hull, & Lankshear, 1996). Digital communications and the use of Information Communication Technology (ICT) are becoming commonplace.

Changing work practices create the need for rising proficiency with existing and emerging literacies. Included within the emerging literacies needed at work are the rising use and understanding of screens, discussion, navigation and familiarity with mixed genres and multimedia. Multimedia is defined by Mayer (2005, p. 5) as the use of several media to present information and where combinations may include text, graphics, animation, pictures, video and sound. Similarly, Ivers and Barron (2006, p. 2) suggest that multimedia involves presenting words (such as printed text or spoken text) and pictures (such as illustrations, photos, animation or video). These authors explain that hyper-environments, hypertext and hypermedia have added to the complexity and sophistication of multimedia definitions by providing electronic, nonlinear approaches to moving through information. However, rather than referring to these as the use of multimedia, throughout this chapter these are referred to as the use of multimodal texts.

A semiotic system or mode is a system of signs and symbols that allow humans to share meaning. Anstey and Bull (2006) explain five different semiotic systems – or modes – for communicating with shared understandings using different signs and symbols. They are:

- Linguistic – oral and written language
- Visual – still and moving images
- Auditory – music and sound effects
- Gestural – facial expressions and body language
- Spatial – layout, arrangement and organisation of objects and space, e.g. garden landscaping, table-setting.

Multimodal texts are those which utilise more than one semiotic system to make meaning. Multimodal texts can combine the linguistic and the visual, such as photo stories, or the use of the linguistic, the visual and the auditory, as in the case of music videos. Readers of multimodal texts may also be considered as viewers. A multimodal text can utilise all five modes. Kress (2003) makes the point that nearly every text is multimodal and acknowledges that even a written text, which uses the linguistic mode, is multimodal if it also uses grammar. He argues that the use of grammar adds additional meaning beyond the printed words.

In recent work, Kalantzis and Cope (2008) recognise emerging semiotic systems beyond those mentioned already. These authors are partly in agreement with the point that Kress makes, but they subdivide the linguistic semiotic system into written and oral language. However, in addition to this, they also argue a case for recognising the shared meaning that occurs through tactile representation, which includes touch, smell and taste. In order to get more of a sense of this newly recognised mode of representation, they write, "forms of tactile representation include kinaesthesia, physical contact, skin sensations (heat/cold, texture, pressure), grasp, manipulable objects, artefacts, cooking, eating and aromas" (p. 203).

Recognising this emerging semiotic system of shared meaning through the tactile mode is particularly important for the teaching of Design and Technology education. Accordingly it becomes important to consider the ways in which an artefact can be considered as a form of text. Such a text would need to be able to be read through shared understandings and shared meanings such as that which might occur between craftspeople, tradespeople and artisans – the people who make things. Makers, and the teachers of makers, would agree that they indeed read artefacts like a text. People who look at and handle made objects and artefacts are often involved in feeling, reading and deconstructing them. Pacey (1999, p. 67) calls this 'thinking with the hands'. Consider practices also like tasting wine or food, or of the Maori wood carver who speaks about the importance of being able to 'read the grain'.

This section shows that what constitutes a text is undertaking some considerable development in the context of our changing world and how we as social beings rely on different semiotic systems to assist us to derive and share meaning. To conclude this section of the chapter, however, the two related notions of consumption and production of texts need to be explained. In these new times, the expanded notion of a text broadens from the idea of writing a text to notion of text production. Similarly, the notion of text consumption refers to engagement with an existing text, in essence a broadening of the concept of 'reading' a text. These two broadened concepts play a significant role in the analysis and discussion that follows later in the chapter. The next section provides an overview of the curriculum development process and locates curriculum writers, teachers and students as agentic actors in this process.

Section 2: Developing Curriculum

This second section discusses the process of curriculum development and provides a three phase model. Each phase denotes a corresponding division of labour and involves a range of different actors in a range of different activities and practices. Significantly, each of the phases requires the use and development of different literate practices. This three phase model provides an organisational framework for the remainder of the discussion presented in Sections 2, 3 and 4 in

this chapter. Section 2 provides detailed contextual information, Section 3 overviews the curriculum practices of the teachers and Section 4 begins to look at the student engagement.

It is a relatively simple task to contrast two different conceptualisations of curriculum as texts. In the first, curriculum is a written document. In the other, curriculum is a lived experience and therefore what Anstey and Bull (2006) call a live text. The process of curriculum development, which includes design and implementation, involves and shows how teachers and learners participate in a sequence of projects and endeavours that require a variety of highly literate practices and which involve the production and consumption of texts.

The three phase model set out below is used to guide this discussion. The first phase focuses on the 'curriculum design'. This involves the design and development of the official curriculum document. This is usually a state-wide project that is undertaken by a small and select group of expert teachers in the field and some major stakeholders. This group is convened by the Curriculum Manager who has responsibility for developing this curriculum document. The design of the curriculum is detailed through the production of a printed text. The curriculum document goes through a rigorous consultation process seeking feedback from the teachers in the field and other stakeholders. This results in the curriculum document going through numerous drafts (see Figure 1).

The second phase involves the subject area teachers' engagement with the initial curriculum document. Once the official curriculum document is accepted and accredited, teachers read and interpret this text in view of their previous experience and existing knowledge bases. Initially this phase involves teachers consuming this text, but consumption quickly turns to production as teachers make their own interpretations of the document. Further text production occurs as the teachers begin to act on their interpretations and design and construct an appropriately correspond-

Figure 1. The curriculum development process

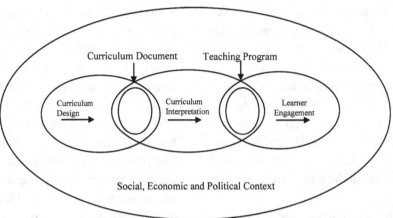

ing teaching program. This transformation of the written curriculum text as teachers interpret the document becomes the basis of the live text that is an enacted teaching program. This curriculum interpretation and transformation is the basis of this second phase. Barlex (2007) argues that engaging learners in ways that enables them to develop creativity, problem-solving, and collaboration can be a demanding task. Teachers are often supported in this phase through a wide range of professional learning activities, for example teacher subject area professional associations that hold professional learning activities, publish journal articles on innovative and exemplary practices, and run teacher conferences.

The third phase begins with the enactment or implementation of the teaching and learning program and the pedagogical interaction between teachers and students. The learners in the program consume this live curriculum text and work to produce or construct their own texts as they make their own interpretations. At the centre of this third phase is the engagement by the learners. Amongst the array of texts produced by each learner are the pedagogical artefacts and multimodal texts. This chapter argues that collectively the sum of these artefacts and multimodal texts can be read and interpreted and that they create a narrative of the student learning in the program. The quality of

the collection of artefacts and multimodal texts that learners produce provides the teachers and others with evidence of the students' learning and understanding. The collection of artefacts and multimodal texts include all of the various pages in the students' design and research portfolio, the made product and the evaluation report.

THE CURRICULUM CONTEXT ACROSS VICTORIA

The next part of this second section provides an overview of the curriculum context in which Design and Technology education operates in secondary schools throughout Victoria. The significance of the description that follows is that it is constructed with reference to an array of formal curriculum and assessment documents. The complexity of the means for arriving at the description begins to reveal the demands being placed on the teachers in this field as they develop their own literate practices for the requirements of their workplaces (schools) in order to be able to interpret the curriculum and assessment requirements as specified through the set of curriculum and assessment documents associated with their work.

The curriculum for Design and Technology education is simplistically characterised by the sequence of three related concepts: design, make and evaluate. This sub-section unpacks these three concepts through a brief review of the curriculum and assessment requirements for Design and Technology education as it is currently taught within Victorian secondary schools. In particular, this unpacking occurs through how these documents imply that Design and Technology be taught at what is generally considered to be the high stakes end of secondary schooling assessment – namely, Year 12. High stakes lead to high accountability. This chapter builds on the assumption that high stakes and accountability ensures that much effort goes into detailing and thoroughly explaining the curriculum and assessment requirements for this final year of schooling. For thoroughness the Victorian Essential Learning Standards (VELS), the curriculum framework that guides the development of programs from Prep to Year 10, is mentioned. This is then followed by discussion of the curriculum and assessment documentation that guides teaching and learning for Year 12 programs. These documents are used as the primary source to begin to understand this subject area of Design and Technology education. The main curriculum documents for Year 12 Design and Technology are the Study Design. Like all the Study Designs at Year 11 and 12 level, these have been written as stand alone documents. Therefore, these subject specific Study Designs (Year 11 and 12 curriculum documents) represent each subject area in its purest form.

Under the Australian Constitution each of the eight Australian states and territories has responsibility for education within its own jurisdiction. Accordingly, each state and territory has developed different state-wide curriculum frameworks along with its own senior secondary certificates to signify successful completion of senior secondary schooling. In Victoria students have an option between two senior secondary certificates; the mainstream Victorian Certificate of Education (VCE) and the more recently developed Victorian Certificate of Applied Learning (VCAL). Preced-

ing these senior school certificate programs is the curriculum framework to guide the learning from Prep to Year 10 – see http://vels.vcaa.vic.edu.au/essential/interdisciplinary/design/index.html. Together these three curricula (VELS for Prep to Year 10; VCE and VCAL for Years 11 and 12) ensure that students can study a variety of forms of Design and Technology across the state at all levels of secondary schooling.

The VCE usually runs across Years 11 and 12 of secondary school though some schools get some of their higher achieving students started during Year 10. Each of the subjects offered in the VCE are called a 'study area'. Within the VCE there is a selection of approximately 90 study areas and some 30 VCE Vocational Education and Training (VET) programs available. Each study area is subdivided into four units. A VCE program usually consists of approximately 20 to 24 units taken over two years. Units 1 and 2 are generally considered to be at Year 11 level and can be completed as single units or as part of a sequence. Units 3 and 4 are more difficult and demanding and are considered to be at Year 12 level. Students undertaking Unit 3 in a study area are usually expected to do the corresponding Unit 4 and therefore complete the sequence. The VCAA (Victorian Curriculum and Assessment Authority) (2007) explain that the Unit 3 and 4 sequence in each VCE study area has three graded assessments, either two school-based assessments and one external examination, or one school-based assessment and two external examinations.

To successfully complete the VCE a student must complete sixteen units, with a minimum of four Unit 3 and 4 sequences. It is compulsory to do English as one of the study areas and each student must complete at least three units in English, and four units if they want to get an Equivalent National Tertiary Entrance Rank (ENTER) score. To successfully complete their VCE, students need to complete English as a compulsory study and three other Unit 3 and 4 sequences.

The main curriculum documents for Years 11 and 12 are the VCE Study Designs (VCAA, 2006) and the corresponding Assessment Handbooks (VCAA, 2008). This is further complemented by information published by the VCAA in the Supplement to their February 2008 Bulletin No. 56 (VCAA, 2008a). In addition to this there are the commercial textbooks such as Livett and O'Leary (2007), which is written to address the requirements of this particular Study Design and the Top Design exhibition held at the Melbourne Museum each year. This exhibition is generally regarded as displaying VCE School-Assessed Tasks (SATs) that showcase excellent student projects completed by some of the Year 12 student cohort of the previous year (http://museumvictoria.com. au/MelbourneMuseum/Education/Education-Programs/Top-Designs-2008/). Used together, the study design, the assessment handbook, the commercial textbooks, and the Top Design exhibition are source documents that have an intertextual relationship to the teachers (and students) in the field. Together these texts assist teachers to construct a coherent understanding of the teaching and learning requirements for VCE Design and Technology education across Victoria. Teaching the program adds a further and additional live text into this mix.

Teese (2005) suggests that the curriculum for VCE is characterised by great diversity with students being offered many options. Standing as testimony to this statement are the 120 Study Designs that have been developed for the VCE, 30 of which are VCE VET programs. Of the other 90, there are three different specialist technology studies available at VCE. Each of the three is detailed in their own Study Design which is developed and accredited by the VCAA. These are: Food and Technology (2006–2010), (VCAA, 2005); Systems Engineering (2007–2010), (VCAA, 2006a); and Design and Technology (2007–2011), (VCAA, 2006). In the context of secondary schools these studies are highly gendered. In some cases this is in contrast with employment in the related fields.

Food and Technology incorporates food studies with an emphasis on food preparation, storage, menu design and cooking. In 2007, across the approximately 270 providers throughout the state:

- 5000 completed Unit 1
- 4700 completed Unit 2
- 3424 completed Unit 3
- 3190 completed Unit 4.

It is estimated that approximately 95% of students enrolled in this study area are female.

Systems Engineering covers the integration of mechanical, electro-technological and control systems. In 2007, across the approximately 100 providers across the state:

- 1700 completed Unit 1
- 1600 completed Unit 2
- 900 completed Unit 3
- 826 completed Unit 4.

Similarly, it is estimated that approximately 95% of students enrolled in this study area are male.

Design and Technology covers design, material processes and production and evaluation using materials like metal, wood, textiles, plastics and ceramics. In 2007, across the 300 providers throughout the state:

- 5770 completed Unit 1
- 5474 completed Unit 2
- 3915 completed Unit 3
- 3688 completed Unit 4.

At first glance it appears that the Design and technology study area is more evenly distributed along gender lines; however of the students who choose to work primarily in the medium of wood and timber as their main material some 90% are male, while of those students who choose to work in textiles, it is estimated that 95% are female.

This section contains detailed contextual curriculum information that is significant to each and every Design and Technology teacher working in secondary schools across Victoria. The purpose of building this contextual information is to provide an overview to the range of texts that teachers need to read and consume in order to be able to begin to do the creative developmental side of their educational work. To be able to find, understand and interpret this information, teachers need to have and be developing their own literate practices which they need to use, to consume, interpret and produce a range of further curriculum texts. The following section looks more specifically at the role and practices of teachers within Design and Technology education. The ability to read, consume and interpret curriculum documents constitutes a significant aspect of the 'working knowledge' of these teachers (McLeod, 2000).

Section 3: Teaching Design and Technology

The previous section set out a three stage model for curriculum development and provided contextual information for the Design and Technology curriculum in Victorian secondary schools. This section turns to the role of teachers in this process. As previously stated this can be divided into a design stage and then a development and implementation stage. In the first stage of designing the curriculum there are only a relatively small number of approximately a dozen Design and Technology teachers involved. In the context of the Year 12 program, this stage culminates in the direct production of the VCE Study Design. However, all Design and Technology teachers are required to be able to make interpretations of these documents and be able to develop and enact an appropriately aligned teaching program for the Year 12 students which they teach. The design and production of a VCE Study Design is a lengthy and detailed process. Study Designs have a useful life of approximately four or five

years and decisions are made about the need and degree of reviewing necessary. Substantial reviews begin with a call for Expressions of Interest. Most respondents who are chosen to undertake the review are experienced leading teachers, or relevant stakeholders. Amongst the stakeholders are representatives from higher education, the VET sector and industry.

In this initial stage of curriculum design, one member of the writing team is designated as the chief writer. The team is given a standard template and encouraged to write up the document through numerous drafts. Consultations occur, new ideas are contemplated and issues arising from the experience of teaching the existing course are addressed. Drafts of the Study Design are opened up to scrutiny by going through consultation and discussion. All the teachers and major stakeholders in the field are invited to read and comment on the drafts. Once completed, the finished and approved Study Design needs to be in schools by March of the year prior to its intended implementation. Therefore, the process of reviewing an existing Study Design begins some two years prior to its introduction into schools.

At the core of all Design and Technology education programs across the state is the design process. While the design process is often referred to in the singular, this is more accurately a plural, 'processes of design' (de Vries, 2007). It is argued that these processes are to be used in a flexible manner as the need, situation and circumstances dictate. Typically however, the processes of design are represented in pedagogical texts as a generic series or cycle of steps to be followed as a guiding framework. Livett and O'Leary (2007, p20) explain the design process in their textbook for pedagogical purposes as a sequence of eight steps. These are:

1. Identify the need:
   ◦ Recognise the situation.
   ◦ Clarify the problem in a design brief.

 - Analyse the design problem and situation.
 - Decide on the brief's specification and criteria for evaluating its solution (the end product).

2. Research:
 - Research the topic area.
 - Organise and analyse your information.
 - Work out what information is relevant to your brief and how the results of your research will influence the design and production.

3. Ideas:
 - Brainstorm and experiment with shape, colour, function, materials and construction techniques.

4. Design options:
 - Formulate realistic ideas, solutions or design options that fulfil the brief.

5. Deciding on a preferred option:
 - Identify the most probable solution by comparison with the brief (using evaluation criteria). This may involve combining features from a range of design options.

6. Planning for production:
 - Create working drawings.
 - Organise and plan the construction process to realise your solution.

7. Production:
 - Make the product (or a fully operating prototype).

8. Testing and evaluating:
 - Conduct a series of tests to assess the effectiveness of your solution.
 - Consult with the user of the product about suitability of the product (how well does it fulfil their need?)
 - Reflect on the processes used in design and production – consider their effectiveness and efficiency.

These steps are presented as a linear arrangement. Many make the point that the processes of design need to be considered a flexible process that is moulded to suit task, situation and circumstances, (de Vries, 2007, p.30); despite this fact there are expectations from teachers and examiners that students will follow this designated process. A brief review of the Table of Contents in the VCE textbook written by Livett and O'Leary (2007) reveals that seven of the eleven chapters have the word 'design' in the chapter title. The second chapter is specifically entitled 'The Design Process'. Interestingly, the steps and sequence in the design process are both contested and confirmed using similar and different terms across a number of other textbooks used in the teaching of Design and Technology (for example, Collins, Cornius-Randall, Annetts, Annetts, Hampson, McMurtie, Parsons, & Simpson, 2006).

The simplistic notion of design, make and evaluate appears in different variations but is never far away. Regardless of the differences or the number of steps described in each or any version of the design process, it is interesting to note that the final two steps often correspond with the make and evaluate stages, while all of the proceeding steps align to the design stage. It is worth considering whether this emphasis indicates the amount of effort that needs to put into the design and planning stages relative to those of making/producing and evaluating.

YEAR 12 DESIGN AND TECHNOLOGY CURRICULUM AND ASSESSMENT

The curriculum for the Year 12 Design and Technology education program is detailed in Units 3 and 4 of the Study Design. In addition, the design of the assessment regime provides further details and insight into the design of the teaching program. Units 3 and 4 both have three Areas of Study and three Outcomes to be satisfied. For the assessment

Table 1. Assessment of Units 3 and 4 either through School Assessed Coursework (SAC) or the School Assessed Task (SAT)

Unit 3			Unit 4		
Outcome 1	Outcome 2	Outcome 3	Outcome 1	Outcome 2	Outcome 3
SAC	SAC	SAT	SAC	SAT	SAT

of these, there are three types of assessments specified. These are: the School-Assessed Coursework (SAC); the School-Assessed Task (SAT); and a final 90 minute examination. Often the requirements for the SAC are completed through some form of written and oral assignment work. There are three SACs to be completed for Units 3 and 4. Outcomes 1 and 2 of Unit 3 and Outcome 1 of Unit 4 are assessed through SACs, involving coursework assignments to be assessed by the students' teacher through the year.

The SAT (School Assessed Task) takes the form of a student specific project (design, make and evaluate) that extends over the two semesters of Year 12 and results in the student developing a design portfolio, a production project and an evaluation report. These three components in the SAT correspond to the same task or project and can be seen to provide evidence of the students' understanding and creativity with respect to the design process. The SAT satisfies the requirements of Unit 3 Outcome 3 and Unit 4 Outcomes 2 and 3 (see Table 1).

The next part of this section provides a brief overview of the particular curriculum requirements as specified in the curriculum and assessment documents for the heavily documented high stakes end of secondary schools. Teachers gain their understanding of the programming requirements through close and collective readings of the Study Design, the Assessment Handbook, the VCAA Bulletin Supplement, the textbooks and the work of students in previous years. Teachers need to be able to interpret, synthesise and transform this information. Appreciation of the role of the teachers in this process begins to show the com-

plexities of the literate practices which teachers need in order to understand and interpret the array of curriculum documents when developing their programs. Clearly students would need a great deal of assistance to reach an understanding of what is required of them as learners through these same source documents. Hence the need for the teacher to explain, mediate and scaffold the students to understand the expectations and requirements of the curriculum.

Teachers are trained to break the codes in these curriculum documents. They pass their understandings on to the students that they teach. The teachers act as the mediators. In order to succeed in Design and Technology, students too need to crack the codes, deconstruct the requirements and demonstrate their understandings and proficiency with each stage of the design process. Further, to do this successfully, students need to understand about the production of their own texts and be able to provide the examiners with what they want to see. In this way, the curriculum and pedagogy in design and technology education become bound to the production of the various texts and products that demonstrate understanding and proficiency with each stage in 'the processes of design'. Each of the various artefacts and products are closely aligned with the pedagogy of this subject area.

Section 4: The Student's Engagement Through the Completion of 'the SAT'

The overview of the main requirements of the current senior secondary VCE Design and Technology Study Design in the previous section provides details of the requirements associated with the SAT. It also shows that the basic curriculum rendition of design, make and evaluate remains in place. Significantly, each of these requires a different, though related means of understanding and abilities to complete. In order for students to demonstrate their understanding and proficiency with each of these stages, the pedagogy is directed at scaffolding the student so that they can produce a range of performative products. The quality of this collection of related artefacts and multimodal texts stands as the evidence of their learning. In order to show understanding and proficiency with design, the student produces and presents a collection of artefacts and/or multimodal texts in response to each step of the design process. The students present these as their portfolio. In order to show understanding and proficiency with making, the students produce a substantial product. To show their ability to evaluate, the students produce an evaluation report which directly addresses appropriately derived, project specific, evaluation criteria. In fact deriving appropriate design briefs and evaluation criteria are a significant aspect of each project undertaken by the students.

All Year 12 SAT projects across the state of Victoria require a student to work through the designing, making and evaluating of a substantial project. In the textiles area this can be a special purpose garment like an evening gown or a child's outfit for a particular occasion. In the wood and metals area it can be a piece of furniture that is all wood, all metal, or composites, such as a games table or a lamp. Interestingly, it is the traditions associated with the individual experience and training of the teachers often recruited from specific fields and trades together with the existing equipment and workshop layouts within schools (architecture) which tend to see programs favour specific mediums (wood, metals, textiles, glass, etc.). This dedication of work/learning to particular mediums is not the intention or requirement of the curriculum.

Figure 2 below shows the completed artefacts designed and made by a group of students from the same class working to the same design brief. The design brief required students to design a lamp that would provide mood lighting in a formal area of a house and which used at least three different types of material in its construction. These finished artefacts show that many quite different solutions are possible in response to the same design brief. The multitude of appropriate responses is a key feature of this field. Hence the requirement for creativity to generate and develop options, then to articulate selection of preferences through justifiable evaluation. As in other fields of study in the school curriculum students need to show their working out. All of which is independent of making the final product.

When teachers and students talk about the SAT in this field this is code for the substantial design, make and evaluation project which is completed by each student. This project is the centrepiece of the Year 12 Design and Technology education curriculum. The SAT project makes up 50 per cent of the final study score; the final 90 minute examination is worth 30 per cent and the three coursework assignments (SACs) are together worth 20 per cent. To successfully complete the SAT, students need to submit a portfolio, an artefact or product and an evaluation report. Explicit curriculum and assessment documentation makes the SAT a good example for understanding the interrelationship between the pedagogy and the products of the pedagogy. These products of the pedagogy are predominantly multimodal texts. Collectively, all of these completed products (the multimodal texts) that emerge from the pedagogy form a complex narrative which in this case is the story of the students' engagement with the SAT and therefore their understanding and proficiency with the design process.

Each year a selection is made of the best of the Unit 3 and 4 SAT student projects which are put on display at the Melbourne Museum at the Top Design Exhibition. Examples of student work

Figure 2. Mood lighting project

are reproduced in the Top Design catalogue, on the corresponding CD in the catalogue, and on the exhibition website hosted by the Melbourne Museum. Some of these appear in the Figure 3 below. The finished artefacts represent just one of the multi-modal texts amongst many which are produced by each student. While the excellence of the finished collection of artefacts and multimodal texts is seductive it is important to understand that each student project entails much more than the finished products.

Immediately apparent in the review of the students' work that appears at Top Design is the gendered divide in the materials and processes typically used to satisfy the curriculum requirements of the SAT. The male students tend to use wood and develop their portfolios using computer-aided drawings and renderings, while the female students tend to do textiles and develop very creative and artistic portfolios. Livett (personal

communication 2008) suggests that the gender profile is close to 95% of males using wood and 95% females doing textiles. Exceptions exist and include the work of a past student, Kim Tran, whose work, depicted in this chapter, provides an exception to the gendered nature of woodwork within secondary schools. Interestingly, a number of female textiles students reported frustration at having to choose between wood and textiles as they wanted to do both.

The gendering of materials in Design and Technology education is a very interesting issue. On one level, it reflects stereotypical masculine and feminine traditions, yet in industry, there are male and female fashion designers, there are male and female chefs and cooks and there are young men and women working in furniture design and manufacture. One researcher who works in Design and Technology education recently asked whether the gender divide in this field might be 'due to

Figure 3. 'Decadent denim for the modern Marie Antoinette' submitted by Brooke Geradi from Ballarat High School. The 'Landscape Architectural Storage' Cabinet, submitted by Tom Baulch from Geelong College. 'Bella Rosa' a dress for her formal, submitted by Kate Kelso from Toorak College Mt Eliza. All are SAT projects for Units 3 and 4 (Year 12), exhibited at Top Design in 2008

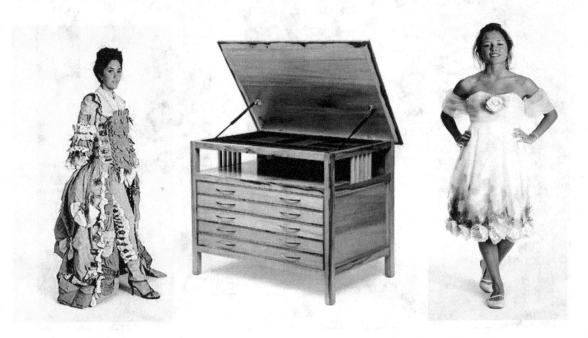

a long traditional acculturation by teachers over the years who have projected wood as male and textiles as female and that this socialization has simply become a schools community expectation and 'normal' due to a collective teacher projected image of the material' (Anonymous, personal communication, 2008).

A visit to the Top Design exhibition sparks many reactions, some of excitement and some more critically reflective. Most Design and Technology teachers see what is being exhibited and compare this with what occurs in their own classrooms. The exhibits provide scaffolding to the teachers particularly novice teachers. These comparisons though are not always positive, this experience leads some teachers to suggest that there is a class divide evident through the use of expensive materials in some student projects and they immediately ask questions about inequitable access to materials, processes and resources. One

teacher of nearly thirty years experience reported no longer taking students to visit the Top Design exhibition as the student projects being exhibited there are mostly from elite private schools and were of projects that would be near impossible to complete with the limited materials, tools and equipment he had available at his school.

Another teacher suggested that the projects on display were made from materials that were not even accessible to students in government schools. One Head of Department that was interviewed from a government secondary school explained that, he found himself asking how others could be expected to compete with these seemingly very well funded and resourced projects. Clear differences are apparent between the programs that are run in some government and private schools. One teacher and Head of Department from a private school explaining to me that he had photos of all his students' finished work at the school because

Table 2. List of ten criteria for the SAT as published by the VCAA

CRITERIA FOR THE AWARD OF GRADES
The extent to which the design folio demonstrates:
1 skill in developing a client or end-user profile, developing
    a design brief and evaluation criteria;
2 skill in carrying out research and developmental work;
3 skill in developing creative and viable design options and
    justifying the preferred option;
4 skill in preparing working drawings and a production work plan.
The extent to which the design folio and the production work demonstrate:
5 understanding of the characteristics and properties of the materials used.
The extent to which the production work and accompanying
documentation demonstrate:
6 skill in the application of processes;
7 skill in the use of tools, equipment and machines;
8 skill in completing the product to specified and accepted
    standards of quality.
The extent to which the evaluation report and the visual display, or the storyboard or multimedia presentation demonstrate:
9 skill in evaluating and promoting the product.
The extent to which the evaluation report demonstrates:
10 skill in evaluating the effectiveness and efficiency of the design

the school had paid a professional photographer to come in, set up a small studio and take photos of the students' work. A well known curriculum writer in the field was also critical of some of the projects on display but based her criticism more on workload issues citing the excessive amount of time that was being spent by some students on their projects.

Teachers making these criticisms do not highlight these inequities for the purpose of seeing these extras taken away from the students who attend these private schools, on the contrary the teachers I spoke with would like to see these being provided and accessible to all students.

THE ASSESSMENT REGIME

A detailed analysis of the assessment regime for the Year 12 Design and Technology requirements shows that this field of study is firmly focused on the teaching and learning of 'the design process'. Marking for The SAT uses ten criteria, each of which is worth five marks. These are published each year in the Supplement to the VCAA Bulletin for VCE, VCAL and VET in February of each year.

The criteria for 2008 are set out below in Table 2. These criteria reflect the curriculum focus on the design process. While the criteria are related to a substantial project, the criteria can be seen to reflect the design, make and evaluate process. It was shown earlier in this chapter that the first six of the eight steps in the design process described in the VCE textbook (Livett & O'Leary, 2007) related to the design phase, with step seven relating to the production stage and step eight relating to evaluation. The ten criteria mirror this same emphasis. The first four criteria relate to designing, one bridges both design and production, the next three to production, the penultimate criterion relates to marketing and promotion not mentioned in the design process of Livett and O'Leary (2007), and the final criterion relates to evaluation.

Design and Technology teachers working in the high stakes end of Year 12 programs invariably try to provide students with access to examples of previous students' work that have been successful in gaining high marks. These examples are intended as models to guide and be emulated by the students albeit in a changed application. Most teachers will also provide students with checklists of products that need to be included in their major project. These checklists describe the products (multimodal texts) which mostly take the form of portfolio pages. In turn, these portfolio pages show evidence of the students' engagement with the design process.

The collection of products that the students produce typically takes the form of multimodal texts presented as pages in a portfolio. Portfolios provide evidence of student engagement with each step in the design process. They become the visual record of the application of the design process to the students' chosen SAT project. The portfolio shows the designing, the research, the development of the ideas, annotated design options and working drawings. Photos are used to show the production stage of the product. The final evaluation report too, is presented as part of the portfolio. Collectively, these texts tell the narrative of the students' engagement with the design process.

THE NEXUS BETWEEN: MULTIMODAL TEXTS, 'THE DESIGN PROCESS', PEDAGOGY AND LEARNING

This section shows the intended student engagement through each stage in the design process as described by Livett and O'Leary (2007). The study showed that each of the steps in the design process creates products in the form of multimodal texts. In turn, these emerging multimodal texts provide a form of evidence aligned to each step in the design process. These texts take many forms; they utilise numerous text formats and, significantly, they are derived from a pedagogy that utilises and integrates multimodal communication, interpretation, representation and articulation.

For many, the design process is thought to begin when the designer is given a design brief to work to. However, the brief is derived from a perceived need. Hence, the first step in the design process depicted in the VCE textbook is about 'Identifying the need'. To successfully demonstrate engagement with this stage, students begin to produce pages for their design portfolio. In particular though, they need to show evidence of identification and establishment of need, for which a design-related solution is to be formulated. As part of building the authenticity of the project, students are expected to find a real client who has a need which forms the basis of the students design solution and project. The students are required to explicitly articulate the need and to show recognition of the situation and clarification of the problem. They also need to begin to analyse the design problem and decide on the specifications for the brief along with appropriate evaluation criteria.

Typically, this part of the design process leads to the production of a number of pages that begin the portfolio. These include a profile of the client and/or end user and a design brief. The client and/or end user profile is developed after talking and consulting with the client and/or end user groups. These discussions are used to gather information about the likes and dislikes, the context, the functional requirements, possible material and appearance preferences. The design brief is also presented as a key page in the portfolio. This provides the initial specification for the product, service, system or environment that is needed. The brief provides information on the situation and circumstances. It needs to state what is flexible, what is in need of further consideration and refinement and what is fixed as a constraint. The specifications detailed in this brief then become the foundation leading to the development of the evaluation criteria for the project which are used to guide the design process. These usually appear in the portfolio following the brief. Livett and O'Leary (2007) explain that typically there are six to eight criteria associated with the project: its function, appearance and safe use, and a further four to six criteria that are associated with the design and production process. Most criteria are derived from the brief whilst some are implied. This pattern whereby students develop portfolio pages in response to each step of the design process is fundamental to success in this subject area.

The second step of the design process is about conducting research. In this stage the design problem is fully explored. Students usually utilise Information Communication Technologies (ICT) to gather information and research different facets of the project. Such aspects of the problem as historical developments, aesthetics, materials, production techniques, construction details, er-

gonomics and availability of accessories such as furniture hardware are researched. Some examples representative of this research are documented as multimodal texts and appear as the next series of pages in the student's portfolio. In Figure 4 below we can see from this folio page where the student is researching, finding and building ideas. There is an interplay here where ideas are developed conceptually through harvesting of photographs, sketching and annotated notes. Big feature ideas

Figure 4. A page from a student's portfolio (submitted by Lauren Bardin from Yarra Valley Grammar School and exhibited at Top Design in 2008)

are read, de-constructed and worked through building new and numerous options to be further thought through and developed.

In Figure 5 below the same student provides an example of her development work. She is working through different options associated with various aspects of her design, though in development work most appear as variations on the same theme. Notice also that the student works through thinking about both the front and the back view of the garment. It is interesting how many students need to be reminded to think about the whole garment when they design. Initially some tend to think only about the front view.

A wide range of ideas need to emerge out of the research. These ideas need to be expanded on, developed further, refined and evaluated. Mitcham and Holbrook (2006) explain the way that design constitutes a distinctive way of turning making into thinking. Designers are required to think through the making. Like the ideas themselves, a range of communication methods can be used to develop the ideas. Designers and makers are generally not known for their writing of essays to

Figure 5. Freehand sketches of possible aspects (submitted by Lauren Bardin from Yarra Valley Grammar School and exhibited at Top Design in 2008)

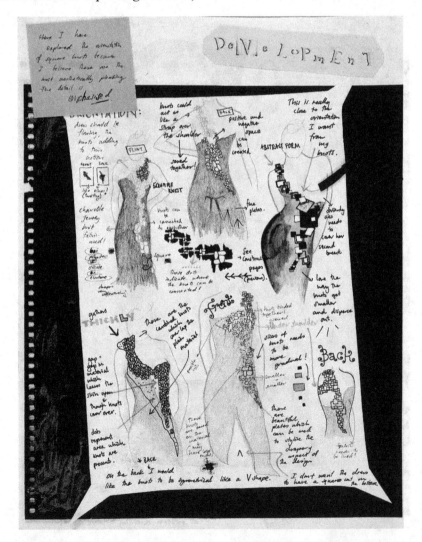

explain their thinking. Rather, most designers use sketching and pictorial representation as a form of brainstorming without words. Sketching and annotated designs, pictorial drawings, orthogonal drawings, diagrams and layouts, mock ups and modelling are examples of the formats and texts that designers and makers use to communicate their designs and design ideas. Figure 6 below shows the research and inspiration pages from the portfolio of Kim Tran. Notice the photograph at the bottom left hand side of the 'research and inspirations' page. This image morphs through the design. It appears in an altered form in the design sketches that appear in the bottom right hand corner of the desk ideas page.

Working with, and through the ideas, leads to design options being developed from these initial explorations. Annotated sketches are an example of how designers keep track of, and develop, particular ideas. Designers know when serious design options are developed, as each are required to satisfy the original need of the client and to fulfil the requirements as specified in the design brief and evaluation criteria. If the designs do not do this they need to be modified and developed further, or discarded. Once about four viable options have been developed, a choice needs to be made as to a preferred option. This is the selection of the design option which best satisfies the need, the design brief and the evaluation criteria. Students need to show the evaluation and selection process for deciding the best option. Therefore the four options, the preferred option and the basis of the selection process need to be communicated and articulated through the pages of the portfolio.

The sixth step in the design process is 'Planning for production'. Within this stage the designer uses models, mock-ups, prototypes and 3D computer images (see Figure 7). An initial production plan and flowchart are developed showing timelines and sequence of operations for the production. A complete list is described of all materials, quantities and sizes, and all equipment and process

Figure 6. Research and inspiration being worked through as design ideas (produced by Kim Tran and exhibited at Top Design in 2004)

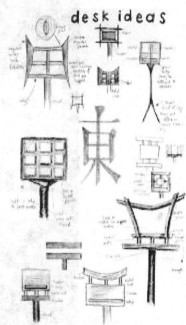

requirements. In recent times, a risk assessment analysis for the project may be included into the portfolio along with material and process safety information.

The seventh step in the process is the production. Here the designer makes the product or artefact. As the designer moves from conception to execution and becomes the maker, they need to demonstrate safe and efficient work practices with tools, materials and equipment. They also need to demonstrate any product or material testing that has occurred and to record their progress throughout a log of the production work. If any modification needs to be made during production, these changes need to be explained and documented. The actual finished product stands as the record of the production stage. However the sub-phases of the production and the final product can also be represented using photographs for the visual

record. These can be annotated and become part of the portfolio.

The photographs that make up the portfolio page in Figure 8 when read together as a group show different views and different facets of the completed artefact. Reading the images on the page we can see a finished artefact though no timber music stand project exists before us. Through these representations we can see the proportions, the colour, the lines, the materials, and the finish, the working out of details such as the tilt and height adjustment, and even the metal spaces that connect the back rest with the ledge support. As a viewer, we are required to read the design and to read the artefact through the visual representation of the artefact. Therefore it is important for students to understand how texts work. This text and these representations are consciously and strategically constructed and presented to us to read in a par-

Figure 7. A prototype or mock-up for a music stand (submitted by Kim Tran and exhibited at Top Design in 2004)

ticular way. The producer (student) positions us as readers to consume her text in a way that is of benefit to her as a student (see Figure 8).

The final step in the design process is the evaluation. Here, the student/designer/maker needs to assess the effectiveness of their design solution. The student needs to address and respond to all of the evaluation criteria that have been articulated previously in the project. The student needs to return to and interact with the client and/or end user and record their responses to the product. Importantly the student also needs to show that they have reflected upon the whole process of the project. This step is usually completed through a brief and focused evaluation report. This text makes up the final pages in the student's portfolio.

DISCUSSION

Multiliterate citizens need to understand and develop literate practices that are appropriate to the literacies and texts of the twenty-first century and also how these texts work and how to use them (Cope & Kalantzis, 2000; Anstey & Bull, 2006). A text needs to convey and share meaning between a producer and a receiver about aspects of experience in the world. Multimodal texts utilise and build meaning through communication using the combination of more than one mode of representation. Portfolios that are produced as part of Design and Technology education are produced to convey meanings to the receiver/reader/viewer. Students who succeed in secondary school know that they need to demonstrate their learning. Design and Technology students show their understanding, their thinking and even their journey towards reaching understanding through the production of these texts. Therefore, uppermost in the students' considerations about audience when producing these texts are their teacher and examiners.

Accordingly, these texts need to be carefully crafted not just to confirm understanding but to provide evidence of their depth and range of understanding. In some ways, this is tantamount

Figure 8. The final production (submitted by Kim Tran and exhibited at Top Design in 2004)

to giving the examiners what they want. Taken for granted is that students understand what is expected. Making it clear and explicit to students that the focus of Design and Technology education is on them showing proficiency with the design process, goes some of the way towards ensuring this occurs. Hence, there is the need for the pages of their portfolios to correspond with each of the steps in the design process.

Portfolio pages have other considerations that assist in developing cohesion and flow. The content of the projects, from the generation of ideas that first appear, through to rough sketches; need to be shown to be developing. In the first instance these ideas need to be shown as partial. Further ideas on aspects of the project need to be shown being tried out; some working and others not working out. The pages that illustrate this process are not likely to be the actual, very first working out of these ideas. Instead the pages of the portfolio need to be consciously constructed to show exemplars of some of the research and some of the working through of ideas in the development stage. In another way, collectively, these pages need to flow as a coherent text. The text/portfolio which the students produce needs to articulate the narrative of the learner's practice. This text needs to show the journey and tell the story – the student's engagement with the design process.

Most prominent within the portfolio are texts that use image and written texts. This combination of modes provides a relatively quick and efficient means of conveying meaning (Guthrie, 2003). Again though, different genres and text forms are used within the pages of the portfolio, depending on the type of communication utilised at each of the various stages of the design process (Welch, 2007). The form of these texts is set to expand dramatically as the digital natives bring their ICT skills to bear on the subject area.

Yet another consideration is whether text or image is presented to the reader first, as this can have a bearing on the message that is conveyed. Central to the reading of the portfolio, as with other

texts, is the experience of the reader. Examiners are selected from the experienced and practicing teachers within the field. They have accumulated understanding and knowledge for reading these texts. Examiners are experienced teachers who have taught Design and Technology for many years themselves. Experienced examiners in this field explain how they can accurately read through a student's portfolio and assess it in ten minutes. They have highly developed pedagogical content knowledge. They know what is involved in teaching at this level. They are so experienced that they can typically predict the difficulties and misunderstandings that might occur at different points in the process. In short, the examiners want to see creative and thoughtful engagement with each step in the design process when they read a student's portfolio.

Teachers could be considered poor teachers if they provide checklists and models to their students. At worst, the students may copy them and, at best, they may use them to try to understand the nuances of the design process. They could lead the student through the process and begin to reduce the learning to following a formula. On the other hand, such actions may represent a very strategic form of teaching in that it makes explicit and provides detail on exactly what the student needs to do to satisfy and succeed with their required tasks at this high stakes end of schooling.

While common in Visual Communication programs, practice with visual and design literacy, with text layout and consideration of the way that texts can be positioned in order to lead readers through a text is not generally practiced within Design and Technology. However as shown in the analysis above it is an important aspect of Design and Technology education. Conscious construction of texts for performativity may not necessarily be a goal of Design and Technology education, but it should be. These texts are vital in the teaching and learning that occurs through this subject. Reading, consuming, deconstructing, drafting, producing and constructing multimodal texts in conscious, critical ways like how it occurs through Design and Technology education is a desired ability and requirement associated with multiliterate citizens of the twenty-first century.

Once these students enter the workforce should they work in the design field in some capacity they will need to know how to present their work to those working in the industry. In this context portfolios take on an additional meaning. The theory of portfolios as a body of work that show what an individual can do is often about promotion and exhibition of ability and showing successful past projects. Portfolios are used in industry for getting work and employment not necessarily as a means of working through the processes of design as they have been in the context of school. The portfolio as multimodal text has different purposes in different contexts. Much responsibility falls on the teachers. At the outset they need to use their life experience to read, consume and interpret the range of curriculum documents. They also need to build a coherent understanding through the curriculum represented in the Study Design. They need to analyse the assessment requirements to see what knowledge and skills are being sought and valued. Once the aims and outcomes being sought are understood, it falls to the teacher to build, or produce, a developmental pathway that will efficiently and effectively model, coach and scaffold learners through the meaning making to achieve the required understandings. Next the developmental pathway needs to be enacted as a learning program. This involves creative, appropriately structured and effective pedagogical communication and interactions. It involves guiding the students' learning as well as understanding and being able to communicate with young people who live within youth culture – a culture that is typically somewhat different to that of their teachers.

CONCLUSION

As Daker (2006) explains we need to develop new language, new literacies, 'in order to both understand our brave new world and learn how to live a meaningful existence in it', (p.1). This chapter begun with a discussion of different text and text forms and located these within new technologies and changing work practices - within new times. It also provided a three stage model by which to review and understand curriculum development. Next came an examination of the texts associated with the teaching and learning that occurs in Design and Technology education in secondary schools across Victoria. It discusses a range of different texts and semiotic systems. The analysis centres on the consumption and production of multimodal texts as they relate to the participants working in the field of Design and Technology education. The discussion uses teaching in upper secondary school to show that teachers need to utilise very highly developed literate practices in their own work of consuming, interpreting and producing texts associated with curriculum development work. Teachers build their understanding of the requirements and expectations in this field of study through actively reading an array of curriculum related texts which together provide a deep intertextual meaning. Further to this, this chapter implicitly explores whether the language of multiliteracies offers teachers of design and technology a means to articulate and discuss their work with other educators outside of their field.

At the heart of the curriculum and pedagogy for Design and Technology education is the design process. Students, like their teachers, are also involved in consuming, interpreting and producing texts. In the instance of Design and Technology education, the students show their engagement with the design process by producing multimodal texts specific to their projects and which show the various stages of the design process. The evidence of student engagement is played out and recorded as pages in the students' portfolio. In order to become multiliterate citizens who are actively involved in the construction of their social futures, students need to be inducted and scaffolded in order to become proficient with a wide range of emerging literacies. An integral part of the new and emerging literacies is understanding of and proficiency with multimodal texts. The field of Design and Technology education plays a part in students developing particular literate practices as they work towards these understandings.

REFERENCES

Adamthwaite, K., Ellis, D., Lowe, P., Rocca, R., Wesley, A., & Worth, M. (2006) *Cambridge Senior Design and Technology*. Melbourne, Australia: Cambridge University Press.

Anstey, M., & Bull, G. (2006). *Teaching and learning multiliteracies: changing times, changing literacies*. Newark, DE: International Reading Association.

Barlex, D. (Ed.). (2007). *Design & technology for the next generation: a collection of provocative pieces, written by experts in their field, to stimulate reflection and curriculum innovation*. Whitchurch, Australia: Cliffeco Communications

Billett, S. (2006). *Work, change and workers*. Dordrecht: Springer

Collins, S., Cornius-Randall, R., Annetts, P., Annetts, S., Hampson, R., McMurtie, Y., et al. (2006). *Switched on: technology Stage 4*. Milton: Wiley & Sons.

Cope, B., & Kalantzis, M. (2000). *Multiliteracies: literacy learning and the design of social futures*, London: Routledge.

Cowley, D. (2007). *Design and Technology: The Leading edge VCE Units 3 & 4*, Melbourne: Pearson Education.

Daker, J. (Ed.). (2006). *Defining technological literacy: towards an epistemological framework*. Basingstoke: Palgrave MacMillan.

De Vries, M. (2007). Philosophical reflections on the nature of design & technology, in Barlex D (ed). Design & technology: for the next generation: *a collection of provocative pieces, written by experts in their field, to stimulate reflection and curriculum innovation*. Whitchurch: Cliffeco Communications. pp. 20-33.

Freebody, P., & Luke, A. (2003). Literacy as engaging with new forms of life: the "four roles" model. In Anstey M & Bull G (Eds), *The literacy lexicon* (2nd Ed., pp. 51-65). Sydney: Pearson Education.

Garner, S., & Evans, M. (1996). Communications in design. In J. Williams, & Williams, A., (ed.), *Technology education for teachers* (pp. 111-135). Melbourne: MacMillan Education.

Gee, J., Hull, G., & Lankshear, C. (1996). *The new work order: behind the language of the new capitalism*. Sydney: Allen & Unwin.

Guthrie, K. (2003). *Visual communication and design: VCE Units 1 – 4*. Melbourne: Thomson Social Science Press

Ivers, K., & Barron, A. (2006). *Multimedia projects in education: designing, producing and assessing*, (3rd Ed.). Westport: Libraries Unlimited.

Kalantzis, M., & Cope, B. (2008). *New Learning: Elements of a Science of Education*. Melbourne: Cambridge University Press.

Kimbell, R., & Stables, K. (2008). *Researching design learning: issues and findings from two decades of research and development*. Dordrecht: Springer.

Kress, G. (2003). *Literacy in the new media age*. London: Routledge.

Kress, G., & Van Leeuwen, T. (1996). *Reading images: a grammar of visual design.* London: Routledge.

Kress, G., & Van Leeuwen, T. (2001). *Multimodal discourses: the modes and media of contemporary communication.* London: Edward Arnold.

Lankshear, C., & Knobel, M. (2003). *New literacies: changing knowledge and classroom learning.* Buckingham, UK: Open University Press.

Linton, H. (2003). *Portfolio design* (3rd Ed.). New York: Universe Publishing.

Livett, J., & O'Leary, J. (2007). *Design and Technology,* (2nd Ed.). Melbourne: Thomson & Social Science Press.

Mayer, R. (2005). Introduction to multimedia learning. In R. Mayer, (Ed.), *The Cambridge Handbook of Multimedia learning* (pp.1-16). New York: Cambridge University Press.

McLeod, J. (2001). Teacher' Working Knowledge: The Value of Lived Experience. *UltiBase Article,* November. Retrieved January 15, 2009 from http://ultibase.rmit.edu.au/Articles/nov01/mcleod1.pdf.

Mitcham, C., & Holbrook, J. B. (2006). Understanding technological design. In J. Daker, (ed.) *Defining technological literacy: towards an epistemological framework* (pp. 105-120). Basingstoke: Palgrave MacMillan.

Pacey, A. (1999). *Meaning in technology.* Cambridge, MA: MIT Press.

Petrina, S. (2007). *Advanced teaching methods for the Technology classroom.* Hershey, PA: Information Science Publishing.

Teese, R. (2005). For which young people do schools work well and why? In S. Richardson, & M. Prior, (Eds.), *No time to lose: the well being of Australia's children* (pp.240-254). Melbourne: Melbourne University Press.

Unsworth, L. (2001). *Teaching multiliteracies across the curriculum: changing contexts of text and image in classroom practice.* Buckingham, UK: Open University Press.

VCAA (2005). *Food and Technology: Victorian Certificate of Education Study Design.* East Melbourne: Victorian Curriculum and Assessment Authority.

VCAA (2006). *Design and Technology: Victorian Certificate of Education Study Design.* East Melbourne: Victorian Curriculum and Assessment Authority.

VCAA (2006a). *Systems Engineering: Victorian Certificate of Education Study Design.* East Melbourne: Victorian Curriculum and Assessment Authority.

VCAA (2007). *VCE and VCAL Administrative Handbook 2008.* East Melbourne: Victorian Curriculum and Assessment Authority.

VCAA (2008). *VCE Design and Technology Assessment Handbook 2007 – 2011.* East Melbourne: Victorian Curriculum and Assessment Authority.

VCAA (2008a). *VCAA Bulletin VCE, VCAL and VET,* (56), Supplement 1,..

VCAA. (2008b). *VCE Statistics.* Retrieved from VCAA website http://www.vcaa.vic.edu.au/vce/statistics/2007/statssect2.html.

VCAA & Melbourne Museum. (2008). Top Design exhibition and catalogue. Retrieved May 4th 2008, from http://museumvictoria.com.au/MelbourneMuseum/Education/Education-Programs/Top-Designs-2008/.

Welch, M. (2007). The pupil as designer. In D. Barlex, (ed). *Design & technology for the next generation: a collection of provocative pieces, written by experts in their field, to stimulate reflection and curriculum innovation* (pp. 120-139). Whitchurch: Cliffeco Communications.

Welch, M., Barlex, D., & Lim, H. (2000). Sketching: fried or foe to the novice designer? *International Journal of Technology and Design Education, 10*, 125–148. doi:10.1023/A:1008991319644

Williams, P. J. (2009) Technological literacy: a multliteracies approach for democracy. *International Journal of Technology and Design Education* 19 237 – 254; Retrieved from http://www.springerlink.com/content/fm0383v317315u60/fulltext.pdf

Chapter 11
Multimedia, Oral History, and Teacher Education:
From Community Space to Cyberspace

Jenifer Schneider
University of South Florida, USA

James R. King
University of South Florida, USA

Deborah Kozdras
University of South Florida, USA

James Welsh
University of South Florida, USA

Vanessa Minick
University of South Florida, USA

ABSTRACT

The study took place at a Catholic PreK-8 school/parish where two faculty instructors taught under-graduate methods courses. At the parish site, the pre-service teachers worked with elementary students to create a range of multi-media projects. These projects showcased the oral histories of the people, places, and events of the school and church community and allowed the pre-service teachers to inte-grate technology into their teaching. The researchers analyzed observational, interview, and textual data and found a range of behaviors that reflected the pre-service teachers' familiarity/unfamiliarity with technology, teaching, and the community in which they were learning. As a result, their attempts at learning through and teaching with technology, along with our attempts to teach with and learn through technology, revealed a multiplicity of enactments of fast literacies (Schneider, King, Kozdras, Minick, & Welsh, 2006). In this chapter, we share examples from the themes of our analysis, which reflect Kinzer's (2005) notion of the "intersection" between school, community, and technology.

DOI: 10.4018/978-1-60566-842-0.ch011

INTRODUCTION

We have observed pre-service teachers' innovative uses of technology, from their personal use of text messaging to their completion of coursework using a variety of word processing programs. However, when faced with the stresses of teaching (an emerging skill) with technology (an emerging skill) they may fall back on their personal classroom experiences as students and gravitate to the familiarity of traditional literacies. Within the habitus of required school literacies, we pondered how we could convince teachers to make their teaching real and engage students in communication for real purposes. Kinzer (2005) pointed to a space for teachers' authenticity at the intersection of schools, communities, and technology. He suggested that "one cannot help but be struck that technology can extend the boundaries of classrooms" (p. 66). In order to extend the boundaries of the pre-service teacher experience, we engaged pre-service teachers, in-service teachers, and their students in face-to-face literacy learning within and beyond their community spaces. We used cyberspace as a virtual communication medium to showcase oral histories of the people, places, and events of a parochial school community. In this paper we report the results of this project and in particular, its impact on our teaching and the learning of our pre-service teachers.

BACKGROUND

Literacy researchers, theorists, and organisations have called for changes in educational curriculum to include "New Literacies" (e.g., Alvermann, 2002; Lankshear & Knobel, 2003; National Council of Teachers of English, 2005; New London Group, 1996). In order to promote these new digitally-based, multi-mediated literacies, The International Reading Association has stated, "The Internet and other forms of information and communication technology (ICT) are redefining the nature of literacy. To become fully literate in today's world, students must become proficient in the new literacy of ICT" (International Reading Association, 2001). Our current project is undertaken in the context of newer, media-based literacies, shaped by suggestions from Kalantzis and Cope (2004) and Kinzer (2005) to connect real-world experiences to school literacies.

Problems with Integrating Technology

In response to the call for the integration of technology into schools, Hobbs (2006) reported a problematic trend in teachers' implementation of digital literacies - the resistance of literacy teachers to infuse technology into their lessons. While many science and mathematics teachers have readily adopted technology into their programs, literacy teachers tend to choose print in preference to multimedia applications. Hobbs speculated that teachers may view technology as a threat to the tradition of print literacies. In addition, other researchers have found that educators may refrain from using technology because they consider it an "out-of-school" literacy. For example, Bromley (2006) found that teachers are suspicious of the increasing informality of Internet writing as a form of non-school literacy. Similarly, Turbill and Murray (2006) found that primary grade Australian teachers viewed technology as play, and therefore not what traditionally is considered to be literacy. McKenna (2006) also noted that teachers might resist technology because they associate it with popular culture, another non-school literacy. Discounting literacy on the grounds that it fails the standard of literacy is an argument that is counter to newer theorizing in what are called the "new literacies" (Knobel & Lankshear, 2006; New London Group, 1996).

Turbill and Murray (2006) proposed that teachers may be reluctant to use technology because they are afraid of what they have not tried. They suggested that the problems might emanate from the colleges of education where teacher educators do not model the use of technology. Further, McKenna and Robinson (2005) noted that teachers tend to model their instruction based on what they were exposed to as students. If these models do not include technology use their own practices tend to be void of them as well. In agreement with Turbill and Murray (2006) as well as McKenna and Robinson (2005), we maintain that technology integration into literacy instruction must at least begin at the teacher education level. At this point in their training, pre-service teachers are trying out new techniques and developing their philosophies of practice. Perhaps one of the reasons why pre-service teachers fail to use technology in their literacy lessons is because they are not provided with models, encouragement and opportunity.

Authentic Integration

If teacher educators integrate technology for real purposes, they will likely move learning experiences outside of the college classroom walls. Kinzer (2005) described how technology can (and should) extend the boundaries of the classroom. He emphasised three fundamental components necessary to enable significant impact on learning: community, school, and technology. Furthermore, Kinzer noted that communicating through digital technologies requires literacy skills that include, but also extend beyond, the traditional notions of reading and writing. He notes that being literate means having the ability to compose multimedia messages using multiple modalities. In this context, "real" communication technology should involve students, businesses, parents, and teachers within authentic contexts and modeled in pre-service teachers' courses.

To this end, multi-genre projects have been deployed to afford authentic contexts by having students create content-area topics and writing (Romano, 2000). In such projects, textual, audio, and visual genres may be used (Tompkins, 2004). In order to make such multimediated projects suc-

cessful in terms of knowledge building, Bereiter and Scardamalia (2003) argue students should be able to inject their own ideas into such projects as well as develop ways of representing, organizing, and connecting with their work.

In particular, Lanman and Wendling (2006) noted that utilizing oral histories with students allows teachers to create conditions to adapt curricula, engage students, gather community support, and meet educational standards. Teachers' use of oral history as frameworks for classroom projects can transform their lessons by including their students' voices and ownership. In this way students see the power of history as a living force within their own lives and communities (Sitton, Mehaffy & Davis, 1983). Oral history (also known as oral biography, oral chronicles, and life history) involves interviewing a person or a group to get an inside perspective into what it was or is like to live as the member of a particular group within a society (Baum, 1987; Chaunce, 1994; Sitton, Mehaffy & Davis, 1983; Thompson, 1988; Zimmerman, 1982). More generally, surveying a group of people can create a picture of that group's collective experience. A broader oral history project can be a way of preserving a cohesive piece of local culture and history, allowing students to verify their findings, analyse interviews, and place the data in an accurate historical context. The following questions, best describe the focus of the study:

What are the effects, both socially and educationally, when we seek to place teacher education within a functioning community outside of the boundaries of traditional institutional settings? How do community, school, and technologies intersect to impact learning, teaching, theory, and research? How does the use of technology impact on pre-service teachers' acquisition of literacy methods when that use is embedded in community-based oral histories?

In this study, the researchers designed and analyzed a project that intended to teach traditional literacy methods to pre-service teachers, while simultaneously creating new literacies, within a bounded social group. The project that brought these initiatives together was a multi-genre, oral history project. Within the context of an oral history project, we investigated the process of integration of technology into pre-service teacher education in literacy.

METHODS

The study took place at a Catholic PreK-8 school during the spring semester. One of the faculty instructors served on the advisory board at the school and received support for the project from the school administration. Several teachers from different grade levels volunteered their classes to participate. Each week, two faculty instructors taught their respective undergraduate methods courses back-to-back at the parish site, giving the pre-service-teacher participants six hours to work with elementary students and receive course instruction.

Participants

Students

Approximately 250 elementary students participated in this project. The students were boys and girls who were in three Kindergarten classes (n=63), two first grade classes (n=59), two second grade classes (n= 64), and two sixth grade classes (n=68). The pre-service teachers worked with beginning readers and writers (age range=4-8; males=98; females =88; race = predominantly Caucasian with many students of Latino descent) as well as fluent readers and writers from sixth grade (age range=11-13; males= 33; females=35; race=predominantly Caucasian with many students of Latino descent). During staggered times in each class session, the grade levels of elementary students worked in 12 groups, each headed by two to three pre-service teachers (n=32). Each grade

level worked with the pre-service teachers on a particular project over a range of class sessions. The Kindergarten students attended one session, first grade attended three sessions, second grade attended six sessions, and sixth grade attended ten.

Pre-Service Teachers

The two methods classes enrolled 32 students, who were predominantly 21-25 year old, Caucasian females. The group also included four Black females, five older Caucasian females, three Hispanic females, and two Caucasian males. Eight of these 32 undergraduate students were part of a Laptop Initiative within the College of Education and they had each purchased an Apple laptop computer and had received special training in software applications such as iMovie and Garageband. Other pre-service teachers also had other personal laptop computers in addition to other equipment.

The two methods courses were required units and students registered for the courses knowing that they were linked and taught off campus. For the course requirements, the pre-service teachers determined students' reading and writing abilities, identified appropriate texts, used shared, guided, and modeled writing to help students write across genres, and then used iMovie, iPhoto, PowerPoint, and Keynote to create oral history projects with the students.

Faculty

The university faculty included one female Caucasian Associate Professor and one male Caucasian Professor. The professors co-taught during two previous summer experiences at a community center in which they taught the same courses, utilized similar methods, and also required students to produce multi-media projects. The two faculty instructors taught the pre-service teachers relevant course content, monitored online discussions, supervised teaching sessions, modeled instructional strategies, and coordinated with the school administration and staff. The faculty also interacted with parents of the elementary students and interested members of the school and parish community. One faculty member arranged for guests to volunteer for the oral history project as interviewees. She also collected documents from the parish. She took on this role because the school's media centre was under construction and they did not have a media specialist on staff. In addition, she was a former student at the school so she had access to individuals and knowledge of the school's history.

Research Assistants

Two doctoral students (two Caucasian females) collected data throughout the project. They observed and wrote field notes in all class sessions and tutoring sessions. They wrote methodological and analytic reflections and interviewed the children, pre-service teachers, and faculty instructors. They also supported the pre-service teachers' instruction by modeling and sharing materials.

Technology Support Personnel

Two staff members (one Caucasian male and one African American male) from the Florida Center for Instructional Technology, a resource centre in the College of Education, provided training and support to all personnel throughout the project. During the first three class sessions, the technology support team trained the students in using video cameras, digital cameras, and various software programs. During the remaining 13 sessions held at the elementary school, they brought laptops, cameras, iPods, recording equipment and assisted the pre-service teachers and students as they collected information and created their projects.

Study Events and Procedures

The first three meetings for the methods classes were held at the university. The faculty members taught the remaining 13 sessions at the parish school. At the school, the pre-service teachers worked with the children in a large parish hall. The pre-service teachers worked in teams of two or three and they were matched with groups of five or six students. During the first 90 minutes of class time, the pre-service teachers worked with primary grade students (K-2 on a rotating schedule) followed by 90 minutes of team teaching with small groups of 6th-grade students. After lunch, the faculty members and researchers held a joint debriefing session to reflect on the teaching time. Then each professor taught his or her respective course content for the remaining two hours (60 minutes for each course).

Project Description

For the reading methods course, the pre-service teachers developed pattern book lessons, conducted repeated readings for fluency, completed informal reading inventories, and Running Records (Clay, 1993). For the writing methods course, the pre-service teachers used various instructional strategies (modeled, shared, interactive writing) and analyzed student written products using a six traits model (Culham, 2003). In the project context, these assignments were embedded in the activities that allowed the students to create oral history projects that generated electronic representations of their learning.

Kindergarten. The Kindergarten students collected family stories about the school or parish. Prior to working with the pre-service teachers, each child took home a page of directions that asked a family member to tell the child a story about a favorite memory. The children drew pictures that were scanned into a computer. Pre-service teachers recorded the children as they narrated their stories.

First Grade. Over three weeks, the first graders created digital photo storybooks about the school and parish. Each team selected a topic and then used a pattern book format to guide the composing of their group books. Using shared writing (McKenzie, 1985) the pre-service teachers helped the students to photograph, plan, and write the text that complemented their digital photos.

Second Grade. The pre-service teachers worked with second graders for six class sessions. Each team selected a focus person (e.g., pastor, teacher, hall staff, lunchroom director). The groups created interview questions, interviewed the focus person, wrote biographies, and created multi-media presentations of each biography.

Sixth Grade. The pre-service teachers worked with sixth graders for 10 weeks. The sixth graders worked in teams to investigate the texts, the tales, and the traditions of the school and parish. The sixth graders researched historical documents and interviewed key informants. The students presented their research in multi-media formats including videos and PowerPoint presentations using written, oral, and visual texts.

Project Reveal. Upon the completion of all of the projects, the research team created a website depository for the projects. On the final day of the research project at the school, each grade level invited their parents to join them for the Oral History Project reveal. The K-2 projects were shared during the first session and the 6th-grade projects were shared in the second session. The faculty members provided an overview of the project and then highlighted a few examples. The parents and students joined the pre-service teachers in small groups to view each of the final projects.

Data Sources

In order to document the project, data collection occurred over the 16 week spring semester. We collected data to record the process of the creation of the oral history projects as well as the final products.

Field notes. The researchers observed the processes of pre-service teachers creating the multi-genre oral history projects, wrote notes, and recorded their methodological and analytical reflections. The researchers also observed course instructional times and recorded field notes.

Photo-ethnography. One member of the research team used photo-ethnography as the primary method of data collection (Pink, 2006). She circulated throughout the room capturing the teaching process through digital photos.

Student Products. Our student-generated data set included 50 family memory recordings (narration and images), 12 digital photo-stories created in the form of pattern books (narrated text and images), 12 biographies created using PowerPoint, Keynote, or iMovie (narration, images, movement), and 12 research projects created using iMovie, PowerPoint, or Keynote (scripted narration, images, movement).

Course Documents. We collected course documents including posted lesson plans created by the instructors, Blackboard reflections, email communications created by the pre-service teachers, and parent communications.

Debriefing sessions. Each week, the research team held sessions to review observational data and to discuss emerging findings which often led to instructional changes. These sessions were digitally recorded.

Data Analysis

We used a multi-leveled (n=4), collaborative grounded theory model (King, Schneider, Kozdras, & Welsh, 2007) that utilized debriefing sessions to form tentative hypotheses based on the research questions. Hypotheses were checked at all four levels (professors, graduate assistants, pre-service teachers, and elementary students). We used constant comparative analysis (Bogdan & Biklen, 1998) to sort our data into meaningful themes to determine the effects of placing teacher education within a functioning community outside of the boundaries of traditional institutional settings and how the community, school, and technology intersected to impact on learning, teaching, theory, and research. These data were read for categories and compared across readers using the constant comparative method (Bogdan & Biklen, 1998). The categorical results of these readings were used to guide the debriefing sessions between the four researchers that occurred following each class meeting. The lesson plans, email, and parent communications were used to recreate the chronology of the project and to determine the instructional directions provided to the pre-service teachers. The texts from the pre-service teachers' online Blackboard reflections were analyzed using the constant comparative method (Bogdan & Biklen, 1998) in order to discern patterns in the pre-service teachers' assessment of the students and their reflections on the teaching process.

RESULTS

Throughout the project, we found a range of behaviors that reflected pre-service teachers' familiarity/unfamiliarity with technology, teaching, and the community in which they were learning. As a result, their attempts at learning through and teaching with technology, along with our attempts to teach with and learn through technology, revealed a multiplicity of enactments of fast literacies (Schneider, King, Kozdras, Minick, & Welsh, 2006). Fast literacies here are defined as the purposeful use of digital media as learning contexts. Below, we share the themes that described the intersection between school, community, and technology. Using the intersection as a metaphor, we found the transportation theme significant in discussing how the learning flowed within groups and between the learning groups and the greater community—we call these our "flow" themes. However, despite our intentions, there were many times when learning was interrupted—we labeled these instances as "crash" themes. We begin with

flow themes to illustrate the regular, working aspects of the project and then proceed with crash themes to show the complexity of the activity. Despite the obstacles, the activity created many overall successful learning intersections.

Flow Themes

We noted a variety of instances where learning "flowed". These were areas where we noticed significant learning extensions and connections among the constituent groups.

University, School, Community Intersection

The elementary students and the pre-service teachers cooperated in groups. The experience created a collective intelligence within their respective communities, in that they were able to share with larger, "real" communities (e.g., parents in "the reveal celebration", and on the Internet). In this situation, the students witnessed the same event, felt and thought the same things, and processed the same information, creating a group with a concrete, real experience producing a condition of "collective effervescence" (Csikszentmihalyi, 1990).

Connectivity and Intermediality

During the process, many of the students were constantly making text-to-self connections. They compared the past to the present and how things were the same and different, which connected them to the project. Personal connecting kept them internally motivated and in a mode of inquiry (Tovani, 2000). Similarly, the pre-service teachers were gaining a sense of the community and understanding of the history of the parish and school. Many pre-service teachers remarked that they were impressed with the students and would consider working in a school that was similar. Other students, who were unfamiliar with the school or unfamiliar with the Catholic faith began to understand that world from the students' perspectives, thereby gaining insights into culturally relevant pedagogy.

The students' and pre-service teachers' connections were captured and transmediated across an array of multimedia projects that involved students in digital storytelling, movie making, and animation (Semali & Pailliotet, 1999). The students made connections across texts (e.g., yearbooks, documents, interview testimony) and communicated the school's history and traditions to a broader audience using oral language, visual images, and text. The comprehensiveness of the students' work is broad. Over 70 multimedia projects were posted on the university website and later transferred to the parish website. The projects are representative of the experience of the students, their teachers, their parents, and volunteers. The students' excitement and the pre-service teachers' pedagogy were captured in time to be shared with the school, the wider community and in a global context.

Altruistic Engagement

Although there were trials in the completion of this monumental task, we were all focused on success. Despite the stress felt by the pre-service teachers, they and their students were immersed in and committed to the completion of the project. For example, throughout the process elementary students carefully researched their topics and created artistic works to include in their digital stories. Throughout the learning process, the pre-service teachers assisted the students with using both traditional literacy (reading and writing) as well as using digital media literacies (digitized audio recordings, PowerPoints, iMovies) in order to research and compose their projects. Some of the time and effort pre-service teachers spent in making these projects more audience-friendly took place outside of the class context, either at home or in the technology lab at the College of

Education. Likewise, community members also volunteered their time to meet with the students and share their knowledge. The classroom teachers felt the excitement and were also immersed in the process, providing support and encouragement as the project unfolded.

Mediacentric Productions

Although the elementary students had varying degrees of experience with technology, collectively (and with the aid of the FCIT technology team) they were able to create products that were seen to be impressive by their parents and the research team. This was the positive outcome from our collective reliance on audience as a motivator. The students could barely contain their excitement in the room as the website videos and slideshows were presented to the parents and parish community. This was especially true when the students appeared in the videos or when their artwork was featured.

Crash Themes

When a field project occurs, there are logistical, academic, and social considerations that need to be addressed. There are also many occasions when all of the players do not receive equal accommodation or consideration. Finally, there are layers of power that oftentimes lie conspicuously bare creating additional conflict. Within these locations of difference - in perception, in ability, in position and in favour - the following themes reflect the tensions among the constituents as these considerations were addressed.

Audience

Throughout the project, the various types of audiences caused moments of uncertainty and shifting product expectations. For example, the pre-service teachers were "watched" by their professors and the other members of the research team. They were the subjects of our record keeping when we circled the room with clipboards and cameras to document their work. The pre-service teachers knew that we were evaluating their performance for a grade in two courses. At the same time, the children were watched by the pre-service teachers and the professors. The children "received" approximations of literacy instruction and technology integration as the captive audience of the pre-service teachers, when these teachers-in-training attempted to apply various methods and techniques. The children understood that their work was going to be shared with the rest of the school, and specifically, with their parents. Yet their work was often high-jacked by the pre-service teachers so that the quality could be controlled. Throughout the project work, the children's parents served as an invisible audience—one that could stop a sixth grader from using "inappropriate" language or control the level of silliness in the projects. The parents also functioned as a target for approval. Many of the students were excited to share their projects. Their parents served as informants for their work with many coming into the school to be interviewed. For the research team, the parents represented an entire community that would potentially approve of the work done by the university. The parents could complain to the school if the project quality was poor or alternatively compliment the research team and pre-service teachers if the learning was worthwhile and the products impressive. In this context our professional and personal reputations were at stake. The hierarchy of audiences was at times difficult to navigate. Our findings regarding audience are consistent with the development of audience in composing (i.e., Wollman-Bonilla, 2001; Bracewell, 1978). In addition, we add the layering of audience and the possible weight of that sedimentation on the elementary students.

Collaboration and Roles

We found that teaching duos or trios created many opportunities for pre-service teachers to become overly reliant on their partners, to standout, or to "hide" within the group. Depending on the varying situations that occurred in the project, pre-service teachers deployed what appeared to be different teaching identities. The different enactment of identities, combined with the perspectives from different observers of the pre-service teachers, allowed the instructional/research team to assemble cases for each of the pre-service teachers. The same variability was true for the instructional/research team. There were occasions when the instructors were overly reliant on individuals with technology skills or, due to differences in personality or teaching style, gave the students mixed messages about expectations or performance while alternating leadership or supporting roles. Within the team and levels of participant structures, all participants (instructional, research, pre-service) took on various roles and, as a result, had multiple views of the experience and academic expectations. These individuals combined to form groups that functioned on a continuum, from highly functioning to dysfunctional. Many of the pre-service teachers were in their first semester in the elementary education program so the instructors provided assistance in pacing lessons and understanding goals.

Off-Site Resentment

This experience was held off-site (not on the university campus) so that our pre-service teachers could actually teach students. As a result of these conditions, there were many instances of context clashes. For example, because we were in a situated religious context, differences in spiritual beliefs sometimes created additional tensions. One student's religious beliefs prohibited photography and he requested that he not be included in any type of photograph or film that would be publicly displayed. Given that this was a multi-media project with the end products exhibited on a website, this request altered the nature of his group's project as well as the student's instructional positioning. Whereas all of the other 6th grade projects included video and photographs, his group's project was a simulated video game that included much of his own commentary about the school.

In another example of context clashing, one of the professor's relationship with the school created tensions. Some pre-service teachers felt that she was conducting the project for the benefit of her family or to elevate her status within the community. On the other hand, she was concerned about the community's perception of the projects and continually mentioned the website to remind the pre-service teachers that people would view their work. She was also responsible for coordinating the logistics within the school, scheduling interviews, and communicating with the community. The project created a great deal more work than any other type of on-site literacy course.

The offsite location also caused travel problems for some students. Although the school was only 10 miles from the university, many of the pre-service teachers commuted from distant counties. Some students who lived on campus relied on each other for transportation, which at times caused tensions between the pre-service teachers.

Because our pre-service teachers actually worked with students, they were required to have teaching materials to facilitate their role in the project. Their creation of mini-classrooms created an additional expense that caused a great deal of stress for some of the pre-service participants. Those who could afford to purchase easels, to bring in laptops and cameras, and to buy markers and other materials were more instructionally effective. With an easel, students did not have to observe writing that was upside down. With laptops, more students had opportunities to use multi-media. The purchase and use of quality art supplies created visually appealing materials and props.

Equipment Malfunction or Dysfunction

Most of the crashes in technology occurred because the pre-service teachers lacked knowledge of how to create multi-media products and therefore could not teach students how to make them either. We also experienced problems because all of the equipment (laptops, iPods, scanners, cameras) were brought from the university to the school. The transporting of equipment was a challenge and this responsibility fell to one person. So, if the designated transporter was stuck in traffic, the pre-service teachers and students were forced to create "filler" activities until the technology arrived. We also had issues with connectivity because the parish hall in which we taught was not equipped for wireless communication. The research team bought the school a router and asked for its installation, but when problems arose, the technology person for the school was difficult to find. All of these technology issues resulted in difficulties in allowing students to fully participate in the project.

FUTURE TRENDS

Perhaps one of the reasons why pre-service teachers often fail to use technology in their literacy lessons is because they are not provided with models, encouragement and opportunities. Creating the type of project described in this paper is logistically, mentally, and socially challenging. Teacher educators must be invested in the outcomes and truly believe in the benefits in order to orchestrate projects between community, school, and technology. At the end of every community experience, the research/instruction team recognized that it was difficult. However, before long, we were analyzing data, revisiting decisions, and making plans for the next experience. From this research we have discovered issues worthy of discussion and in need of future research.

Group Dynamics

As implicated in the crash themes, group dynamics play a major role in the success of a community technology project. The requirements for collaborative teaching and working with different types of learners from a community that is not one's own can be challenging for pre-service teachers. In the field of business, Tuckman's (1965) model is often cited as the seminal research that has labeled how groups develop and progress to achieve goals. Tuckman found that groups move through four stages—forming, storming, norming, and performing. We also found that our groups followed similar stages over time. However, as suggested by previous research (Johnson, Johnson, & Smith, 1991; Millis & Cottell, 1998; Smith, 1996), we never considered modeling how the groups should work together, the roles they could take, or the problems they might experience. We now understand the problems that occur in this scenario and we know that the groups will take time to coalesce. For teacher educators, this information could be used to better prepare pre-service teachers for group experiences. Providing them with more pre-project, in-class time to form groups and plan may have helped the group dynamics prior to working with the students. Our advice for teacher educators is to run a trial project in which the pre-service teachers could have time to practice with the technology in a more relaxed setting and establish group norms and performance goals for the project before they actually work with the children.

Researcher Considerations

The most significant finding for researchers was the efficacy we found using collaborative grounded theory (King et al, 2007). As evidenced in the data analysis, many of the crash themes were identified through researcher notes and collaborative post-session debriefing. As previously mentioned, although we noticed and discussed a variety of

lessons to be drawn in terms of "illuminating" problems (Newton, 2003), these crash themes may or may not apply in another situation. In fact, in examining our data analysis process, we identified the crash themes through our researcher observation notes and post-class debriefing sessions where we would discuss significant observations. In both notes and conversations, our researcher critiques of the situation brought forth many themes of crash, which logically stand out from the overall process of flow. Using the analogy of a highway, instances of uninterrupted driving (flow) toward a location (goal) may go unnoticed by the observer. Alternatively, congestion, crashes and other detractions from the process (e.g., thwarting instructional goals and desires) become areas of attention from a critical perspective. Interestingly, and importantly, most flow themes were realized through a close inspection of the products and the photo-ethnography of the process. Through the photo-ethnography, we hoped to capture the creative moments of the process in action. Bringing back an actual visual representation of the process re-minded (reengaged our minds) us of the many instances of smooth learning.

CONCLUSION

As was indicated in the flow themes, at times students reached optimal learning experiences as they worked as "autotelic workers" (Csikszentmihalyi, 1990) where the "work" became a flow experience toward a common goal. This common goal involved a personal link between the students, their school, their families, and the community; as well as using technology to extend the boundaries of the classroom (Kinzer, 2005). Optimal experiences occurred when the students were totally immersed in their work (personal connections). They sorted through old photos and yearbooks (school culture connections), carefully planned interview questions (community connections) and their mode of presentation (technology connections). During work time, they were active, creative, concentrated, and motivated (real-world/ audience connection). In these flow activities, the teacher candidates, the goal of the project, and the innovation of technology provided a combined force of scaffolding (Vygotsky, 1978) opportunities through a model of gradual release of responsibility. The activities and projects focused on the students and all adults involved were focused on helping them to achieve their goal. However, these modalities were simultaneously challenging and rewarding (new technologies, writing, editing, real audience, new literacies).

Ultimately, the context clashes, travel issues, financial strains, and equipment ownership were evidenced in the lack of buy-in from some of the pre-service teachers. Two of the pre-service teachers dropped the course, and others began to mentally or physically shut down by calling in sick or failing to complete assignments. Others reacted to the stressors in more subtle ways, choosing to gossip or cause problems within their group by "forgetting" equipment, props, or paperwork.

While we agree with taking education into real world contexts, we do not have a model for how the multiple stakeholders lay claim to the products that emanate from such a shared enterprise. It is, after all, difficult if not impossible to accommodate everyone's desire. What we presented is a series of conflicts and convergences that occurred when we tried to accomplish educational and technological training in a real-world setting.

ACKNOWLEDGMENT

The authors gratefully acknowledge support from the Florida Center for Instructional Technology.

REFERENCES

Alvermann, D. (2002). *Adolescents and literacies in a digital world*. New York: Peter Lang.

Baum, W. K. (1987). *Oral history of the local historical society.* Nashville, TN: American Association for State and Local History.

Berieter, C., & Scardamalia, M. (2003). *Learning to work creatively with knowledge*. Retrieved August 4, 2008 from http://www-personal.umich. edu/~jaylemke/courses/ED750/Scardamalia_Bereiter_KBuilding.pdf.

Bogdan, R., & Biklen, S. (1998). *Qualitative research in education: An introduction to theory and methods.* Needham Heights, MA: Allyn & Bacon.

Bracewell, R. (1978, March). *The development of audience awareness in writing.* Paper presented at the Annual Meeting of the American Educational Research Association, Toronto.

Bromley, K. (2006). Technology and writing. In M.C. McKenna, L. Labbo, R.D. Kieffer, & D. Reinking, (Eds.), *International handbook of literacy and technology: Volume II.* (pp. 349-361). Mahwah, NJ: Lawrence Erlbaum Associates.

Chaunce, S. (1994). *Oral history and the local historian.* London: Longman.

Clay, M. (1993). *An observation survey of early literacy achievement.* Portsmouth, NH: Heinemann.

Csikszentmihalyi, M. (1990). *Flow: The psychology of optimal experience.* New York: Harper Perennial.

Culham, R. (2003). *6+1 traits of writing: The complete guide to grades three and up.* Northwest Regional Laboratory. New York: Scholastic.

Hobbs, R. (2006). Multiple visions of multimedia literacy: Emerging areas of synthesis. In M.C. McKenna, L. Labbo, R.D. Kieffer, & D. Reinking, (Eds.), *International handbook of literacy and technology: Volume II.* (pp. 15-28). Mahwah, NJ: Lawrence Erlbaum Associates.

International Reading Association. (2001). *Integrating literacy and technology in the curriculum: A position statement*. Retrieved May 25, 2008 from http://www.reading.org/resources/issues/positions_technology.html

Johnson, D. W., Johnson, R. T., & Smith, K. (1991). *Cooperative learning: Increasing college faculty instructional productivity (ASHE-ERIC Higher Education Report No. 4)*. Washington, DC: The George Washington University, School of Education and Human Development.

Kalantzis, M., & Cope, B. (2004). Designs for learning. *E-learning, 1*, 38–43. doi:10.2304/elea.2004.1.1.7

King, J., Schneider, J., Kozdras, D., & Welsh, J. (2007, April). *Transforming L/literacies into d/Designs: Fast literacies faster pedagogies*. Paper presented at the Annual Meeting of the American Educational Research Association, Chicago.

Kinzer, C. K. (2005). The intersection of schools, communities, and technology: Recognizing children's use of new literacies. In R.A. Karchmer, M.H. Mallette, J. Kara-Soteriou, & D. J. Leu, (Eds.), *Innovative approaches to literacy education: Using the Internet to support new literacies*. (pp. 65-82). Newark, DE: International Reading Association.

Knobel, M., & Lankshear, C. (2006). *The new literacies sampler*. New York: Peter Lang.

Lankshear, C., & Knobel, M. (2003). *New literacies: Changing knowledge and classroom learning*. Buckingham, UK: Open University Press.

Lanman, B. A., & Wendling, L. M. (2006). *Preparing the next generation of oral historians: An anthology of oral history education*. Lanham, MD: Rowman & Littlefield.

McKenna, M. (2006). Introduction: Trends and trajectories of literacy and technology in the new millennium. In M. McKenna, L. Labbo, R. Kieffer, & D. Reinking (Eds.). *International handbook of literacy and technology: Volume II* (pp. xi-xviii). Mahwah, NJ: Erlbaum.

McKenna, M. C., & Robinson, R. D. (2005). *Teaching through text* (4th ed.). Boston: Allyn & Bacon.

McKenzie, M. G. (1985). Shared writing: Apprenticeship in writing. *Language Matters, 1-2*, 1–5.

Millis, B. J., & Cottell, P. G. (1998). *Cooperative learning for higher education faculty*. American Council on Education, Series on Higher Education. Phoenix, AZ: The Oryx Press.

National Council of Teachers of English. (2005). *Multimodal literacies*. Retrieved April 29, 2007 from www.ncte.org/about/over/positions/category/media/123213.htm?source-gs

New London Group. (1996). A pedagogy for multiliteracies: Designing social futures. *Harvard Educational Review, 66*, 60–92.

Newton, J. (2003). Implementing a teaching and learning strategy. *Studies in Higher Education, 28*(4), 427–441. doi:10.1080/0307507032000122279

Pink, S. (2006). *Doing visual ethnography* (2nd Ed.). London: Sage Publications Inc.

Romano, T. (2000). *Blending genre, altering style: Writing multigenre papers*. Portsmouth, NH: Boynton/Cook Heinemann.

Schneider, J., King, J., Kozdras, D., Minich, V., & Welsh, J. (November, 2006). *Power, performance, and perspective in a pre-service teacher/elementary student collaborative research/teaching project*. Paper presented at the Annual Meeting of the National Reading Conference, Los Angeles, CA.

Semali, L., & Pailliotet, A. (1999). *Intermediality*. Boulder, CO: Westview.

Sitton, T., Mehaffy, G. I., & Davis, O. L. (1983). *Oral history: A guide for teachers (and others)*. Austin, TX: University of Texas Press.

Smith, K. A. (1996). Cooperative learning: Making "group work" work. In T.E. Sutherland & C.C. Bonwell (Eds.), *Using active learning in college classes: A range of options for faculty: New Directions for Teaching and Learning* (No. 67). San Francisco: Josey-Bass.

Thompson, P. (1988). *The voice of the past: Oral history (2nd Ed.)*. Oxford, UK: Oxford University Press.

Tompkins, G. (2004). *Teaching writing: Balancing process and product*. Upper Saddle River, NJ: Pearson Prentice Hall.

Tovani, C. (2000). *I read it but I don't get it*. Portland, ME: Stenhouse.

Tuckman, B. (1965). Developmental sequence in small groups. *Psychological Bulletin, 63*, 384–399. doi:10.1037/h0022100

Turbill, J., & Murray, J. (2006). Early literacy and new technologies in Australian schools: Policy, research, and practice. In M.C. McKenna, L. Labbo, R.D. Kieffer, & D. Reinking, (Eds.), *International handbook of literacy and technology: Volume II.* (pp. 93-108). Mahwah, NJ: Lawrence Erlbaum Associates.

Vygotsky, L. S. (1978). *Mind in society: The development of higher psychological processes*. Cambridge, MA: Harvard University Press.

Wollman-Bonilla, J. (2001). Can first grade writers demonstrate audience awareness? *Reading Research Quarterly, 36*, 184–201. doi:10.1598/RRQ.36.2.4

Zimmerman, W. Z. (1982). *Instant oral biographies*. New York: Guarionex.

Section 3
The Literacy of Gaming

Chapter 12
The Hidden Literacies of Massively Multiplayer Online Games

P. G. Schrader
University of Nevada, USA

K. A. Lawless
University of Illinois, USA

ABSTRACT

Given the multitude of available options, citizens of a globalized, knowledge-based society must have the ability to locate, evaluate, and apply information across sources. Further, the manner in which information is consumed around the globe has become increasingly multimodal. Unfortunately, students are rarely presented with formal opportunities to engage in and with multiliteracies. As a result, there are very few opportunities for researchers to understand the nature of skills necessary to function in a multiliterate world. In serving this purpose, this chapter examines the multiliteracies associated with Massively Multiplayer Online Games (MMOGs). Specifically, it will examine the nature and affordances of the associated technologies as they pertain to the multiliteracies of consumption and production. A call for additional research with direct ties to education is also addressed.

INTRODUCTION

Over the last century, media and our notion of "text" have evolved. Newspapers and magazines from the early 1900s are easily indentified by their abundant use of text, tight columns, and small fonts while employing relatively few images (Crow, 2006; Kress, 2003; Kress & Van Leeuwen, 2001). By contrast, the multimodal aspects of modern media have become more pronounced (Kress &

DOI: 10.4018/978-1-60566-842-0.ch012

Van Leeuwen, 2001). At a minimum, characters and image are used together to communicate information, challenging our traditional definition of "text." More generally, words, images, and other elements function as simple components of a larger, complex frame (Kress, 2005). Collectively, these attributes and the technological characteristics of emerging technologies have allowed for new and highly complex environments, notably ones in which users interact and exchange information.

Modern technology affords the presentation of information in a variety of modes (e.g., audio, visual, video, text, spatial, etc.). One only needs to consider any news website to verify this point. A single article might have videos, sound bytes, advertisements, and animations woven into the text. In addition, one might consider commercial websites, media kiosks, or smartphone interfaces and they will see that this scenario is far from isolated or unique. As a result, there has been a shift in what it means to be literate and productive in a modern, multimodal world (Goldman, 2004; Kitson, Fletcher, & Kearney, 2007; Leu, 2000; New London Group, 1996). In this sense, "reading" and "literacy" rely not only on the content within each element, but also each element's position, relationships among elements, as well as aspects of the reader (Kress, 2005; RAND Reading Study Group, 2002).

Beyond the attributes of presentation and transmission, the affordances of modern media have also influenced the way we access and interpret information. On a global scale, users may find information via television, papers, magazines, blogs, forums, and/or podcasts, just to name a few. By contrast to previous generations, there has been a multimodal explosion associated with all classes of media on nearly any topic, which may be accessed from virtually any resource. Although the interpretation of multiple sources is not a new concept, the ubiquity of these resources have made it necessary to further examine the complex skills associated with locating, evaluating, and implementing information (Schrader, Lawless, & McCreery, in press; Spivey & King, 1989). Often termed multiple source comprehension (or intertextuality), these skills are integral in a multiliterate world.

Unfortunately, multiple source comprehension introduces complexities beyond those typically present in single source learning. For example, a learner must not only determine the relevance of a particular resource but also make this evaluation in relation to other resources. Competing sources may afford alternate perspectives or provide conflicting information, challenging the learner to critically evaluate and compare these points of view. However, connecting information across resources can be a daunting task, particularly for individuals with low domain knowledge, interest, or motivation (Lawless & Kulikowich, 1996, 1998). This challenge is exacerbated when information is presented in multiple formats, which requires the reader to simultaneously interpret information across sources and modes.

Technology has clearly provided new affordances for the presentation of information. As a result, contemporary environments also allow users to participate in the creation and exchange of information in dynamic ways (Dede, 2008; Schrader et al., in press). On the World Wide Web (WWW), there has been a shift from a passive information retrieval system to a dynamic, interactive model in which users are active participants in authoring, editing, evaluating, and disseminating content (Dede, 2008; O'Reilly, 2005). Often termed Web 2.0, the modern Internet and WWW have changed the way people share their views (e.g., blogs), engage in communities of practice (e.g., social networks), and collaborate on ideas (e.g., wikis) (Dede, 2008; Jenkins, 2006, 2007, 2008). When compared to previous generations, these venues and tools imply an entirely different set of skills to be productive (Goldman, 2004).

Collectively, the presentation, consumption, and production of information across resources and modes have given rise to a wide array of educational difficulties. Although 17 million students in the United States regularly use the Internet in school (Pew Internet and American Life, 2001, 2005), we know very little about the skills students require to negotiate these information environments (Lawless & Schrader, 2008). As a result, little emphasis is placed on training students to become competent 21st century learners within formal school settings (Manning, Lawless, Gomez, McLeod, Braasch, & Goldman, 2008). This is not only true of the United States, but countries like Australia and the United Kingdom where there is a similar push toward understanding multiliteracies and the associated educational contexts (Kitson et al., 2007; New London Group, 1996). However, it would seem that students are ill-prepared to overcome the complexities associated with multiliteracies in the 21st century, at least formally (Apple, 2007; Gee, 2006; Leu, 2000). This lack of attention to the complexities of multimodal learning in schools is not only problematic for students, but also leaves researchers without an authentic context in which to examine the emergence and development of these skills.

Fortunately, there are many informal environments (e.g., outside of school) in which highly sophisticated multiliteracy practices are regularly applied. Specifically, Massively Multiplayer Online Games (MMOGs) provide an authentic example of multiliteracies in practice (Schrader, Lawless & McCreery, 2009). Within the game, players collaborate, exchange resources, and interpret strategies from various sources. They accomplish this by interpreting movement, images, sound, and text collectively. Outside the game, players locate, evaluate, and synthesize a range of information for the purpose of play. Similarly, the same culture is responsible for creating much of this information and they do so in a variety of formats, including images, video, sound, and text.

Overall, MMOGs and their encapsulating culture provide a rich context in which we might examine the authentic application of multiliteracies (Hayes, 2007; Schrader et al., 2009; Schrader & McCreery, 2007). This chapter will examine the nature of these skills in a highly popular MMOG, the *World of Warcraft* (WoW). The strategies players exhibit in contexts like these inform our understanding of multiple source comprehension and multiliteracies and how they may relate to more formal educational environments.

Multiliteracy in the 21st Century

In the United States, data indicate that the use of resources like the World Wide Web (WWW)

has steadily increased over the past several years (see Pew Internet and American Life, 2001, 2005, 2007). In 2004, 87% of American students regularly accessed the Internet. By 2007, that statistic rose to 94% of students, the majority of whom used it as a principal resource for school related research (Pew Internet and American Life, 2007, 2008). Students are using the Internet to communicate, research, and play (Pew Internet and American Life, 2005). Although there may be little formal training for students to leverage the skills necessary to utilize the Internet (Apple, 2007; Gee, 2006; Schrader et al., 2009), these data suggest that the Internet is becoming ubiquitous with this population.

The trends present in American education appear to mirror those in the globalized workplace. Manpower, a world leader in the employment services industry, regularly examines societal and global workforce trends. Data from a survey of more than 52,000 employers from 27 countries around the world indicated that companies are using more technology and that there is a trend toward the virtualization of work and employees (Manpower, 2007). From a global perspective, professionals are being hired based on their skills and abilities, rather than their geographic location. Further, there is little evidence to suggest that these trends will diminish. When asked about their expectations for the next 10 years, most employers (87%) speculated that they would conduct more interviews virtually and 81% anticipated that more people would work from home on a regular basis (Manpower, 2007).

Whether for work or school, researchers assert that the ways users embrace and implement new technologies greatly influences the manner in which we communicate, exchange ideas, collaborate, and work (Dede, 2008; Jenkins, 2006, 2007; Manpower, 2007). For example, *Wikipedia* and other wikis are constructed upon the epistemology of negotiated compromise (Dede, 2008). Participants use the wiki to debate facts, edit excerpts, and openly argue their views in an effort to achieve conceptual agreement. This is in stark contrast to the static analog (i.e., the encyclopedia), about which readers have no ability to change the entries. Further, a source like Wikipedia is unbounded and contains both "just-in-time" publications as well as those on any topic valued by society (Dede, 2008; Jenkins, 2008).

In contrast to *Wikipedia*, social networking sites like *Facebook* or its immersive, 3-D cousin, *Second Life*, are designed to provide a virtual platform for friends and colleagues to gather and socialize. While wikis leverage social participation for the purpose of knowledge construction, social networks have a different purpose (Lawless & Schrader, 2008). These networks allow users to post and comment on photographs, share links and videos, and exchange other multimodal details of their lives. Sometimes called social bookmarking, the potential for peers to evaluate, edit, and comment on these media provides an entirely new mechanism for participants to locate and filter online content (Lawless & Schrader, 2008).

Whether focused on a manuscript, socialization, or some other purpose, users of these resources typically create images, videos, texts, or other multimodal artifacts in an effort to communicate their views. More importantly, facile users implement these tools in seamless ways where the message is principal but the mode of transmission is functional and irrevocably tied to the message (i.e., images, videos, text). As a consequence, it is not sufficient to regard only the elemental literacy skills associated with learning in virtual environments; rather, greater emphasis is placed upon the multiliteracies associated with these contexts. In particular, researchers have previously described issues associated with navigation, intertextuality, and multimodality as they pertain to literacy.

Navigation

In general, literacy is often described as a transactive process that takes place among the text, the reader, and the context in which the text is read (Leu & Kinzer, 2003; RAND Reading Study Group, 2002). From this perspective, reading is constructive, interactive, and socially cued (Alexander & Fox, 2004; Leu & Kinzer, 2000; Rosenblatt, 1994; Ruddell & Unrau, 2004; Shanahan, 1990). However, these views of reading and text comprehension typically pertain to static, traditional texts. Unfortunately for theorists, the modern examples of multiliteracies and texts are much more dynamic than that. Fundamentally, hypermedia is generally nonlinear, intertextual, and multimodal (Chen & Macredie, 2002; Dillon, McKnight, & Richardson, 1990). These characteristics invite and require cognitive demands beyond those inherent in static texts and single source learning (Lawless & Schrader, 2008).

At a minimum, hypermedia users must interact with and navigate the environment in order to comprehend information (Lawless & Schrader, 2008). However, navigation itself is fraught with challenges including, understanding where the reader is currently, where they have been, and where they are going in relation to the overall "text" (Lawless & Schrader, 2008; Lawless, Schrader, & Mayall, 2007). As a cognitive process, navigation is layered on top of existing, traditional literacies (e.g., decoding, interpreting), thus adding complexity to the simplest of hypermedia examples. When considering more dynamic, though less understood, examples (e.g., immersive 3D worlds), these challenges are multiplied many times.

Intertextuality

Overlying navigation, intertextuality is a characteristic present in all texts (Hartman & Hartman, 1993; Orr, 1986). In general, reading and writing involves selecting, organizing, and connecting content from source texts (Spivey, 1984; Spivey & King, 1989). However, the importance of intertextuality with respect to hypertext is elevated by virtue of hypermedia's relational design and the process of navigation (Lawless & Schrader,

2008). As with any "text," hypertexts present content from authors' necessarily unique and sometimes idiosyncratic perspectives. Alone, this accounts for competing views, presentation styles, and a variety of other barriers to understanding information across texts. However, the ease by which content is added to the World Wide Web (WWW), linked, and accessed compounds these concerns.

Hypertext users must first search for and locate information (Bruce, 2002). Users must make an initial plan or establish a set of goals related to the information and continually evaluate their progress (Bruce, 1997; 2002). Once located, users must interpret and synthesize the information in relation to the greater context and their broad understanding. At a meta-level, users must also determine whether or not the information is relevant to the task as well as consider their overall progress in achieving their information related goals. Ultimately, once the users successfully locate, evaluate, and navigate the information, they must implement the newly acquired ideas. Collectively, these strategies represent a minimal, yet necessary, set to be successful in the 21st century (Bruce, 1997, 2002; Leu, 2000; Society of College, National and University Libraries, 1999).

Multimodality

Beyond navigation and the issues associated with intertextuality, hypermedia is traditionally multimodal. Graphics and text are typically woven together to communicate information and an overall "appeal" for the site. Kress (2005) argued that the components of any media are interpreted on multiple levels. For example, readers interpret static text and images as individual sources of information. However, readers also construct meaning from the relationships among these elements. Specifically, they evaluate the selection of icons, the placement of images, and the holistic quality of the entire "text." Something as simple as font choice might suggest a certain

level of sophistication while color might indicate a particular mood or quality (Kress, 2003, 2005; Kress & Van Leeuwen, 2001).

Beyond static presentation of visual information, researchers have also addressed the challenges associated with interpreting visual images (Monaco, 2000; Rose, 2005). Classical psychologist J. J. Gibson (1986) identified the many affordances associated with the visual field in a static physical space. These affordances lead one to detect characteristics of the environment like an object's relative location, texture, and illumination. However, he asserted that motion and corresponding changes in visual information yield a complete picture of the environment, offering cues about such elements as volume, distance, and size (Gibson, 1986). With respect to modern technology, motion is nearly ubiquitous. As a result, several researchers have examined the concept of visual and moving images as it relates to learning and literacy (Madden, Chung, & Dawson, 2008; Monaco, 2000; Parker, 1999; Rose, 2005).

Interpreting information from film requires the viewer to detect subtle signs and cues about the media, negotiating a balance between denotative and connotative meaning (Monaco, 2000). Unlike traditional text, the room for ambiguity or interpretation of film is relatively small. Imagination plays a minor part in the exchange. However, viewers must still evaluate the many possible metaphors, characters' effect, and the use of various techniques to communicate cinematic mood. In this sense, understanding film and movies is very important to working with static narratives or texts in which the reader must identify plot elements, interpret motives, and understand the overall context (Monaco, 2000).

In addition to viewing movies, modern technologies have empowered users with the possibility of creating new media. Parker (1999) describes the importance of narrative in the creation of moving media. He argues that there is a crucial connection between selecting segments, editing, and composing with narrative literacy. Similarly,

Madden et al., (2008) summarize the distinction between *filming* and *editing*. Although both are multimodal, filming entails the selection of the visio-spatial perspective, the elements involved, and motion as method to communicate ideas (e.g., panning, zooming, etc.). By contrast, editing is the essential process of making meaning by placing and arranging these shots in a particular, relevant order (Burn & Parker, 2001, 2003). Together, these two aspects of film creation define the *mode* of the moving image, or kineikonic mode.

In isolation, there are many evident challenges associated with interpreting static visual elements or producing moving images. However, these challenges are exacerbated by the ease in which multiple modes are blended and combined. Modern tools demand that authors must not only understand the nature of the information, but they must make meaningful decisions associated with the media and method of presentation. According to Kress (2005), the informational affordances associated with an image are considerably different than those associated with text. Similarly, video and audio hold additional and distinct affordances in the way audiences interact with ideas. When creating resources, authors are required to determine which mode, or combination of modes, most accurately or appropriately communicates their message. For example, an author might select video rather than text and image as an appropriate media to create a tutorial on *dancing the foxtrot*. Although the author might use different views and soundtracks, they might also overlay graphics of dance steps and or text to further enhance and convey the lesson. Regardless of the media or outcome, the meta-processes and multiliteracies associated with creating multimodal messages are highly complex. These skills require careful consideration, particularly given the technological needs of 21st century citizens (Leu, 2000).

Multiliteracies and WoW

Collectively, many researchers describe the skills associated with a multiliterate world as 'new literacies' (Coiro, 2003; Coiro, Knobel, Lankshear, & Leu, 2008). Unfortunately, students are not well prepared to perform these activities (Apple, 2007; Gee, 2006). Part of the issue lies with the nature of education in countries like the United Kingdom and the United States where standardized testing has become the driving force behind education and its funding (Gee, 2006; Harrison, 2006; USDOE, 2007; Wickens & Sandlin, 2007). As a result, we overlook important connections that technology may provide to these digital natives. We are failing to formally prepare students to meaningfully consume or produce information with modern technology. We neither address their ability to think critically nor engage mindfully with the knowledge-based society in which they live (Apple, 2007; Gee, 2006). Although our students are digital natives with respect to these tools, educators are missing the opportunity to use technology to connect with this population (Pellegrino, Goldman, Bertenthal & Lawless, 2007).

Informally, research indicates that American students write extensively using multimodal resources (e.g., emails, social networks, and instant messages) (Pew Internet and American Life Project, 2008). Unfortunately, parents and students in the United States do not perceive these media activities to be writing even though most parents (83%) and school age children (86%) agree that writing is an important skill for success in the 21st century (Pew Internet and American Life Project, 2008). Students' responses to questions about writing instruction highlight the issues with their preparation. Most American students (82%) agree that general writing instruction could be improved and another 78% agree that computer-based writing instruction could be improved. While it may be argued that students' informal participation in multimodal authorship facilitates literacy development, little is being done in formal settings to teach these tools. Beyond the examples already described, immersive environments provide a broad context for the application of multiliteracies. Specifically, within each Massively Multiplayer Online Game (MMOG) and the associated, encapsulating culture, players are presented with opportunities to author, consume, and exchange multimodal resources (Hayes, 2007; Sanford & Madill, 2007; Steinkuehler, 2006).

While MMOGs are sometimes discounted as a research context or considered trivial due to their emphasis on "fun," there is an extensive body of literature that outlines the merits and importance of games in education (see Gee, 2003; Young, Schrader, & Zheng, 2006; Squire, 2006; Squire & Jenkins, 2003). Regardless of one's perspective on MMOGs, the fact remains that videogames have become a permanent fixture in our society (Schrader et al., 2009). They are a social phenomenon and the associated culture produces vast entertainment and information resources that are both produced and consumed by gamers (Hayes, 2007; Steinkuehler, 2006; Steinkuehler, Black, & Clinton, 2005).

Kress (2005) suggested when considered collectively, the technological and social contexts provide the frame for modern 'text' comprehension. According to Kress, a 'text' includes icons and images, video, sound, and the interaction of all included elements. From this perspective, MMOGs represent a microcosm of the knowledge society and members exhibit the socially cued multiliteracies necessary to function in that society. For this reason, MMOGs present an ideal frame to examine multiliteracies in a modern, global culture.

With more than 10 million paid subscriptions, the *World of Warcraft* (WoW) is the world's most popular MMOG (Blizzard Entertainment, 2008). This is a statistic with which the authors are both well aware and also intimately familiar. Combined, they have several years experience both researching and playing WoW. As such, the remainder of this chapter is dedicated to describing the specific

multiliteracies associated with WoW using the authors' familiarity with the game to describe WoW's affordances. Further, results of a short, self-report survey of gamers' literacy practices while playing WoW are used to support the claims.

Throughout, it is important to note that we acknowledge that WoW has been created for the purpose of entertainment. As such, we do not examine outcomes or skills from MMOG environments as they might transfer to educational contexts. Rather, we seek to use WoW as a research environment where multiliteracies are an authentic part of the culture. This deeper knowledge base will allow us to better develop instruction in existing and emergent environments that share similar salient features (e.g., social scaffolds, diverse networks of information, etc.). In so doing, we may ultimately narrow the gap between the demands of a virtualized workplace and the preparation of students to function in that world. To this end, the following questions guided our discussion and interpretation of the results:

1) Based on the authors' extensive experience, what are the multiliteracies associated with WoW?

2) How do players utilize multiliteracies within the World of Warcraft?

3) How do players utilize multiliteracies outside the immediate game environment?

4) Do players use resources socially or to acquire information?

Affordances of WoW

WoW is a three-dimensional, immersive environment in which players control a virtual character so they may interact with the world and other players within that world (Schrader & McCreery, 2007; Young et al., 2006). Researchers have described environments such as WoW as intentional epistemic systems, designed experiences, and goal directed, collaborative environments (Schrader, Young, & Zheng, 2006; Squire, 2006; Young et al., 2006). The game affords multiple actions and players use the tools to work with others in an effort to accomplish complex tasks (e.g., quests, content progression, etc.).

While the method and manner of interaction within the game is nearly infinite, there are a few characteristics of the environment that relate directly to our understanding of multiliteracies. First, the game affords motion through a virtual world and sound that accompanies this interaction. Using these mechanisms, players are able to gain a lot of information about the game and the context. For example, objects that accrete and occlude provide information about location, distance, and proximity. Players often utilize information like this to make decisions about navigation, how they interact with objects, and how they work with others in the environment to solve complex problems.

In addition to motion and sound, the game allows for several complex modes of communication. The most obvious form is the in-game chat, a text-based system allowing players to communicate. In chat, players can use pre-programmed functions to constrain their audience. Specifically, they can type to a private message to a single player, a somewhat private message to all players in their immediate group, or an even broader message to the members of their entire guild (a subset of online peers). In a more public sense, players can also use the chat functionality to send a public message to any player within a certain physical distance. For example, they can decide whether they want to type to people within 15 virtual yards (i.e., using the */say* command) or type to people in the same virtual city (i.e., using the */yell* command). Every received message is presented in the chat window using a different color. This color-coding ultimately allows players to combine the visual information with the content to make decisions about the nature of the messages (i.e., public or private) and how they should respond.

In addition to communication, the chat system also serves as a log of players' interaction with the world. Specifically, the log presents text-based reports of important actions in the game via the chat interface. If a player fails to strike a target, text associated with "you miss" may appear in the window. However, this is not the only way in which players glean information about their actions in the world. For example, they may use the graphic animations or the associated sounds to determine if an action was successful or a failure. In a complex task, if a member of a player's current group yelps and falls over, they may be dead or just feigning death. In this case, the final assessment requires players to consider information from multiple channels and across modes (e.g., visual and text). This information is also color-coded, allowing players to more readily distinguish chat text from log text. The game also allows players to create new text-windows to further separate the messages.

Text and motion are perhaps the most obvious modes by which players interpret information within WoW, however they are not the only ones. Other modes include sound (both ambient and event driven), maps, mailboxes, banks, and other in-game resources. These tools are part of the game and dynamically update with respect to changes in the environment. For example, as a player moves throughout the virtual world, noises occur all around their avatar. By manipulating the sound field, WoW can make the roar of an enemy come from any direction, thus giving the player more information about their environment. Similarly, a player's location on one of two interactive maps is updated based on their position in the game. A full-screen map provides a large-scale view of a broad area. A smaller, more permanent map functions like a compass, helping to orient the player in the virtual space. The mini-map also uses visual icons to represent the hostility of creatures (passive, aggressive, or friendly) or the presence of resources in the immediate area (within 30 yards).

Individually, each tool provided within the game offers specific cues about the players' environment. Collectively, the information from these sources allows gamers to act and achieve their goals. Similarly, these resources provide gamers with the necessary means of communication and feedback to collaborate with other individuals who are committed to common goals. Forty or more players can work together to collect resources, kill opponents, or overcome obstacles. However, in-game actions would be impossible if players were unable to interpret information from multiple modes across these intratextual resources. Overall, these in-game accomplishments are made possible by players' ability to effectively apply multiliteracies apparent within WoW.

Beyond the game itself, WoW is also an emergent and thriving information and social culture (Steinkuehler, 2008). A plethora of online affinity spaces support the game and this virtual culture. This extended community also serves as an important context for game communication and collaboration. The discourse practices encapsulated within and across these spaces help to facilitate game play, provide an environment for socialization, and are a conduit for the creation and dissemination of artifacts for entertainment purposes. Examples of such resources include discussion forums, game play databases, wikis, video logs and user guides. To demonstrate the breadth of multiliteracies required by the players to fully participate in the WoW culture we discuss three specific examples in more depth: the official WoW website and forums, WoWwiki, and sites hosting machinima (e.g., machinima. com or youtube).

Blizzard Entertainment hosts one of the most active WoW support sites (see http://www.warcraft.com and http://forums.worldofwarcraft. com). Within this site, players of all ability levels (noobie to master) exchange information with each other. Expert players hired by Blizzard, also monitor the discussions. Their role includes editing or deleting inappropriate content, answering player queries, and highlighting important posts for the community to view. Previous research has shown that forums are not merely used to develop, share, and exchange information, but are also a site for strong mentorship amongst players as well as a place for socialization and the development of social capital (McCreery, Schrader, & Lawless, 2008; Steinkuehler & Williams, 2006). Moreover, the discussions that unfold within the forum site have a high propensity for intertextuality and multimodal communication. Players frequently reference other messages within the site, provide links to resources external to the forum, and include graphical representations of themselves and the information they are sharing.

The interaction among players supports the notion that WoW is inherently social and collaborative. In addition, many WoW-related websites function in similar, collaborative ways. Outside the game, players use websites to leverage the distributed intelligence of the community in order to develop more formalized resources. WoWwiki.com is one such resource. WoWwiki differs from forums because it strives to capitalize on the vast size and varied areas of expertise within the larger WoW community. Wikis in general are community-edited websites and WoWwiki uses these features to distribute the burden of creating and disseminating information. As such, WoWwiki is made up entirely of user contributions. Players can edit, correct, and add information to the site while they view it. As a result, rather than having to wait for a small group of people to update the information as it becomes available, the information on WoWwiki is as up to date and comprehensive as possible. In addition, rather than having information strung out across a number of individual posts and isolated threads as many forums do, information in WoWwiki is integrated and organized into cohesive and unified documents around relevant topics. These characteristics of WoWwiki are extremely useful because game developers regularly update and change the content of WoW. WoWwiki's dynamic and ever evolving nature allows it to change with the game, ensuring that the documents contained within the site never become outdated. As with all wikis, the speed by which content may become available coincides with the potential for inaccuracies. However, WoWwiki is regularly monitored and edited by experts, including players and site managers.

In addition to online communities and distributed knowledge spaces, WoW is an important component of online culture. A highly interesting aspect of this online culture is machinima. Machinima is a highly popular, real-world filmmaking technique that leverages interactive 3D virtual spaces like WoW to create animated movies. Within a particular machinima video, events and character movements programmed by the games that are visible onscreen are captured using special software. This animation is then edited, narrated, or set to an audio track. Many machinima videos are created to help others learn about a particular facet of the game or how to accomplish a particular task. However, many other machinima videos are created purely for entrainment purposes. Common among this genre are machinima music videos or other forms of audio dubbing (e.g., Southpark). In this sense, machinima is an example of emergent gameplay. It is a process of putting game tools to unexpected uses, and a form of artistic computer game modification. Regardless, machinima represents a new form of literacy that is particularly prominent among gamers. Large repositories of WoW machinima are available online including machinima.com and Youtube's machinima channel, www.youtube.com/user/machinima.

Survey of Gamers

To further explore the affordances and multiliteracies within WoW, an informal survey of gamers was conducted during the spring of 2007. A total of 745 participants responded to a recruitment message posted to each server's official forum located on Blizzard's public WoW website. The sample included 630 males (84.6%), 110 females (14.8%), and 5 (0.7%) who did not report a gender. More than half of the respondents (51.1%)

indicated that they fell between the ages of 18 and 22 and 83.5% reported they were 30 years or younger. The mean age of participants was 24.4 years. Nearly all players (96.2%) reported high levels of skill with their main character suggesting that this population excelled within this context. These demographic data reflected nearly identical trends when compared to existing data from more than 30,000 MMOG players (Yee, 2006).

Four separate scales were administered to participants inquiring about behaviors performed simultaneously with game play (i.e., Out-of-Game Resource Use ($\alpha = 0.81$), The Reason for Use (Out-of-Game) ($\alpha = 0.67$), In-Game Resource Use ($\alpha = 0.79$), and Reason for Use (In-Game) ($\alpha = 0.72$)). The "in-game resource use" and "outside the game resource use" scales employed a 5-point scale from 1-never to 5-always and pertained to behaviors associated with locating information while actively playing WoW. The "reason for use" scales employed a 5-point scale from 1-not at all useful to 5-very useful and pertained to whether the tool was used for social or informational purposes. Appendix A presents a set of sample items from each of these scales.

Methods for Acquiring In-Game Information

The data confirm that players reported utilizing a variety of "in-game" tools while actively playing the game. Players reported that they regularly access in-game chat about items (55.5%), about quests (44.5%), and about strategies (49.2%). In addition to the text-based systems, players reported leveraging graphic systems to find information. For example, the majority of players reported high levels of use for the mini-map or compass (86.7%) and full screen map (77.1%). Although the compass is in use without user intervention, the full screen map overwrites all other onscreen information. As such, the player must remember what actions are taking place in the game while simultaneously determining their virtual location and direction.

Similarly, the data indicate that players access several tools that provide social cues and information. Specifically, they regularly access popup screens that indicate which members of their guild are online (83.2%) as well as their other friends (76.8%). In many cases, these screens will provide immediate information about who is online, but they also provide other data. The screens indicate members' last login, player notes, guild rank, and more. It would also seem that players are only interested in finding information about friends and guild-mates. The majority of participants reported that they do not access information about players who have been ignored (74.5%). Players may be using these tools for social reasons so they can create groups and accomplish in-game challenges.

Collectively, all participants also reported several activities linked to the use of resources external to the WoW environment. Most participants specified that they always or almost always access external websites that contained information about game items (69%) and tips or information to complete quests (64.6%). In terms of social networking, 44% of respondents indicated that they access official online discussion forums simultaneous with game play. Further, the majority of respondents (58.7%) reported that they rely on their guild's online forums. In addition to text, audio communication using a VoIP program such as Ventrilo was very high (74.8%) and nearly one third of players reported using online video (28.4%).

What becomes clear from these data is that there are multiple methods that players leverage to accrue information about WoW. Text, sound, and video all play some role both within and outside the WoW environment. Further, players are exploring these ideas while they actively play the game. Although players search for content within (e.g., item links, quest logs, Non-Player Character, or NPC, dialogue, etc.) and outside the game, it appears that players show a high propensity to accrue information from external resources. More importantly, players appear to leverage existing technologies to collaborate with other gamers using external resources rather than tools provided within the gaming software itself.

Reasons for Using Tools

Clearly, immersive environments like WoW present information in a variety of formats. Although each has a different quality and function (e.g., chat for communication, video for environmental cues, sound for events within and outside of direct view, etc.), these data confirm that they are well used. These data also indicate that players use these tools for different purposes. Further, many of the tools afford a variety of objectives. For example, many players reported using the mini-map compass with great frequency. Although the tool can be used socially, they appear to use this tool to acquire information about their environment (94.6%). Similarly, the in-game mailbox is designed to send asynchronous messages to other players, but these data indicate that the mailbox is also used for information related objectives (57.6%); relatively few players use it for social purposes (13.4%).

By contrast, these data indicate that players also use tools for their social affordances. Specifically, players report using the guild tabs (59.7%), friend tab (71%), and ignore list (66.8%) for social reasons. These reasons may include searching for party members, joint questing, or simply to catch up on the latest social events. Although this may not be surprising given the social nature of these resources, the tools also afford players the ability to plan, strategize, and gather information about their human resources when attempting complex tasks.

Regardless of the purpose of their use, the tools embedded within WoW clearly afford a variety of actions and goals. The tools themselves provide information visually, via text, and other iconographic representations. Overall, players negotiate a complex bevy of resources to glean usable information. More importantly, these players interpret varying messages across resources during active gaming sessions. Although these data are self-reporting and should be interpreted with caution, the results, when interpreted in conjunction with the authors' combined play experiences, suggest that the game's affordances, the variety of resources within it, and the intentional use of resources and tools provide evidence of highly sophisticated multiliteracies within WoW.

Outside the game, players use a variety of resources for both social purposes as well as those related to retrieving information. With respect to external websites, players report using them for research. Most indicated using sites about items (96.2%), strategies (97.5%), and quests (97.1%) to locate and retrieve information. We acknowledge that these sites were created with a focus on information. However, most sites are also designed and developed to facilitate communication, social tagging, and user contribution.

Although players do not appear to meaningfully engage with the social tools embedded in many websites, they appear to interact with social networks in more diverse ways. The data suggest several trends in terms of social participation. First, players appear to interact with various social groups based on their degree of membership. A highly personal membership to a community such as a guild corresponds to social purposes of the forum (44.3%). A less personal membership in a group (i.e., the official WoW forums) corresponds to interaction in both social (25.8%) and knowledge-related reasons (37.5%). When the group membership becomes less obvious, as with the global WoW community, players report using the forums to acquire information (59.3%). Second, there appears to be a negative trend in terms of the flow of information in the community. Although players report accessing forums and websites for information, very few actually make knowledge-related posts (13.9%).

These data indicate that the properties of these in- and out-of-game resources afford multiple uses.

At a minimum, players use these resources for social and informational reasons. More notably, the prompts were framed from the perspective of active play. Specifically, players use these tools while actively playing the game. This concurrence corresponds to a set of sophisticated multiliteracies. However, the ability to interpret information from a variety of modes is one thing; the ability to do so while making decisions about the purpose of the tool while actively engaged in other sophisticated tasks is another.

Discussion and Implications

At a minimum, the data reported here indicate that there are abundant multiliteracies associated with WoW and its encapsulating culture. Within the game, the developers have embedded tools like mailboxes, chat, animation, and sound. Players utilize visual cues to determine things like location, size, proximity, and the results of action. They use sound to expand their virtual awareness. Typically, text carries a number of affordances that are used to exchange ideas and socialize. Beyond this, WoW developers have also included the ability to send private or group messages as well as internal hyperlinks to items and quests. Independently, each resource provides players with a tremendous amount of information. Collectively however, these multimodal tools enable players to leverage all aspects of the environment in highly complex ways. Ultimately, players' holistic interaction with the contextual resources creates a feedback system that ultimately informs players' actions, problem solving, and collaboration.

Although WoW is limitless in terms of players' opportunities and the associated multiliteracies are profound, the tools external to the game are equally noteworthy. In general, the affordances of the modern WWW do not limit users to information consumption; they involve an equal capacity for information production (Dede, 2008; O'Reilly, 2005). In terms of WoW, players collaborate, create, and exchange information using social networks like the official WoW forums. Similarly, players have created distributed knowledge networks (i.e., Wikis) that all members can edit, update, and utilize. Yet another example of production is the use of multimedia to share information, strategies, or humor. It is evident from this and other research that players use these multimodal tools to locate, access, and exchange information across sources (see McCreery et al., 2008; Schrader et al., 2009). Examined collectively, these data suggest that players exhibit profound multiliteracies as a result of participation in WoW and the surrounding culture.

These two aspects of WoW, the in-game and out-of-game experiences, come together in a rich landscape of information, tools, resources, and social interactions. The 3D persistent worlds of games like WoW and their encapsulating culture provide contexts that require the utilization of multiple literacies to bridge these important areas. Players must simultaneously attune to a barrage of information through and across a multitude of modalities. They make informed decisions, solve problems, and collaborate as a result of their ability to negotiate this complicated network of ideas. Further, players harvest information from all available resources, across channels and modes, while they are actively engaged in complex in-game tasks. Overall, the many contexts associated with WoW require a sophisticated choreography of multiliteracy practices that is rarely evident in formal educational environments.

Unfortunately, our understanding of the powerful interactions in MMOG settings is only in its infancy. As a community of researchers, we know relatively little about the development and employment of these practices within MMOGs. For example, research has demonstrated that novice players use external discussion forums as a place to access the "wisdom" of more experienced and expert players (McCreery et al., 2008; Schrader & McCreery, 2007). Unfortunately, we have yet to address how these collaborations within forums develop; what content more experienced and less experienced members contribute to the discussions; what stimulates these contributions (e.g., response to a direct question or spontaneous response); and how patterns of interactions across "generations" of game members emerge.

Admittedly, research of this nature is highly complex and may require new, unproven methodologies. However, it is also likely to inform our understanding of more formal environments. In particular, MMOGs present an informal space to examine multiliterate learning practices than more formal learning settings, such as traditional K-12 classrooms, do not. Literacy research associated with MMOGs is poised to facilitate the intentional, orchestrated development of similar skills. The similarities and differences between environments will also enable comparisons between features, such as collaboration and peer learning in formal and informal educational settings. Current implementations in traditional educational contexts are mixed at best.

Regardless of the approach, it is crucial to continue research associated with multiliteracies. We have long established the need to understand how users leverage multimodal learning resources (Kitson et al., 2007; Kress, 2005; New London Group, 1996). Further, one cannot ignore current trends toward market globalization, a knowledge-based society, and the affordances of Web 2.0 (Alexander, 2008; Goldman, 2004; Leu, 2000; Manpower, 2007; O'Reilly, 2005). The demand for these skills is clear and in the end, students must develop 21st century skills in order to function in modern society. Understanding the hidden multiliteracies associated with MMOGs is a viable path to that end.

REFERENCES

Alexander, B. (2008). Web 2.0 and emergent multiliteracies. *Theory into Practice, 47*, 150–160. doi:10.1080/00405840801992371

Alexander, P. A., & Fox, E. (2004). A historical perspective on reading research and practice. In R. B. Ruddell & N. J. Unrau (Eds.), *Theoretical models and processes of reading* (5ᵗʰ ed., pp. 33-68). Newark, DE: International Reading Association.

Apple, M. W. (2007). Ideological success, educational failure? On the politics of No Child Left Behind. *Journal of Teacher Education, 58,* 108–116. doi:10.1177/0022487106297844

Blizzard Entertainment. (2008). *World of Warcraft R Reaches New Milestone: 10 Million Subscribers.* Retrieved June 13, 2008 from: http://www.blizzard.com/us/press/080122.html.

Bruce, C. S. (1997). *Seven Faces of Information Literacy.* Adelaide, Australia: AUSLIB Press.

Bruce, C. S. (2002). Information literacy as a catalyst for educational change: A background paper. In *Proceedings Information Literacy Meeting of Experts,* Prague, The Czech Republic. Retrieved October 14, 2007 from, http://dlist.sir.arizona.edu/archive/00000300/.

Burn, A., & Parker, D. (2001). Making your mark: Digital inscription, animation and a new visual semiotic. [ECI]. *Education Communication and Information, 1*(2), 155–179. doi:10.1080/14636310120091913

Burn, A., & Parker, D. (2003). Tiger's big plan: Multimodality and the moving image. In C. Jewitt & G. Kress (Eds.), *Multimodal Literacy* (pp. 56-72). New York: Peter Lang.

Chen, S. Y., & Macredie, R. D. (2002). Cognitive styles and hypermedia navigation: Development of a learning model. *Journal of the American Society for Information Science and Technology, 53,* 3–15. doi:10.1002/asi.10023

Coiro, J. (2003). Reading comprehension on the Internet: Expanding our understanding of reading comprehension to encompass new literacies. *The Reading Teacher, 56*(5), 458–464.

Coiro, J., Knobel, M., Lankshear, C., & Leu, D. J. (2008). *Handbook of New Literacies.* Hillsdale, NJ: Lawrence Erlbaum Associates.

Crow, D. (2006). *Left to right: The cultural shift from words to pictures.* Lausanne, Switzerland: AVA Publishing.

Dede, C. (2008). New horizons: A seismic shift in epistemology. *EDUCAUSE Review, 43*(3), 80–81.

Dillon, A., McKnight, C., & Richardson, J. (1990). Navigation in hypertext: A critical review of the concept. In D. Diaper, D. Gilmore, G. Cockton, & B. Shackel (Eds.), *Human-Computer Interaction: INTERACT 90* (pp. 58-592). Amsterdam: Elsevier.

Gee, J. P. (2003). *What video games have to teach us about learning and literacy.* New York: Palgrave/St. Martin's.

Gee, J. P. (2006). Foreword. In D. W. Shaffer, *How computer games help children learn* (pp. ix-xii). New York: Palgrave/Macmillan.

Gibson, J. J. (1986). *The ecological approach to visual perception.* Hillsdale, NJ: Lawrence Erlbaum Associates.

Goldman, S. R. (2004). Cognitive aspects of constructing meaning through and across multiple texts. In N. Shuart-Ferris & D. M. Bloome (Eds.), *Uses of intertextuality in classroom and educational research* (pp. 313-347). Greenwich, CT: Information Age Publishing.

Harrison, C. (2006). Sustaining myths, necessary illusions, and national literacy policies: Some U.S. and U.K. comparisons. *The Elementary School Teacher, 107*(1), 121–131.

Hartman, D. K., & Hartman, J. A. (1993). Reading across texts: Expanding the role of the reader. *The Reading Teacher, 47*(3), 202–211.

Hayes, E. (2007). *Computer and video gaming and IT proficiency: An exploratory study*. Paper presented at the Annual Meeting of the American Educational Research Association, Chicago, IL.

Jenkins, H. (2006). *Convergence culture: Where old and new media collide*. New York: New York University Press.

Jenkins, H. (2007). From YouTube to YouNiversity. *The Chronicle of Higher Education Review, 53*(24), 9.

Jenkins, H. (2008). Public intellectuals in the new-media landscape. *The Chronicle of Higher Education, 54*(30), 18–20.

Kitson, L., Fletcher, M., & Kearney, J. (2007). Continuity and change in literacy practices: A move towards multiliteracies. *Journal of Classroom Instruction, 41*(2), 29–41.

Kress, G. (2003). *Literacy in the new media age*. New York: Routledge.

Kress, G. (2005). Gains and losses: New forms of texts, knowledge, and learning. *Computers and Composition, 22*, 5–22. doi:10.1016/j.compcom.2004.12.004

Kress, G., & Van Leeuwen, T. (2001). *Multimodal discourse: The modes and media of contemporary communication*. New York: Oxford University Press.

Lawless, K. A., & Kulikowich, J. M. (1996). Understanding hypertext navigation through cluster analysis. *Journal of Educational Computing Research, 14*(4), 385–399.

Lawless, K. A., & Kulikowich, J. M. (1998). Domain knowledge, interest, and hypertext navigation: A study of individual differences. *Journal of Educational Multimedia and Hypermedia, 7*(1), 51–70.

Lawless, K. A., & Schrader, P. G. (2008). Where do we go now? Understanding research on navigation in complex digital environments. In J. Coiro, M. Knobel, C. Lankshear, & D. J. Leu (Eds.), *Handbook of new literacies,* (pp. 267-296). Hillsdale, NJ: Lawrence Erlbaum Associates.

Lawless, K. A., Schrader, P. G., & Mayall, H. J. (2007). Acquisition of information online: Knowledge, navigational strategy and learning outcomes. *Journal of Literacy Research, 30*(3), 289–306.

Leu, D. J., Jr. (2000). Literacy and technology: Deictic consequences for literacy education in an information age. In M. L. Kamil, P. Mosenthal, P. D. Pearson, & R. Barr (Eds.), *Handbook of reading research.* (Vol. 3, pp. 743-770). Mahwah, NJ: Erlbaum.

Leu, D. J. Jr, & Kinzer, C. K. (2000). The convergence of literacy instruction with networked technologies for information and communication. *Reading Research Quarterly, 35*(1), 108–127. doi:10.1598/RRQ.35.1.8

Leu, D. J., Jr., & Kinzer, C. K. (2003). *Effective literacy instruction: Implementing best practice* (5th ed.). Upper Saddle River, NJ: Merrill/Prentice-Hall.

Madden, M., Chung, P. W. H., & Dawson, C. W. (2008). The effect of a computer-based cartooning tool on children's cartoons and written stories. *Computers & Education, 51*, 900–925. doi:10.1016/j.compedu.2007.09.008

Manning, F. H., Lawless, K. A., Gomez, K. G., McLeod, M., Braasch, J., & Goldman, S. R. (2008). *Sources of information in the classroom: Characterizing instruction through a model of multiple source comprehension for inquiry learning.* Paper presented at the annual meeting of the Association of Psychological Science, Chicago, IL.

Manpower, (2007). *A manpower report: The virtual world of work.* Milwaukee, WI: Manpower Inc. Retrieved June 13, 2008 from http://www.manpower.com/research/research.cfm.

McCreery, M., Schrader, P. G., & Lawless, K. A. (2008, April). *The social engagement of information: What MMOGs can teach us about multi-text environments.* Paper presented at the Annual meeting of the American Educational Research Association, New York. Monaco, J. (2000). *How to read a film: The world of movies, media, and multimedia (art, technology, language, history, theory).* New York: Oxford University Press.

New London Group. (1996). A pedagogy of multiliteracies: Designing social futures. *Harvard Educational Review, 66*(1), 60–92.

O'Reilly, T. (2005). *What is Web 2.0?: Design patterns and business models for the next generation of software.* Sebastopol, CA: O'Reilly Network. Retrieved June 13, 2008 from http://www.oreillynet.com/pub/a/oreilly/tim/news/2005/09/30/what-is-web-20.html.

Orr, L. (1986). Intertextuality and the cultural text in recent semiotics. *College English, 48,* 811–823. doi:10.2307/376732

Parker, D. (1999). You've read the book, now make the film: Moving image media, print literacy and narrative. *English Education, 33*(1), 24–35. doi:10.1111/j.1754-8845.1999.tb00160.x

Pellegrino, J. W., Goldman, S. G., Bertenthal, M., & Lawless, K. A. (2007). Technology in teacher training: The what works and why project. In L. S., Smolin, K. A., Lawless, & N. Burbules (Eds.), *National Society for the Study of Education Yearbook.* Columbia: Teachers College, Columbia University.

Pew Internet & American Life. (2007). *Teen/parent survey on writing, final topline, 11/21/07.* Retrieved June 13, 2008 from http://www.pewinternet.org/datasets/Teens_Writing_November_2007_Topline.doc.

Pew Internet & American Life Project. (2001). *The Internet and education: Findings of the Pew Internet & American Life Project.* Retrieved March 12, 2007 from http://www.pewInternet.org/reports.

Pew Internet & American Life Project. (2005). *The Internet at school.* Retrieved March 12, 2007 from http://www.pewinternet.org/PPF/r/163/report_display.asp.

Pew Internet & American Life Project. (2008). *Writing, technology and teens.* Retreived June 13, 2008 from http://www.pewinternet.org/PPF/r/247/report_display.asp.

RAND Reading Study Group. (2002). *Reading for understanding: Toward an R&D program in reading comprehension.* Santa Monica, CA: Rand Education. Also available at http://www.rand.org/multi/achievementforall/reading/

Rose, G. (2005). Visual methodologies. In G. Griffin (Ed.), *Research methods for English studies* (pp. 67-89). Edinburgh, UK: Edinburgh University Press.

Rosenblatt, L. M. (1994). The transactional theory of reading and writing. In R. B. Ruddell, M. R. Ruddell, & H. Singer (Eds.), *Theoretical models and processes of reading* (4th ed., pp. 1057-1092). Newark, DE: International Reading Association.

Ruddell, R. B., & Unrau, N. J. (1994/2004). Reading as a meaning-construction process: The reader, the text, and the teacher. In R. B. Ruddell & N. J. Unrau (Eds.), *Theoretical models and processes of reading* (5th ed., pp. 1462-1521). Newark, DE: International Reading Association.

Sanford, K., & Madill, L. (2007). Understanding the power of new literacies through video game play and design. *Canadian Journal of Education, 30*(2), 432–455.

Schrader, P. G., Lawless, K. A., & McCreery, M. (2009). Intertextuality in massively multiplayer online games. In R. E. Ferdig (Ed.) *Handbook of research on effective electronic gaming in education, Vol III,* (pp. 791-807). Hershey, PA: Information Science Reference.

Schrader, P. G., & McCreery, M. (2007). The acquisition of skill and expertise in massively multiplayer online games. *Educational Technology Research & Development.* Retrieved October 10, 2007 from http://www.springerlink.com/content/n2496u376825u512/.

Schrader, P. G., Young, M. F., & Zheng, D. P. (2006). Teachers' perceptions of video games: MMOGs and the future of preservice teacher education. *Innovate, 2*(3). Retrieved February 22, 2006 from http://www.innovateonline.info/index.php?view=article&id=125

Shanahan, T. (1990). Reading and writing together: What does it really mean? In T. Shanahan (Ed.), *Reading and writing together: New perspectives for the classroom* (pp. 1-18). Norwood, MA: Christopher-Gordon.

Society of College, National and University Libraries. (1999). *Information skills in higher education.* London, UK: SCONUL. Retrieved October 5, 2007 from, http://www.sconul.ac.uk/groups/information_literacy/papers/Seven_pillars2.pdf.

Spivey, N. N. (1984). *Discourse synthesis: Constructing texts in reading and writing* (Outstanding Dissertation Mono- graph Series). Newark, DE: International Reading Association.

Spivey, N. N., & King, J. R. (1989). Readers as writers composing from sources. *Reading Research Quarterly, 24*(1), 7–26. doi:10.1598/RRQ.24.1.1

Squire, K., & Jenkins, H. (2003). Harnessing the power of games in education. *Vision, 3*(6), 5–33.

Squire, K. D. (2006). From content to context: Videogames as designed experience. *Educational Researcher, 35*(8), 19–29. doi:10.3102/0013189X035008019

Steinkuehler, C., Black, R., & Clinton, K. (2005). Researching literacy as tool, place, and way of being. *Reading Research Quarterly, 40*(1), 7–12.

Steinkuehler, C., & Williams, D. (2006). Where everybody knows your (screen) name: Online games as "third places." *Journal of Computer-Mediated Communication, 11*(4), article 1.

Steinkuehler, C. A. (2006). Why game (culture) studies now? *Games and Culture, 1*(1), 97–102. doi:10.1177/1555412005281911

Steinkuehler, C. A. (2008). Cognition and literacy in massively multiplayer online games. In J. Coiro, M. Knobel, C. Lankshear, & D. Leu (Eds.), *Handbook of Research on New Literacies*, (pp. 611-634). Mahwah NJ: Erlbaum.

U.S. Department of Education. (2007). Ed.gov: Reauthorization of No Child Left Behind. Retrieved June 13, 2007 from http://www.ed.gov/nclb/landing.jhtml.

Wickens, C. M., & Sandlin, J. A. (2007). Literacy for what? Literacy for whom? The politics of literacy education and neocolonialism in UNESCO- and World Bank sponsored literacy programs. *Adult Education Quarterly*, *57*(4), 275–292. doi:10.1177/0741713607302364

Young, M. F., Schrader, P. G., & Zheng, D. P. (2006). MMOGs as learning environments: An ecological journey into Quest Atlantis and the Sims Online. *Innovate, 2*(4). Retrieved March 20, 2006 from http://www.innovateonline.info/index.php?view=article&id=66

APPENDIX A

Table 1. Survey Sample Items

	Noobie	Competent	Proficient	Expert
Please rate your expertise with respect to your current Main Character:				

Out-of-Game Resource Use:

Table 2. How often do you do the following while you are ACTIVELY playing the World of Warcraft?

	Never				Always
View the official World of Warcraft Forums:	1	2	3	4	5
View your guild's online forum:	1	2	3	4	5
View other online discussion forums:	1	2	3	4	5
Access websites about game items:	1	2	3	4	5
Access websites about strategies:	1	2	3	4	5
Access websites for quest information:	1	2	3	4	5
Use an instant messenger-type program:	1	2	3	4	5
Use voice programs like Ventrilo:	1	2	3	4	5
Access videos:	1	2	3	4	5
Use an external email program:	1	2	3	4	5
Post to online forums:	1	2	3	4	5

Out-of-Game Resource Use:

Table 3. Why do you use the following?

	Mostly Social				Mostly Informational	N/A
View the official World of Warcraft Forums:	1	2	3	4	5	6
View your guild's online forum:	1	2	3	4	5	6
View other online discussion forums:	1	2	3	4	5	6
Access websites about game items:	1	2	3	4	5	6
Access websites about strategies:	1	2	3	4	5	6
Access websites for quest information:	1	2	3	4	5	6
Use an instant messenger-type program:	1	2	3	4	5	6
Use voice programs like Ventrilo:	1	2	3	4	5	6
Access videos:	1	2	3	4	5	6
Use an external email program:	1	2	3	4	5	6
Post to online forums:	1	2	3	4	5	6

In-Game Resource Use:

Table 4. While you are ACTIVELY playing the World of Warcraft, how often do you use the following in-game resources?

	Never				Always
Use in-game chat about items:	1	2	3	4	5
Use-in game chat about quests:	1	2	3	4	5
Use in-game chat about strategies:	1	2	3	4	5
Use the in-game mailbox:	1	2	3	4	5
Use the full screen map:	1	2	3	4	5
Use the minimap (or compass):	1	2	3	4	5
Access an NPC:	1	2	3	4	5
Use the guild tab:	1	2	3	4	5
Use the friends tab:	1	2	3	4	5
Access my ignore list:	1	2	3	4	5
Access the quest log text:	1	2	3	4	5

In-Game Resource Use:

Table 5. Why do you use the following?

	Mostly Social				Mostly Informational	N/A
Use in-game chat about items:	1	2	3	4	5	6
Use-in game chat about quests:	1	2	3	4	5	6
Use in-game chat about strategies:	1	2	3	4	5	6
Use the in-game mailbox:	1	2	3	4	5	6
Use the full screen map:	1	2	3	4	5	6
Use the minimap (or compass):	1	2	3	4	5	6
Access an NPC:	1	2	3	4	5	6
Use the guild tab:	1	2	3	4	5	6
Use the friends tab:	1	2	3	4	5	6
Access my ignore list:	1	2	3	4	5	6
Access the quest log text:	1	2	3	4	5	6

Chapter 13
Multiliteracies and Games:
Do Cybergamers Dream of Pedagogic Sheep?

Pam Wright
Latrobe University, Australia

David Skidmore
Padgate, UK

ABSTRACT

Digitalization of modern society has lead to rapid changes and innovative ways of communicating. Changes in the way people perceive belonging to society are reflected in the multiple methods of participation, communication, learning and engaging. Knowledge has become synonymous with how we can locate, use and find new information in a networked world rather than what it is we already know. The quest for knowledge in this digital and globalized society forces interaction with multiple modes of information. In this multi-literate society, educators must find opportunities for students to interact and interpret the multitude of new literacies. This chapter discusses how multi-literacies are bound up in computer games and how educators can employ these games through play, study and creation to shift students from consumers to creators of interactive narratives. The chapter provides some strategies for implementing the games in the curriculum. It also raises questions about computer game use in the primary classroom, and calls for an integrated approach to teacher and trainee teacher professional development in the area of computer gaming.

INTRODUCTION

This chapter focuses on commercial computer games within the primary curriculum and the various learning opportunities that these can provide. It additionally explores trainee teacher attitudes towards the use of such games in the classroom and goes on

DOI: 10.4018/978-1-60566-842-0.ch013

to explore how the development of multi-literacies, when using these games, can be extended through both modifying and creating computer games.

When technology becomes more abundant and seamlessly woven into our daily lives, new types of literacies are emerging (Buckingham, 1993; The New London Group, 1996; Cope & Kalantzis, 2000; Lankshear & Knobel, 2003). The New London Group (1996) brought, to our attention, the notion of multiliteracies. They explained that in modern society there were emerging a number of different types of literacies, which were equally as important (if not more so, as they require new approaches to pedagogy and curriculum) as our traditional understanding of what it means to be literate. These emerging literacies are often made up from a multitude of media and may incorporate many different media at the same time. Some of these new literacies can be defined as: audio, visual, film, computer, TV and web.

However, it would be a mistake to view any of these in isolation since there seems to be cross over between the different mediums. The Oxford English Dictionary (OED) is currently collecting 'new' words that have developed from gaming, texting and street language in order to produce an alternative dictionary. It is argued that 'youth culture' has a big influence upon the social learning of developing adults. Such influences are often dismissed as 'fads' or 'seven day wonders', but the long term influence cannot be denied. Consider the 1970s'/1980s' impact of the Dungeons and Dragons series. Initially presented as comic books they went on to inspire Fantasy Weekends and then computer games. People actually carried their fantasy identities into the real world and those 'included', i.e. other players, would acknowledge this identity. Skidmore (1994) argues that such rituals are used to communicate inclusivity and exclusivity to onlookers. Given the demise of 'popular' comic books, the publication 'Shoot', a football magazine aimed at 9 – 16 year old males in the UK, was discontinued in June 2008 because of faltering sales (Daily Mail, 18/6/08), other outlets have developed to replace them. There are so many computer games on the market that this publication is no longer of youth interest. In the UK and USA the demise of comic books and the rise of computer game engagement have led to serious concerns about school leavers' reading abilities (Goldlove, 2008). What is not recognized is the evolvement of literacy in this argument. Some academics have recognized the impact of

youth culture and are producing the works of Shakespeare in text-speak and experimenting with computer games, the results have yet to be released (Daily Express, 17/5/08).

BACKGROUND

The New London Group (1996) argue that literacy learning in this century needs to take account of new media that shape the way language is used. Technology has changed the way we not only operate in a globalized society, but also our means of communicating and subsequently the language we use. Often educators are in a dilemma; between 'txtng and your sincerley'. According to O'Rouke (2002), educators need to provide opportunities for student engagement at a critical level. She suggests that to prepare multiliterate students they need opportunities to both express themselves and make sense of the world through multiple modes of communication (linguistic/textual, visual/graphical, musical/audio, spatial, gestural) sometimes all operating simultaneously.

Using computer games in the classroom can help to provide these opportunities. Computer games, particularly commercial computer games, tend to present themselves in a multimodal fashion, combining linguistic/textual with engaging visuals and seamlessly weaving audio and mood music into the game. Through game play, students can develop their spatial awareness in an alternative way to the traditional means. That isn't to say that it is better, just different. In today's technological world, this is a useful skill particularly with geographical information systems becoming more commonplace and affordable.

Traditional literacies can be supported by playing computer games in the classroom. By carefully selecting a commercial game such as those based on books (there are numerous games of this type; the *Agatha Christie* series or *Jules Verne* series) students can enhance their literacy learning. These types of games can help aid comprehension and understanding, by including multiple modes of information. Students can then be asked to not only demonstrate their linguistic comprehension, but also their comprehension and understanding of how other forms of media help them to engage with the 'text' through analysis of modes such as visual, spatial, musical. A different form of comprehension is achieved because students become participants in the game and have a certain amount of control over outcomes. This means that literacy learning is no longer a passive act, but one where students have moved from mere consumer to becoming a director.

Once game play has shifted towards the development of games, then students become creators of media. Rourke (2002) reasons that they then critique the effectiveness of the communication modes they have chosen to use, the appropriateness for particular audiences, and the content of the message that has actually been delivered.

Technology has altered many aspects of our lives, including communication and learning. According to Siemens:

"Learning needs and theories that describe learning principles and processes should be reflective of underlying social environments." Siemens, G. www.connectivism.ca

Siemens is currently developing Connectivism as a new theory of learning. He argues that by including technology and connection making, as learning activities, it begins to move learning theories into a digital age. At the foundation of this theory are new literacies or digital literacies. Siemens states that competence is derived from forming connections. These connections make much use of multiple, digital sources. Knowledge is now acquired in differing ways from how it was a few decades ago. The way that knowledge is used, its shelf-life and sources rely on technology and connections. Digital networking is now important for future citizens; they need to interpret information from multiple sources, be able to evaluate the available information and communicate virtually. Here mode and choice of mode is a significant issue (Kress, 2003). The ability to acquire new knowledge becomes more important than what we already know.

Siemen's blog, on Connectivism, contains an interesting thread about pedagogy and technology. The following 'reply' highlights the importance of emerging literacies and the changes technology has brought about.

"Daniel:

It's true that we use the term "pedagogy" to differentiate between what is worthwhile in learning and what is not.

.... Our father wanted to teach us 'useful skills' and one of them was fixing the car. We always avoided this as much as possible, preferring to play video games. It was the early 1980s, so this included basic technology problems like getting the tape recorder to play back the game, how to cheat in the game and many times how to modify the code (in GWBasic). In 2008 these skills turn out to be much more useful than knowing how to fix a car. Unless you're in the desert alone and your car breaks down and you have a whole bunch of tools and replacement parts with you, of course."

Posted by Daniel | March 16, 2008 9:35 PM http://connectivism.ca/blog/2008/03/pedagogy_ first_whatever.html

New ways of communicating develop through the use of social and virtual networks and with computer games perhaps it is valid for us to consider gaming as one of these new literacies.

"The video game is now considered as everything from the <u>ergodic</u> (work) to the <u>ludic</u> (play); as narrative, simulation, performance, remediation, and art; a potential tool for education or an object of

study for behavioural psychology; as a playground for social interaction; and, of course, as toy and a medium of entertainment."

(Wolf & Perron, 2003, p.2)

No longer is it just the stereotypical geek who plays computer games, but an enormous proportion of younger members of society, nor is gaming exclusive to youth, many adults play a variety of computer games. This can easily be evidenced through the online game, *Jewel Quest II*, where the amount of 'mums', 'dads', 'grans', 'nannas' and 'grandpas', as opponents, abound. This must be read with some caution as there are also players named Dumbledore and Vixen (see above regarding carrying fantasy identity into everyday life) of which we are sure that they are neither! It would be unusual though for gamers to create such boring pseudonyms. The perception of computer games as the domain of children could be the reason why they are often seen as a low art form and lack the credibility of traditional media (Newman, 2004).

Buckingham and Burn (2007) challenge us to think about games as new forms of literacy. In relation to their stance on the legitimacy of game literacy, they argue that:

"...a more specific semiotic analysis would suggest that games function in linguistic terms both through the indicative mood (that is, showing us the world) but also in the imperative mood (that is, urging us to take action upon that world)."

(Buckingham & Burn, 2007, p. 327).

Put simply, Game Literacy is being literate about computer games, being able to read games through, critical analysis of the game, characters and genre, understanding how games work, understanding the rules and knowing what to expect. Being Game Literate stimulates a different way of thinking, communicating and collaborating with peers, which can be translated and effectively used pedagogically.

Communicating with peers in an acceptable way, i.e. conforming to the group norm is a crucial part of belonging/inclusivity. Given that an increasing amount of social networking is carried out on the internet (MySpace, facebook, Digg for social tagging, Instant Messaging, such as MSN, etc) and the first point of similarity is, often, game literacy, this can be a useful tool. The negative aspect of using the internet is that it becomes more credible than that which is actual. It enters the factual – actual continuum at the very left hand of the scale. To explain: the factual – actualcontinuum is offered as a mode of explanation for the failure of health promotion (Richman & Skidmore, 1984). Factually we know that smoking is harmful, but actually someone will know a relative who smoked 60 full strength cigarettes every day from the age of 14 until they died at 98 after being knocked down by a bus leaving an all night party; the coroner reported that she had the lungs of a young girl. With regard to the internet, the opposite is true. It is similar to: I read it in a book, it was in the newspaper and so on. For example, it has become a 'truth' in statistical analysis that Chi-square can be used on any type of data. So what? It is also asserted that the 15th century punishment of 'drawing' involved a person being tethered to two horses which were then sent off in different directions. In fact 'drawing' was the disembowelment of a person whilst they were still alive. The point being that if the majority of people believe something it becomes a truth. Hence history, scholarly works and statistics become watered down and meaningless.

Computer games can provide valuable learning experiences but they will only be as good as the knowledge programmed into them. In the middle ages the people who shaped the development of civilization were the scholars, those who could read and write. This meant that they controlled the propaganda machinery that led to the belief, for example, that Richard the Third was a hunched backed horror-bag. He may have been a lovely bloke who bought his mother chocolates and flowers but his supporters did not control the press! This must be considered when we argue the case for 'gaming' in education.

Gaming in the classroom or the study of gaming is not mainstream. While many teachers currently use computer games as part of their customary classroom activities, they tend to opt for educational games. That is: games that have been created (usually by educators) for the specific purpose of teaching a particular subject. It is important here for us to distinguish between the two main types of computer games; firstly educational games and secondly commercial computer games.

Educational games tend to concentrate on specific learning areas such as: spelling, grammar, vocabulary, and mathematics games. Children playing these games are required to practice skills and are often graded and given feedback on their performance (in a non-threatening manner) in order to encourage and motivate them to progress. More often than not, they tend to be drill and practice games where children can become easily bored if they are overexposed to them. However, these educational games are missing critical and higher order thinking, collaborative activities, complex problem solving, interesting storylines and multiple ways of interacting with the game (Rice, 2007).

Successful commercial computer games on the other hand, have all this. They have a certain level of complexity in their storylines and problems. They regularly rely on the use of higher order thinking skills to solve intricate problems and enable progression within the game. According to Gee (2003) commercial computer games have great potential as learning tools, as many require complex problem solving, collaboration, theory testing, and evaluation, all components of experiential learning. It is precisely these skills which keep children and young people engaged with such games and which makes them motivated to improve their performance. They also have built

in rewards such as getting to the next level, which enters the communication cycle: I've got to level six on the '*Lethal Reaper*' game.

With much research on the topic of the literacies being developed, used and acquired when playing commercial computer games, why, then, are teachers not employing them more fully? Why do they seem to prefer to use educational computer games? Frequently, teachers seem to view the use of computer games simply as extension activities, time fillers, or rewards for children who complete work on time rather than as an integral part of the curriculum (Halverson, 2005; Prensky, 2006; Schrader, Zheng, & Young, 2006;). In addition, to this lack of integration, many of the educational games (which tend to be the first preference for teachers) are limited in their ability to generate the same type of deep learning that can occur in commercial computer games. Prensky (2006) argues that they tend to be boring and repetitive, consisting mainly of drill and skill activities or as he calls it: "drill and kill." This relates to the above point regarding the demise of reading. Why read when you can play it out on a computer game? Educational packages may be comparable to a book, whereas commercial games equate to the video.

To address the questions raised in the previous section perhaps the reasons that teachers rely on tried and tested educational games has some relation to public perception. Much media attention has been devoted to the ill-effects of children and young people playing computer games. Most citing extreme cases where children who have played violent computer games, go on to commit violent acts, others attribute childhood obesity to lengthy stints playing computer games. It is rare to read a newspaper article or watch a media clip that does not use scare-mongering tactics when discussing computer games or one that actually promotes the benefits of computer game play. This pervades popular opinion where it circulates as fact. Of course, there is nothing new in such scare tactics, the publicity about the film 'A Clockwork

Orange', in the 1960s, led to a thirty year ban in cinemas and video releases in the UK. The fear was that it would lead to youth violence; however, statistics suggest that youth violence has been fairly constant since the end of the Second World War to the present day, i.e. no increase despite the growth of violent films, videos and computer games. However, no growth in youth violence does not sell newspapers! Consequently, with the advent of the internet, a gory crime in some small outback town can now make the nationals and convince the rest of us that violence is on the increase. The modern message appears to be that it is all the fault of these computer games that teach kids to steal cars and kill people.

Parents frequently express their concern about the time their children spend playing computer games. It is common to hear cries of "I'd rather my child go outside to play than spend hours playing mindless computer games". It is accepted as fact that computer game playing is a waste of time; that it is mindless fun and that children would be best to expend their energy by playing outdoors. It is the influence of the media that furnishes these strong reactions towards games. By the same rationale, many parents are reluctant to allow their children to play outside because of the threat of violence and/or abduction. It started with television (the violence stimulates imitation in children) and spread to video games. We guess the kids can't win. There is little reaction regarding texting and computer game narrative killing the language. *C u 2morra* may make sense but we run the risk of becoming on-going comedy sketches: *F U N E X? S V F X*....a famous Wiley sketch from the 1980s: *Have you any eggs? Yes, we have eggs.* Translating Shakespeare into text language may introduce youths to his works but isn't this violence upon the language? However, working together with commercial computer gamers could enhance, not only the language but, also, the view of literature. The adaptation of comic novels, such as 300 Spartans, has revived an interest in classical history and led to the release

of *Beowulf*. The next step is the computer game which may stimulate interest in the book. In the 1970s' film versions of historical events, such as *Beckett, The Lion in Winter* and *A Man for All Seasons* saw an increase in library withdrawals for that period of history. Computer games could serve a similar function.

In spite of the bad press and low cultural value placed on games, there has recently been a flurry of research into the educational benefits of playing computer games. Educational researchers are becoming more aware of the multifaceted learning opportunities that computer games can offer.

Games themselves, provide some sort of narrative, but these tend to stray from the traditional linear narrative. According to BECTA (2005) good games have storylines, key characters or clear conclusions. The narrative can be complex, yet at the same time so subtle it does not overbear the gaming experience. A good example of this is one of the hidden object genre games "*Big City Adventure San Francisco*" where players are required to move around a virtual replica of the city and collect hidden objects. At the same time, players are provided with information about the city and important events. After playing the game, one of the authors really wasn't aware that they had taken in much of the information. However, a few months later, a TV documentary on San Francisco revealed how much had been learned about the great earthquake of 1906, subsequent fires, the politics of the time, and various areas of the city. This supports the point that good games immerse the player in an imaginative story with plot twists, strong characters and often non-linear storylines (BECTA, 2005). It is also important to recognize the differences between narrative as it relates to games and as it relates to other media. Juuls (2001), states that games deal with narrative differently because of the context, interactivity and the role of the player. He argues that games themselves are interactive narratives and Newman (2004), concurs, maintaining that games enable narrative that is fully interactive. In the computer game, the player controls consciousness rather than the author as with traditional narrative.

Imagine this applied to history. The game sees Henry the Second imprison his wife and take issue with his three sons: Richard, Geoffry and John. Each son wants to be king after Henry, John feels he is the favorite, Richard is the most powerful and Geoffry is ignored. Elenor (the queen) favors Richard, the King favors John. The player is given various options to play and will see the outcome of each action. If done well it could inspire a player to engage with history. Of course, games come in different guises and some may be more appropriate than others.

Different Types of Commercial Games

There are many different types of computer game, but the gaming industry and academia is still struggling to develop a consistent definition of genre. We would argue that some genres are more suited to learning purposes and development of multiliteracies within the formal educational setting. In Table 1, we provide a broad section of genres, which is by no means exhaustive.

Benefits of Games in the Classroom

Gee (2003) asserts that good computer games are based on sound learning principles. Most studies, however, have concentrated on using games with secondary school students rather than students in primary schools (BECTA, 2005; Squire, 2005) or out of school time (Kafai, 2006). We propose that the primary curriculum is very much suited to learning with and about games.

The table above highlights the benefits and new literacies, which are developed by game play. Collaboration is probably the most commonly observed behaviour when playing games, yet is probably the most surprising to those who glean their information about games from the Media. Game players also communicate globally; within

the game, outside the game, about the game. The BECTA (2005) report states that the success of games lies in how information is presented to gamers. Information is presented 'just in time' to be used to solve problems that are challenging but do-able. Challenges progress once mastery is complete. This keeps players motivated and engaged.

Gamers often share knowledge and expertise in game communities, gamers know how and where to find information within these communities to help them progress through the game making them multiliterate.

How Games can be Used in the Classroom

There are many ways in which educators can effectively employ games in the classroom. *Sim City* or the *Tycoon Games* could be used to help students understand the connections between business and the environment. Real time strategy games can be integrated into the curriculum, as in Gee's (2007) research on *Age of Mythology*, where students were compelled to read around the subject of Mythology, create art works and writing relating to Mythology.

Adventure games lend themselves to whole class discussions such as Rylands' use of *Myst* to enhance creative writing amongst his students. A current study is also investigating the learning opportunities that might be gleaned by comparing traditional narrative with interactive narrative. The study aims to combine adventure games that are based on books such as Verne's *Journey to the End of the Earth* with shared reading sessions, to discover effects on learning and literacy (Wright, forthcoming).

Game playing in the classroom, no doubt motivates and immerses students in learning, but as teachers we can move our students a step further, from simply being consumers of games to becoming creators (Kafai, 2006). Modifying, or 'Modding' games provides a step towards this shift. Some games have editable levels, such as the platform game *SuperGran* along with many others. Students are able to direct and create game play. A more integrated approach to developing

such skills can also be taken with '*The Movies*', a sim-type game in which the player directs the storyline and becomes the creator of films and the Movie Studio. Within the game, players are

Table 1. Game Genres. Developed from teaching resources available at ACMI (http://www.acmi.net.au/)

Genre	Description	Pedagogy
Platform	Relatively simple games where the player chases or avoids characters by jumping onto platforms. • *Sonic the Hedgehog* • *Super Mario*	Can be used in the study of games, for example, to study characters, storylines and plots, graphics, rules, outcomes, etc.
First Person Shooter (FPS)	The aim is usually to battle some sort of enemy. The player is placed behind a weapon or even a vehicle which is in constant view to enhance the impression of being part of the game. Often associated with violence. • *Doom* • *Quake* • *Grand Theft Auto* • *Halo*	Possibly not well-suited to formal educational settings, particularly the primary classroom due to their often violent content. However they could still be used to discuss the study of games; genre, plot, character, graphics, use of music, etc. These types of games are ideally suited to the development of <u>Machinima</u> (this is discussed in the next section of the chapter) within the classroom.
Simulation	Usually refers to games that involve simulating the real environment, such as learning to play golf, fly a plane, drive a car, or even dissect a frog. • *V8 Super Cars* • *Flight Simulator* There is another type of simulation game, which crossed the boundary between simulation and real time strategy. Games such as; • *Sim City,* • *Roller Coaster Tycoon,* • *The Movies,* all involve some simulation of environment but require the player to strategize and direct play.	These games could be used to help develop sporting skill. Alternatively games such as *Lemonade Tycoon*, can help students better understand business and economic concepts, whilst *Sim City* games can be used to teach about environment, civics and citizenship.
Real Time Strategy (RTS)	Players strategically direct play. Play could be battles or building empires. The game progresses in 'real time' rather than turn-by-turn. • *Empires* • *Command and Conquer* • *Age of Mythology* • *Civilization*	Games such as *Age of Mythology* or *Civilization* have been used to help students understand difficult concepts, such as Mythology or the way history shapes our present (Squire, 2005)
Role Playing (RPG)	Players are required to complete a lengthy quest, overcoming obstacles along the way. • *Morrowind* • *Everquest* • *Baldur's Gate* • *Neverwinter Nights*	Such games can be used in a combination of ways between the strategies listed for RTS and MMOGs.
Massively Multi-player Online Game MMOG	Similar to the RTS games, where players direct and strategize. Can involve battles and quests but require interaction between players. Can be played in teams and players are able to interact globally with other players. • *Runescape* • *World of Warcraft*	Research by Schrader et. al., (2006) reveals much communication and collaboration between players. Our own experiences of using *Runescape* in the classroom has shown similar results and additionally highlighted critical thinking, problem solving skills, cooperative and peer learning.

continued on following page

Table 1. continued

Genre	Description	Pedagogy
Adventure	Adventure games are based on a strong storyline. Players use problem solving skills to overcome obstacles and solve puzzles to progress in the game. Often more linear in nature but newer games of this type allow more player-directed outcomes and endings, such as Agatha Christie's *Peril at End House*. Some are based on books such as the *Agatha Christie* series, *Sherlock Holmes* or the *Jules Verne* series. • *Myst* • *Azada* • *Dream Chronicles II*	Tim Rylands, a teacher in the UK has successfully used *Myst* to help develop creative writing amongst his students. *Agatha Christie Peril at End House* has been used to help a group of primary students in Australia with their studies in forensic science (ASSISTM). Games based on books such as the *Jules Verne* series are currently being used in conjunction with shared reading to help develop literacy amongst primary students.
Hidden Object	This is one of the newer genres emerging. Objects are camouflaged and players are required to retrieve them. • *Travelogue 360° Paris* • *Big City Adventure San Francisco* Some games mix Hidden Object and Adventure to provide more stimulating play, such as the *Sherlock Holmes* series.	Games such as *Travelogue 360° Paris* could be used in Humanities to give students a feel of being in Paris. Students could collect facts and information and compare game to real life.

able to create Machinima. Machinima combines game design, film making and animation to produce animated films from computer games. There are many examples on the Machinima website www.machinima.com some using *The Sims*, others based on *Quake* or *Halo* and many more.

Ewan Macintosh describes a wealth of ideas on how to use commercial computer games in the classroom to promote learning and multiliteracies in his blog titled; "Thinking Out of the (X) Box: Gaming to Expand Horizons in Creative Writing." His use of games for learning span the genres from *Brain Training* and *Nintendogs* to *Rollercoaster Tycoon* and *Guitar Hero*, with ideas for implementation. In addition, the Learning and Teaching Scotland's Consolarium has numerous ideas, examples, plans, discussions and links to further reading on the subject of game-based learning. The Australian Centre for the Moving Image (ACMI) has a whole unit of work for primary students targeting game literacy. It involves learning about genre, analyzing game narrative, thinking critically about game characters, and creating characters. This could be followed up by getting students to create their own games in a simple environment such as *Scratch* or *Alice*. This

is what Buckingham and Burn (2007) discuss in their paper on Game Literacy as a discipline (see http://www.acmi.net.au/global/docs/sonic_education_pack.pdf).

Involvement in developing one's own future is nothing new. Cognitive and behaviour therapy has recognized for some thirty years that clients' involvement in creating their own therapy is far more successful than that dominated by a therapist (Thornicroft, 2004). In other words, when a person is party to a decision, they have an invested interest in making sure the decision is acted upon.

When thinking about teaching with and about games, constructivist principles can provide educators with opportunities to build authentic, learner-centered, collaborative experiences into their curriculum. These, in turn, support higher-order thinking, critical reflection, and experiential learning processes. When looking at the study of games, teachers need to provide authentic learning experiences and engage learners in a dialogic process that gives them opportunities to articulate their understanding (Petraglia 1998).

Introducing Games to Pre-Service Teachers

Schrader, Zheng, and Young (2006) argue that there are many benefits to be derived from the pedagogical use of commercial computer games, particularly massively multiplayer online games (MMOGs). However, their research found that many pre-service teachers are not yet fully aware of the pedagogical benefits and uses of these games, and they suggest that teacher preparation programs need to incorporate opportunities for pre-service teachers to experiment with and reflect upon commercial games. Similarly, Squire (2005) argues that teachers need opportunities to experience and reflect upon game use within the classroom and to consider how they can effectively use games as learning tools.

Studies have found that it is vitally important for pre-service teachers to be exposed to situated learning (Jones 2002). Research into pre-service teacher attitudes towards using commercial computer games within the curriculum found that trainee teachers were conservative towards the use of commercial games in the primary classroom (Wright, in press). The study involved two different cohorts of pre-service primary teachers, but this section deals only with the data from the second cohort as the materials used with that cohort and mode of delivery were much improved.

Trainee teachers were given a short course titled '*Gaming in the Primary Curriculum*', which was delivered online. Trainee teachers were required to read a number of texts on the subject (Kirriemuir & Macfarlane, 2004 ; Gee, 2003; Prensky, 2006; Squire, 2005), then experiment with games, research appropriate games and evaluate them in terms of learning opportunities. Online focus groups were used in the form of grouped-discussion board postings to explore their attitudes towards the use of commercial games in the primary curriculum.

In an attempt to model the use of games in the classroom, some trainee teachers became inspired by watching the video clips of *Rylands* using *Myst* to enhance literacy, suggesting that this model opened their eyes to innovative ways of introducing games into the curriculum. Many realized that computer games can promote inquiry and discussion. Around 15% of pre-service teachers in the study felt compelled to apply their learning experiences in their next teaching assignment and described how they used computer games in their classrooms.

70% of participants were able to discuss the interdisciplinary benefits of commercial computer games as learning tools. However, they generally displayed some reticence towards the use of MMOGs, a finding in line with the research of Schrader et al. (2006) who found that many pre-service teachers are not yet fully aware of the pedagogical benefits and uses of these games and they suggest that teacher preparation programs need to incorporate opportunities for pre-service teachers to experiment with and reflect upon commercial games. Similarly, Squire (2005) argues that teachers need opportunities to experience and reflect upon game use within the classroom and to consider how they can effectively use games as learning tools.

These findings suggest that pre-service teachers not only need hands-on experience and opportunities to reflect, but also need to see such instruction done successfully before they can apply what they have learned to new situations (Wright & Vongalis-Macrow, 2006). This finding helps to answer the question posed earlier in this chapter: Teachers and student teachers need to be convinced of the benefits to learning that can stem from using games within the curriculum, but they also need to see *how* to do this effectively.

CONCLUSION

This chapter has explored the potential use of 'commercial' computer games as a pedagogical tool. It is argued that such games can influence communication, problem solving and social interaction. With more innovation these games could provide an introduction for higher order learning skills, for instance: exploring history or visiting classical literature. They could also banish boredom from the classroom and place motivation for learning into the hands of the student.

REFERENCES

BECTA. (2005). *Learning lessons from digital games: What can games teach us about narrative?* Coventry, UK: BECTA.

Buckingham, D. (1993). *Changing literacies: Media education and modern culture.* London: Tufnell Press.

Buckingham, D., & Burn, A. (2007). Game literacy in theory and practice. *Journal of Educational Multimedia and Hypermedia, 16*(3), 323–349.

Cope, B., & Kalantzis, M. (Eds.). (2000). *Multiliteracies: Literacy learning and the design of social futures.* London: Routledge.

Gee, J. (2003). *What video games have to teach us about literacy and learning.* New York: Palgrave Macmillan.

Gee, J. (2007). *Good video games and good learning: Collected essays on video games, learning, and literacy.* New York: P. Lang.

Goldlove, B. (2008). Reading ability in school leavers: The computer generation. *Daily Mail conference report,* 22.5.08.

Halverson, R. 2005. What can K-12 school leaders learn from video games and gaming? *Innovate 1*(6). Retrieved March 2008, from http://www.innovateonline.info/index.php?view=article&id=81

Hovland, C. I., & Weiss, W. (1976). *Source credibility: Truth and publishing. Social Comment.* New York.

Jonassen, D., Davidson, M., Campbell, J., & Haag, B. B. (1995). Constructivism and computer-mediated communication in distance education. *American Journal of Distance Education, 9*(2), 7–23.

Juuls, J. (2001). Games telling stories. A brief note on games and narratives. *The International Journal of Computer Game Research, 1*(1). Retrieved May, 2008, from http://www.gamestudies.org/0101/juul-gts/

Kafai, Y. B. (2006). Playing and making games for learning: Instructionist and constructionist perspectives for game studies. *Games and Culture, 1*(1), 36–40. doi:10.1177/1555412005281767

Kirriemuir, J., & Macfarlane, A. (2004*). Literature review in games and learning.* Bristol: NESTA Futurelab.

Kress, G. (2003). *Literacy in the new media age.* London: Routledge.

Lankshear, C., & Knobel, M. (2003). *New literacies: Changing knowledge and classroom learning.* Buckingham, UK: Open University Press.

Macintosh, E. (2008). *Thinking out of the (X) Box: Gaming to expand horizons in creative writing.* Retrieved September, 2008, from http://edu.blogs.com/edublogs/2007/10/thinking-out-of.html

Newman, J. (2004). *Videogames.* London: Routledge.

O' Rourke, C. (2002). Engaging students through ICTs: A multiliteracies approach. *TechnKnowLogia,* (April – June), 57-59.

Petraglia, J. (1998). The real world on a short leash: The (mis)application of constructivism to the design of educational technology. *Educational Technology Research and Development, 46*(3), 53–65. doi:10.1007/BF02299761

Prensky, M. (2006). *Don't bother me Mom—I'm learning.* St. Paul, MN: Paragon House.

Rice, J. W. (2007). Assessing higher order thinking in video games. *Journal of Technology and Teacher Education, 15*(1), 87–100.

Richman, J. I., & Skidmore, D. (1984). *Promoting health: Research report*. Manchester, UK: Manchester Polytechnic.

Schrader, P. D., Zheng, D., & Young, M. (2006). Teachers' perceptions of video games: MMOGs and the future of preservice teacher education. *Innovate, 2*(3). Retrieved March, 2008, from http://www.innovateonline.info/index.php?view=article&id=125

Siemens, G. (2004). Connectivism: A learning theory for the digital age. *elearnspace*. Retrieved May, 2008, from http://www.elearnspace.org/Articles/connectivism.htm

Skidmore, D. (1994). *The ideology of community care*. London: Chapman and Hall.

Squire, K. (2005). Changing the game: What happens when video games enter the classroom? *Innovate, 1*(6). Retrieved March, 2008, from http://www.Innovateonline.info/index.php?view=article&id=82

Street, B. (1995). *Social literacies*. London: Longman.

Thornicroft, J. (2004). *Cognitive behaviour therapy*. London: Routledge.

Wright, P. (in press). Trainee teachers' e-Learning experiences of computer play. *Innovate*.

Wright, P., & Vongalis-Macrow, A. (2006). *Integrating ICT into pre-service education: Reframing teacher education*. Paper presented at the British Educational Research Association Annual Conference, University of Warwick, September. Retrieved March 2008, from http://www.leeds.ac.uk/educol/documents/168675.doc

Chapter 14

Learning from Computer Games:
Literacy Learning in a Virtual World

Robyn Henderson
University of Southern Queensland, Australia

ABSTRACT

This chapter builds on James Gee's (2003) description of the playing of computer games as the learning of a new literacy. To investigate this form of literacy learning from a player's perspective, the author created an avatar and joined the online community of the Massively Multiplayer Online Game, the World of Warcraft™ produced by Blizzard Entertainment®. This autoethnographic approach to exploring the game's linguistic, visual, audio, spatial and gestural elements of design provide an insider's perspective of the meaning-making resources that were on offer. The chapter concludes with a tentative consideration of how understandings about the literacies used within a virtual world might inform the learning of literacies in schools and other educational institutions.

INTRODUCTION

It is widely recognised that computer games have become a major form of entertainment for many young people. In fact, recent reports by GfK Australia (2008a) and the media (e.g. "Games consoles wrap up boom festive season," 2008) indicated that 175,000 Sony PlayStations were sold in Australia in the five weeks prior to Christmas in 2007 and that sales of the Nintendo DS and the Nintendo Wii were also in the tens of thousands during that period. At

the end of 2008, GfK Australia (2008b) reported that sales of games consoles had continued to increase with "double digit revenue growth in 2008" (p. 2). Because this suggests that digital technologies play a substantial role in the entertainment practices of so many young people, it is imperative that educators learn more about the practices that young people are using in their out-of-school lives and consider how these might inform school or other forms of institutional learning.

Views about the value of computer games, which are played on a range of technological devices including computers, games consoles and even

DOI: 10.4018/978-1-60566-842-0.ch014

mobile telephones, are diverse and have been conceptualised broadly as "a harmless diversion at best, a vile corruptor of youth at worst" (Brown & Thomas, 2006). Negative views surface regularly, especially in relation to apparent links between violence in computer games and aggressive behaviours (e.g. "Violent games make users more aggressive," 2006). Indeed, if we go back to the 1980s, the US Surgeon General announced that games were among the top health risks facing American citizens (see Squire, 2002). Such negative perceptions seem to originate in commonsense understandings that game-playing, even if not harmful to mental health, is a waste of time and is contributing to a population of socially disinterested, sedentary and obese young people.

At the other end of the spectrum are positive stories about computer games. Many of these have focused on the experiences and skills that may be transferred from the virtual world to the 'real' world. For example, there is the regularly cited example of Stephen Gillett, who apparently drew on his experiences as a guild leader in the computer game *World of Warcraft*™ as an important qualification to 'win' the position of senior director of engineering operations at Yahoo!® (Brown & Thomas, 2006; Prensky, 2006). Another widely publicised example involves reports that surgeons who engage in digital game playing are much better in simulations of keyhole surgery than those who do not ("Nurse, hand me the latest video game," 2007; Prensky, 2006). As Steinkuehler (2006) pointed out, the media tends "to greet every new technology with stories of salvation or damnation (and relatively little between)" (p. 50).

Whilst positive examples are sometimes dismissed as media hype or exaggeration, there is a developing body of work that highlights the literacy practices of computer games (e.g. Gee, 2003, 2004; Martin & Murray, 2006; McClay, Mackey, Carbonaro, Szafron, & Schaeffer, 2007; Steinkuehler, 2004). Gee (2003) argues that learning to play a computer game is "learning a new literacy" (p. 13) and that games draw on

successful learning principles and provide considerable evidence about how learning might be enhanced in contexts such as schools. In Gee's (2004) opinion, young people's exposure to the language and symbols of digital technologies means that they are engaged with compelling and motivating learning that may draw on different forms of thinking, interacting, and valuing from those usually promoted by schools.

Because games are developed to be sold, their designers are cognisant of players' needs. According to Gee (2005b), "good game designers are practical theoreticians of learning" who have to consider how "to get new players to learn their long, complex, and difficult games" (p. 5). Some of the learning principles that operate in games involve empowering players and engaging them in problem-solving tasks. For example, games expect players to be producers, not just consumers; they require risk-taking; they are "pleasantly frustrating"; they give verbal information "just-in-time" and "on demand"; and they situate "the meanings of words in terms of the actions, images, and dialogues that they relate to" (Gee, 2005a, p. 36). Furthermore, players are expected to perform before being competent, whereas schools "often demand that students gain competence through reading texts before they can perform in the domain that they are learning" (p. 37). Through such principles, games "trigger deep learning that is itself part and parcel of the fun" (Gee, 2005b, p. 15).

With Gee's work in mind, this chapter considers the literacies that are required for playing a particular computer game. If learning to play a computer game *is* "learning a new literacy" (Gee, 2003, p. 13), then we need to explore this notion further, as there is substantial evidence that the playing of computer games is a popular past time for young people in today's world. This chapter, then, will contribute to our understandings of the digital literacy practices of computer games. Such an investigation is essential for educators who want to know more about the literacies used by their students in contexts outside of formal education.

Using The New London Group's (1996) notion of multiliteracies and elements of multimodal design, the chapter will investigate the resources that were used by one player in the activities and practices of one computer game. It will explore the linguistic, visual, audio, spatial and gestural elements of meaning-making, and the combinations of these, that were used as the game was played. The chapter will conclude by reflecting on the game's literacies and considering how teachers might build on students' knowledge of such literacies – sometimes referred to as their "funds of knowledge" (Moll, Amanti, Neff & Gonzales, 1992) – to ensure that success in literacies outside-of-education can be used as the foundations for successful literacy learning within educational institutions.

BACKGROUND

It has been widely recognised that the proliferation of new technologies has meant the development of new and hybrid literacies (e.g. Snyder, 1996; The New London Group, 1996). For many young people, daily social and cultural practices revolve around the use of digital technologies, including computers, mobile telephones and games consoles. All of these involve literacy practices, such as navigating websites, understanding text messages, finding particular pieces of information about playing games, and writing, composing or designing emails, machinimas (machine cinema produced within the virtual world of games) and chat within games. What is particularly interesting, however, is that there is evidence that some of these literacy practices are not always understood as 'literacies', even by those who engage in them. As Henderson and Honan (2008) found, many teachers are quick to dismiss games as leisure activities with little or no value to school learning or to literacy learning. Additionally, it appears

that many young people, even though "heavily embedded in a tech-rich world," do not always believe "that communication over the internet or text messaging is writing" (Lenhart, Arafeh, Smith & Macgill, 2008, p. ii).

For teachers, though, it is important to recognise the literacy practices that are involved, because school literacy learning has traditionally tended to privilege a narrow range of literacy practices and this has had the effect of advantaging some learners in the literacy classroom and marginalising others. Gee (2004) explained that some children "get an important head start" to the learning of school literacies and academic language before they begin school and receive ongoing support through their lives outside of school (p. 3). By contrast, other children have to rely solely on their school experiences for learning the literacies and academic language required for success in school settings. Indeed, there is a growing body of research that has shown that clear links and connections between the literacy practices of home and the literacy practices of educational contexts are essential for academic literacy success (Comber, Badger, Barnett, Nixon, & Pitt, 2001; Gregory & Williams, 2000). Comber and Kamler's (2004, 2005) collaborative classroom work on "turn-around pedagogies," for example, has demonstrated the benefits of building on the "funds of knowledge" that students bring to school (Moll et al., 1992). Yet recent research indicates that this understanding may not have yet translated into an understanding of the usage of technologies and digital texts in students' home lives (Honan, 2006; Merchant, 2007). Furthermore, efforts by governments and school systems, in countries like Australia, to make computers available to students in all classes has tended to focus attention on access issues, rather than considering the knowledges that students are developing as they use digital technologies in their everyday lives.

With computer games playing a major role in the leisure time of so many of today's young people (Young, Schrader & Zheng, 2006), it is important for teachers to have knowledge about the literacies of game playing, as a way of identifying potential bridges to the learning of literacies that are privileged in educational contexts. The playing of computer games very clearly requires young people to make sense of a range of meaning-making resources, as it is widely recognised that the reading of digital texts incorporates "non-linear, multi-layered, intertextual" components as well as "reading images and other semiotic sign systems" (Sanford & Madill, 2007, p. 434). Whilst differences between the reading of digital texts and traditional print-based texts have been well documented (e.g. Gambrell, 2005; Merchant, 2007; Snyder, 1996), it has been argued that there is a need to investigate the knowledge-building processes and multimodal capacities that are occurring as digital literacies are being used in young people's everyday lives (Burke & Rowsell, 2007; Merchant, 2007). As Merchant (2007) highlighted, there is a concern if "a whole range of cultural resources fails to be translated into cultural capital by the school system" (p. 253). A rethinking is critical if educators are going to capitalise on opportunities for young people to use everyday literacy knowledges to inform learning in educational contexts.

Most of the research in this area, however, has investigated the benefits of learning games in terms of social interactions and problem-solving capacities (e.g. Johnson, 2005; Steinkuehler & Williams, 2006; Young et al., 2006), learning principles (Compton-Lilly, 2007; Gee 2003, 2005a, 2005b, 2005c), issues around identity (Bulfin & North, 2006; Gee, 2003; Turkle, 2003), or the use of computer games as texts in the classroom (e.g. Beavis, 2006; Beavis & Charles, 2005; Beavis & O'Mara, 2006; Ikpeze & Boyd, 2007; McGinnis, 2007). According to Squire (2002), one of the gaps in the educational research on game-playing has been in the area of "putting aside preconceptions and examining gamers on their own terms" (p. 3).

To look at this area, then, this chapter approaches computer games from a player's perspective. I decided that an understanding of the world of computer games required personal experience of a games environment or virtual world. Joining "the video-game literacy club," as Norton-Meier (2005) called it (p. 431), provided a way of rethinking taken-for-granted assumptions about the literacies of electronic games as well as a way of seeing a game through the eyes of a "digital immigrant" (Prensky, 2001). Whilst the literacy practices of the screen view of one computer game – the Massively Multiplayer Online Game of *Lineage II* – has been described by Steinkuehler (2007), the focus was to identify the literacy practices from a "contemporary point of view" and from a "traditional point of view" (pp. 300-301). Steinkuehler's analysis highlighted the "dense representations" that players need to be able to 'read' both "quickly and adeptly" in the screen view of games (p. 300), as well as the way that players have to demonstrate "fluency and participation in a thoroughly *literate* space of icons, symbols, gestures, action, pictorial representations, and text" (p. 301).

What is different about the analysis in this chapter is that it focuses on the literacy practices required in a computer game from the perspective of a new player or 'newbie'. It does not consider the potential of games for classroom learning, which has been the focus of other research (e.g. Jenkins, Klopfer, Squire, & Tan, 2003; Squire & Jenkins, 2003). Instead, it sets out to consider the literacy practices used in gaming environments and how understandings of these might inform school literacy learning.

AN AUTOETHNOGRAPHIC RESEARCH APPROACH

This chapter's exploration of literacies used in computer games is confined to one Massively Multiplayer Online Game (MMOG) that has millions of players globally – the *World of Warcraft*™ produced by Blizzard Entertainment® (2004a). A recent press release indicated that it has over 11.5 million subscribers (Blizzard Entertainment, 2008, December 23). The game was chosen because of its popularity and because research suggests that it has wide appeal across age and sociocultural groups (Yee, 2008). It was also one of the games played regularly by many young people I knew and they advocated that it was a 'good' example to buy and try. As a MMOG, the game provides a virtual world where all players log in via an internet connection and are 'seen' in the world as characters called avatars. The game can be played at any time during the day or night and players from across countries 'mix' in this online environment.

This investigation will explore experiences of one player, myself, who was a novice at navigating and negotiating the game's virtual world. My approach is based on the view that an insider perspective (Gee, 1996; Lankshear & Knobel, 2007) can offer significant understandings about how technology is experienced (Kerawalla & Crook, 2002). In taking an autoethnographic approach (Ellingson, 1998; Ellis & Bochner, 2000), where I document my own experiences in the virtual world of a computer game as valid topics of investigation, I wanted to be able to combine my experiences as a game 'newbie' with my understandings about literacies.

As Steinkuehler (2006) explained, participation in an online gaming community involves "participation in a Discourse community" where "an individual comes to understand the world (and themselves) from the perspective of that community" (p. 40). Not only did I expect to learn a new Discourse, but I knew that I would be bringing multiple perspectives to that community, as a researcher and educator in the area of literacies and as a self-proclaimed "digital immigrant" (Prensky, 2001) with little experience of computer games. I was also aware that my background would probably mean that I would view the virtual *World of*

Warcraft™ through an educational lens. Whilst mindful that the information gathered would not be generalisable across other players or other games, I wanted to experience first-hand the literacies of the game and to see whether they were different from the literacies I was used to experiencing on a daily basis.

I draw on the multiliteracies work of The New London Group (1996), particularly their discussion of design elements and "the increasing complexity and inter-relationship of different modes of meaning" (p. 78). The New London Group identified five elements of design – linguistic, visual, audio, spatial and gestural – and the potential for these to work together in dynamic, multimodal combinations. As Steinkuehler (2007) noted, the literacy practices that comprise computer games are "not isolated and autonomous but, rather, interrelated in complex and mutually defining ways" (p. 303):

*At the **macro level**, participating over time in MMOGs entails not only (inter)action in the game's virtual environment but also the production and consumption of online fandom content in the form of discussion boards, website contributions, creative endeavours such as writing stories, and the like. At the **micro level** of a given moment in an individual's game play, participation means movement across multiple "attentional spaces" (Lemke, n.d.). (Steinkuehler, 2007, p. 303)*

This chapter will draw mainly on my initial experiences in the game as a player. By describing my first entry to the game and the resources available on the screen interface, I consider how meaning is made in the game in relation to linguistic, visual, audio, spatial and gestural elements of textual design and the micro and macro levels discussed by Steinkuehler (2007).

A PLAYER'S USE OF LITERACIES IN THE GAME

On Entering the Game: Visual, Audio and Linguistic Design

The virtual world of the *World of Warcraft*™ is accessed by entering a user identification and password. From that beginning moment, the computer screen is a text, a two-dimensional surface inscribed with meaning. Yet, once the world is accessed, that text appears to be a three-dimensional space. In this sense, the entire virtual world is a text that is 'read' by players, yet it is also changed by players as they move through the world of the game. To begin playing the game, a new player has to make a series of decisions in relation to designing a character known as an avatar. The first decision is whether to join the Alliance or the Horde, the two warring factions of the game. This is followed by a series of choices relating to race, class, gender and appearance, including skin colour, hair colour, hairstyle and body markings. The centre of the computer screen displays an image of the player's avatar and the player is able to trial various appearances before making a final decision. This customisation process relies on visual design, with the player using the computer mouse to click on icons which change the avatar's appearance.

The visual appearance of the avatar is the focus of this activity. However, text boxes provide linguistic descriptions of each faction, race and class, thereby contextualising the player's decisions in terms of the virtual world of the game and the history of the factional conflict that the world has experienced. Supporting information is also provided in the *Game manual* (Blizzard Entertainment, 2004b) which is provided when the game is purchased. My decisions resulted in the design of a female Human (race) Paladin (class), described by the manual as "a virtuous defender of the weak and a tireless enemy of the undead" with "a useful mix of healing and defensive spells" (p. 80). This description marked an intertextuality with the traditional good-bad binaries of fantasy narratives and positioned me as a strong and honourable character within the game's narrative. The final design step involved providing a name for the avatar. This linguistic process was constrained by the rules of the game – that no two avatars on a server may have the same name, that names have to be between 2 and 12 characters long, and that commercial names are prohibited. However, the potential for imagination was otherwise unlimited, again perhaps linked to the fantasy theme.

Once an avatar has been designed, a player's introduction to the virtual world of the game is through a movie-like introduction that is linked to the player's choice of race and class. My introduction – the one for Human Paladins – began with a camera-view looking upwards at the stone walls of Stormwind City, one of the larger cities of the game's world, before pulling away from the city walls and moving through the forest outside the city. Initially the visuals were accompanied by a drum roll, followed by a chorus with orchestral music. After the first few seconds, a voice-over began to describe the location as one of the "last bastions of human power in the world" and provided a brief history of the "savage war" that had engulfed it. The voice spoke directly to me: "You must defend the kingdom against the foul mongrels that encroach upon it and hunt down the subversive traitors that seek to destroy it from within."

I was positioned by the voice-over and the combination of visual, audio and linguistic elements as playing an important role in defending the kingdom. The visual images presented a place of grandeur and beauty, with the invisible camera seeming to fly through the trees of the forest to a resting place outside the cathedral in Northshire Valley. At this point, I realised that the avatar I had designed – at Level 1, the beginning level of the game – had appeared in front of a cathedral. The music had stopped, but sounds of nature, especially birds, were evident. Using the mouse,

I was able to move my avatar – walk, run or jump – in an apparent three-dimensional space. I could choose to enter the cathedral, walk into the fields or the forest, or approach other avatars or non-player characters. Whilst the opening movie had positioned me as a listener and as a potential hero in the Kingdom of Azeroth – and I simply had to listen to the story as it was being told – I was no longer being told anything and I was no longer a passive participant. I was now faced with learning how to 'play' the game and to become an active participant. From an initial, albeit brief, position as a consumer of information, I was now able to direct and decide how my avatar would operate in the virtual world. I had to become an active producer within the game (Gee, 2005a, 2005b).

Games are designed to allow players to progress their avatar from the beginning levels through to more complex and difficult levels. In the case of the *World of Warcraft*™, avatars begin at Level 1 and progress to Level 60 by accepting and completing quests, and the purchase of game 'add-ons' allows further progression to Level 70 and to Level 80. Games generally provide opportunities for beginning players to be "free to explore, try things, take risks, and make new discoveries" (Gee, 2004, p. 66) and, in the *World of Warcraft*™, initial play occurs in a relatively safe location where a Level 1 avatar may explore and complete simple quests. Yellow explanation marks above the heads of non-player characters (NPCs) invite beginning players to accept quests. By using the mouse to right-click on a NPC, a dialogue box opens and the player is able to read what is required. Such quests usually involve killing 'monsters' of some type, collecting the 'loot' that is 'dropped' when monsters die, or collecting items from the environment, then reporting to a particular NPC. Quest completion is rewarded by experience points as well as other goods.

As the player's avatar moves from level to level, quests become more complex and take more time, but they reap greater rewards. Additionally, many quests are designed to take the avatar to areas of the Kingdom of Azeroth that the avatar has not explored previously. This means that more of the virtual world becomes available and a player is able to make decisions about where the avatar might travel and about what types of quests are undertaken.

Reading the Computer Screen Interface: Visual and Linguistic Modes of Meaning

To accompany an avatar's arrival in the virtual world, the *Game manual* (Blizzard Entertainment, 2004b) provides information about the computer screen interface, although the game's packaging advertises that the "interface is so intuitive, you may never need to read the manual." I was grateful, however, for the manual's advice about how to 'read' the screen, as it offers extensive visual and linguistic information. The cursor itself is a source of visual information. Although usually visible in the image of a gauntlet, the cursor is able to change shape and indicate particular sources of information within the game. For example, when it is moved over a vendor, it becomes a bag, indicating that goods may be bought and sold from that character. At other times, it takes the shape of a book, a scroll or a magnifying glass.

The outer edges of the computer screen display various forms of information. Figure 1 shows the screen as it appeared when I had progressed to Level 60. At the beginning of the game, the layout was the same but not all slots around the edges of the screen contained information. Although many players customise the screen by downloading modifications available from the internet, I used the layout provided by the game.

The top left-hand corner of the screen provided details about my avatar – portrait and name – as well as health and mana bars that showed whether my avatar needed food or drink. The top right-hand corner provided a display of icons to indicate which spells were active, as well as a day/night clock and a small map which could be zoomed

Figure 1. The screen interface for the World of Warcraft™ (© 2009 Blizzard Entertainment. Used with permission.)

in and out. The avatar's position on the map was always visible and the name of the location was displayed above the map. A row of slots across the full width of the bottom of the screen provided about a dozen spaces for spells, weapons and other items, five spaces for backpacks, and seven that contained icons enabling access to other important game information, including character details, quest log, spell book, world map and 'help'. New avatars begin with one backpack and the player is able to buy or collect others during the game. Each backpack opens up to reveal a number of slots, sometimes as many as 16, so that food, drink, weapons and loot from killing monsters are able to be carried.

Although many slots on the screen are empty at the beginning stages of the game, each may be filled with an icon which represents something that the avatar possesses, whether an aura, a spell or a material possession. Experienced players often have over 100 icons that can be displayed and 'read'. An experienced player might have about 50 slots containing spells and other items, plus five backpacks with up to 16 slots each. In Figure 1, two backpacks are open showing icons inside that represent a whole range of goods that the avatar possessed at that particular point in time. Above these slots is an Experience (XP) Bar. Its colour indicates whether the avatar is rested or not and how far through a level the avatar has progressed. There is also a row of slots down the right hand-side of the screen, as well as additional rows which may be accessed from the bottom of the screen.

As a beginning player, I was immediately aware that the screen could present large amounts of

Figure 2. Linguistic information for one spell icon in the World of Warcraft^{TM}

> **Seal of the Crusader**   Rank 6
> 136 Mana
> Instant cast
>
> Fills the Paladin with the spirit of a crusader for 30 sec, granting 371 melee attack power The Paladin also attacks 40% faster, but deals less damage with each attack. Only one Seal can be active on the Paladin at any one time.
>
> Unleashing this seal's energy will judge an enemy for 20 sec, increasing Holy damage taken by up to 161. Your melee strikes will refresh the spell's duration. Only one judgement per Paladin can be active at any one time.

information in visual form, with icons, symbols and colours presenting information. Linguistic information played a much lesser role in terms of 'reading the screen', although the movement of the cursor over many of the slots provided a description of the contents. This was particularly the case with spells, where the player could be reminded about the particular spell, its rank, how much mana it used and its effects. As demonstrated in Figure 2, the amount of linguistic information provided for the icon of one spell – the 'Seal of the Crusader' – was considerable. The description provided complex and detailed information that the player could access whenever needed. In this way, many of the visual design elements on the screen were augmented by access to information presented in linguistic form.

In the bottom left-hand corner of the screen was the chat log, which displayed several channels of chat simultaneously. These multiple layers of communication included general messages from other players in the nearby area, private messages from other players, discussions between players working as a team or party on a raid, and

sometimes messages from the game developers. Only eight lines of chat are visible on the screen at any one time, although it is possible to scroll through the log to view the chat that has occurred since logging into the game. Whilst the chat log is a linguistic element of the screen, the text is colour-coded, thus providing a short-hand visual reference to the types of communication that are displayed.

The chat log was the section of the screen that I struggled to read. To monitor chat whilst I also engaged in the multifaceted tasks of 'playing the game' – such as moving my avatar, protecting my avatar from attack, monitoring health, trying to use appropriate spells and game strategies and so on – meant reading multiple sources of visual and linguistic information simultaneously. This multitasking seemed far too difficult at first. Individually, each was a fairly simple task, but the game required expert manipulation of the mouse to enact the actions and movement of my avatar at the same time as reading and monitoring the information displayed around the outer edges of the screen (as already described) and 'reading' the environment displayed in the central area of the screen (as will be discussed in the next section).

Additionally, I could not always make sense of the abbreviated language that was used on the chat channels, even though it was not unlike text messaging. This became much easier once I knew some of the conventions that were used widely. For example, it helped to know that *SW* referred to Stormwind City, that *kk* was an abbreviation for *okay* and that *lfg* meant *looking for group* – a call for players to join a temporary group for a specific purpose within the game. These, of course, are only a few of the abbreviations in use. Although some were game specific, there was also widespread use of more generally used text messaging abbreviations, including *u* for *you* and *r* for *are*. Although such communication has often been criticised by the media as a lesser form of language (e.g. "Has txt kild the ritn wd?", 2007), it fulfils the need for players to communicate quickly with other players within the context of a complex game.

Reading the screen, then, involved monitoring a plethora of information, including my avatar's health and mana levels, the spells that were in use, geographical location, and communications amongst players, to name just a few. As Steinkuehler (2007) pointed out, complex screen displays are common to Massively Multiplayer Online Games and it is difficult initially to know how to read "the seeming sundry assortment of images, bar graphs, texts, icons, and symbols" (p. 300). Early in my experiences of the *World of Warcraft*™, I felt that I could not cope effectively with all of the information that was available. Over time, with practice, I learnt how to make sense of the complex visual and linguistic elements that were available on the screen. Although reading the screen was a major part of this, it was not all that was required. Communicating with other players via chat, for example, was an important social aspect of the game and being able to use this linguistic form of communication quickly and effectively was essential. I very quickly learnt to use the text abbreviations that others used, as

well as to not worry about the spelling or typing errors that I made.

Other Sources of Linguistic Information

Visual design elements played a key role in the playing of the game and provided condensed representations of detailed information. Even though there were few linguistic elements on the screen itself, I have explained how players could access linguistic descriptions of the information presented as icons. Additionally, dialogue boxes – such as the player's quest log which contains information about the player's multiple current quests – could be opened and viewed. These provided opportunities for more conventional reading, as the left-to-right and top-to-bottom conventions of traditional print-based materials generally applied. Similarly, locations within the game have books that may be read and players sometimes collect, carry and deliver letters and scrolls. Letters can be 'written' and sent to players within the game via letterboxes which are conveniently placed outside the inns where avatars go to rest, eat and drink. All of these provide opportunities for players to read print in seemingly conventional ways, even though the texts are electronic ones displayed on the computer screen.

Further information to assist with game playing, however, can be obtained by going beyond the game. Websites or fandom sites – such as the official *World of Warcraft*™ site (Blizzard Entertainment, 2008), the *Unofficial World of Warcraft* site (IncGamers Ltd, 2007) and numerous online databases of information, frequently asked questions and answers, and blogs (e.g. Thott, 2008) – provide information and tips that players can use to facilitate problem-solving within the game. The movement from the game to other electronic sources of information is an important component of the way that Massively Multiplayer Online Games operate. A player's 'reading' of the game, then, goes beyond the multiple sources of information *on* the screen to other sources available *beyond* the screen from internet sites. In other words, players "engage in multiple forms of recognizable and coherent literacy practices" *within* and *beyond* the game (Steinkuehler, 2007, p. 302). The capacity to move quickly out of the game, then search for and locate information from various internet sites before returning to the game, was one that I found difficult. What I learnt, however, was that asking other players for assistance via chat often tapped into the expertise of other players who were willing to share knowledge or tell me where particular types of information could be found.

Audio, Spatial and Gestural Design

Although the game interface provides many opportunities for reading visual and linguistic elements, other elements of design are also important. Audio elements are evident in the background music and other sounds that can be heard when the avatar is in particular locations of the virtual world. These sounds often indicate how safe the location is for the avatar or they indicate particular actions that are in progress, such as the sounds of digging for minerals or blacksmithing weapons or armour. Other sounds, such as the sound of walking or running and the sound of battle, are audio components of the game. As a player, I was quite aware that particular sounds offered indications of place and action, even to the extent of sometimes knowing that other players were nearby. Audio elements of design were also used for communication within the game. For example, some non-player characters 'talked' and there was always the potential for avatars to talk and make other sounds such as laughing and crying. Additionally, many players use communication software such as Skype to maintain real-time voice communication with other players.

Spatial design elements are also integral to game play. Knowing how to manipulate my avatar within the three-dimensional representation of the world of Azeroth was essential to survival. Being able to turn quickly, to scan the surroundings through 360 degrees, to find particular locations, to manoeuvre through buildings, and to travel, whether by foot, rail, horse or griffin, were necessary skills obtained through becoming expert with a computer mouse or with particular key strokes of the computer keyboard. However, it was not only important to be able to manipulate the avatar in particular ways. It was also important to be able to read maps, to follow directions and to use clues to find particular locations. The world of the game incorporates two continents as well as islands, and avatars are able to move through forests and caves and across mountain ranges, plains, deserts and snow-covered terrain. Making sense of each location that is visited requires geographic and architectonic knowledges that relate to landscape and architecture respectively (see The New London Group, 1996).

To make meaning in the game, players also have to engage with gestural design elements of meaning-making. The 'reading' of bodies – of other avatars and of non-player characters – is an important requirement in the game and it relies on knowledge about the race and class of other avatars, the talents and skills that are generally associated with particular lifeforms, and previous experiences within the game. Players dress their avatars in particular ways and loot or buy armour, clothing and weapons, which enable them to present particular 'images' to others in the game. Additionally, the player can draw on 'emote' abilities and can decide that their avatar will applaud, beg, bow, cry, dance, sleep and so on. These make meaning though the gestural mode, although in some cases audio elements are also involved and a linguistic description of particular behaviours is entered automatically into the chat log.

REFLECTING ON THE GAME'S LITERACIES

My exploration of the design elements that were evident to me as a player in the *World of Warcraft*™ indicated that players draw on broad and complex modes of meaning. During game-play on a computer screen, players are involved in a massive reading task – not only reading the traditional texts that are used as part of the game, including (electronic) books, scrolls and dialogue boxes, but also reading visual icons and making sense of audio, spatial and gestural information (see also Steinkuehler, 2007). Whilst the game's traditional texts require fairly conventional practices, such as left-to-right and top-to-bottom reading, players are also expected to monitor multiple sources of meaning presented in multimodal forms and to move quickly to and from different parts of the screen and sometimes beyond the screen. Players are not only consumers of multiple forms of meaning, but they are also producers of meaning, engaging in multiple forms of communication with other players and with non-player characters.

Until I experienced the game, I had not understood how complex a computer game could be, nor had I anticipated how difficult and challenging its literacies would be. Players monitor, access and use multiple sources of information in precisioned ways, and the multiplicity becomes more complex as players' avatars progress through the higher levels of the game. Although I agree with Mortensen's assessment that playing the *World of Warcraft*™ "encourages and demands multitasking" (2006, p. 404), that term seems to under-rate the complex co-ordination or orchestration of skills and the integrated utilisation of design elements that allow players to be successful.

While making sense of "dense representations" and drawing on "constellations of literacy practices" in order to "mediate virtual action" (Steinkuehler, 2007, pp. 300-301), a player has to think quickly, make snap decisions about which spells or talents to use, move the avatar and

monitor the avatar's health and mana, while also communicating with other players and remaining aware of possible dangers. Indeed, skills in information literacies are essential to game play. Knowing how to locate information in an effective and efficient way and being able to use that information to construct new meanings and to problem-solve are critical to the game, but they have also been identified as necessary skills to deal with the "diverse information choices" that permeate the lives of people in the 21st century (Bundy, 2004, p. 3).

As Gee's (2005a, 2005b, 2005c) research has demonstrated, games are designed around successful learning principles and players learn to use situated literacies in the context of the game as they play. This situated learning moves players through the game's levels and through increasingly complex tasks. Successful quests, for example, require players to use conventional literacy practices, such as reading and following instructions and clues. However, these conventional practices around linguistic information are embedded within a virtual world where visual images, sound effects (audio), movement and gestures provide opportunities for players to 'read the world' and to construct meaning within that context. The player continually constructs meaning through action, designing narratives, and communicating with other players and non-player characters. Communication in the chat log, for example, might include player-to-player discussions about the game, about game strategies, or about issues beyond and unrelated to the game.

FUTURE DIRECTIONS: BUILDING ON STUDENTS' KNOWLEDGE OF LITERACIES

This chapter has considered the linguistic, visual, audio, spatial and gestural elements of design in the *World of Warcraft*™ and presented insights into game playing in a virtual world. Although these are insights gained from one novice player, they have demonstrated the significance and complexity of literacies within such an environment and suggest that more than lip service needs to be paid to the literacy experiences of young people who play computer games in their out-of-school hours.

It is quite probable that some students spend more hours each day playing computer games than attending school. I found that long periods of time, generally well in excess of two hours, were essential to enable effective participation in aspects of the game. Short stints in the game were not always useful, especially if my avatar had to travel from one place to another within the virtual world. Indeed, part of the reason that I felt I was unsuccessful as a team player was that I was unwilling to commit the amount of time that many other players seemed willing to devote. I was always entering the world on a strict time limit, willing to play but unwilling to commit to playing for a long period of time. In many respects, this may have meant that I missed out on some of the valuable social experiences, interactions and events that captivate so many players (Mortensen, 2006; Steinkuehler, 2004).

As was explained near the beginning of this chapter, considerable research has indicated that it is important to understand and build on the funds of knowledge about literacies that students bring to school (Moll et al., 1992). According to Kamler and Comber (2005), students' out-of-school literacies are resources on which school literacy learning can build and these should not "remain invisible and under-valued in the school context" (p. 5). Kamler and Comber advocate that teachers should look for evidence of their students' "capabilities, interests, strengths and cultural investments" (p. 6). The question, then, is what funds of knowledge do players acquire while playing computer games? And how might these be used to inform literacy learning in school contexts?

In terms of the literacies of computer games, I came to the conclusion that players had to draw on a range of practices, some conventional and some not. There were certainly many times when I felt illiterate in the virtual world, struggling to make meaning quickly enough and experiencing some difficulties with trying to keep up with the multiple sources of information that were available simultaneously. Yet the game provided me with multiple opportunities to hone skills at consuming and producing meaning in multimodal ways that I had not previously experienced. For many young people, it would seem that these ways of making meaning are part of everyday practices, whereas they were new experiences for me.

Major differences between my everyday experiences of literacies and my experiences in the virtual world included the density and range of iconic and symbolic meanings on the computer screen, the interface of the game. It was not that linguistic design – often regarded as the most important in classrooms – was not important in this context, but that it worked in conjunction with other modes. Additionally, to play the game and to complete quests, I had to be able to locate, evaluate and use information – that is, to develop effective information literacy practices (see Bundy, 2004). On many occasions, I needed to go beyond what was offered by the game itself, to ask other players for assistance or to search for information from websites that offered hints and clues to the difficult aspects of particular quests. To be a successful player, then, I had to become an expert problem-solver and I needed to develop information literacy strategies that enabled me to move intertextually within and outside the game. In Gee's (2005a) terms, I searched for information when I felt that I was "ready for it" and needed it (p. 36).

Nevertheless, there was never a right way to solve problems within the game and different players are able to find solutions in different ways. What I learnt was that the game was never about finding 'the' answer to a problem. It was always about finding 'an' answer. And, as Gee (2005a) highlighted, games offer opportunities to "take risks, explore, and try new things" (p. 35). It was possible to trial (or 'perform') a solution, or even to trial and re-trial multiple solutions. In this way, games foster performance before competence and offer opportunities to "explore, think laterally and rethink goals" (Gee, 2005a, p. 36). One wonders whether schooling can provide the opportunities that games offer – for learning to occur through creative and active problem-solving across multimodal texts.

For teachers wanting to capitalise on students' learning from games, there is still much to find out about the specific literacy practices that players develop. However, my experiences suggest that players make meaning from multiple modes; that they often pool their expertise and are used to co-operating and co-ordinating with other players (see also Gee, 2005a); that they learn to problem-solve, and that they develop strategies that enable them to be information literate within the environment of the game. It would seem critical that teachers think about how they might build on those strengths to develop the literacies that are privileged in classroom contexts. It would also seem important that students themselves consider the skills that games have taught them, so that they are aware of how they might transfer those skills to other contexts.

Whilst I recognise that not all educators would necessarily want to experience computer games from a player's perspective, it is an experience that offers considerable learning about the complex resources that must be used to make meaning and to accomplish the game's goals. There are, however, other ways for teachers to learn about the literacies of computer games. As computer games are texts used in popular culture and are part of the daily literacy experiences of many students, educators might utilise opportunities for students to share these texts in the classroom and make comparisons with more conventional classroom texts, a strategy recommended by a number of researchers (see Beavis, 2006; Beavis & Charles, 2005; Beavis & O'Mara, 2006; Ikpeze & Boyd, 2007; McGinnis, 2007). As Kamler and Comber

(2005) noted, opportunities to link students' social practices from home and the community with the practices of education are one way of turning around the deficit discourses that so often pervade educational contexts.

In relation to my experiences as a novice player of a computer game, there seemed to be a resonance with the work of Marie Clay on beginning reading and the training of reading recovery teachers (see Clay, 1993). As a player trying to be literate in a virtual world, I had to learn how to use many of the strategies that Clay wrote about – searching for information, using information, self-monitoring, cross-checking on information and self-correcting (pp. 40-41). I had to attend to multiple aspects of the text, although these were the multiple design elements of a multimodal text, not the print texts that were the focus of Clay's work. Instead of focusing on "the aspects of printed texts (letters, words, pictures, language, messages, stories)" (p. 7), the five elements of design – linguistic, visual, audio, spatial and gestural – and combinations of these were significant. From a future research perspective, I suspect that Clay's work might offer ways of teasing out some of the specific practices that are used by players as they negotiate the virtual world of games such as the *World of Warcraft*™.

CONCLUSION

Widespread use of computer games and the accompanying employment of multimodal elements of design, incorporating linguistic, visual, audio, spatial and gestural elements, prompts a (re)consideration of school literacy learning and how it might build on the literacy practices with which many young people have become familiar. It would seem that the multimodality of today's computer games has provided opportunities for young people to become literate in ways that we do not necessarily know or recognise. Yet we need to know about them if we wish to use them as funds of knowledge on which to build other literacy knowledges.

Whilst the autoethnographic investigation described in this chapter confirms the multimodal nature of the literacies of one computer game from the point of view of one player, there would seem to be much work to be done in mapping these literacies against the literacies that are going to be needed for successful literate lives in the world of the future. Further research is needed to enable this mapping and to see how educators might build on the literacies that have been learned and practised in computer games and to find their relationships to the literacies that are privileged and taught in schools.

NOTE

Blizzard Entertainment®: Blizzard Entertainment is a trademark or registered trademark of Blizzard Entertainment, Inc. in the U.S. and/or other countries. All rights reserved.

World of Warcraft™: World of Warcraft and Blizzard Entertainment are trademarks or registered trademarks of Blizzard Entertainment, Inc. in the U.S. and/or other countries.

REFERENCES

Beavis, C. (2006). *Lara meets literacy: Computer games and English*. Retrieved April 19, 2007, from http://www.sofweb.vic.edu.aa/english

Beavis, C., & Charles, C. (2005). Writing, English and digital culture. In B. Doecke & G. Parr (Eds.), *Writing = learning* (pp. 229-246). Kent Town, Australia: Wakefield Press.

Beavis, C., & O'Mara, J. (2006). Preparing English teachers for a changing world. In B. Doecke, M. Howie & W. Sawyer (Eds.), *"Only connect... "*: *English teaching, schooling and community* (pp. 349-355). Kent Town, Australia: Wakefield Press.

Blizzard Entertainment. (2004a). *World of Warcraft*™ [Game]. Irvine, CA: Blizzard Entertainment.

Blizzard Entertainment. (2004b). *World of Warcraft*™*game manual*. Irvine, CA: Blizzard Entertainment.

Blizzard Entertainment. (2008). *Welcome to World of Warcraft.com*. Retrieved June 1, 2008, from http://www.worldofwarcraft.com/index.xml

Blizzard Entertainment. (2008, December 2008). *World of Warcraft subscriber base reaches 11.5 million worldwide*. Retrieved January 10, 2009, from http://www.blizzard.com/us/press/081121.html

Brown, J. S., & Thomas, D. (2006). You play World of WarCraft? You're hired!: Why multiplayer games may be the best kind of job training. *Wired Magazine, 14*(4). Retrieved April 3, 2006, from http://www.wired.com

Bulfin, S., & North, S. (2006, September 27-29). *The literate places and spaces in/between: Reframing the school-home binary*. Paper presented at the National Conference of the Australian Systemic Functional Linguistics Association, University of New England, Armidale, Australia.

Bundy, A. (2004). *Australian and New Zealand information literacy framework: Principles, standards and practices*. Underdale, Australia: Australian and New Zealand Institute for Information Literacy.

Burke, A., & Rowsell, J. (2007). Assessing multimodal learning practices. *E-learning, 4*(3), 329–341. doi:10.2304/elea.2007.4.3.329

Clay, M. M. (1993). *Reading Recovery: A guidebook for teachers in training*. Auckland, New Zealand: Heinemann Education.

Comber, B., Badger, L., Barnett, J., Nixon, H., & Pitt, J. (2001). *Socio-economically disadvantaged students and the development of literacies in school: A longitudinal study* (Vol. 1). Adelaide, Australia: University of South Australia.

Comber, B., & Kamler, B. (2004). Getting out of deficit: Pedagogies of reconnection. *Teaching Education, 15*(3), 293–310. doi:10.1080/1047621042000257225

Comber, B., & Kamler, B. (Eds.). (2005). *Turnaround pedagogies: Literacy interventions for at-risk students*. Newtown, Australia: Primary English Teaching Association.

Compton-Lilly, C. (2007). What can video games teach us about teaching reading? *The Reading Teacher, 60*(8), 718–727. doi:10.1598/RT.60.8.2

Ellingson, L. L. (1998). "Then you know how I feel": Empathy, identification, and reflexivity in fieldwork. *Qualitative Inquiry, 4*(4), 492–514. doi:10.1177/107780049800400405

Ellis, C., & Bochner, A. P. (2000). Autoethnography, personal narrative, reflexivity: Researcher as subject. In N. K. Denzin & Y. S. Lincoln (Eds.), *Handbook of qualitative research* (2nd ed., pp. 733-768). Thousand Oaks, CA: Sage Publications.

Gambrell, L. B. (2005). Reading literature, reading text, reading the Internet: The times they are a'changing. *The Reading Teacher, 58*(6), 588–591. doi:10.1598/RT.58.6.8

Games consoles wrap up boom festive season. (2008, January 19-20). *The Courier Mail*, p. 24.

Gee, J. P. (1996). *Social linguistics and literacies: Ideology in discourses* (2nd ed.). London: Falmer Press.

Gee, J. P. (2003). *What video games have to teach us about learning and literacy*. New York: Palgrave Macmillan.

Gee, J. P. (2004). *Situated language and learning: A critique of traditional school*. New York: Routledge.

Gee, J. P. (2005a). Good video games and good learning. *Phi Kappan Phi Forum, 85*(2), 33–37.

Gee, J. P. (2005b). Learning by design: Good video games as learning machines. *E-learning, 2*(1), 5–16. doi:10.2304/elea.2005.2.1.5

Gee, J. P. (2005c). *Why video games are good for your soul: Pleasure and learning*. Melbourne, Australia: Common Ground Publishing.

GfK Australia. (2008a). *Entertainment media* [web page]. Retrieved January 18, 2008, from http://www.gfk.com.au/

GfK Australia. (2008b). *GfK RT newsletter 3 - 2008*. Retrieved January 10, 2009, from http://www.gfkrt.com/news_events/quarterly_newsletter/index.en.html

Gregory, E., & Williams, A. (2000). *City literacies: Learning to read across generations and cultures*. London: Routledge.

Has txt kild the ritn wd? (2007, October 2). *theage.com.au (Fairfax Digital)*. Retrieved October 2, 2007, from http://www.theage.com.au/news/in-depth/

Henderson, R., & Honan, E. (2008). Digital literacies in two low socioeconomic classrooms: Snapshots of practice. *English Teaching: Practice and Critique, 7*(2), 85–98.

Honan, E. (2006). Deficit discourses within the Digital Divide. *English in Australia, 41*(3), 36–43.

Ikpeze, C. H., & Boyd, F. B. (2007). Web-based inquiry learning: Facilitating thoughtful literacy with WebQuests. *The Reading Teacher, 60*(7), 644–654. doi:10.1598/RT.60.7.5

IncGamers Ltd. (2007). *Worldofwar.net: The unofficial WoW site*. Retrieved June 1, 2008, from http://www.worldofwar.net/

Jenkins, H., Klopfer, E., Squire, K., & Tan, P. (2003). Entering the education arcade. *ACM Computers in Entertainment, 1*(1), 1–11. doi:10.1145/950566.950567

Johnson, S. (2005). *Everything bad is good for you: How today's popular culture is actually making us smarter*. New York: Riverhead Books.

Kamler, B., & Comber, B. (2005). Designing turn-around pedagogies and contesting deficit assumptions. In B. Comber & B. Kamler (Eds.), *Turn-around pedagogies: Literacy interventions for at-risk students* (pp. 1-14). Newtown, Australia: Primary English Teaching Association.

Kerawalla, L., & Crook, C. (2002). Children's computer use at home and at school: Context and continuity. *British Educational Research Journal, 28*(6), 751–771. doi:10.1080/0141192022000019044

Lankshear, C., & Knobel, M. (2007). Researching new literacies: Web 2.0 practices and insider perspectives. *E-learning, 4*(3), 224-240. doi:10.2304/elea.2007.4.3.224

Lenhart, A., Arafeh, S., Smith, A., & Macgill, A. R. (2008). *Writing, technology and teens*. [Report]. Washington, DC: PEW Internet and American Life Project & The National Commission on Writing.

Martin, C., & Murray, L. (2006). Editorial: Digital games in the twenty-first century. *Learning, Media and Technology, 31*(4), 323–327. doi:10.1080/17439880601022940

McClay, J. K., Mackey, M., Carbonaro, M., Szafron, D., & Schaeffer, J. (2007). Adolescents composing fiction in digital game and written formats: Tacit, explicit and metacognitive strategies. *E-learning, 4*(3), 273–284. doi:10.2304/elea.2007.4.3.273

McGinnis, T. A. (2007). Khmer rap boys, X-Men, Asia's fruits, and Dragonball Z: Creating multilingual and multimodal classroom contexts. *Journal of Adolescent & Adult Literacy, 50*(7), 570–579. doi:10.1598/JAAL.50.7.6

Merchant, G. (2007). Mind the gap(s): Discourses and discontinuity in digital literacies. *E-learning, 4*(3), 241–254. doi:10.2304/elea.2007.4.3.241

Moll, L. C., Amanti, C., Neff, D., & Gonzales, N. (1992). Funds of knowledge for teaching: Using a qualitative approach to connect homes and classrooms. *Theory into Practice, XXXI*(2), 132–141.

Mortensen, T. E. (2006). WoW is the new MUD. *Games and Culture, 1*(4), 397–413. doi:10.1177/1555412006292622

Norton-Meier, L. (2005). Joining the video-game literacy club: A reluctant mother tried to join the "flow". *Journal of Adolescent & Adult Literacy, 48*(5), 428–432. doi:10.1598/JAAL.48.5.6

Nurse, hand me the latest video game. (2007, February 21). *The Australian*, p. 3.

Prensky, M. (2001). Digital natives, digital immigrants. *On the Horizon, 9*(5). Retrieved February 12, 2006, from http://www.marcprensky.com/writing

Prensky, M. (2006). *"Don't bother me Mom - I'm learning!"* St. Paul, MN: Paragon House.

Sanford, K., & Madill, L. (2007). Understanding the power of new literacies through video game play and design. *Canadian Journal of Education, 30*(2), 432–455.

Snyder, I. (1996). *Hypertext: The electronic labyrinth*. Carlton South, Australia: Melbourne University Press.

Squire, K. (2002). Cultural framing of computer/ video games. *Game Studies, 2*(1). Retrieved April 5, 2006, from http://gamestudies.org/0102/ squire/

Squire, K., & Jenkins, H. (2003). Harnessing the power of games in education. *Insight, 3* (Vision 1). Retrieved 26 June, 2008, from http://www. iaete.org/insight/articles.cfm?&id=26

Steinkuehler, C. (2004). Learning in massively multiplayer online games. In Y. B. Kafai, W. A. Sandoval, N. Enyedy, A. S. Nixon & F. Herrera (Eds.), *Proceedings of the Sixth National Conference of the Learning Sciences*. Mahwah, NJ: Erlbaum.

Steinkuehler, C. (2006). Massively multiplayer online video gaming as participation in a discourse. *Mind, Culture, and Activity, 13*(1), 38–52. doi:10.1207/s15327884mca1301_4

Steinkuehler, C. (2007). Massively multiplayer online gaming as a constellation of literacy practices. *E-learning, 4*(3), 297–318. doi:10.2304/ elea.2007.4.3.297

Steinkuehler, C., & Williams, D. (2006). Where everybody knows your (screen) name: Online games as "third places". *Journal of Computer-Mediated Communication, 11*(4). doi:10.1111/ j.1083-6101.2006.00300.x

The New London Group. (1996). A pedagogy of multiliteracies: Designing social futures. *Harvard Educational Review, 66*(1), 60–92.

Thott. (2008). *Thottbot: World of Warcraft database*. Retrieved June 1, 2008, from http:// thottbot.com/

Turkle, S. (2003). Collaborative selves, collaborative worlds: Identity in the Information Age. In J. A. Inman, C. Reed & P. Sands (Eds.), *Electronic collaboration in the humanities: Issues and options* (pp. 3-12). Mahwah, NJ: Lawrence Erlbaum Associated.

Violent games make users more aggressive. (2006). *The Australian*. Retrieved January 10, 2006, from http://www.theaustralian.news.com.au

Yee, N. (2008). *The Daedalus Project*. Retrieved January 19, 2008, from http://www.nickyee.com/ daedalus

Young, M., Schrader, P. G., & Zheng, D. (2006). MMOGs as learning environments: An ecological journey into Quest Atlantis and The Sims Online. *Innovate, 4*(2). Retrieved April 2, 2006, from http://www.innovateonlin/info

Compilation of References

Abalhassan, K. M. I. (2002). *English as a foreign language instruction with CALL multimedia in Saudi Arabian private schools: A multi-case and multi-site study of CALL instruction.* Unpublished PhD, Indiana University of Pennsylvania.

Abu Bakar, M., & Abdul Rahim, R. (2005). *A preliminary report on teaching of Malay as a second language in Singapore schools: An analysis of initial data from the Singapore pedagogy Coding Schema.* Retrieved December 7, 2007, from http://crpp.nie.edu.sg/file.php/337/RRS05-003 final version.pdf

Adams, C. (2007). On the 'informed use' of PowerPoint: Rejoining Vallance and Towndrow. *Journal of Curriculum Studies, 39*(2), 229–233. doi:10.1080/00220270601175246

Adams, T. (2006). PowerPoint, habits of mind, and classroom culture. *Journal of Curriculum Studies, 38*(4), 389–411. doi:10.1080/00220270600579141

Adamthwaite, K., Ellis, D., Lowe, P., Rocca, R., Wesley, A., & Worth, M. (2006) *Cambridge Senior Design and Technology.* Melbourne, Australia: Cambridge University Press.

Al-Ahaydib, M. E. A. (1986). *Teaching English as a foreign language in the intermediate and secondary schools of Saudi Arabia: A diagnostic study.* Unpublished PhD, University of Kansas.

Aland, J. (2004). The impact of digital technologies on contemporary visual arts education. *Australian Art Education, 27*(2), 4–21.

Alexander, B. (2008). Web 2.0 and emergent multiliteracies. *Theory into Practice, 47,* 150–160. doi:10.1080/00405840801992371

Alexander, P. A., & Fox, E. (2004). A historical perspective on reading research and practice. In R. B. Ruddell & N. J. Unrau (Eds.), *Theoretical models and processes of reading* (5th ed., pp. 33-68). Newark, DE: International Reading Association.

Al-Juhani, S. O. (1991). *The effectiveness of computer-assisted instruction in teaching English as a foreign language in Saudi secondary schools.* Unpublished PhD, University of Denver.

Al-Kahtani, S. (2004). Deterrents to CALL in Saudi Arabia. *Essential Teacher, 1*(3), 26–30.

Al-Kahtani, S. A. (2001). *Computer-assisted language learning in EFL instruction at selected Saudi Arabian universities: Profiles of faculty.* Indiana University of Pennsylvania, PA.

Al-Kamookh, A. (1983). *A survey of the English language teachers' perceptions of the English language teaching methods in the intermediate and secondary schools of the eastern province in Saudi Arabia.* Kansas: University of Kansas.

Al-Mazroou, R. A. Y. (1988). *An evaluative study of teaching English as a foreign language in secondary schools in Saudi Arabia as perceived by Saudi EFL teachers.* Unpublished M.A, Southern Illinois University, Carbondale.

Alvermann, D. E. (2002). *Adolescents and literacies in a digital world.* New York: Peter Lang.

Alvermann, D. E. (2002). Effective literacy instruction for adolescents. *Journal of Literacy Research, 34*(2), 189–208. doi:10.1207/s15548430jlr3402_4

Alvermann, D. E., Moon, J. S., & Hagood, M. C. (1999). *Popular culture in the classroom: Teaching and researching critical media literacy.* Newark, DE: International Reading Association.

Anderson, J. D. (1993). Power, privilege, and public education: Reflections on savage inequalities. *Educational Theory, 43*(1), 1–10. doi:10.1111/j.1741-5446.1993.00001.x

Anderson, R. E., & Ronnkvist, A. (1999). The presence of computers in American schools. *Teaching, learning and computing: 1998 national survey.* (Center for Research on Information Technology and Organizations Report No. 2). Retrieved April 25, 2006, from http://www.crito.uci.edu/tlc/findings/Computers_in_American_Schools/reprot2_text_tables.pdf

Anstey, M., & Bull, G. (2004). *The literacy labyrinth* (2nd Ed.). Sydney: Pearson Education Australia.

Anstey, M., & Bull, G. (2006). *Teaching and learning multiliteracies: changing times, changing literacies.* Newark, DE: International Reading Association.

Apple, M. W. (2007). Ideological success, educational failure? On the politics of No Child Left Behind. *Journal of Teacher Education, 58*, 108–116. doi:10.1177/0022487106297844

Archer, L. (2007). Kevin Rudd promises computers for every student. *news.com.au.* Retrieved January 20, 2009, from www.news.com.au/story/0,23599,22754187-2,00.html?from=public_rss

Archibald, A. (2004). *Writing in a second language.* Retrieved February 13, 2008, from http://llas.ac.uk/resources/goodpractice.aspx 157

Atkinson, C. (2005). *Beyond bullets: People communicating with people.* Retrieved March 29, 2008, from http://socialble media.typepad.com/beyond-bullets/

Attewell, P. (2001). The first and second digital divides. *Sociology of Education, 74*(3), 252–259. doi:10.2307/2673277

Australian Council of Deans of Education. (2001). *New learning: A charter for Australian education.* Canberra, Australia: Australian Council of Deans of Education.

Australian Labor Party. (2007). *The Australian economy needs an education revolution* (Policy paper). Retrieved January 20, 2009, from www.alp.org.au/download/now/education-revolution.pdf

Aviram, A. (2001). The integration of ICT and education: From computers in the classroom, to mindful radical adaptation of educational systems to the emerging cyber culture. *Journal of Educational Change, 1*, 331–352. doi:10.1023/A:1010082722912

Baelstri, D., Ehrman, S., & Ferguson, D. (Eds.). (1992). *Learning to design, designing to learn: Using technology to transform the curriculum.* New York: Taylor and Francis.

Bakhtin, M. M. (1981). *The dialogic imagination: Four essays by M. M. Bakhtin.* Austin: University of Texas Press.

Bamford, A. (2006). *The Wow Factor: Global research compendium of the arts in education.* Berlin: Waxmann.

Barlex, D. (Ed.). (2007). *Design & technology for the next generation: a collection of provocative pieces, written by experts in their field, to stimulate reflection and curriculum innovation.* Whitchurch, Australia: Cliffeco Communications

Barnes & Noble. (2006). *SparkNotes LLC.* Retrieved 26 May, 2008, from http://www.sparknotes.com/lit/

Barron, B. J. S. (1998). Doing with understanding: Lessons from research on problem and project-based learning. *Journal of the Learning Sciences, 7*(3/4), 1179–1187.

Barton, D., & Hamilton, M. (2000). Literacy practices. In D. Barton, M. Hamilton, & R. Ivonic (Eds.), *Situated literacies: Reading and writing in context (pp. 7-15).* New York: Routledge.

Baruch, Y. (1999). Response rates in academic studies: A comparative analysis. *Human Relations, 52*(4), 421–438.

Bates, J. M. (1997). Measuring predetermined socio-economic 'inputs' when assessing the efficiency of educational outputs. *Applied Economics, 29*, 85–93. doi:10.1080/000368497327434

Batstone, R. (2002). Making sense of new language: A discourse perspective. *Language Awareness, 11*(1), 14–29. doi:10.1080/09658410208667043

Baum, W. K. (1987). *Oral history of the local historical society.* Nashville, TN: American Association for State and Local History.

Beach, R. (2000). Using media ethnographies to study response to media as activity. In A. Watts Paillotet & P. Mosenthal (Eds.), *Reconceptualizing literacy in the media age* (pp. 3-39). Stamford, CT: JAI Press.

Beavis, C. (2006). *Lara meets literacy: Computer games and English.* Retrieved April 19, 2007, from http://www.sofweb.vic.edu.aa/english

Beavis, C., & Charles, C. (2005). Writing, English and digital culture. In B. Doecke & G. Parr (Eds.), *Writing = learning* (pp. 229-246). Kent Town, Australia: Wakefield Press.

Beavis, C., & O'Mara, J. (2006). Preparing English teachers for a changing world. In B. Doecke, M. Howie & W. Sawyer (Eds.), *"Only connect... ": English teaching, schooling and community* (pp. 349-355). Kent Town, Australia: Wakefield Press.

Becker, H. J. (1999). Internet use by teachers: Conditions of professional use and teacher-directed student use. *Teaching, learning and computing: 1998 national survey.* (Center for Research on Information Technology and Organizations Report No. 1). Retrieved April 14, 2006, from http://www.vermontinstitutes.org/tech/research/i-use-teach.pdf

BECTA. (2001). *Primary Schools of the Future–Achieving Today.* London: British Educational Communications and Technology Agency.

BECTA. (2005). *Learning lessons from digital games: What can games teach us about narrative?* Coventry, UK: BECTA.

Belle, G. G., & Soetaert, R. (2001). Breakdown into the virtual user-involved design and learning. *Journal of Technology and Teacher Education, 9*, 31–42.

Benigno, V., Bocconi, S., & Ott, M. (2007). Inclusive education: Helping teachers to choose ICT resources and to use them effectively. *eLearning Papers, 6*, 1-13.

Berieter, C., & Scardamalia, M. (2003). *Learning to work creatively with knowledge.* Retrieved August 4, 2008 from http://www-personal.umich.edu/~jaylemke/courses/ED750/Scardamalia_Bereiter_KBuilding.pdf.

Biesenbach, L. S., & Weasenforth, D. (2001). E-mail and word processing in the ESL classroom: How the medium affects the message. *Language Learning & Technology, 5*(1), 135–165.

Billett, S. (2006). *Work, change and workers.* Dordrecht: Springer

Black, R. (2005). Access and affiliation: The literacy and composition practices of English language learners in an online fanfiction community. *Journal of Adolescent & Adult Literacy, 49*, 118–128. doi:10.1598/JAAL.49.2.4

Black, R. (2006). Language, culture, and identity in online fanfiction. *E-Learning, 3*, 170–184. doi:10.2304/elea.2006.3.2.170

Bligh, A. (2002). *Qld State schools to share in more than $18 million to boost ICTs.* Retrieved September 20, 2008, from http://www.education.qld.gov.au/itt/learning/docs/ictl-grant-1instal.doc

Blizzard Entertainment. (2004). *World of Warcraft™* [Game]. Irvine, CA: Blizzard Entertainment.

Blizzard Entertainment. (2004). *World of Warcraft™game manual.* Irvine, CA: Blizzard Entertainment.

Blizzard Entertainment. (2008). *Welcome to World of Warcraft.com.* Retrieved June 1, 2008, from http://www.worldofwarcraft.com/index.xml

Blizzard Entertainment. (2008). *World of Warcraft Reaches New Milestone: 10 Million Subscribers.* Retrieved June 13, 2008 from: http://www.blizzard.com/us/press/080122.html.

Blizzard Entertainment. (2008, December 2008). *World of Warcraft subscriber base reaches 11.5 million worldwide.* Retrieved January 10, 2009, from http://www.blizzard.com/us/press/081121.html

Bloch, J. (2004). Second language cyber rhetoric: A study of Chinese second language writers in an online usenet group. *Language Learning & Technology, 8*(3), 66–82.

Bloch, J. (2006). Abdullah's blogging: A generation 1.5 student enters the blogosphere. *Language Learning & Technology, 11*(2), 128–141.

Bogdan, R., & Biklen, S. (1998). *Qualitative research in education: An introduction to theory and methods.* Needham Heights, MA: Allyn & Bacon.

Bonk, C. J., & King, K. S. (Eds.). (1998). *Electronic Collaborators: Learner-Centered Technologies for Literacy, Apprenticeship, and Discourse.* Mahwah, NJ: Lawrence Erlbaum Associates.

Bracewell, R. (1978, March). *The development of audience awareness in writing.* Paper presented at the Annual Meeting of the American Educational Research Association, Toronto.

Brazilai-Nahon, K. (2006). Gaps and bits: Conceptualizing measurement for digital divide/s. *The Information Society, 22*(5), 269–278. doi:10.1080/01972240600903953

Bromley, K. (2006). Technology and writing. In M.C. McKenna, L. Labbo, R.D. Kieffer, & D. Reinking, (Eds.), *International handbook of literacy and technology: Volume II.* (pp. 349-361). Mahwah, NJ: Lawrence Erlbaum Associates.

Bronack, S. (2006, Spring). Learning unplugged: The Internet divide in American schools. *Electronic Magazine of Multicultural Education, 8*(1). Retrieved August 22, 2006, from http://www.eastern.edu/publications/emme/2006spring/bronack.html

Brown, J. S., & Thomas, D. (2006). You play World of WarCraft? You're hired!: Why multiplayer games may be the best kind of job training. *Wired Magazine, 14*(4). Retrieved April 3, 2006, from http://www.wired.com

Bruce, C. S. (1997). *Seven Faces of Information Literacy.* Adelaide, Australia: AUSLIB Press.

Bruce, C. S. (2002). Information literacy as a catalyst for educational change: A background paper. In *Proceedings Information Literacy Meeting of Experts,* Prague, The Czech Republic. Retrieved October 14, 2007 from, http://dlist.sir.arizona.edu/archive/00000300/.

Bruton, A. (2005). Process writing and communicative-task-based instruction: Many common features, but more common limitations? *Teaching English as a Second or Foreign Language, 9*(3), 1–31.

Buckingham, D. (1993). *Changing literacies: Media education and modern culture.* London: Tufnell Press.

Buckingham, D. (1993). English and media studies: Making the difference. *English Quarterly, 25*(4), 8.

Buckingham, D., & Burn, A. (2007). Game literacy in theory and practice. *Journal of Educational Multimedia and Hypermedia, 16*(3), 323–349.

Bulfin, S., & North, S. (2006, September 27-29). *The literate places and spaces in/between: Reframing the school-home binary.* Paper presented at the National Conference of the Australian Systemic Functional Linguistics Association, University of New England, Armidale, Australia.

Bulger, M., Mayer, R. E., & Almeroth, K. C. (2008). Measuring learner engagement in computer-equipped college classrooms. *Journal of Educational Multimedia and Hypermedia, 17*(2), 129–144.

Bundy, A. (2004). *Australian and New Zealand information literacy framework: Principles, standards and practices.* Underdale, Australia: Australian and New Zealand Institute for Information Literacy.

Burke, A., & Rowsell, J. (2007). Assessing multimodal learning practices. *E-learning, 4*(3), 329–341. doi:10.2304/elea.2007.4.3.329

Burn, A., & Parker, D. (2001). Making your mark: Digital inscription, animation and a new visual semiotic. [ECI]. *Education Communication and Information, 1*(2), 155–179. doi:10.1080/14636310120091913

Burn, A., & Parker, D. (2003). Tiger's big plan: Multimodality and the moving image. In C. Jewitt & G. Kress (Eds.), *Multimodal Literacy* (pp. 56-72). New York: Peter Lang.

Burns, R. (2000). *Introduction to Research Methods.* (4th ed.). Frenchs Forest, Australia: Pearson Education.

Butzin, S. M. (2000). Project CHILD: A decade of success for young children. *Technology Horizons in Education Journal, 27*(11). Available online http://www.thejournal.com/magazine/vault/A2882B.cfm

Canale, M., & Swain, M. (1980). Theoretical bases of communicative approaches to second language teaching and testing. *Applied Linguistics, 1*(1), 1–47. doi:10.1093/applin/1.1.1

Carley, K. (1990). Content analysis. In R. E. Asher (Ed.), *The encyclopedia of language and linguistics* (pp. 725-730). Edinburgh: Pergamon Press.

Carley, K. (1993). Coding choices for textual analysis: A comparison of content analysis and map analysis. *Sociological Methodology, 23*, 75–126. doi:10.2307/271007

Carley, K., & Palmquist, M. (1992). Extracting, representing, and analyzing mental models. *Social Forces, 70*(3), 601–636. doi:10.2307/2579746

Carvin, A. (2002, April 1). Digital divide still very real. *Cnet News.* Retrieved April 17, 2007, from http://news.com.com.Digital+divide+still+very+real/2010-1071_3-872138.html

Castek, J., Coiro, J., Hartman, D. K., Henry, L. A., Leu, D. J., & Zawilinski, L. (2007). New literacies, new challenges, and new opportunities. In M. B. Sampson, P. E. Linder, F. Falk-Ross, M. M. Foote, & S. Szabo (Eds.), *Multiple literacies in the 21st century: The twenty-eighth yearbook of the college reading association (pp. 31-50).* Logan, UT: College Reading Association.

Cazden, C. (2000). Four innovative programs: A postscript from Alice Springs. In B. Cope & M. Kalantzis (Eds.), *Multiliteracies: Literacy learning and the design of social futures* (pp. 321-348). London: Routledge.

Celce-Murcia, M. (2007). Rethinking the role of communicative competence in language teaching. In E. A. N. Soler & M. P. S. Jordà (Eds.), *Intercultural language use and language learning.* Netherlands: Springer Netherlands.

Cellular-News. (2009). *Student Arrested for Refusing to Stop Texting in Class.* Retrieved February 22, 2009, from http://www.cellular-news.com/story/36173.php

CEO Forum on Education & Technology. (1999, February). *Professional development: A link to better learning* (Year 2 STaR report). Washington, DC: Author.

Chambers, D. P., & Stacey, K. (2005). Developing and using multimedia effectively for undergraduate teacher education. *Australasian Journal of Educational Technology, 21*(2), 211–221.

Chandler, J. (2003). The efficacy of various kinds of error feedback for improvement in the accuracy and fluency of second language student writing. *Journal of Second Language Writing, 12*, 267–296. doi:10.1016/S1060-3743(03)00038-9

Chandler-Olcott, K., & Mahar, D. (2003). "Tech-savviness" meets multiliteracies: Exploring adolescent girls' technology-related literacy practices. *Reading Research Quarterly, 38*, 356–385. doi:10.1598/RRQ.38.3.3

Chaunce, S. (1994). *Oral history and the local historian.* London: Longman.

Chen, S. Y., & Macredie, R. D. (2002). Cognitive styles and hypermedia navigation: Development of a learning model. *Journal of the American Society for Information Science and Technology, 53*, 3–15. doi:10.1002/asi.10023

Chen, Y. H. (2005). Computer mediated communication: The use of CMC to develop EFL learners' communicative competence. *Asian EFL Journal, 7*(1), 167–182.

Chesher, C. (2005). *Blogs and the crisis of authorship.* Retrieved May 29, 2008, from http://incsub.org/blogtalk/?page_id=40.

Clarke, C. (2003). *Towards a unified e-learning strategy.* Consultation Document, Department for education and skills. UK: UK Department of Education and Skills.

Clarke, M. A. (2007). *Creativity in modern foreign languages teaching and learning.* Higher Education Academy Report.

Clay, M. (1993). *An observation survey of early literacy achievement.* Portsmouth, NH: Heinemann.

Clay, M. M. (1993). *Reading Recovery: A guidebook for teachers in training.* Auckland, New Zealand: Heinemann Education.

Coiro, J. (2003). Reading comprehension on the Internet: Expanding our understanding of reading comprehension to encompass new literacies. *The Reading Teacher, 56*(6), 458–465.

Coiro, J. (2007). *Exploring changes to reading comprehension on the Internet: Paradoxes and possibilities for diverse adolescent readers.* Unpublished doctoral dissertation. University of Connecticut, Storrs.

Coiro, J., & Dobler, B. (2007). Exploring the comprehension strategies used by sixth-grade skilled readers as they search for and locate information on the Internet. *Reading Research Quarterly, 42*(2), 214–257. doi:10.1598/RRQ.42.2.2

Coiro, J., Knobel, M., Lankshear, C., & Leu, D. J. (2008). *Handbook of New Literacies.* Hillsdale, NJ: Lawrence Erlbaum Associates.

Cole, D. R., & Throssell, P. (2008). Epiphanies in action: Teaching and learning in synchronous harmony. *The International Journal of Learning, 15*(7), 175–184.

Cole, D., & Moyle, V. (In press). Cam-capture literacy and its incorporation into multiliteracies. In D. Pullen, & D. Cole (Eds.), *Multiliteracies and Technology enhanced Education: Social Practice and the Global Classroom.* Hershey, PA: IGI Global.

Cole, M. (1996). *Cultural psychology: A once and future discipline.* Cambridge, MA: Harvard University Press.

Collins, S., Cornius-Randall, R., Annetts, P., Annetts, S., Hampson, R., McMurtie, Y., et al. (2006). *Switched on: technology Stage 4.* Milton: Wiley & Sons.

Collis, B. A., & Lai, K. W. (1996). Information technology and children from a classroom perspective. In B. A. Collis, G. A. Knezek, K. W. Lai, K. T. Miyashita, W. J. Pelgrum, T. Plomp, & T. Sakamoto (Eds.), *Children and computers in school* (pp. 43-68). Mahwah, NJ: Erlbaum.

Comber, B., & Kamler, B. (2004). Getting out of deficit: Pedagogies of reconnection. *Teaching Education, 15*(3), 293–310. doi:10.1080/1047621042000257225

Comber, B., & Kamler, B. (Eds.). (2005). *Turn-around pedagogies: Literacy interventions for at-risk students.* Newtown, Australia: Primary English Teaching Association.

Comber, B., Badger, L., Barnett, J., Nixon, H., & Pitt, J. (2001). *Socio-economically disadvantaged students and the development of literacies in school: A longitudinal study* (Vol. 1). Adelaide, Australia: University of South Australia.

Compton-Lilly, C. (2007). What can video games teach us about teaching reading? *The Reading Teacher, 60*(8), 718–727. doi:10.1598/RT.60.8.2

Connecticut Alliance for Great Schools (CTAGS). (n.d.). *The achievement gap.* Retrieved August 26, 2006 from http://www.ctags.org/gap.php

Cooper, M. (2002). *Does the digital divide still exist? Bush administration shrugs, but evidence says "Yes".* Washington, DC: Consumer Federation of America. Retrieved April 15, 2007, from http://www.comsumerfed.org/DigitalDivideReport20020530.pdf

Coorey, P. (2007). Rudd vows education revolution. *The Sydney Morning Herald,* Jan 23, 2007. Retrieved January 20, 2009, from www.smh.com.au/news/national/rudd-vows-educationrevolution/2007/01/22/1169330827940.html?page=fullpag

Cope, B., & Kalantzis, M. (1997). *Productive diversity: A new Australian model for work and management.* Annandale, Australia: Pluto Press.

Cope, B., & Kalantzis, M. (2000). Designs for social futures. In B. Cope & M. Kalantzis (Eds.), *Multiliteracies: Literacy learning and the design of social futures* (pp. 203-238). London: Routledge.

Cope, B., & Kalantzis, M. (Eds.). (2000). *Multiliteracies: Literacy learning and the design of social futures.* London: Routledge.

Cowley, D. (2007). *Design and Technology: The Leading edge VCE Units 3 & 4,* Melbourne: Pearson Education.

Cox, M., & Abbot, C. (Eds.). (2004). *A review of research literature relating to ICT and attainment.* Coventry, Becta/London: Deparment of Children, School and Families.

Crow, D. (2006). *Left to right: The cultural shift from words to pictures.* Lausanne, Switzerland: AVA Publishing.

Csikszentmihalyi, M. (1990). *Flow: The psychology of optimal experience.* New York: Harper Perennial.

Cuban, L. (2001). *Oversold and underused: Computers in the classroom.* Cambridge, MA: Harvard University Press.

Cuban, L. (2004). Meeting challenges in urban schools. *Educational Leadership, 61*(7), 64–69.

Cuban, L., Kirkpatrick, H., & Peck, C. (2001). High access and low use of technologies in high school classrooms: Explaining an apparent paradox. *American Educational Research Journal, 38*(4), 813–834. doi:10.3102/00028312038004813

Culham, R. (2003). *6+1 traits of writing: The complete guide to grades three and up.* Northwest Regional Laboratory. New York: Scholastic.

Daker, J. (Ed.). (2006). *Defining technological literacy: towards an epistemological framework.* Basingstoke: Palgrave MacMillan.

Daley, E. (2002). *Multimedia literacy.* Retrieved 22/11/2008, from http://www.si.umich.edu/about-SI/news-detail.htm?NewsItemID=136

Davis, D. (2008). *First we see: The national review of visual education.* Canberra, Australia: Australian Government.

Davis, L. (Ed.). (2003). *Shakespeare matters: History, teaching, performance.* Newark, DE: University of Delaware Press.

Dawes, L. (2001). What stops teachers using new technology? In M. Leask (Ed.), *Issues in teaching using ICT* (pp. 61-79). Florence, KY: Routledge.

DCSF. (2004). Department for Children, Schools and Families (UK). *ICT in schools survey 2004.* Retrieved January 10, 2009, from http://publications.teachernet.gov.uk/default.aspx?PageFunction=productdetails&PageMode=publications&ProductId=DFES-1122-2004& Dearing, R. (1997). *Higher education in the learning society. London, United Kingdom: National Committee of Inquiry into Higher Education.* Retrieved July 26, 2007, from http://www.leeds.ac.uk/educol/ncihe/

de Certeau, M. (1984). *The practice of everyday life.* Berkeley, CA: University of California Press.

De Vries, M. (2007). Philosophical reflections on the nature of design & technology, in Barlex D (ed). Design & technology: for the next generation: *a collection of provocative pieces, written by experts in their field, to stimulate reflection and curriculum innovation.* Whitchurch: Cliffeco Communications. pp. 20-33.

Deaney, R., Ruthven, K., & Hennessy, S. (2004). *Teachers developing practical theories of the contribution of ICT to subject teaching and learning: An analysis of cases from English Secondary School.* Cambridge, UK: University of Cambridge.

Dede, C. (1997). Rethinking how to invest in technology. *Educational Leadership,* (November): 12–16.

Dede, C. (2008). New horizons: A seismic shift in epistemology. *EDUCAUSE Review, 43*(3), 80–81.

Delpit, L. (1995). *Other people's children: Cultural conflict in the classroom.* New York: Free Press.

DETYA. (2000). *Learning for the knowledge society: An education and training action plan for the information economy.* Canberra, Australia: Department of Education, Training and Youth Affairs. Retrieved November 4, 2007 from http://www.dest.gov.au/sectors/school_education/publications_resources/summaries_brochures/learning_for_the_knowledge_society.htm

Dewan, S., & Riggins, F. J. (2005). The digital divide: Current and future research directions. *Journal of Association for Information Systems, 6*(2), 298–337.

Dillon, A., McKnight, C., & Richardson, J. (1990). Navigation in hypertext: A critical review of the concept. In D. Diaper, D. Gilmore, G. Cockton, & B. Shackel (Eds.), *Human-Computer Interaction: INTERACT 90* (pp. 58-592). Amsterdam: Elsevier.

Dimitriadis, G., & McCarthy, C. (2001). *Reading and teaching the postcolonial: From Baldwin to Basquiat and beyond.* New York: Teachers College Press.

Dolence, M. G., & Norris, D. M. (1995). *Transforming Higher Education: A Vision for Learning in the 21st Century.* Ann Arbor, MI: Society for College and University Planning.

Donnelly, K. (2006). The Muffled Canon. *The Weekend Australian,* May 5th, 2006, 20. Ethell, R. G., & McMeniman, M. (2000). Unlocking the knowledge in action of an expert practitioner. *Journal of Teacher Education, 51*(2), 87–101.

Dornan, R., Rosea, L., & Wilson, M. (2003). *Within and beyond writing process in the Secondary English classroom.* Upper Saddle River, NJ: Allyn and Bacon, Pearson Education.

Dressman, M., O'Brien, D., Rogers, T., Ivey, G., Wilder, P., & Alvermann, D. (2005). Problematizing adolescent literacies: Four instances, multiple perspectives. In J.V. Hoffman, D.L. Shallert, C.M. Fairbanks, J. Worthy, & B. Maloch (Eds.), *55th yearbook of the National Reading Conference* (pp. 141-154). Oak Creek, WI: National Reading Conference.

Dyril, O. E., & Kinnaman, D. E. (1994). Integrating technology into our classroom curriculum. *Technology & Learning, 14*(5), 38–42.

Eagleton, M. B., & Dobler, E. (2007). *Reading the web: Strategies for Internet inquiry.* New York: The Guilford Press.

Eastin, M. S., & LaRose, R. (2000). Internet self-efficacy and the psychology of the digital divide. *Journal of Computer-Mediated Communication, 6*(1), 25–56.

Easy Lingo. (2006). Instant translator English-Arabic. Aramedia.

Editorial Projects in Education (EPE) Research Center. (2007, March). *Technology counts 2007: A digital decade.* Bethesda, MD: Education Week.

Edmiston, B. (2000). Drama as ethical education. *Research in Drama Education, 5,* 63–84. doi:10.1080/135697800114203

Ehrmann, S. (1995). New technology, old trap. *Educational Review, 30*(5), 41–43.

Ellingson, L. L. (1998). "Then you know how I feel": Empathy, identification, and reflexivity in fieldwork. *Qualitative Inquiry, 4*(4), 492–514. doi:10.1177/107780049800400405

Ellis, C., & Bochner, A. P. (2000). Autoethnography, personal narrative, reflexivity: Researcher as subject. In N. K. Denzin & Y. S. Lincoln (Eds.), *Handbook of qualitative research* (2nd ed., pp. 733-768). Thousand Oaks, CA: Sage Publications.

Ellis, R. (2003). *Task-based language learning and teaching.* Oxford, UK: Oxford University Press.

Ellsworth, E. (1989). Why doesn't this feel empowering? Working through the repressive myths of critical pedagogy. *Harvard Educational Review, 59*(3), 303–314.

Engestrom, Y., & Miettinen, R. (1999). Introduction. In Y. Engestrom, R. Miettinen, & R. Punamaki (Eds.), *Perspectives on activity theory* (pp. 1-16). Cambridge, UK: Cambridge University Press.

European University Association. (2007). *Creativity in Higher Education.* Report on the EUA Creativity Project 2006 – 2007. Retrieved on January 15th 2007 from <www.eua.be/fileadmin/user_upload/files/Publications/Creativity_in_higher_education.pdf>

Fairclough, N. (1992). *Discourse and social change.* Cambridge, UK: Polity Press.

Fairclough, N. (2003). *Analyzing discourse.* London: Routledge.

Fairlie, R. W. (2005, September 20). Are we really a notion online? Ethnic and racial disparities in access to technology and their consequences. *FreePress*. Retrieved September 3, 2006, from http://www.freepress.net/docs/lccrdigitaldivide.pdf

Fallows, D. (2004). The Internet and daily life. *Pew Internet and American Life Project*. Retrieved August 17, 2006, from http://www.pewinternet.org/pdfs/PIP_Internet_and_Daily_Life.pdf

Farabaugh, R. (2007). "The Isle Is Full of Noises": Using wiki software to establish a discourse community in a Shakespeare classroom. *Multilingual Matters, 16*(1), 41–56.

Fearn, L., & Farnan, N. (2001). *Interactions: Teaching writing and the language arts.* Boston: Houghton Mifflin Company.

Feeberg, A. (1991). *Critical theory of technology.* New York: Oxford University Press.

Feez, S. (2002). Heritage and innovation in second language education. In A. M. Johns (Ed.), *Genre in the classroom* (pp. 47-68). Mahwah, NJ: Lawrence Erlbaum Associates.

Ferris, D. (2004). The "Grammar Correction" Debate in second language writing: Where are we, and where do we go from here? (and what do we do in the meantime…?). *Journal of Second Language Writing, 13*, 49–62. doi:10.1016/j.jslw.2004.04.005

Ferris, D. (2007). Preparing teachers to respond to students' writing. *Journal of Second Language Writing, 16*, 165–193. doi:10.1016/j.jslw.2007.07.003

Finger, G., Russell, G., Jamieson-Proctor, R., & Russell, N. (2007). *Transforming learning with ICT: Making IT Happen!* Sydney: Pearson.

Forsyth, I. (1996). *Teaching and learning materials and the Internet.* London: Kogan Page.

Fosnot, C. (1996). *Constructivism: Theory, perspectives, and practice.* New York: Teachers College Press.

Franks, A., Durran, J., & Burn, A. (2006). Stories of the three-legged stool: English, media, drama, from critique to production. *English Education, 40*(1), 63–78.

Fredricks, J. A., Blumenfeld, P. C., & Paris, A. H. (2004). School engagement: Potential of the concept, state of the evidence. *Review of Educational Research, 74*(1), 59–109. doi:10.3102/00346543074001059

Freebody, P. (2007). Building literacy education: pasts, futures, and "the sum of effort". In A. Simpson (Ed.). *Future Directions in Literacy: International Conversations conference 2007*, (pp. 96 – 114). Sydney: Sydney University Press.

Freebody, P., & Luke, A. (1990). Literacies programs: Debates and demands in cultural context. *Prospect: Australian Journal of TESOL, 5*(3), 7–16.

Freebody, P., & Luke, A. (2003). Literacy as engaging with new forms of life: the "four roles" model. In Anstey M & Bull G (Eds), *The literacy lexicon* (2nd Ed., pp. 51-65). Sydney: Pearson Education.

Freesmith, D. (2006). The politics of the English curriculum: Ideology in the campaign against critical literacy in The Australian. *Engineers Australia, 41*(1), 25–30.

Freire, P., & Macedo, D. (1987). *Reading the word and world.* South Hadley, MA: Bergin & Garvey.

Friedman, T. L. (2005). *The world is flat: A brief history of the twenty-first century.* New York: Farrar, Straus, & Giroux.

Fulford, C. P. (2001). A model of cognitive speed. *International Journal of Instructional Media, 28*(1), 31–42.

Gagnon, G., & Collay, M. (2001). *Constructivist learning design.* Retrieved 06/02/2006, from http://www.prainbow.com/cld/cldp.html

Gambrell, L. B. (2005). Reading literature, reading text, reading the Internet: The times they are a'changing. *The Reading Teacher, 58*(6), 588–591. doi:10.1598/RT.58.6.8

Games consoles wrap up boom festive season. (2008, January 19-20). *The Courier Mail*, p. 24.

Gardner, H. (1993). *Frames of mind: the theory of multiple intelligences*. New York: Basic Books.

Garner, S., & Evans, M. (1996). Communications in design. In J. Williams, & Williams, A., (ed.), *Technology education for teachers* (pp. 111-135). Melbourne: MacMillan Education.

Gates, W. H. (2007, March). Written testimony of William H. Gates, Chairman, Microsoft Corporation: Before the committee on Health, Education, Labor and Pensions, U.S. Senate. *Business Week*. Retrieved March 14, 2007, from http://www.businessweek.com/bwdaily/dnflash/content/mar2007/db20070307_617500.htm

Gee, J. (1994). Orality and literacy: from the savage mind to ways with words. In J. Maybin & J. Clevedon (Eds), *Language and literacy in social practice*. Multilingual Matters Ltd & The Open University.

Gee, J. (2007). *Good video games and good learning: Collected essays on video games, learning, and literacy*. New York: P. Lang.

Gee, J. P. (1996). *Social linguistics and literacies: Ideology in discourses* (2nd ed.). London: Falmer Press.

Gee, J. P. (2000). New people in new worlds: Networks, the new capitalism and schools. In B. Cope & M. Kalantzis (Eds.), *Multiliteracies: Literacy learning and the design of social futures* (pp. 43-68). New York: Routledge.

Gee, J. P. (2003). *What video games have to teach us about learning and literacy*. New York: Palgrave/St. Martin's.

Gee, J. P. (2004). *Situated language in learning: A critique of traditional schooling*. London: Routledge.

Gee, J. P. (2005). Good video games and good learning. *Phi Kappan Phi Forum*, *85*(2), 33–37.

Gee, J. P. (2005). Learning by design: Good video games as learning machines. *E-learning*, *2*(1), 5–16. doi:10.2304/elea.2005.2.1.5

Gee, J. P. (2005). *Why video games are good for your soul: Pleasure and learning*. Melbourne, Australia: Common Ground Publishing.

Gee, J. P. (2006). Foreword. In D. W. Shaffer, *How computer games help children learn* (pp. ix-xii). New York: Palgrave/Macmillan.

Gee, J. P. (2006). Self-fashioning and shape-shifting: Language, identity, and social class. In D. Alvermann, K. Hinchman, D. Moore, S. F. Phelps & D. R. Waff (Eds.), *Reconceptualizing the literacies in adolescents' lives* (2nd ed., pp. 165-185). Mahwah, NJ: Lawrence Erlbaum Associates.

Gee, J., Hull, G., & Lankshear, C. (1996). *The new work order: behind the language of the new capitalism*. Sydney: Allen & Unwin.

GfK Australia. (2008a). *Entertainment media* [web page]. Retrieved January 18, 2008, from http://www.gfk.com.au/

GfK Australia. (2008b). *GfK RT newsletter 3 - 2008*. Retrieved January 10, 2009, from http://www.gfkrt.com/news_events/quarterly_newsletter/index.en.html

Gibson, J. J. (1986). *The ecological approach to visual perception*. Hillsdale, NJ: Lawrence Erlbaum Associates.

Gibson, S., & Oberg, D. (2004). Visions and realities of Internet use in schools: Canadian perspectives. *British Journal of Educational Technology*, *35*(5), 569–585. doi:10.1111/j.0007-1013.2004.00414.x

Gilster, P. (1997). *Digital literacy*. New York: John Wiley.

Gitsaki, C., & Taylor, R. P. (2000). *Internet English: WWW-based communication activities*. Oxford: Oxford University Press.

Goldlove, B. (2008). Reading ability in school leavers: The computer generation. *Daily Mail conference report*, 22.5.08.

Goldman, S. R. (2004). Cognitive aspects of constructing meaning through and across multiple texts. In N. Shuart-Ferris & D. M. Bloome (Eds.), *Uses of intertextuality in classroom and educational research* (pp. 313-347). Greenwich, CT: Information Age Publishing.

Goodson, I. F., & Mangan, J. M. (1996). Computer literacy as ideology. *British Journal of Sociology of Education, 17*(1), 65–79. doi:10.1080/0142569960170105

Goodyear, P., & Jones, C. (2003). Implicit theories of learning and change: Their role in the development environments for higher education. In S. Naidu (Ed.), *Learning and teaching with technological practices.* London: Kogan Page.

Goslee, S., & Conte, C. (1998). *Losing ground bit by bit: Low-income communities in the information age.* Retrieved August 12, 2006, from the Benton Foundation Web site: http://www.benton.org/PUBLIBRARY/losing-ground/home.html

Green, B., & Bigum, C. (1993). Aliens in the classroom. *Australian Journal of Education, 37*(2), 119–141.

Green, J. M. (1993). Student attitudes toward communicative and non-communicative activities: Do enjoyment and effectiveness go together? *Modern Language Journal, 77*(1), 1–10. doi:10.2307/329552

Gregory, E., & Williams, A. (2000). *City literacies: Learning to read across generations and cultures.* London: Routledge.

Guerra, J. C. (2004). Emerging representations, situated literacies, and the practice of transcultural repositioning. In M.H. Kells, V. Balester & V. Villanueva (Eds.), *Latino/a discourses: On language, identity and literacy in education* (pp. 7 – 23). Portsmouth, NH: Heinemann.

Guri-Rosenblit, S. (1998). Future agendas of distance-teaching and mass-orientated universities. Universities in a digital age: Transformation, innovation, and tradition. *Proceedings of the seventh EDEN (European Distance Education Network) Annual Conference* (June 1998). Budapest: European distance education network.

Guthrie, K. (2003). *Visual communication and design: VCE Units 1 – 4.* Melbourne: Thomson Social Science Press

Gutiérrez, K. D., Baquedano-López, P., & Alvarez, H. H. (2001). Literacy as hybridity: Moving beyond bilingualism in urban classrooms. *The best for our children:*

Critical perspectives on literacy for Latino students (pp. 122-141). Columbia University: Teachers College.

Gutierrez, K. D., Baquedano-Lopez, P., Alvarez, H., & Chiu, M. M. (1999). Building culture of collaboration through hybrid language practices. *Theory into Practice, 38*(2), 87–93.

Hagood, M. (2003). New media and online literacies: No age left behind. *Reading Research Quarterly, 38,* 387–391. doi:10.1598/RRQ.38.3.4

Hall, G. E., & Hord, S. M. (1984). *Change in schools: Facilitating the process.* New York: State University of New York Press.

Halpin, R. (1999). A model of constructivist learning in practice: Computer literacy integrated into elementary mathematics and science teacher education. *Journal of Research on Computing in Education, 32*(1), 128–138.

Halverson, R. 2005. What can K-12 school leaders learn from video games and gaming? *Innovate 1*(6). Retrieved March 2008, from http://www.innovateonline.info/index.php?view=article&id=81

Hargittai, E. (2002). Second-level digital divide: Differences in people's online skills. [from http://www.markle.org/downloadable_assets/hargittai-secondleveldd.pdf]. *First Monday, 7,* •••. Retrieved October 14, 2005.

Harrison, C. (2006). Sustaining myths, necessary illusions, and national literacy policies: Some U.S. and U.K. comparisons. *The Elementary School Teacher, 107*(1), 121–131.

Hartman, D. K., & Hartman, J. A. (1993). Reading across texts: Expanding the role of the reader. *The Reading Teacher, 47*(3), 202–211.

Has txt kild the ritn wd? (2007, October 2). *theage.com. au (Fairfax Digital).* Retrieved October 2, 2007, from http://www.theage.com.au/news/in-depth/

Hay, L. E. (2000). Educating the net generation. *School Administrator, 57*(54), 6–10.

Hayes, E. (2007). *Computer and video gaming and IT proficiency: An exploratory study.* Paper presented at the

Annual Meeting of the American Educational Research Association, Chicago, IL.

Henderson, A. T., & Berla, N. (Eds.). *A new generation of evidence: The family is critical to student achievement.* Boston: Center for Law & Education. (ERIC Document Reproduction Service No. ED375968).

Henderson, R., & Honan, E. (2008). Digital literacies in two low socioeconomic classrooms: Snapshots of practice. *English Teaching: Practice and Critique, 7*(2), 85–98.

Hennessy, S., Deaney, R., & Ruthven, K. (2003). *Pedagogic strategies for using ICT to support subject teaching and learning: An analysis across 15 case studies.* Cambridge, UK: University of Cambridge.

Henry, L. A. (2005). Information search strategies on the Internet: A critical component of new literacies. *Webology, 2.* Available at http://www.webology.ir/2005/v2n1/a9.html

Henry, L. A. (2006). SEARCHing for an answer: The critical role of new literacies while reading on the Internet. *The Reading Teacher, 59*(7), 614–627. doi:10.1598/RT.59.7.1

Henry, L. A. (2006, December). *What reading demands does searching on the Internet require? A review of the literature.* Paper presented at the annual meeting of the National Reading Conference. Los Angeles, CA.

Henry, L. A. (2006, May). *Investigation of literacy skills and strategies used while searching for information on the Internet: A comprehensive review and synthesis of research.* Paper presented at the annual convention of the International Reading Association, Chicago, IL.

Herrington, J., Reeves, T. C., Oliver, R., & Woo, Y. (2004). Designing authentic activities in web-based courses. *Journal of Computing in Higher Education, 16*(1), 3–29. doi:10.1007/BF02960280

Hill, S., & Mulhearn, G. (2007). Children of the new millennium: Research and Hirsch, E. D. (1987). *Cultural literacy: What every American needs to know.* Boston: Houghton Mifflin.

Hirsch, L., Saeedi, M., Cornillon, J., & Litosseliti, L. (2004). A structured dialogue tool for argumentative learning. *Journal of Computer Assisted Learning, 20,* 72–80. doi:10.1111/j.1365-2729.2004.00068.x

Hobbs, R. (1998). The seven great debates in the media literacy movement. *The Journal of Communication, 48*(1), 6–32. doi:10.1111/j.1460-2466.1998.tb02734.x

Hobbs, R. (2006). Multiple visions of multimedia literacy: Emerging areas of synthesis. In M. C. McKenna, L. Labbo, R. D. Kieffer, & D. Reinking, (Eds.), *International handbook of literacy and technology: Volume II.* (pp. 15-28). Mahwah, NJ: Lawrence Erlbaum Associates.

Holdich, C., & Chung, P. (2003). A 'computer tutor' to assist children to develop their narrative writing skills: Conferencing with HARRY. *International Journal of Human-Computer Studies, 59,* 631–669. doi:10.1016/S1071-5819(03)00086-7

Holloway, S., & Valentine, G. (2001). "It's only as stupid as you are": Children's and adults' negotiation of ICT competence at home and at school. *Social & Cultural Geography, 2,* 25–42. doi:10.1080/14649360020028258

Honan, E. (2006). Deficit discourses within the Digital Divide. *English in Australia, 41*(3), 36–43.

Hovland, C. I., & Weiss, W. (1976). *Source credibility: Truth and publishing. Social Comment.* New York.

Hoxby, C. M. (1997). *Local property tax-based funding of public schools.* Heartland Policy Study No. 82. Retrieved September 18, 2008 from http://www.heartland.org/

Huddlestone, B. (2008). *Teachers' attitudes and beliefs: a case study of ICT use in a catholic classroom.* Unpublished honours thesis. University of Tasmania, Locked Bag, Australia.

Hulbert, J., & Wetmore, J. K., & York, R. (2006). *Shakespeare and youth culture.* New York: Palgrave Macmillan.

Hunter, C. S. J., & Harman, D. (1985). *Adult illiteracy in the United States.* New York, NY: McGraw Hill.

Hutcheson, G. D. (2005). Moore's Law: the history and economics of an observation that changed the world. *Electrochemical Society Interface, 14*(1), 17–21.

Hyland, K. (2003). Genre-based pedagogies: A social response to process. *Journal of Second Language Writing, 12*, 17–29. doi:10.1016/S1060-3743(02)00124-8

Hyland, K. (2007). Genre pedagogy: Language, literacy and second language writing instruction. *Journal of Second Language Writing, 12*, 3–15.

Ikpeze, C. H., & Boyd, F. B. (2007). Web-based inquiry learning: Facilitating thoughtful literacy with WebQuests. *The Reading Teacher, 60*(7), 644–654. doi:10.1598/RT.60.7.5

IncGamers Ltd. (2007). *Worldofwar.net: The unofficial WoW site*. Retrieved June 1, 2008, from http://www.worldofwar.net/

International Reading Association. (2001). *Integrating literacy and technology in the curriculum: A position statement*. Retrieved May 25, 2008 from http://www.reading.org/resources/issues/positions_technology.html

Ito, M. (2007). Technologies of the childhood imagination: Yugioh, media mixes, and everyday cultural production. In J. Karanagis (Ed.), *Structures of participation in digital culture* (pp. 88-110). New York: Columbia University Press.

Ivers, K. (2003). *A teacher's guide to using technology in the classroom*. Westport, CT: Libraries Unlimited.

Ivers, K., & Barron, A. (2006). *Multimedia projects in education: designing, producing and assessing*, (3rd Ed.). Westport: Libraries Unlimited.

Jenkins, H. (1992). *Textual poachers: Television fans & participatory culture*. New York: Routledge.

Jenkins, H. (2006). *Confronting the challenges of participatory culture: Media education for the 21st century*. MacArthur Foundation White Paper.

Jenkins, H. (2006). *Convergence culture: Where old and new media collide*. New York: New York University Press.

Jenkins, H. (2007). From YouTube to YouNiversity. *The Chronicle of Higher Education Review, 53*(24), 9.

Jenkins, H. (2008). Public intellectuals in the new-media landscape. *The Chronicle of Higher Education, 54*(30), 18–20.

Jenkins, H., Clinton, K., Purushotma, R., Robinson, A. J., & Weigel, M. (2006). *Confronting the challenges of participatory culture: Media education for the 21st Century*. Chicago: The MacArthur Foundation.

Jenkins, H., Klopfer, E., Squire, K., & Tan, P. (2003). Entering the education arcade. *ACM Computers in Entertainment, 1*(1), 1–11. doi:10.1145/950566.950567

Jenkins, J. (1999, March). Teaching tomorrow: The changing role of teachers in the connected classroom. Paper presented at the *EDEN 1999 Open Classroom Conference*, Balatonfured, Hungary. Retrieved June 28, 2007 from http://www.eden-online.org/papers/jenkins.pdf#search=%22%22EDEN%201999%20Open%20Classroom%20Conference%22%22

Jetnikoff, A. (2003). Expanding our literacy repertoires: Using film in senior English Classrooms in Queensland. *Australian Screen Education, 33*, 78–82.

Jetnikoff, A. (2005). Adaption: A case in point about adapting films from books. *Engineers Australia, 143*, 88–94.

Jetnikoff, A. (2006). Combating cyclops: Critical approaches to media literacy and popular culture in senior English. *English in Australia, 41*(1), 37.45.

Johnson, D. W., Johnson, R. T., & Smith, K. (1991). *Cooperative learning: Increasing college faculty instructional productivity (ASHE-ERIC Higher Education Report No. 4)*. Washington, DC: The George Washington University, School of Education and Human Development.

Johnson, S. (2005). *Everything bad is good for you: How today's popular culture is actually making us smarter*. New York: Riverhead Books.

Jonassen, D., Davidson, M., Campbell, J., & Haag, B. B. (1995). Constructivism and computer-mediated communication in distance education. *American Journal of Distance Education, 9*(2), 7–23.

Jones, R. H., Garralda, A., Li, D., & Lock, G. (2006). Interactional dynamics in online and face-to-face peer-tutoring sessions for second language writers. *Journal of Second Language Writing, 15*, 1–23. doi:10.1016/j.jslw.2005.12.001

Junger, G. (1999). *Ten Things I Hate About You.* Screen Writers: Mc Cullah Lutz, K. & Smith, K. Produced by Jeffrey Chernov, Touchstone Pictures.

Juuls, J. (2001). Games telling stories. A brief note on games and narratives. *The International Journal of Computer Game Research, 1*(1). Retrieved May, 2008, from http://www.gamestudies.org/0101/juul-gts/

Kafai, Y. B. (2006). Playing and making games for learning: Instructionist and constructionist perspectives for game studies. *Games and Culture, 1*(1), 36–40. doi:10.1177/1555412005281767

Kalantzis, M., & Cope, B. (2000). A multiliteracies pedagogy: A pedagogical supplement. In Cope, B. & Kalantzis M. (Eds.), *Multiliteracies: Literacy learning and the design of social futures* (pp. 239-248). London: Routledge.

Kalantzis, M., & Cope, B. (2004). Designs for learning. *E-learning, 1*, 38–43. doi:10.2304/elea.2004.1.1.7

Kalantzis, M., & Cope, B. (2008). *New Learning: Elements of a Science of Education.* Melbourne: Cambridge University Press.

Kalantzis, M., Cope, B., & Harvey, A. (2003). Assessing multiliteracies and the new basics. *Assessment in Education: Principles . Policy & Practice, 10*(1), 15–26.

Kamberelis, G. (2001). Producing heteroglossic classroom (micro) cultures through hybrid discourse practice. *Linguistics and Education, 12*, 85–125. doi:10.1016/S0898-5898(00)00044-9

Kamler, B., & Comber, B. (2005). Designing turn-around pedagogies and contesting deficit assumptions. In B. Comber & B. Kamler (Eds.), *Turn-around pedagogies:*

Literacy interventions for at-risk students (pp. 1-14). Newtown, Australia: Primary English Teaching Association.

Kapitzke, C., & Bruce, B. C. (2006). *Libr@ries: Changing information space and practice.* Mahwah, NJ: Lawrence Erlbaum Associates.

Karolides, N. J. (Ed.). (2000). *Reader response in secondary and college classrooms.* Mahwah, NJ: L. Erlbaum.

Katz, J. (2000). *Geeks: How two lost boys rode the Internet of Idaho.* New York: Broadway Books.

Katz, J., Rice, R., & Aspden, P. (2001). The Internet 1995-2000: Access, civic involvement and social interaction. *The American Behavioral Scientist, 45*(3), 405–419.

Kearsley, G. (1998). *A guide to on-line education.* Retrieved November 28, 2007, from http:www.gwis.circ.gwu.edu/~etl/online.html

Kerawalla, L., & Crook, C. (2002). Children's computer use at home and at school: Context and continuity. *British Educational Research Journal, 28*(6), 751–771. doi:10.1080/0141192022000019044

Kerrey, B., & Iskason, J. (2000). *The power of the internet for learning. Final report of the web-based education commission.* Retrieved November 5, 2007, from http://www.ed.gov/offices/AC/WBEC/FinalReport/index.html

Kimbell, R., & Stables, K. (2008). *Researching design learning: issues and findings from two decades of research and development.* Dordrecht: Springer.

Kinchin, I. M., & Alias, M. (2005). Exploiting variations in concept map morphology as a lesson-planning tool for trainee teachers in Higher Education. *Journal of In-service Education, 31*(2), 569–592. doi:10.1080/13674580500200366

King, J., Schneider, J., Kozdras, D., & Welsh, J. (2007, April). *Transforming L/literacies into d/Designs: Fast literacies faster pedagogies.* Paper presented at the Annual Meeting of the American Educational Research Association, Chicago.

Kinzer, C. K. (2005). The intersection of schools, communities, and technology: Recognizing children's use of new literacies. In R.A. Karchmer, M.H. Mallette, J. Kara-Soteriou, & D. J. Leu, (Eds.), *Innovative approaches to literacy education: Using the Internet to support new literacies.* (pp. 65-82). Newark, DE: International Reading Association.

Kirkland, D. E. (2008). "The Rose That Grew from Concrete": Postmodern blackness and new English education. *English Journal, 97*(5), 69–75.

Kirriemuir, J., & Macfarlane, A. (2004). *Literature review in games and learning.* Bristol: NESTA Futurelab.

Kissler, L. (1997). Beyond the text. In R. Salome & J. Davis (Eds.), *Teaching Shakespeare into the twenty-first century.* Athens, OH: Ohio UP.

Kitson, L., Fletcher, M., & Kearney, J. (2007). Continuity and change in literacy practices: A move towards multiliteracies. *Journal of Classroom Instruction, 41*(2), 29–41.

Kleiman, G. M. (2000). *The digital classroom: Myths and realities about technology in K-12 schools.* Cambridge, MA: Harvard Education Press.

Kleiner, A., & Lewis, L. (2003, October). *Internet access in U.S. public schools and classrooms: 1994-2002.* (NCES 2004-011). Retrieved September 3, 2006, from the National Center for Education Statistics Web site http://nces.ed.gov/pubs2004/2004-011.pdf

Kliman, B. W. (Ed.). (2001). *Approaches to teaching Shakespeare's Hamlet.* New York: Modern Language Association.

Knezek, D. (2008). *NETS statement. ISTE.* Retrieved January 28, 2009, from http://www.iste.org/AM/Template.cfm?Section=NETS

Kniveton, B. (2004). The influences and motivations on which students base their choice of career. *Research in Higher Education, 72*, 47–59.

Knobel, M., & Lankshear, C. (2002). Cut, paste, and publish: The production and consumptions of zines. In D.

Alvermann (Ed.), *Adolescents and literacies in a digital world* (pp.164-185). New York: Peter Lang.

Knobel, M., & Lankshear, C. (2006). *The new literacies sampler.* New York: Peter Lang.

Kobayashi, H., & Rinnert, C. (2007). Task response and text construction across first and second language writing. *Journal of Second Language Writing, 7*, 1–23.

Koper, R., & Manderveld, J. (2004). Educational modelling language: Modelling reusable, interoperable, rich and personalised units of learning. *British Journal of Educational Technology, 35*(5), 537–551. doi:10.1111/j.0007-1013.2004.00412.x

Kozol, J. (1991). *Savage inequalities.* New York: Crown Publishers.

Kraidy, M. (1999). The global, the local, and the hybrid: A native ethnography of glocalization. *Critical Studies in Mass Communication, 16*, 456–476. doi:10.1080/15295039909367111

Kraidy, M. (2005). *Hybridity or the cultural logic of globalization.* Philadelphia: Temple University.

Kress, G. (2003). *Literacy in the new media age.* London: Routledge.

Kress, G. (2005). Gains and losses: New forms of text, knowledge, and learning. *Computers and Composition, 22*, 5–22. doi:10.1016/j.compcom.2004.12.004

Kress, G., & Van Leeuwen, T. (1996). *Reading images: a grammar of visual design.* London: Routledge.

Kress, G., & Van Leeuwen, T. (2001). *Multimodal discourse: The modes and media of contemporary communication.* New York: Oxford University Press.

Krippendorf, K. (1980). *Content analysis: An introduction to its methodology.* Beverly Hills, CA: Sage Publications.

Kubota, R. (1997). A reevaluation of the uniqueness of Japanese written discourse. *Written Communication, 14*, 460–480. doi:10.1177/0741088397014004002

Kubota, R. (1998). An investigation of first to second language transfer in writing among Japanese university students: Implications for contrastive rhetoric. *Journal of Second Language Writing, 7,* 69–100. doi:10.1016/S1060-3743(98)90006-6

Kumar, R. (2002). Managing risks in IT projects: An options perspective. *Information & Management, 40*(1), 63–74. doi:10.1016/S0378-7206(01)00133-1

Kvale, S. (1996). *InterViews: An introduction to qualitative research interviewing.* Thousand Oaks, CA: Sage.

Labbo, L. (2004). Seeking synergy between postmodern picture books and digital genres. *Language Arts, 81,* 202.

Lam, E. (2000). L2 literacy and the design of the self: A case study of a teenager writing on the Internet. *TESOL Quarterly, 34,* 457–483. doi:10.2307/3587739

Lam, E. (2006). Re-envisioning language, literacy, and the immigrant subject in new mediascapes. *Pedagogies: An International Journal, 1,* 171–195. doi:10.1207/s15544818ped0103_2

Lam, E. (2006). Culture and learning in the context of globalization: Research directions. *Review of Research in Education, 30,* 213–237. doi:10.3102/0091732X030001213

Lamb, A., & Johnson, L. (2006). Key words in Instruction, Blogs and Blogging Part II. *School Library Media Activities, 22*(9), 40–44.

Land, S. M., & Hannafin, M. J. (1996). *Student-centred learning environments: Foundations, assumptions and implications.* Paper presented at the National Convention of the Association for Educational Communications and Technology, Indianapolis: IN.

Lankshear, C. (2007). Introduction. In M. Knobel & C. Lankshear (Eds.), *A new literacies sampler.* New York: Peter Lang.

Lankshear, C., & Knobel, M. (2002). Do we have your attention? New literacies, digital technologies and the education of adolescents. In D. Alvermann (Ed.), *Adolescents and literacies in a digital world* (pp.19-39). New York: Peter Lang. Lapp, J., & Flood, D. (1995). Broadening the lens: Toward an expanded conceptualization of literacy. In K.A. Hinchman, D.J. Leu, & C.K. Kinzer (Eds.), *Perspectives on literacy research and practice* (pp. 1-16). Chicago: National.

Lankshear, C., & Knobel, M. (2003). *New Literacies Changing Knowledge and Classroom Learning.* Philadelphia: Open University Press.

Lankshear, C., & Knobel, M. (2007). Researching new literacies: Web 2.0 practices and insider perspectives. *E-learning, 4*(3), 224-240. doi:10.2304/elea.2007.4.3.224

Lankshear, C., Snyder, I., & Green, B. (2000). *Teachers and Technoliteracy: Managing literacy, technology and learning in schools.* St. Leonards, Australia: Allen & Unwin.

Lanman, B. A., & Wendling, L. M. (2006). *Preparing the next generation of oral historians: An anthology of oral history education.* Lanham, MD: Rowman & Littlefield.

Lapan, T., Hinkelman, J., Adams, A., & Turner, S. (1999). Understanding rural adolescents' interests, values and efficacy expectations. *Journal of Career Development, 26*(2), 107–124.

Larson, J., & Marsh, J. (2005). *Making Literacy Real: Theories and Practices for Learning and Teaching.* London: Sage Publications.

Laurinen, L., & Marttunen, M. (2007). Written arguments and collaborative speech acts in practicing the argumentative power of language through chat debates. *Computers and Composition, 24,* 230–246. doi:10.1016/j.compcom.2007.05.002

Lave, J., & Wenger, E. (1991). *Legitimate peripheral participation.* New York: Cambridge University Press.

Lave, J., & Wenger, E. (1991). *Situated learning: Legitimate peripheral participation.* Cambridge: Cambridge University Press.

Lawless, K. A., & Kulikowich, J. M. (1996). Understanding hypertext navigation through cluster analysis. *Journal of Educational Computing Research, 14*(4), 385–399.

Lawless, K. A., & Kulikowich, J. M. (1998). Domain knowledge, interest, and hypertext navigation: A study of individual differences. *Journal of Educational Multimedia and Hypermedia, 7*(1), 51–70.

Lawless, K. A., & Schrader, P. G. (2008). Where do we go now? Understanding research on navigation in complex digital environments. In J. Coiro, M. Knobel, C. Lankshear, & D. J. Leu (Eds.), *Handbook of new literacies,* (pp. 267-296). Hillsdale, NJ: Lawrence Erlbaum Associates.

Lawless, K. A., Schrader, P. G., & Mayall, H. J. (2007). Acquisition of information online: Knowledge, navigational strategy and learning outcomes. *Journal of Literacy Research, 30*(3), 289–306.

Lazarus, W., Biemans, H. J. A., & Wopereis, I. (2005). Differences between novice and experienced users in searching information on the World Wide Web. *Journal of the American Society for Information Science American Society for Information Science, 51*(6), 576–581.

Lê, Q. (2007). 'Health informatics: An intercultural perspective'. *Proceedings of MEDINFO 2007 - Building Sustainable Health Systems,* 20 – 24 August 2007, Brisbane, Australia, (pp. 1194-1198).

Leander, K. M. (2003). Writing travelers' tales on new literacyscapes. *Reading Research Quarterly, 38*(3), 392–397.

Leander, K., & McKim, K. (2003). Tracing the everyday 'sittings' of adolescents on the internet: A strategic adaptation of ethnography across online and offline spaces. *Education Communication and Information, 3*(2), 211–240. doi:10.1080/14636310303140

Lee, V. E., & Croninger, R. G. (1994). The relative importance of home and school in the development of literacy skills for middle-grade students. *American Journal of Education, 102*(3), 286–329. doi:10.1086/444071

Lenhart, A., Arafeh, S., Smith, A., & Macgill, A. R. (2008). *Writing, technology and teens.* [Report]. Washington, DC: PEW Internet and American Life Project & The National Commission on Writing.

Lenhart, A., Madden, M., & Hitlin, P. (2005). *Teens and technology: Youth are leading the transition to a fully wired and mobile nation.* Pew Internet and American Life Project. Retrieved May 8, 2006, from http://www.pewinternet.org/pdfs/PIP_Teens_Tech_ July2005web.pdf

Leu, D. J. (2000). Our children's future: Changing the focus of literacy and literacy instruction. *The Reading Teacher, 53*(5), 424–429.

Leu, D. J. (2002). The new literacies: Research on reading instruction with the Internet and other digital technologies. In A. E. Farstrup & S. J. Samuels (Eds.), *What research has to say about reading instruction* (3rd ed., pp. 310-337). Newark, DE: International Reading Association.

Leu, D. J. Jr, & Kinzer, C. K. (2000). The convergence of literacy instruction with networked technologies for information and communication. *Reading Research Quarterly, 35*(1), 108–127. doi:10.1598/RRQ.35.1.8

Leu, D. J., & Reinking, D. (2005). Developing Internet comprehension strategies among poor, adolescent students at risk to become dropouts [Grant proposal]. Grant funded by Institute of Educational Sciences.

Leu, D. J., Ataya, R., & Coiro, J. (2002, December). *Assessing assessment strategies among the 50 states: Evaluating the literacies of our past or our future?* Paper presented at the annual meeting of the National Reading Conference, Miami, FL.

Leu, D. J., Castek, J., Hartman, D. K., Coiro, J., Henry, L. A., & Lyver, S. (2005). Evaluating the development of scientific knowledge and new forms of reading comprehension during online learning. In R. Smith, T. Clark & R. L. Blomeyer, *A synthesis of new research on K-12 online learning* (pp. 30-34). Naperville, IL: Learning Point Associates, North Central Regional Educational Laboratory.

Leu, D. J., Coiro, J., Castek, J., Hartman, D. K., Henry, L. A., & Reinking, D. (2008). Research on instruction and assessment in the new literacies of online reading comprehension. In C. C. Block & S. R. Parris (Eds.), *Comprehension instruction: Research-based best practices* (2nd ed., pp. 321-346). New York: The Guilford Press.

Leu, D. J., Jr. (2000). Literacy and technology: Deictic consequences for literacy education in an information age. In M. L. Kamil, P. Mosenthal, P. D. Pearson, & R. Barr (Eds.), *Handbook of reading research.* (Vol. 3, pp. 743-770). Mahwah, NJ: Erlbaum.

Leu, D. J., Jr., & Kinzer, C. K. (2003). *Effective literacy instruction: Implementing best practice* (5th ed.). Upper Saddle River, NJ: Merrill/Prentice-Hall.

Leu, D. J., Kinzer, C. K., Coiro, J., & Cammack, D. (2004). Toward a theory of new literacies emerging from the Internet and other information and communication technologies. In R. B. Ruddell & N. Unrau (Eds.), *Theoretical models and processes of reading* (5th ed., pp. 1568–1611). Newark, DE: International Reading Association.

Levin, D., & Arafeh, S. (2002). *The digital disconnect: The widening gap between Internet-savvy students and their schools.* Pew Internet & American Life Project. Retrieved May 8, 2006, from http://www.pewinternet. org/PPF/r/67/report_display.asp

Lewis, C. (2007). Internet communication among youth: New practices and epistemologies. In J. Flood, D. Lapp & S.B. Heath (Eds.), *Handbook on teaching literacy through the communicative, visual and performing arts.* Mahwah, NJ: Lawrence Erlbaum Associates.

Lewis, C., & del Valle, A. (2008). Literacy and identity. In L. Christenbury, R., Bomer & P. Smagorinsky (Eds.), *Handbook of adolescent literacy research.* New York: Guilford Press.

Lewis, M. (2002). *Next: The future just happened.* New York: Norton.

Lievrouw, L. A., & Farb, S. E. (2003). Information and equity. *Annual Review of Information Science & Technology, 37,* 499–540. doi:10.1002/aris.1440370112

Lim, C. P. (2004). Learning technology in transition. *British Journal of Educational Technology, 35*(6), 754–755. doi:10.1111/j.1467-8535.2004.00432_11.x

Lim, C. P., & Chai, C. S. (2007a). An activity-theoretical approach to research of ICT integration in Singapore schools: Orienting activities and learner autonomy.

Computers & Education, 43(3), 215–236. doi:10.1016/j. compedu.2003.10.005

Lim, C. P., & Chai, C. S. (2007b). *Teachers' pedagogical beliefs and their planning and conduct of computer-mediated classroom lessons.* Retrieved December 4, 2008, from http://www.blackwellsynergy.com.ezproxy.library. uq.edu.au/doi/pdf/10.1111/j.1467 -8535.2007.00774.x

Lin, A., Wang, W., Akamatsu, N., & Riazi, A. M. (2002). Appropriating English, expanding identities and re-visioning the field: From TESOL to teaching English for glocalized communication (TEGCOM). *Journal of Language, Identity, and Education, 1*(4), 295–316. doi:10.1207/S15327701JLIE0104_4

Lin, C., & Pervan, G. (2003). The Practice of IT Benefits Management in Large Australian Organizations. *Information & Management, 41*(1), 13–24. doi:10.1016/ S0378-7206(03)00002-8

Lin, L., Cranton, P., & Bridglall, B. (2005). *Psychological type and asynchronous written dialogue in adult learning.* Ann Arbor, MI: The University of Michigan Press.

Lindstrom, R. (1994). *The Business Week guide to multimedia presentations: Create dynamic presentations that inspire.* New York: McGraw-Hill.

Linton, H. (2003). *Portfolio design* (3rd Ed.). New York: Universe Publishing.

Lipsitz, G. (1994). *Dangerous crossroads: Popular music, postmodernism and the poetics of place.* New York: Verso.

Littauer, J. S. (2006). *Hamlet: Teacher's guide and student activities.* Retrieved 25 May, 2008, from http://www. sdcoe.k12.ca.us/score/ham/hamtg.html

Littleton, K., & Hakkinen, P. (1999). Learning together: Understanding the process of computer-based collaborative learning. In P. Dillenbourg (Ed.), *Collaborative-learning: Cognitive and computational approaches* (pp. 1-19). Oxford: Elsevier.

Livett, J., & O'Leary, J. (2007). *Design and Technology,* (2nd Ed.). Melbourne: Thomson & Social Science Press.

Livingstone, S. (2003). Children's use of the Internet: Reflections on the emerging research agenda. *New Media & Society, 5*(2), 147–166. doi:10.1177/1461444803005002001

Lockard, J., & Pegrum, M. (Eds.). (2006). *Brave new classrooms: Democratic education and the Internet.* New York: Peter Lang.

Lordusamy, A., Hu, C., & Wong, P. (2001). *Perceived Benefits of EduPAD in enhancing learning.* Paper presented at the AARE Conference. Perth, Australia: Fremantle.

Loretta, K. (2002). Technology as a tool for literacy in the age of information: Implications for the ESL classroom. *Teaching English in the Two-Year College, 30*(2), 129–145.

Luke, A. (2004). Notes on the future of critical discourse studies. *Critical Discourse Studies, 1*(1), 149–152. doi:10.1080/17405900410001674551

Luke, A. (2004). Teaching after the marketplace: From commodity to cosmopolitanism. *Teachers College Record, 106*, 1422–1443. doi:10.1111/j.1467-9620.2004.00384.x

Luke, A., & Freebody, P. (2000). Literate futures: The teacher summary version [of the] report of the Literacy Review for Queensland State Schools.

Luke, A., & Goldstein, T. (2006). Building intercultural capital: [Online supplement to Rogers, T., Marshall, E., & Tyson, C.A. (2006). Dialogic narratives of literacy, teaching, and schooling: Preparing literacy teachers for diverse settings. *Reading Research Quarterly, 41*(2), 202–224. Available at http://dx.doi.org/10.1598/RRQ.41.2.3. doi:10.1598/RRQ.41.2.3

Luke, C. (1997). Media literacy and cultural studies. In S. Muspratt, A. Luke, & P. Freebody (Eds.), *Constructing critical literacies: Teaching and learning textual practice* (pp. 19-50). Creskill, NJ: Hampton Press.

Luke, C. (2000). Cyber-schooling and technological change: Multiliteracies for new times. In B. Cope & M. Kalantzis (Eds.), *Multiliteracies: Literacy learning and the design of social futures* (pp. 69-91). London: Routledge.

Luppicini, R., & Adell, R. (Eds.). (2009). *Handbook of Research on Technoethics.* Hershey, PA: IGI Global.

Lusted, D. (Ed.). (1991). *The media studies book.* London: Routledge.

Macintosh, E. (2008). *Thinking out of the (X) Box: Gaming to expand horizons in creative writing.* Retrieved September, 2008, from http://edu.blogs.com/edublogs/2007/10/thinking-out-of.html

Mack, R. L. (2001). *The digital divide: Standing at the intersection of race & technology.* Durham, NC: Carolina Academic Press.

Madden, M., Chung, P. W. H., & Dawson, C. W. (2008). The effect of a computer-based cartooning tool on children's cartoons and written stories. *Computers & Education, 51*, 900–925. doi:10.1016/j.compedu.2007.09.008

Magnan, S. S. (2007). Reconsidering communicative language teaching for national goals. *Modern Language Journal, 91*(2), 249–252. doi:10.1111/j.1540-4781.2007.00543_3.x

Malone, T. (2007, February). Educators face new technological challenge. *Daily Herald*, February 22, 2007. Retrieved March 22, 2007, from http://www.dailyherald.com/search /printstory.asp?id=284007

Manning, F. H., Lawless, K. A., Gomez, K. G., McLeod, M., Braasch, J., & Goldman, S. R. (2008). *Sources of information in the classroom: Characterizing instruction through a model of multiple source comprehension for inquiry learning.* Paper presented at the annual meeting of the Association of Psychological Science, Chicago, IL.

Manpower, (2007). *A manpower report: The virtual world of work.* Milwaukee, WI: Manpower Inc. Retrieved June 13, 2008 from http://www.manpower.com/research/research.cfm.

Marina, S. (2001). Facing the challenges, getting the right way with distance learning. *At a Distance, 15*(30), 1-8.

Martin, B. (2005). Information society revisited: From vision to reality. *Journal of Information Science, 31*(1), 3–11. doi:10.1177/0165551505049254

Martin, C., & Murray, L. (2006). Editorial: Digital games in the twenty-first century. *Learning, Media and Technology, 31*(4), 323–327. doi:10.1080/17439880601022940

Martin, R. (2007). *Teaching problem-solving skills in writing rather than rules.* Paper presented at the IF-TEALEA National Conference, Melbourne.

Massy, W., & Zemsky, R. 1995. Using Information Technology to Enhance Academic Productivity. Paper presented at *Wingspread Conference*, June. EDUCOM.

Mayer, R. (2005). Introduction to multimedia learning. In R. Mayer, (Ed.), *The Cambridge Handbook of Multimedia learning*(pp.1-16). New York: Cambridge University Press.

Mayer, R. E., & Moreno, R. (2003). Nine ways to reduce cognitive load in multimedia learning. *Educational Psychologist, 38*(1), 42–52. doi:10.1207/S15326985EP3801_6

Mayring, P. (2000). Qualitative content analysis. *Forum: Qualitative Social Research, 1.* Retrieved August 28, 2006, from http://www.qualitative-research.net/fqqs-teste/2-00mayring-e.htm

McClay, J. K., Mackey, M., Carbonaro, M., Szafron, D., & Schaeffer, J. (2007). Adolescents composing fiction in digital game and written formats: Tacit, explicit and metacognitive strategies. *E-learning, 4*(3), 273–284. doi:10.2304/elea.2007.4.3.273

McClure, C. R. (1997). Network literacy in an electronic society: An educational disconnect? In R. Kubey (Ed.), *Media literacy in the information age. Current perspectives: Information and behavior* (pp. 403-439). New Brunswick, NJ: Transaction.

McCreery, M., Schrader, P. G., & Lawless, K. A. (2008, April). *The social engagement of information: What MMOGs can teach us about multi-text environments.* Paper presented at the Annual meeting of the American Educational Research Association, New York. Monaco, J. (2000). *How to read a film: The world of movies, media, and multimedia (art, technology, language, history, theory).* New York: Oxford University Press.

McGinnis, T. A. (2007). Khmer rap boys, X-Men, Asia's fruits, and Dragonball Z: Creating multilingual and multimodal classroom contexts. *Journal of Adolescent & Adult Literacy, 50*(7), 570–579. doi:10.1598/JAAL.50.7.6

McKenna, M. (2006). Introduction: Trends and trajectories of literacy and technology in the new millennium. In M. McKenna, L. Labbo, R. Kieffer, & D. Reinking (Eds.). *International handbook of literacy and technology: Volume II* (pp. xi-xviii). Mahwah, NJ: Erlbaum.

McKenna, M. C., & Robinson, R. D. (2005). *Teaching through text* (4th ed.). Boston: Allyn & Bacon.

McKenzie, M. G. (1985). Shared writing: Apprenticeship in writing. *Language Matters, 1-2*, 1–5.

McLeod, J. (2001). Teacher' Working Knowledge: The Value of Lived Experience. *UltiBase Article,* November. Retrieved January 15, 2009 from http://ultibase.rmit.edu.au/Articles/nov01/mcleod1.pdf.

Mellor, B. (1989). *Reading Hamlet.* Perth, Australia: Chalkface Press.

Merchant, G. (2007). Mind the gap(s): Discourses and discontinuity in digital literacies. *E-learning, 4*(3), 241–254. doi:10.2304/elea.2007.4.3.241

Meredyth, D., Russell, N., Blackwood, L., Thomas, J., & Wise, P. (1999). *Real time: Computers, change and schooling.* Canberra, Australia: Australian Key Centre for Cultural and Media Policy & Macmillan printing group.

Meunier, L. E. (1994). Computer-assisted language instruction in cooperative learning. *Applied Language Learning, 5*(2), 31–56.

Middlehurst, R. (2003). Competition, collaboration and ICT: Challenges and choices for higher education institutions. In M. Van der Wende & M. va der Ven (Eds.). *The use of ICT in Higher Education: A mirror of Europe* (pp. 253-276). Utrecht: Lemma Publishers.

Miles, M. B., & Huberman, A. M. (1994). *Qualitative data analysis* (2nd ed.). Newbury Park, CA: Sage.

Milis, K., & Mercken, R. (2004). The use of the balance scorecard for the evaluation of information and communication technology projects. *International Journal of Project Management, 22*, 87–97. doi:10.1016/S0263-7863(03)00060-7

Miller, M., & Colwill, R. (2003). *Queensland senior English*. South Yarra, Austalia: Macmillan Education Australia.

Millis, B. J., & Cottell, P. G. (1998). *Cooperative learning for higher education faculty*. American Council on Education, Series on Higher Education. Phoenix, AZ: The Oryx Press.

Mitcham, C., & Holbrook, J. B. (2006). Understanding technological design. In J. Daker, (ed.) *Defining technological literacy: towards an epistemological framework* (pp. 105-120). Basingstoke: Palgrave MacMillan.

MOE. (2002). *IT Masterplan*. Retrieved June 9, 2004 from http//www1.moe.gov.sg/iteducation

MOE. (2003). *Malay Language Curriculum*. Retrieved February 21, 2005, from http//www.moe.gov.sg/cpdd/syllabuses.htm

MOE. (2004). *IT in Education*. Retrieved May 21, 2005, from http//www1.moe.edu.sg/iteducation/masterplan/brochure.htm

MOE. (2005). *ICT projects*. Retrieved December 29, 2004, from http//www.moe.gov.sg/schools

Moje, E. (2008). Youth cultures, literacies, and identities in and out of school. In Flood, J., Heath, S.B., & Lapp, D. (Eds.), *Handbook of research on teaching literacy through the communicative arts* (pp. 207-219). Newark, DE: International Reading Association.

Moje, E., Ciechanowski, K., Kramer, K., Ellis, L., Carrillo, R., & Collazo, T. (2004). Working toward third space in content area literacy: An examination of everyday funds of knowledge and Discourse. *Reading Research Quarterly, 39*, 38–70. doi:10.1598/RRQ.39.1.4

Moll, L. C., Amanti, C., Neff, D., & Gonzales, N. (1992). Funds of knowledge for teaching: Using a qualitative approach to connect homes and classrooms. *Theory into Practice, XXXI*(2), 132–141.

Morgan, D. (1986). *Girls' education and career choice: What the research says*. Sydney: NSW Joint Non-Government Schools' P.E.P. Committee.

Mortensen, T. E. (2006). WoW is the new MUD. *Games and Culture, 1*(4), 397–413. doi:10.1177/1555412006292622

Moursund, D. G. (2005). *Introduction to Information and Communication Technology in Education*. Retrieved January 20, 2009, from http://uoregon.edu/~moursund/Books/ICT/ICTBook.html

Muffoletto, R. (1994). Technology and restructuring education: Constructing a context. *Educational Technology, 34*(2), 24–28.

Mumford, E. (1979). *Systems design and human needs. In Bjorn-Anderson et al. The impact of systems change in organizations*. Netherlands: Sijhoff & Noordhoff International Publishers.

National Council of Teachers of English. (2005). *Multimodal literacies*. Retrieved April 29, 2007 from www.ncte.org/about/over/positions/category/media/123213.htm?source-gs

Neo, M., Neo, T. K., & Xiao-Lian, G. T. (2007). A constructivist approach to learning an interactive multimedia course: Malaysian students' perspectives. *Australasian Journal of Educational Technology, 23*(4), 470–489.

Neuendorf, K. A. (2002). *The content analysis guidebook*. Thousand Oaks, CA: Sage Publications.

New Literacies Research Team. (2006). Thinking about our future as researchers: New literacies, new challenges, and new opportunities. In M.B. Sampson, S. Szabo, F. Falk-Ross, M. Foote, & P.E. Linder (Eds.), *Multiple Literacies in the 21st Century: The twenty-eighth yearbook of the college reading association* (pp. 31-50). Logan, UT: College Reading Association.

New London Group. (1996). A pedagogy of multiliteracies: Designing social futures. *Harvard Educational Review, 66*(1), 60–92.

New London Group. (2000). A pedagogy of multiliteracies: Designing social futures. In B. Cope & M. Kalantzis (Eds.), *Multiliteracies: Literacy learning and the design of social futures* (pp. 9-37). London: Routledge.

Newby, T. J., Stepich, D. A., Lehman, J. D., & Russell, J. D. (2000). *Instructional technology for teaching and learning: Designing instruction, integrating computers, and using media* (2nd ed.). New Jersey: Merrill/Prentice Hall.

Newhouse, P. (2001). A follow-up study of students using portable computers at a secondary school. *British Journal of Educational Technology, 32*(2), 209–219. doi:10.1111/1467-8535.00191

Newhouse, P., Trinidad, S. & Clarkson, B. (20002). *Quality pedagogy and effective learning with information and communications technology (ICT)*. Western Australian Department of Education.

Newman, J. (2004). *Videogames*. London: Routledge.

Newton, J. (2003). Implementing a teaching and learning strategy. *Studies in Higher Education, 28*(4), 427–441. doi:10.1080/0307507032000122279

Noel, S., & Robert, J. M. (2003). How the web is used to support collaborative writing. *Behaviour & Information Technology, 22*(4), 245–262. doi:10.1080/0144929031000120860

Noel, S., & Robert, J. M. (2004). Empirical study on collaborative writing: What do coauthors do, use and like? *Computer Supported Cooperative Work: The Journal of Collaborative Computing, 13*(1), 63–89. doi:10.1023/B:COSU.0000014876.96003.be

Noor, R. (2001). Contrastive rhetoric in expository prose: Approaches and achievements. *Journal of Pragmatics, 33*, 255–269. doi:10.1016/S0378-2166(99)00136-8

Norris, P. (2001). *Digital divide: Civic engagement, information poverty, and the Internet worldwide*. Cambridge, UK: Cambridge University Press.

Northcutt, N., & McCoy, D. (2004). *Interactive qualitative analysis: A systems method for qualitative research*. Thousand Oaks, CA: Sage Publications.

Norton-Meier, L. (2005). Joining the video-game literacy club: A relunctant mother tried to join the "flow". *Journal of Adolescent & Adult Literacy, 48*(5), 428–432. doi:10.1598/JAAL.48.5.6

Nurse, hand me the latest video game. (2007, February 21). *The Australian*, p. 3.

Nussbaum, E. (2004, January 11). My so-called Blog. *The New York Times Magazine*, 33-37.

O' Rourke, C. (2002). Engaging students through ICTs: A multiliteracies approach. *TechnKnowLogia*, (April – June), 57-59.

O'Neil, R., Kingsbury, R., & Yeadon, T. (1978). *American Kernel Lessons*. White Plains, N.Y: Longman.

O'Reilly, T. (2005). *What is Web 2.0?: Design patterns and business models for the next generation of software*. Sebastopol, CA: O'Reilly Network. Retrieved June 13, 2008 from http://www.oreillynet.com/pub/a/oreilly/tim/news/2005/09/30/what-is-web-20.html.

Oakley, K. (2007). *Educating for the creative workforce: Rethinking Arts and Education*. Australia Council for the Arts. Retrieved 14 March, 2008 from <www.australiacouncil.gov.au/publications/education_and_the_arts/creative_workforce_rethinking_arts_and_education>

Oh, S., & Jonassen, D. H. (2007). Scaffolding online argumentation during problem solving. *Journal of Computer Assisted Learning, 23*, 95–110. doi:10.1111/j.1365-2729.2006.00206.x

Oppenheimer, T. (1997). The computer delusion. *Atlantic Monthly, 280*(1), 45–62.

Oppenheimer, T. (2003). *The false promise of technology in the classroom and how learning can be saved*. New York: Random House.

Orr, L. (1986). Intertextuality and the cultural text in recent semiotics. *College English, 48*, 811–823. doi:10.2307/376732

Pacey, A. (1999). *Meaning in technology*. Cambridge, MA: MIT Press.

Paige, R. (2002, September). *Introductory letter*. Visions 2020: Transforming education and training through advanced technologies. Retrieved April 15, 2007, from the National Science and Technology council Website, http://www.visions2020.gov/Papers.htm

Palfrey, J., & Gasser, U. (2008). *Born digital: Understanding the first generation of digital natives*. New York: Basic Books.

Palmquist, M. E., Carley, K. M., & Dale, T. A. (1997). Two applications of automated text analysis: Analyzing literary and non-literary texts. In C. Roberts (Ed.), *Text analysis for the social science: Methods for drawing statistical inferences from texts and transcripts*. Hillsdale, NJ: Lawrence Erlbaum Associates.

Papert, S. (1998). *Child power: Keys to the new learning of the digital century*. Talk given at the Imperial College London. Retrieved from http://www.ConnectedFamily.com/frame4/cf0413seymour/recent_essay/cf0413_cherry_2.html

Parayil, G. (2005). The digital divide and increasing returns: Contradictions of information capitalism. *The Information Society, 21*(1), 41–51. doi:10.1080/01972240590895900

Parker, D. (1999). You've read the book, now make the film: Moving image media, print literacy and narrative. *English Education, 33*(1), 24–35. doi:10.1111/j.1754-8845.1999.tb00160.x

Parsad, B., & Jones, J. (2005). *Internet access in U.S. public schools and classrooms: 1994–2003* (NCES 2005-015). Retrieved August, 18, 2006, from the National Center for Education Statistics Website, http://nces.ed.gov/pubs2005/2005015.pdf

Partnership for 21ˢᵗ Century Skills. (2004). Learning for the 21ˢᵗ century. Retrieved August 15, 2006, from http://www.21stcenturyskills.org/reports/learning.asp

Peck, C., Cuban, L., & Kirkpatrick, H. (2002). Techno-promoter dreams, student realities. *Phi Delta Kappan*, (February): 472–480.

Pedroza, H. A. (2003). *English for All (EFA)*. Los Angeles: Sacramento County Office of Education and the Division of Adult Career Education (DACE).

Pelgrum, W. (2001). Obstacles to the integration of ICT in education: Results from a worldwide educational assessment. *Computers & Education, 37*(2), 163–178. doi:10.1016/S0360-1315(01)00045-8

Pellegrino, J. W., Goldman, S. G., Bertenthal, M., & Lawless, K. A. (2007). Technology in teacher training: The what works and why project. In L. S., Smolin, K. A., Lawless, & N. Burbules (Eds.), *National Society for the Study of Education Yearbook*. Columbia: Teachers College, Columbia University.

Peppard, J., & Ward, J. (•••). (n.d.). Beyond Strategic Information Systems: Towards and IS Capability. *The Journal of Strategic Information Systems, 13*(2), 167–194. doi:10.1016/j.jsis.2004.02.002

Perkins, D. (1991). Technology meets constructivism: Do they make a marriage? *Educational Technology, 31*(5), 18–23.

Perry, D., & Smithmier, M. (2005). Peer-editing with technology: Using the computer to create interactive feedback. *English Journal, 94*(6), 23–24.

Petraglia, J. (1998). The real world on a short leash: The (mis)application of constructivism to the design of educational technology. *Educational Technology Research and Development, 46*(3), 53–65. doi:10.1007/BF02299761

Petrina, S. (2007). *Advanced teaching methods for the Technology classroom*. Hershey, PA: Information Science Publishing.

Pew Internet & American Life Project. (2001). *The Internet and education: Findings of the Pew Internet & American Life Project*. Retrieved March 12, 2007 from http://www.pewInternet.org/reports.

Pew Internet & American Life Project. (2005). *The Internet at school*. Retrieved March 12, 2007 from http://www.pewinternet.org/PPF/r/163/report_display.asp.

Pew Internet & American Life Project. (2008). *Writing, technology and teens.* Retrieved June 13, 2008 from http://www.pewinternet.org/PPF/r/247/report_display.asp.

Pew Internet & American Life. (2007). *Teen/parent survey on writing, final topline, 11/21/07.* Retrieved June 13, 2008 from http://www.pewinternet.org/datasets/Teens_Writing_November_2007_Topline.doc.

Pica, T., & Doughty, C. (1985). Input and interaction in the communicative language classroom: A comparison of teacher-fronted and group activities. In S. M. Gass & C. Madden, (Eds.), *Input in Second Language Acquisition.* Rowley, MA: Newbury House.

Pickering, J. (1995). Teaching on the Internet is learning. *Active Learning, 2,* 9–12.

Pink, S. (2006). *Doing visual ethnography* (2nd Ed.). London: Sage Publications Inc.

Plasse, M. (2004). Crossover dreams: Reflections on Shakespeareans and popular culture. *College Literature, 31*(4), 12–18. doi:10.1353/lit.2004.0061

Powell, A. H. (2007). Access(ing), habits, attitudes, and engagements: Re-thinking access as practice. *Computers and Composition, 24*(1), 16–35. doi:10.1016/j.compcom.2006.12.006

Prensky, M. (2001). Digital natives, digital immigrants. *On the Horizon, 9*(5). Retrieved February 12, 2006, from http://www.marcprensky.com/writing

Prensky, M. (2001). Digital natives, digital immigrants. *On the Horizon, 9*(5). Retrieved on 20 January, 2009 from http://www.marcprensky.com/writing/Prensky%20-%20Digital%20Natives%20Digital%20Immigrants%20-%20Part1.pdf

Prensky, M. (2006). *"Don't bother me Mom - I'm learning!"* St. Paul, MN: Paragon House.

Pressley, M. (2006). *What the future of reading research could be.* Paper presented at the Reading Research Conference at the annual meeting of the International Reading Association, Chicago, Illinois.

Pullen, D. (2008) Technoethics in Schools. In R. Luppicini & R. Adell (Eds.), *Handbook of Research on Technoethics* (pp. 680-698). Hershey, PA: IGI Global.

Pullen, D., & Cole, D. (Eds.). (Forthcoming). *Multiliteracies and Technology enhanced Education: Social Practice and the Global Classroom.* Hershey, PA: IGI Global.

Pullen, D., Baguley, M., & Marsden, A. (2009). Back to Basics: Electronic Collaboration in the Education Sector. In J. Salmons & L. Wilson (Eds.), *Handbook of Research on Electronic Collaboration and Organizational Synergy* (pp. 205-222). Hershey, PA: IGI Global.

QBSSS. (2002). *English: Senior syllabus.* Brisbane, Australia: Queensland Board of Senior Secondary Studies.

Queensland Studies Authority. (2007). *Senior visual art 2007.* Spring Hill, Queensland: Queensland Government.

RAND Reading Study Group. (2002). *Reading for understanding: Toward an R&D program in reading comprehension.* Santa Monica, CA: Rand Education. Also available at http://www.rand.org/multi/achievementforall/reading/

RAND Reading Study Group. (2002). *Reading for understanding: Toward an R&D program in reading comprehension.* Retrieved March 3, 2004 from the RAND Corporation Web site: http://www.rand.org/multi/achievementforall/reading/readreport.html

Reagan, T. (1999). Constructivist epistemology and second/foreign language pedagogy. *Foreign Language Annals, 32*(4), 413–425. doi:10.1111/j.1944-9720.1999.tb00872.x

Redd, T. (2003). "Tryin to make a dolla outa fifteen cent": Teaching composition with the Internet at an HBCU. *Computers and Composition, 20,* 359–373. doi:10.1016/j.compcom.2003.08.012

Reil, M. (2000). The future of technology and education: Where are we heading? In D. Watson & T. Downes (Eds.). *Communication and networking in Education* (pp.9-24). Boston: Kluwer Academic Press.

Rice, J. W. (2007). Assessing higher order thinking in video games. *Journal of Technology and Teacher Education, 15*(1), 87–100.

Rice, R. (2002). Primary issues in Internet use: Access, civic and community involvement, and social interaction and expression. In L. Lievrouw & S. Livingstone (Eds.), *The Handbook of New Media: Social shaping and consequences of ICTs* (pp. 105-129). London: Sage.

Richardson, W. (2006). *Blogs, Wikis, Podcasts, and other powerful web tools for classrooms*. Thousand Oaks, CA: Corwin Press.

Richman, J. I., & Skidmore, D. (1984). *Promoting health: Research report*. Manchester, UK: Manchester Polytechnic.

Roberts, T. S. (2005). *Computer-supported collaborative learning in higher education*. Hershey, PA: Idea Group Pub.

Robertson, M., & Williams, M. (2004). *Young People, Leisure and Place: Cross Cultural Prespectives*. New York: Nova Science Publishers.

Robertson, R. (1995). Glocalization: Time-space and homogeneity-heterogeneity. In M. Featherstone, S. Lash & R. Robertson (Eds.), *Global modernities*. London: Sage.

Robinson, K. (2001). *Out of our minds: Learning to be creative*. Chichester, UK: Capstone.

Robinson, S. (1999). Exploring Shakespeare: Dynamic drama conventions in teaching "Romeo and Juliet". *Engineers Australia, 125*, 88–91.

Robyler, M., Edwards, J., & Havriluk, M. (1997). *Integrating educational technology into teaching*. Upper Saddle River, NJ: Prentice-Hall Inc.

Rogers, R. (2006). From cultural exchange to transculturation: A review and reconceptualization of cultural appropriation. *Communication Theory, 15*, 474–503. doi:10.1111/j.1468-2885.2006.00277.x

Rogoff, B. (1995). Observing sociocultural activity on three planes: Participatory appropriation, guided partici-

pation, and apprenticeship. In J.V. Wertsch, P. Delrio & A. Alvarez (Eds.), *Sociocultural studies of mind*. Boston: Cambridge University Press.

Romano, T. (2000). *Blending genre, altering style: Writing multigenre papers*. Portsmouth, NH: Boynton/Cook Heinemann.

Rose, G. (2005). Visual methodologies. In G. Griffin (Ed.), *Research methods for English studies* (pp. 67-89). Edinburgh, UK: Edinburgh University Press.

Rosenblatt, L. M. (1994). The transactional theory of reading and writing. In R. B. Ruddell, M. R. Ruddell, & H. Singer (Eds.), *Theoretical models and processes of reading* (4th ed., pp. 1057-1092). Newark, DE: International Reading Association.

Ross, T., & Bailey, G. (1996). *Technology-based learning: A handbook for teachers and technology leaders*. Australia: IRI/Skylight Training and Publishing, Inc.

Rothstein, R. (2004). *Class and schools: Using social, economic, and educational reform to close the black-white achievement gap*. New York: Teachers College Press.

Rowand, C. (2000, April). *Teacher use of computers and the Internet in public schools*. (NCES 2000-090). Retrieved August 18, 2006, from the National Center for Educational Statistics Website, http://nces.ed.gov/programs/quarterly/Vol_2/2_2/q3-2.asp

Ruddell, R. B., & Unrau, N. J. (1994/2004). Reading as a meaning-construction process: The reader, the text, and the teacher. In R. B. Ruddell & N. J. Unrau (Eds.), *Theoretical models and processes of reading* (5th ed., pp. 1462-1521). Newark, DE: International Reading Association.

Russell, D. R. (1997). Rethinking genre in school and society: An activity theory analysis. *Written Communication, 14*, 504–555. doi:10.1177/0741088397014004004

Russell, T. (1999). *The no significant difference phenomenon*. Chapel Hill, NC: Office of instructional telecommiunications.

Rust, C., Price, M., & O'Donovan, B. (2003). Improving students' learning by developing their understanding of assessment criteria and processes. *Assessment & Evaluation in Higher Education, 28*(2), 147–164. doi:10.1080/02602930301671

Ruthven, K., Hennnesy, S., & Deaney, R. (2004). *Incorporating Internet resources into classroom practice: Pedagogical perspectives and strategies for secondary school subject teachers*. Retrieved May 21, 2004 from http://www.tcrecord.org.

Saettler, P. (1990). *The evolution of American educational technology*. Englewood, CO: Libraries Unlimited.

Salibrici, M. (1999). Dissonance and rhetorical inquiry: A Burkean model for critical reading and writing. *Journal of Adolescent & Adult Literacy, 48*, 628–637.

Salvo, M. (2002). Critical engagement with technology in the computer classroom. *Technical Communication Quarterly, 11*(3), 317–337. doi:10.1207/s15427625tcq1103_5

Sanford, K., & Madill, L. (2007). Understanding the power of new literacies through video game play and design. *Canadian Journal of Education, 30*(2), 432–455.

Savery, J. R., & Duffy, T. M. (2001). *Problem based learning: An instructional model and its constructivist framework*. Indiana University, IN.

Savignon, S. J. (1991). Communicative language teaching. *TESOL Quarterly, 25*(2), 261–277. doi:10.2307/3587463

Saville, M. (forthcoming). Robotics as a vehicle for multiliteracies. In D. Pullen, & D. Cole (Eds.). (Forthcoming). *Multiliteracies and Technology enhanced Education: Social Practice and the Global Classroom*. Hershey, PA: IGI Global.

Sawyer, R. K. (2006). *Explaining creativity*. New York: Oxford University Press.

Scanlon, C. (2009). The natives aren't quite so restless. *The Australian*, 33.

Schcolnik, M., Kol, S., & Abarbanel, J. (2006). Constructivism in theory and in practice. *English Teaching Forum, 4*, 12–20.

Schiller, J. (1997). What do principals do when implementing computer education? *The Practicing Administrator, 14*(4), 36–39.

Schneider, J., King, J., Kozdras, D., Minich, V., & Welsh, J. (November, 2006). *Power, performance, and perspective in a pre-service teacher/elementary student collaborative research/teaching project*. Paper presented at the Annual Meeting of the National Reading Conference, Los Angeles, CA.

Schon, D. A. (1983). *The reflective practitioner: How professionals think in action*. New York: Basic Books.

Schrader, P. D., Zheng, D., & Young, M. (2006). Teachers' perceptions of video games: MMOGs and the future of preservice teacher education. *Innovate, 2*(3). Retrieved March, 2008, from http://www.innovateonline.info/index.php?view=article&id=125

Schrader, P. G., & McCreery, M. (2007). The acquisition of skill and expertise in massively multiplayer online games. *Educational Technology Research & Development*. Retrieved October 10, 2007 from http://www.springerlink.com/content/n2496u376825u512/.

Schrader, P. G., Lawless, K. A., & McCreery, M. (2009). Intertextuality in massively multiplayer online games. In R. E. Ferdig (Ed.) *Handbook of research on effective electronic gaming in education, Vol III*, (pp. 791-807). Hershey, PA: Information Science Reference.

Schrader, P. G., Young, M. F., & Zheng, D. P. (2006). Teachers' perceptions of video games: MMOGs and the future of preservice teacher education. *Innovate, 2*(3). Retrieved February 22, 2006 from http://www.innovateonline.info/index.php?view=article&id=125

Scouter, C. (2003). Foreword. In C. Nicol (Ed.), *ICT Policy: A beginner's handbook*. Paris: Association for Progressive Communications.

See, J. (1994). Technology and outcome-based education: Connection in concept and practice. *The Computing Teacher, 17*(3), 30–31.

Seliger, H. W. (1983). Learner interaction in the classroom and its effect on language acquisition. In H. W. Seliger

& M. H. Long, (Eds.), *Classroom oriented research in second language acquisition* (pp. xi, 305 p). Rowley, MA: Newbury House.

Semali, L., & Pailliotet, A. (1999). *Intermediality.* Boulder, CO: Westview.

Sercue, L. (2004). Intercultural communicative competence in foreign language education: Integrating theory and practice. In O. St.John, K. V. Esch, & E. Schalkwijk (Eds.), *New insights into foreign language learning and teaching.* Frankfurt: Peter Lang.

Shanahan, T. (1990). Reading and writing together: What does it really mean? In T. Shanahan (Ed.), *Reading and writing together: New perspectives for the classroom* (pp. 1-18). Norwood, MA: Christopher-Gordon.

Sharpe, F. (1996). Towards a research paradigm on devolution. *Journal of Educational Administration, 34*(1), 4–12. doi:10.1108/09578239610107138

Shelly, G. B., Cashman, T. J., Gunter, R. E., & Gunter, G. A. (2006). *Teachers Discovering Computers: Integrating technology and digital media in the classroom* (4th Edition). Boston: Course Technology, Thomson Learning.

Shepherd, J. (2005). *Striking a balance: The management of language in Singapore.* New York: Peter Lang.

Shetzer, H., & Warschauer, M. (2000). An electronic literacy approach to network – based language teaching. In W.M. Warschauer, & R. Kern (Eds.), *Networked-based language learning: Concepts and practice* (pp. 171-185). Cambridge, UK: Cambridge University Press.

Siemens, G. (2004). Connectivism: A learning theory for the digital age. *elearnspace.* Retrieved May, 2008, from http://www.elearnspace.org/Articles/connectivism.htm

Silverman, D. (2001). *Interpreting qualitative data.* (2nd ed.). London: Sage Publications.

Sime, D., & Priestley, M. (2005). Student teachers' first reflections on information and communications technology and classroom learning: Implications for initial teacher education. *Journal of Computer Assisted Learning, 21*, 130–142. doi:10.1111/j.1365-2729.2005.00120.x

Sitton, T., Mehaffy, G. I., & Davis, O. L. (1983). *Oral history: A guide for teachers (and others).* Austin, TX: University of Texas Press.

Skelton, T., & Valentine, G. (1998). *Cool places: Geographies of youth culture.* London: Routledge.

Skidmore, D. (1994). *The ideology of community care.* London: Chapman and Hall.

Smerdon, B., Cronen, S., Lanahan, L., Anderson, J., Iannotti, N., & Angeles, J. (2000). *Teachers' tools for the 21st century: A report on teachers' use of technology.* (NCES 2000-102). Retrieved August 18, 2006, from the National Center for Education Statistics Website, http://nces.ed.gov/pubs2000/2000102A.pdf

Smith, B. (2003). Computer-mediated negotiated interaction: An expanded model. *Modern Language Journal, 87*(1), 38–57. doi:10.1111/1540-4781.00177

Smith, K. A. (1996). Cooperative learning: Making "group work" work. In T.E. Sutherland & C.C. Bonwell (Eds.), *Using active learning in college classes: A range of options for faculty: New Directions for Teaching and Learning* (No. 67). San Francisco: Josey-Bass.

Smith, R. *(2002).* Successfully incorporating Internet content and advanced presentation technology into collegiate courses: Lessons, Methodology, and Demonstration. *Massachusetts.*

Snowden, C. (2006). *'Casting a Powerful Spell: The Evolution of SMS', The Cell Phone Reader - Essays in Social Transformation.* New York: Peter Lang Publishers Inc.

Snyder, I. (1996). *Hypertext: The electronic labyrinth.* New York: New York University Press.

Snyder, I. (2008). *The Literacy Wars.* Sydney: Allen and Unwin.

Society of College, National and University Libraries. (1999). *Information skills in higher education.* London, UK: SCONUL. Retrieved October 5, 2007 from, http://www.sconul.ac.uk/groups/information_literacy/papers/Seven_pillars2.pdf.

Solvie, P. (2008). Use of the Wiki: Encouraging Preservice Teachers' Construction of Knowledge in Reading Methods Courses. *The Journal of Literacy and Technology, 9*(2), 58–87.

Spitzer, K. L., Eisenberg, M. B., & Lowe, C. A. (1998). *Information literacy: Essential skills for the information age.* ERIC Clearinghouse on Information and Technology: Syracuse, NY.

Spivey, N. N. (1984). *Discourse synthesis: Constructing texts in reading and writing* (Outstanding Dissertation Mono- graph Series). Newark, DE: International Reading Association.

Spivey, N. N., & King, J. R. (1989). Readers as writers composing from sources. *Reading Research Quarterly, 24*(1), 7–26. doi:10.1598/RRQ.24.1.1

Squire, K. (2002). Cultural framing of computer/video games. *Game Studies, 2*(1). Retrieved April 5, 2006, from http://gamestudies.org/0102/squire/

Squire, K. (2005). Changing the game: What happens when video games enter the classroom? *Innovate, 1*(6). Retrieved March, 2008, from http://www.Innovateonline. info/index.php?view=article&id=82

Squire, K. D. (2006). From content to context: Videogames as designed experience. *Educational Researcher, 35*(8), 19–29. doi:10.3102/0013189X035008019

Squire, K., & Jenkins, H. (2003). Harnessing the power of games in education. *Vision, 3*(6), 5–33.

Stake, R. (1995). *The art of case study research.* Thousand Oaks, CA: Sage.

Steinkuehler, C. (2004). Learning in massively multiplayer online games. In Y. B. Kafai, W. A. Sandoval, N. Enyedy, A. S. Nixon & F. Herrera (Eds.), *Proceedings of the Sixth National Conference of the Learning Sciences.* Mahwah, NJ: Erlbaum.

Steinkuehler, C. (2006). Massively multiplayer online video gaming as participation in a discourse. *Mind, Culture, and Activity, 13*(1), 38–52. doi:10.1207/s15327884mca1301_4

Steinkuehler, C. (2007). Massively multiplayer online gaming as a constellation of literacy practices. *E-learning, 4*(3), 297–318. doi:10.2304/elea.2007.4.3.297

Steinkuehler, C. A. (2006). Why game (culture) studies now? *Games and Culture, 1*(1), 97–102. doi:10.1177/1555412005281911

Steinkuehler, C. A. (2008). Cognition and literacy in massively multiplayer online games. In J. Coiro, M. Knobel, C. Lankshear, & D. Leu (Eds.), *Handbook of Research on New Literacies,* (pp. 611-634). Mahwah NJ: Erlbaum.

Steinkuehler, C., & Williams, D. (2006). Where everybody knows your (screen) name: Online games as "third places". *Journal of Computer-Mediated Communication, 11*(4). doi:10.1111/j.1083-6101.2006.00300.x

Steinkuehler, C., Black, R., & Clinton, K. (2005). Researching literacy as tool, place, and way of being. *Reading Research Quarterly, 40*(1), 7–12.

Sternberg, R. J., & Horvath, J. A. (1995). A prototype view of expert teaching. *Educational Researcher, 24*(6), 9–17.

Stevens, V. (2005). Multiliteracies for collaborative learning environments. *TESL-EJ, 9*(2).

Stokes, S. (2001). Visual literacy in teaching and learning: A literature perspective. *Electronic Journal for Integration of Technology in Education, 1*(1). Retrieved January 21, 2009, from http://ejite.isu.edu/Volume1No1/Stokes.html

Storch, N. (2005). Collaborative writing: Product, process and students' reflections. *Journal of Second Language Writing, 14*, 153–173. doi:10.1016/j.jslw.2005.05.002

Street, B. (1995). *Social literacies.* London: Longman.

Street, B. (2000). Literacy events and literacy practices: Theory and practice in the New Literacy Studies. In M. Martin-Jones (Ed.), *Mutilingual matters.* Philadelphia, PA: J. Benjamins.

Strenski, E., Feagin, C., & Singer, J. (2005). E-mail small group peer view revisited. *Computers and Composition, 22*(2), 191–208. doi:10.1016/j.compcom.2005.02.005

Strickland, R. (1993). Teaching Shakespeare against the grain. In *Teaching Shakespeare today: Practical approaches and productive strategies.* Urbana, IL: National Council of Teachers of English.

Sullivan, K., & Pratt, E. (1996). A comparative study of two ESL writing environments: A computer-assisted classroom and a traditional oral classroom. *System, 24,* 491–501. doi:10.1016/S0346-251X(96)00044-9

Sutherland, R., Armstrong, V., Facer, K., & Fulong, R. (2004). Transforming teaching and learning: Embedding ICT into everyday classroom practices. *Journal of Computer Assisted Learning, 20*(6), 4–13.

Swan, K. (2003). Learning effectiveness: What the research tell us. In J. Bourne & J. C. Moore (Eds.), *Elements of quality online education: Practice and direction* (pp. 13-45). Needham, MA: Sloan Center for Online Education.

Tardy, C. (2005). Expressions of disciplinarity and individuality in a multimodal genre. *Computers and Composition, 22*(3), 319–336. doi:10.1016/j.compcom.2005.05.004

Taylor, P. (1998). Institutional change in uncertain time: Lone ranging is not enough. *Studies in Higher Education, 234,* 269–279. doi:10.1080/03075079812331380246

Teese, R. (2005). For which young people do schools work well and why? In S. Richardson, & M. Prior, (Eds.), *No time to lose: the well being of Australia's children* (pp.240-254). Melbourne: Melbourne University Press.

The International Society for Technology in Education (ISTE). (2008). *National Educational technology Standards (NETS) for teachers.* Retrieved January 21, 2009, from http://www.iste.org/AM/Template.cfm?Section=NETS

Thomas, A. (2007, February). *Avatar as new literacy.* Paper presented at National Council of Teacher of English Assembly of Research. Nashville TN.

Thompson, G. (2002). Interaction in academic writing: Learning to argue with the reader. *Applied Linguistics, 22,* 58–78. doi:10.1093/applin/22.1.58

Thompson, P. (1988). *The voice of the past: Oral history (2ⁿᵈ Ed.).* Oxford, UK: Oxford University Press.

Thorne, S. L. (2006). Pedagogical and praxiological lessons from Internet-mediated intercultural foreign language education research. In J. A. Belz & S. L. Thorne (Eds.), *Internet-mediated intercultural foreign language education.* Boston, MA: Thomson Heinle.

Thornicroft, J. (2004). *Cognitive behaviour therapy.* London: Routledge.

Thott. (2008). *Thottbot: World of Warcraft database.* Retrieved June 1, 2008, from http://thottbot.com/

Tinio, V. (2007). *ICT in education.* Retrieved June 27, 2008 from http://www.apdip.net/publications/iespprimers/ICTinEducation.pdf

Toffler, A. (1971). *Future shock.* London: Pan Books.

Tompkins, G. (2004). *Teaching writing: Balancing process and product.* Upper Saddle River, NJ: Pearson Prentice Hall.

Tovani, C. (2000). *I read it but I don't get it.* Portland, ME: Stenhouse.

Tringali, D. (1993). *Success not stereotyping: Gender perceptions in a low socio-economic school and the effects this has on subject selection and career choice.* Dissertation, The University of Queensland, Australia.

Tuckman, B. (1965). Developmental sequence in small groups. *Psychological Bulletin, 63,* 384–399. doi:10.1037/h0022100

Turbill, J. (2003). Exploring the potential of the digital language experience approach in Australian classrooms. *Reading Online, 6*(7), Retrieved February 7, 2008, from http://www.readingonline.org/international/inter_index.asp?HREF=turbill7.

Turbill, J., & Bean, W. (2006). *Writing Instruction K-6: Understanding process, purpose, audience.* New York: Richard Owen Publishers.

Turbill, J., & Murray, J. (2006). Early literacy and new technologies in Australian schools: Policy, research, and practice. In M.C. McKenna, L. Labbo, R.D. Kieffer, &

D. Reinking, (Eds.), *International handbook of literacy and technology: Volume II.* (pp. 93-108). Mahwah, NJ: Lawrence Erlbaum Associates.

Turkle, S. (2003). Collaborative selves, collaborative worlds: Identity in the Information Age. In J. A. Inman, C. Reed & P. Sands (Eds.), *Electronic collaboration in the humanities: Issues and options* (pp. 3-12). Mahwah, NJ: Lawrence Erlbaum Associated.

Tuzi, F. (2004). The impact of e-feedback on the revisions of second language writers in an academic writing course. *Computers and Composition, 21*, 217–235. doi:10.1016/j.compcom.2004.02.003

Twigg, C., & Oblinger, D. (1996). *The virtual university.* Retrieved January 8, 2009, from http://www.educom.edu/nlii/VU.html

Twombey, C., Shamburg, C., & Zieger, L. (2006). *Teachers as technology leaders.* Washington, DC: International Society for Technology in Education.

Tyner, K. (1998). *Literacy in a digital world: Teaching and learning in the age of information.* Mahwah, NJ: Erlbaum.

U.S. Department of Education (DOE). (2002). *No Child Left Behind Act of 2001.* Washington DC: Author. Retrieved September 22, 2005, from http://www.ed.gov/policy/elsec/leg/esea02/index.html

U.S. Department of Education. (2007). Ed.gov: Reauthorization of No Child Left Behind. Retrieved June 13, 2007 from http://www.ed.gov/nclb/landing.jhtml.

UNESCO. (2003). *Developing and using indicators of ICT use in education.* Retrieved December 22, 2008 from www.unsecobkk.org/ips/ebooks/documents/ICT-indicators.pdf

United States of America Department of Education. (2009). *No child left behind act of 2001.* Retrieved January 15, 2009, from http://www.ed.gov/nclb/landing.jhtml

Unsworth, L. (2001). *Teaching multiliteracies across the curriculum: changing contexts of text and image in classroom practice.* Buckingham, UK: Open University Press.

Valentine, G., Holloway, S., & Bingham, N. (2002). The digital generation: Children, ICT and the everyday nature of social exclusion. *Antipode, 34*, 296–315. doi:10.1111/1467-8330.00239

Van Dijk, T. (2008). *Discourse and power.* New York: Palgrave Macmillan.

Vanithamani, S. (2005). 'Thinking Schools, Learning Nations': Implementation of curriculum review in Singapore. *Educational Research for Policy and Practice, 4*(2-3), 97–113. doi:10.1007/s10671-005-1543-x

VCAA & Melbourne Museum. (2008). Top Design exhibition and catalogue. Retrieved May 4th 2008, from http://museumvictoria.com.au/MelbourneMuseum/Education/Education-Programs/Top-Designs-2008/.

VCAA (2005). *Food and Technology: Victorian Certificate of Education Study Design.* East Melbourne: Victorian Curriculum and Assessment Authority.

VCAA (2006). *Design and Technology: Victorian Certificate of Education Study Design.* East Melbourne: Victorian Curriculum and Assessment Authority.

VCAA (2006). *Systems Engineering: Victorian Certificate of Education Study Design.* East Melbourne: Victorian Curriculum and Assessment Authority.

VCAA (2007). *VCE and VCAL Administrative Handbook 2008.* East Melbourne: Victorian Curriculum and Assessment Authority.

VCAA (2008). *VCE Design and Technology Assessment Handbook 2007 – 2011.* East Melbourne: Victorian Curriculum and Assessment Authority.

VCAA (2008). *VCAA Bulletin VCE, VCAL and VET,* (56), Supplement 1..

VCAA. (2008). *VCE Statistics.* Retrieved from VCAA website http://www.vcaa.vic.edu.au/vce/statistics/2007/statssect2.html.

Violent games make users more aggressive. (2006). *The Australian.* Retrieved January 10, 2006, from http://www.theaustralian.news.com.au

Volk, D., & de Acosta, M. (2003). Reinventing texts and contexts: Syncretic literacy events in young Puerto Rican children's homes. *Research in the Teaching of English*, *38*(1), 8–48.

Vygotsky, L. S. (1978). *Mind in society: The development of higher psychological processes*. Cambridge, MA: Harvard University Press.

Walker, A. (2008). *Early childhood education (ECE) supporting it with ICT*. Unpublished honours thesis, University of Tasmania, Locked Bag, Australia.

Wang, M., & Kang, M. (2005). Cybergogy for engaged learning: A framework for creating learner engagement through information and communication technology. In M. S. Khine (Ed.), *Engaged learning with emerging technologies*. Amsterdam: Springer Netherlands.

Warlick, D. (2005). *Classroom Blogging: A teacher's guide to the blogosphere*. Raleigh, NC: Lulu.

Warschauer, M. (2002). *Technology and social inclusion: Rethinking the digital divide*. Cambridge, MA: MIT Press.

Warschauer, M., & Ware, P. (2006). Automated writing evaluation: Defining classroom research agenda. *Language Teaching Research*, *10*(2), 157–180. doi:10.1191/1362168806lr190oa

Warschauer, M., Knobel, M., & Stone, L. (2004). Technology and equity in schooling: Deconstructing the digital divide. *Educational Policy*, *18*(4), 562–588. doi:10.1177/0895904804266469

Welch, M. (2007). The pupil as designer. In D. Barlex, (ed). *Design & technology for the next generation: a collection of provocative pieces, written by experts in their field, to stimulate reflection and curriculum innovation* (pp. 120-139). Whitchurch: Cliffeco Communications.

Welch, M., Barlex, D., & Lim, H. (2000). Sketching: fried or foe to the novice designer? *International Journal of Technology and Design Education*, *10*, 125–148. doi:10.1023/A:1008991319644

Wellington, J. (2005). Has ICT come of age? Recurring debates on the role of ICT in education, 1982-2004.

Research in Science & Technological Education, *23*(1), 25–39. doi:10.1080/02635140500068419

Wenger, E. (1998). *Communities of practice: Learning, meaning, and identity*. Cambridge, MA: Cambridge University Press.

Wertsch, J. (1998). *Mind as action*. New York: Oxford University Press.

Wesche, M. B., & Skehan, P. (2002). Writing in the secondary classroom: The effects of prompts and tasks on novice learners of French. *Modern Language Journal*, *84*, 171–184.

Wheeler, S. (2000). *The role of the teacher in the use of ICT*. Bohemia, Czech Republic: University of Western Bohemia.

Wickens, C. M., & Sandlin, J. A. (2007). Literacy for what? Literacy for whom? The politics of literacy education and neocolonialism in UNESCO- and World Bank sponsored literacy programs. *Adult Education Quarterly*, *57*(4), 275–292. doi:10.1177/0741713607302364

Will, R. (2006). *Blogs, wikis, podcasts and other powerful web tools for classrooms*. Thousand Oaks, CA: Corwin Press.

Williams, D., Coles, L., Wilson, K., Richardson, A., & Tuson, J. (2000). Teachers and ICT: current use and future needs. *British Journal of Educational Technology*, *31*(4), 307–320. doi:10.1111/1467-8535.00164

Williams, K. (2003). Literacy and computer literacy: Analyzing the NRC's "Being fluent with information technology" [Electronic version]. *The Journal of Literacy and Technology*, *3*. Retrieved July 1, 2006, from http://www.literacyandtechnology.org/v3n1/williams.htm

Williams, P. J. (2009) Technological literacy: a multliteracies approach for democracy. *International Journal of Technology and Design Education* 19 237 – 254; Retrieved from http://www.springerlink.com/content/fm0383v317315u60/fulltext.pdf

Williams, R., Harold, B., Robertson, J., & Southwood, G. (1997). Sweeping decentralization of education decision-making authority: Lessons from England and New Zealand. *Phi Delta Kappan, 78*(8), 626–631.

Willis, P. (2003). Foot soldiers of modernity: The dialectics of cultural consumption and the 21st century school. *Harvard Educational Review, 73*(3), 390–415.

Wind, Y. (2006). Managing creativity. *Rotman Magazine,* Spring/Summer, 20-23.

Wollman-Bonilla, J. (2001). Can first grade writers demonstrate audience awareness? *Reading Research Quarterly, 36,* 184–201. doi:10.1598/RRQ.36.2.4

Wright, P. (in press). Trainee teachers' e-Learning experiences of computer play. *Innovate.*

Wright, P., & Vongalis-Macrow, A. (2006). *Integrating ICT into pre-service education: Reframing teacher education.* Paper presented at the British Educational Research Association Annual Conference, University of Warwick, September. Retrieved March 2008, from http://www.leeds.ac.uk/educol/documents/168675.doc

Wright, S. (2003). *The arts, young children, and learning.* Boston: Allyn & Bacon.

Wright, S. (2004). *Children, meaning-making and the arts.* Frenchs Forest, Australia: Pearson, Prentice Hall.

Yee, N. (2008). *The Daedalus Project.* Retrieved January 19, 2008, from http://www.nickyee.com/daedalus

Yi, S. D., & Kim, H. S. (2005). The value of Korean art and cultural heritage. *Art Education, 58*(5), 18–24.

Yi, Y. (2007). Engaging literacy: A biliterate student's composing practices beyond school. *Journal of Second Language Writing, 16*(1), 23–39. doi:10.1016/j.jslw.2007.03.001

Yildirim, Z. (2005). Hypermedia as a cognitive tool: Student teachers' experiences in learning by doing. *Educational Technology & Society, 8*(2), 107–118.

Young, M. F., Schrader, P. G., & Zheng, D. P. (2006). MMOGs as learning environments: An ecological journey into Quest Atlantis and the Sims Online. *Innovate, 2*(4). Retrieved March 20, 2006 from http://www.innovateonline.info/index.php?view=article&id=66

Zaid, M. A. (1993). *Comprehensive analysis of the current system of teaching English as a foreign language in the Saudi Arabian intermediate schools.* Unpublished Ph.D., University of Colorado at Boulder, Boulder.

Zammit, K., & Downes, T. (2002). New learning environments and the multiliterate individual: A framework for educators. *The Australian Journal of Langauge and Literacy, 25,* 24–36.

Zhao, Y., & Cziko, G. A. (2001). Teacher adoption of technology: A perceptual control theory perspective. *Journal of Technology and Teacher Education, 9,* 5–30.

Zheng, R., & Zhou, B. (2006). Recency effect on problem solving in interactive multimedia learning. *Educational Technology & Society, 9*(2), 107–118.

Zimmerman, W. Z. (1982). *Instant oral biographies.* New York: Guarionex.

Zurawski, N. (1998). *Culture, identity and the Internet.* Retrieved January 20, 2009 from http://www.uni-muenster.de/PeaCon/zurawski/Identity.html

About the Contributors

Darren Lee Pullen is a lecturer in ICT, Professional Studies and Multiliteracies in the Faculty of Education at the University of Tasmania, Australia. He has worked with governments, industry sectors, enterprises (particularly health and training) and the education community to facilitate socio-technical change. His professional focus is on building viable humachine (human-machine) relationships and learning systems. Darren's previous employment includes being a Research Fellow in the health sector, ICT consultant and educator. He currently works as a lecturer and is the principal of an international consultancy firm—Humachine Consultancy. His research interest is in the management of change processes with a particular interest in the micro-meso-macro level relationships between technology innovations and human-machine (humachine) relationships and interactions.

Christina Gitsaki is a Lecturer at the School of Education, The University of Queensland and the Executive Secretary of the Applied Linguistics Association of Australia (ALAA). She has extensive teaching experience in the areas of ESL/EFL and CALL. Her main research interests include second language acquisition and TESOL, the use of ICTs and the Internet for teaching English, Learning Objects design and CALL applications.

Margaret Baguley is a senior lecturer in arts education, curriculum and pedagogy in the Faculty of Education, University of Southern Queensland, Australia. Her teaching and research interests are concerned with the role of visual art in the education of early childhood, primary and secondary students. She has an extensive teaching background across all facets of education, in addition to maintaining her arts practice. An interest in collaborative practice and exhibition underpins her teaching. Dr Baguley's research supervision encompasses studies in visual arts education, children's engagement with the arts, teacher development, museum studies and the value of the arts in the community. In 2008 Margaret received a national award to recognize her outstanding contribution to student learning from the Australian Learning and Teaching Council (ALTC).

* * *

Abbad Mohammed Alabbad completed his B.A. degree at King Saud University in Riyadh, Saudi Arabia and continued his higher education in Morgantown in the United States where he finished his Masters in Linguistics and TESOL in 2001. He is currently working on his PhD research at The University of Queensland, Brisbane, Australia. His main research interests are in the area of Computer-Assisted Language Learning, second language acquisition, and online course design.

Mike Brown, is a Senior Lecturer in the School of Education at the University of Ballarat, Victoria, Australia. Initially, Mike had an industrial background as a Sheetmetal worker and draughtsman. He began his teaching career as a secondary teacher in Technology Studies where he was introduced to a learner-centred pedagogy built around design and problem solving. He worked as a trade instructor teaching Sheetmetal apprentices in the Technical and Further Education (TAFE) sector. For the past fifteen years, he has worked in university based teacher education programs preparing teachers and conducting research in adult, vocational, and Design and Technology education. His most recent research has been through RAVE (Researching Adult and Vocational Education) at the University of Ballarat and has included national studies of Men's learning in and through community contexts, Dual recognition and assessment regimes within VET in schools programs, Applied learning in secondary schools, and Curriculum development in Design and Technology education.

Candance Doerr-Stevens is currently working toward a Ph.D. in critical literacy from the department of Curriculum and Instruction at the University of Minnesota. She has taught writing at the elementary, junior high, and college levels and currently teaches education courses for pre-service and practicing teachers. Candance's current research interests include the emergent literacy practices involved in digital writing, in particular the rhetorical affordances of online role-play and the identity practices involved in the multimodal composition process of digital storytelling.

Robyn Henderson is a Senior Lecturer (Literacies Education) at the Toowoomba Campus of the University of Southern Queensland, Australia. Her current research interests are in the areas of multiliteracies and digital literacies and the relationship between learning digital literacies at home and at school, especially in relation to students who might be marginalised within an education system. She also researches in the areas of academic literacies and the implications of mobility and poverty on school-based literacy learning. All of her work is underpinned by a concern for social justice issues.

Laurie A. Henry is an Assistant Professor of Early Adolescent Literacy at the University of Kentucky. Prior to this appointment, she was a researcher with the New Literacies Research Team at the University of Connecticut where she completed a Ph.D. in Educational Psychology with an emphasis in Cognition and Instruction, Literacy and Technology. Henry's work focuses on early adolescent literacy development, including development of the new literacies of information searching, Internet-based critical reading, expanded definitions of the digital divide, and social equity issues related to the acquisition of digital literacy skills among marginalized youth. Henry teaches undergraduate and graduate courses in literacy education at the University of Kentucky, speaks and consults widely on the new literacies of online reading and writing, and is an active member of several state, national, and international professional organizations. Henry is author of five refereed articles and coauthor of thirteen invited articles and book chapters.

Eileen Honan is Senior Lecturer in English and Literacy Education at The University of Queensland. Her research interests include developing methodological applications in educational research of Deleuze and Guattari's philosophical work, and working with teachers to develop their understanding of theoretical issues related to their literacy teaching practices.

Bridgette Huddlestone is a primary school teacher (specialised in Early Childhood Education) and is the author of an Honours Dissertation "Teachers Attitudes and Beliefs towards ICT in the Catholic classroom". Bridgette has studied a Bachelor of Education at the University of Tasmania, Launceston, and has worked side-by-side with Darren Pullen a lecturer in ICT, Professional Studies and Multiliteracies at the same University. An interest both personally and professionally in the area of Information and Communication Technology in education underpins her teaching and research focus.

Anita Jetnikoff lectures in English Curriculum and Film and Media curriculum Studies at Queensland University of Technology. She is a highly experienced secondary and tertiary teacher. Her research and publication interests include literary theory, literature and cultural studies, teaching and technology, multiliteracies, 'new literacies' and new media, and youth, gender, culture and identity representations in media and literature. She is a documentary film maker. She is the co-author of the new book *Media Remix* due for release in July 2008.

Martin Kerby is the Head of Information Services and Museum Curator/Archivist of St Joseph's Nudgee College Museum in Brisbane, Australia. He was also a foundation member of the Middle School program in 2001. He has written two books, *Undying Echoes* (2001) about the military history of St Joseph's Nudgee College and *Where Glory Awaits* (2005) the military history of St Joseph's Gregory Terrace, another boys' school in Brisbane. Martin is currently working on a PhD examining the life of war correspondent Sir Philip Gibbs. In January 2008 he was awarded a place at the inaugural Australian Government Summer School in History held in Canberra.

James R. King is a Professor in the Department of Childhood Education and Literacy Studies at the University of South Florida in Tampa. There he researches media literacies, critical literacies, and masculinities in educational contexts.

Deborah Kozdras is currently a graduate student in Literacy Studies at the University of South Florida in Tampa where she teaches undergraduate education classes in writing and reading. Her research interests lie in digital media literacies, writing, and connecting literacy learning to youth culture. Currently she is working on her dissertation, documenting the composition processes with which students engage while creating narrative digital videos.

Kimberly A. Lawless is an associate professor of Educational Psychology and Language, Literacy, and Culture at the University of Illinois at Chicago. Dr. Lawless studies how individuals acquire and comprehend information from nonlinear digital environments, focusing on how aspects of the reader, the media, and the task influence navigational strategy and learning outcomes.

Quynh Lê is a Lecturer in Rural Health and the Graduate Research Coordinator at the University Department of Rural Health, Tasmania. Her current research interests include social determinants of health through multilevel analysis and spatial analysis, population health, health informatics and intercultural health. Her research-enhancing activities include co-editor of the on-line international research Journal Language, Society and Culture (1997 – till now), manager of the International Conference on Science, Mathematics and Technology Education (1997) and she has a wide range of publications on health, education, and information technology.

Thao Lê received his PhD in theoretical linguistics at Monash University in 1977. He is a Senior Lecturer in the Faculty of Education, University of Tasmania. He teaches and conducts research in the following areas: research methodology, applied linguistics, TESOL, and e-learning. He was a keynote speaker at several major conferences in computer education and research. Dr. Lê has over one hundred conference papers/articles. His forthcoming book is *Critical Discourse Analysis: An interdisciplinary perspective*.

Donna Mahar, PhD, is Assistant Professor of English and literacy in the Masters of Arts in Teaching Program at Empire State College, the State University of New York's hybrid learning program. She has also been a professor of literacy at the State University of New York's Cortland campus. Formerly a middle school English teacher who achieved National Board Certification as well as local, state, and national recognition for her work with early adolescents, her research on adolescent literacy and information communication technology has been published in academic and practitioner journals. Her current work is concerned with 21st-century literacies as they impact school reform; youth, culture, literacy, and identity studies [YCLI]; and teacher-research.

Vanessa Minick is a doctoral student in the department of Childhood Education and Literacy Studies at the University of South Florida in Tampa. Her research focus concerns composition theory and learning to write.

Jenifer Jasinski Schneider is an Associate Professor in the Department of Childhood Education and Literacy Studies at the University of South Florida in Tampa. Her research focuses on writing development and writing instruction as well as the use of process drama in literacy teaching and learning.

P.G. Schrader is an assistant professor of Educational Technology at the University of Nevada, Las Vegas. Dr. Schrader's recent work involves understanding learning in complex nonlinear digital environments like Massively Multiplayer Online Games and Hypertext. In these contexts, he has examined aspects of expertise, literacy, and the dynamic exchange of information. His work has appeared in a number of journals as well as at national and international conferences. While he's not writing, you might find Dr. Schrader further itemizing his level 70 druid in the World of Warcraft.

Dave Skidmore is currently a Freelance Educational Consultant and was previously Head of Department of Health Care Studies at Manchester Metropolitan University for 14 years. He was at MMU for 26 years where he undertook various positions ranging from lecturer.

Amanda Walker currently fulfils the role of Literacy Leader at a local primary school, providing literacy support for the early childhood area. Amanda has recently completed her Bachelor of Education, graduating with Honours, and worked closely with Darren Pullen, lecturer of ICT and Professional Studies at the University of Tasmania, Launceston and fellow student, Bridgette Huddlestone. Her Honours Dissertation, entitled "Early Childhood Education (ECE) - Supporting it with ICT" was the result of observations that instruction in the use of ICT's in this area was sadly lacking. She believes in the importance of ICT use in both personal and professional pursuits and continues to research to enhance her own knowledge and understanding as a base for her teaching growth.

James Welsh is a doctoral student in the department of Childhood Education and Literacy Studies at the University of South Florida in Tampa. His research focus is new literacies, with particular attention to critical media literacy in elementary education. In addition, James coordinates support for technology integration at the USF College of Education through his work at the Florida Center for Instructional Technology (FCIT).

Peter White has been a lecturer in computer assisted language learning in the School of Languages and Comparative Cultural Studies at The University of Queensland. He has a background in applied linguistics, computing and public policy.

Pam Wright has an Honours degree in History from Lancaster University (UK) and also has a Masters degree in Managing Information Technology from the University of Salford (UK). Pam has extensive experience in e-learning having been an early adopter and has previously been employed as an advisor to teachers using e-learning. Pam has lectured in universities and colleges in both England and Australia. She currently coordinates the ICT programmes for the Faculty of Education (Bundoora) at La Trobe University, where she also teaches in the postgraduate program: the areas are; Using Multimedia for Learning, Learning Technologies in Education and Teaching, Learning with Computer Games and Learning in Virtual Environments. Wright has been successful in three recent grant applications relating to the uses of ICT and learning and she has contributed to a number of journal articles.

Abduyah Ya'akub is a graduate from the Nanyang Technological University, in Singapore, and has recently completed her PhD at the University of Queensland. She has taught Malay Language in Singaporean secondary schools, and worked with the Singapore Ministry of Education on planning and developing curriculum. Her research has focused on identifying the changes of social and cultural practices when digital technologies are used in school. A particular interest is the connections between literacy, technology and disadvantage.

Index

A

achievement gap 57, 58, 71, 72, 74, 79
active engagement 153
active learner 88, 91, 97, 152
activity theory 20, 34, 35
adequate yearly progress (AYP) 71
altruistic engagement 192
androgynous 26, 29
appropriation 33, 36, 37, 38, 40, 41, 42, 43,
    44, 45, 47, 48, 49, 50, 51, 54
Australian Centre for the Moving Image
    (ACMI) 227, 228
authentic integration 187
Autoethnography 232, 247
autotelic 195
avatar 207, 232, 237, 238, 239, 240, 241,
    242, 243, 244

B

Blizzard Entertainment 206, 208, 213, 236,
    237, 238, 239, 241, 246
brainstorming 177
British Educational Communications
    and Technology Agency (BECTA)
    11, 12, 13, 14, 225, 226, 230

C

Chi-square 223
civic pluralism 36, 38, 39, 40, 42, 43, 45,
    48, 50, 51
communities of practice 20, 24, 26, 27, 30,
    31, 32, 40, 150
computer aided design (CAD) 133

computer-assisted language learning (CALL) 8
    8, 90, 91, 92, 93, 94, 96, 97, 98,
    99, 100, 101, 103
computer mediated communication (CMC)
    101, 118, 119
connectivism 222, 231
constructivism 88, 89, 91, 99, 100, 103
creative juxtaposition 40
critical discourse analysis (CDA) 80, 81, 82
critical literacy
    5, 38, 50, 144, 145, 146, 156
cultural heritage 105, 142, 144
curriculum design 163, 167
curriculum development
    160, 161, 163, 164, 167, 181

D

debriefing 185, 189, 190, 191, 195
designs of meaning framework 36
dialogic interplay 38, 42
digital age 1, 4, 6, 7, 8, 16, 80
digital divide 71, 74, 75, 77, 78, 79
digital immigrants 4, 13, 235, 236
digital literacies 7, 56, 185, 186, 222, 232,
    235, 248
digital natives 4, 10, 131
digital revolution 10
digital texts 232, 234, 235
disorganized rips 21, 22, 23
drill and kill 224
Dungeons and Dragons 221

E

Easy Lingo 94, 101
education revolution 10, 14, 15